Facing Fascism and Confronting the Past

Facing Fascism and Confronting the Past

German Women Writers from Weimar to the Present

Edited by Elke P. Frederiksen and
Martha Kaarsberg Wallach

State University of New York State Press

Published by
State University of New York Press

Printed in the United States of America

For information, address State University of New York Press, State University Plaza, Albany, NY 12246

Production by Kelli Williams
Marketing by Fran Keneston

Library of Congress Cataloging-in-Publication Data

Facing fascism and confronting the past: German women writers from Weimar to the present / edited by Elke P. Frederiksen and Martha Kaarsberg Wallach.

p. cm.

Includes bibliographical references and index.

ISBN 0-7914-4579-8 (alk. paper)—ISBN 0-7914-4580-1 (pbk. : alk. paper)

1. German literature—20th century—History and criticism. 2. German literature—Women authors—History and criticism. 3. German literature—Jewish authors—History and criticism. 4. Authors, German—20th century—Political and social views. 5. Fascism in literature. I. Frederiksen, Elke. II. Wallach, Martha Kaarsberg.

PT405 .F295 2000
830.9'9287'0904—dc21 99-049785

10 9 8 7 6 5 4 3 2 1

In friendship dedicated to
Ute Countess Baudissin

CONTENTS

Part III. Individual Women's Voices against Fascism

Part IV. Exile and the Holocaust

Part V. Women's Voices after 1945

List of Illustrations

Acknowledgments

The idea for this volume dates back to an international conference entitled "German Women Writers from Weimar to the Present: Facing Fascism and Confronting the Past," which was co-sponsored by the Goethe Institute Washington and the University of Maryland at College Park in 1993. The Director of the Goethe Institute Washington, Ute Countess Baudissin, conceived of the idea for such a conference, which she co-chaired with Elke Frederiksen and Martha Kaarsberg Wallach. Both editors are deeply indebted to Countess Baudissin for her support and friendship. The volume is therefore dedicated to her. We are grateful to the late Peter Wallach who provided help, advice, and encouragement and named both our conference and this volume. Thanks also go to Norman Frederiksen for his support and advice in editing and with computer problems.

We thank our universities for financial assistance of this project; the University of Maryland at College Park provided significant conference support and Central Connecticut State University an AAUP Research Grant that helped finance completion of the manuscript.

We would also like to thank the following publishers for permitting us to reprint text selections and illustrations: the Artothek: Spezialarchiv für Gemäldefotografie, Farrar, Straus and Giroux, the Kupferstichkabinett der Staatlichen Museen zu Berlin, New Directions, Suhrkamp, University of North Carolina Press, Random House, the Virginia Museum of Fine Arts, and the Watkins Loomis Agency. In particular, we thank The Feminist Press for permission to include Ruth Kluger's essay. Several librarians, colleagues, and graduate assistants provided help and guidance with searches and documentation; thanks are due to Arnd Goebel, Suzana Habibovic, Joan Packer and Emily Chasse of CCSU, Beth Muellner and Roxane Riegler of UMD, Johannes Ziegler of the Staatsbibliothek Berlin, Eckart Schiele of the Gedenkstätte Deutscher Widerstand, Berlin, Irina Hundt and Harry Smith of Berlin, Germany. Special thanks go to John Hargraves of Connecticut College for translating Elke Liebs's chapter, to CCSU colleagues David Blitz and Francis Keefe for help with editing manuscripts of non-native speakers of English and to James Peltz for his friendly advice in guiding the manuscript through the acquisition stage of publication.

Introduction

Elke P. Frederiksen and Martha Kaarsberg Wallach

The Holocaust and Nazi era emerged in the early postwar years as a topic in popular culture and the media, and scholarly research on the Third Reich has increased noticeably since the 1970s in both Germany and in the United States (Martin). Only a few historical studies, however, that appeared in the late 1970s and early 1980s have focused on women and fascism, in particular on women's activities and their roles during the Nazi years (e.g., Jill Stephenson, Renate Bridenthal). In the late 1980s and 1990s , research entered a new phase. Not only has the number of publications increased, but the theoretical discussions have become much more sophisticated. At their center is a theoretical debate over terminology, women's roles (not only as victims but also as perpetrators and collaborators), and specifically over the relationship of feminist scholarship to research on National Socialism. Whereas most of this scholarship is still conducted by historians and sociologists in the United States and in Germany (Gisela Bock, Claudia Koonz, Christina Thürmer-Rohr, Lerke Gravenhorst, Alison Owings), scholars of German literature have very recently joined the debate (e.g., Sigrid Weigel, Elaine Martin, Marie-Luise Gättens). But there is still a scarcity of scholarly work on women's literary and cultural representations of the Nazi era, in the United States as well as in Germany.

Our project *Facing Fascism and Confronting the Past: German Women Writers from Weimar to the Present,* is the first English-language book-length treatment of the topic, which spans almost the entire twentieth century (from the 1920s to the 1990s) and discusses texts by a wide variety of women writers of very diverse backgrounds, many of them Jewish. The book includes an autobiographical account of a Holocaust survivor's experiences as well as sixteen scholarly articles.

This volume will be significant for American and German readers because it gives a voice to Jewish, but also non-Jewish women writers from German-speaking countries who were silenced during the Nazi years. It focuses on these authors' literary attempts to confront the Nazi past, but it also discusses younger writers and filmmakers (e.g., Drewitz, Wolf, Sander) who wrote or created their works after 1945. These women emphasize the fascist past and the consequences of fascism for the postwar period, in an attempt to come to terms with this historical phenomenon on the one hand, but also in order to deal with fascist and patriarchal tendencies in their own societies in the 1950s, 1960s, 1970s, and 1980s. In light of the recent political events in Europe such as the unification of Germany, the discussions presented here are particularly relevant. Issues of gender, patriarchy, and fascism are central to the analyses of texts by authors such as Nelly Sachs, Anna Seghers, Elisabeth Langgässer, Ingeborg Drewitz, Grete Weil, Christa Wolf, and others.

Facing Fascism and Confronting the Past . . . is a contribution to the ongoing debate about fascism that has only recently begun to investigate literary texts by women writers. Contributors to this volume are all established scholars in literary and cultural studies, from the United States, Germany, and Denmark. They share common concerns with historians and sociologists, whose studies have centered on language, responsibility, guilt, morality, racism, and sexism (Martin). They ask similar questions, but they address them in different ways. As Sara Lennox states in her commentary:

> Our training in textual analysis can help other scholars of National Socialism to understand how discourses, representations, interpretations already influence how participants experience and evaluate events and that they affect again how participants or observers construct an account of what happened and what it meant. We can explore why the Nazi period is represented in certain ways rather than others, whence those representations derive, what sorts of writers employ what kind of textual forms, and how and why representations of fascism change over time. (Conclusion: New Scholarly Perspectives, 287)

Of particular interest methodologically will be the insights gained from a differentiated view of a victim-perpetrator-collaborator dialectic, while keeping in mind the shifts and displacements that occur when historical events are changed into specific perceptions of history, which are then translated into literary form (Ryan, 16).

Ruth (Angress) Kluger's moving account of her Holocaust experiences opens this volume. She is a critically acclaimed author in Europe and a renowned scholar in the United States and abroad, whose text will appear in this volume in English for the first time.

Ruth Kluger was a child survivor of concentration camps at Theresienstadt and Auschwitz, managed a transfer to a labor camp by lying about her age, and then escaped together with her mother and a friend. Almost half a century later she decided to write about her experiences. "Growing Up in the Eye of the Firestorm" is written in a reflective style. We hear of childhood memories followed by reflections and interpretations, sometimes the adult author's reflections and interpretations, sometimes her recollections of earlier musings. Kluger remembers the losses her family suffered during the Holocaust, the deaths of her father, her brother, an aunt. She thinks about childhood incidents in Vienna experiencing prejudices against Jews. "Sketches from Birkenau" give us glimpses of the social disintegration in the camps, the heat, the hunger, the suffering of the old and infirm. Most dramatic is the description of her experiences in the labor camp: her survival because she is able to pass for a fifteen-year-old, the back-breaking work, the cold, the ever-greater scarcity of food. Kluger's text is of significance for our volume not only on account of the subject matter and her spellbinding narrative style, but also because she touches on many issues that recur in the discussions in this volume such as *Trauerarbeit* (grief work) and *Vergangenheitsbewältigung* (coming to terms with the past), antisemitism, the interrelation of gender, fascism, and patriarchy, the mother-daughter relationship.

In the section "From Weimar to National Socialism," Gisela Brinker-Gabler investigates the circumstances of early German modernists' (Expressionist) involvements with fascism, namely those that created a "new woman" to accompany the movement's "new man." Pointing out the "new woman's" traditional association with nature and matter, she demonstrates how the "new man" continues in his role as dominator. Brinker-Gabler is especially interested in the effects of the male's subject-position and his representation of this "new woman" on the Expressionist woman writer. Juxtaposing poems by Gottfried Benn (1886–1956) and Else Lasker-Schüler (1869–1945), she compares male and female writers' expressions of experience and desire. While "woman" is objectified and identified with nature in Benn's poem, Lasker-Schüler's text presents "man" and "woman" as contrasting images of lifelessness and fullness of life, which is based on Lasker-Schüler's negotiation of the Expressionist construction of "woman" and her own reality as a woman. The poet offers no illusions about nature as refuge and suggests this dream-like state to be dangerous.

Ritta Jo Horsley also concentrates on the question of subjectivity by focusing on female identities in the 1920s and 1930s as portrayed in the novels of Irmgard Keun (1905–1982). Keun lived and wrote in Germany during the Weimar period and in exile after the fascist takeover. Horsley examines several historical and literary representations of the "new woman" in her extensive introduction, as she questions the myth of the sexually and economically independent woman during the time of the Weimar Republic. Horsley shows how Keun's novels reflect sociopolitical realities of the Weimar period and the Third Reich. The heroines in novels such as *Das kunstseidene Mädchen* (1932) (*The Artificial Silk Girl*) are independent women in an identity crisis. With the Nazi takeover, Keun's female protagonists seem to become more passive and fearful (e.g., *D-Zug dritter Klasse*, 1938; *Express Train Third Class*).

While both Brinker-Gabler and Horsley analyze literary texts in relation to pre-fascist and fascist ideology, Elaine Martin connects literary questions more explicitly with sociohistorical ones. She refers to the scholarship by Claudia Koonz and Christina Thürmer-Rohr, borrowing from them a double gaze that emphasizes a victim-perpetrator dialectic. Martin investigates the autobiographical literature of six women who wrote during the Third Reich, in order to gain deeper insight into the reasons for these women's participation in National Socialism. Martin links the issue of gender to the disturbing connection between sexual desire and violence, which she recognizes in both male and female Nazis' fantasies. But Martin also discovers and suggests that several of these authors' attempts at questioning National Socialism may be the first step toward resistance, since National Socialism thrived on blind and silent allegiance.

The following section, "Individual Women's Voices against Fascism," focuses more specifically on well-known Jewish women writers and their reactions to fascism and in particular to National Socialism. Gertraud Gutzmann outlines the ways in which Anna Seghers practiced "literary antifascim" and how she remained true to her belief in the power of the literary text and its ability to impact political processes. While referring to Seghers's exile works *The Seventh Cross* (1942) and *Transit* (1944 in English translation; 1948 in German), Gutzmann presents a close reading of the short story "Der Ausflug der toten Mädchen" (1946) ("The Excursion of the Dead Girls"), which she interprets as Seghers's "fictional articulation of literature's function in post-fascist Germany" (Gutzmann). The author's commitment to reeducating German youth after the Nazi experience is particularly evident in that text, which explores the circumstances why human beings participate in, tolerate, and condone the persecution of others.

While Seghers wrote her texts of the 1930s and 1940s in exile, Gertrud Kolmar's little-explored correspondence with her sister Hilde is an invaluable document about Jewish life inside Germany during World War II. Monika Shafi reads it as a literary text which makes up an integral part of Kolmar's oeuvre. This correspondence is the only source for the extremely reclusive poet's personal voice. Central to Kolmar's letters are the construction and representation of the self that provided her with the means of self-exploration and resistance, very different from her "unified, teleological" poetic self. Shafi describes Kolmar's process of self-inscription: Kolmar moves away from the assimilated bourgeois Jewish life both physically and mentally; she criticizes others in the ghetto for living in their "German" past, denying their Jewishness; she studies Hebrew; she chooses a gypsy woman as the embodiment of the heroic self that she seeks; she has a relationship with a factory coworker. Ultimately, a comparison with Antigone seems appropriate, with Kolmar defying her oppressors through letter writing.

By juxtaposing Elisabeth Langgässer's novel *Proserpina* (1933/49) with her daughter Cordelia Edvardson's autobiographical text *Gebranntes Kind sucht das Feuer* (1989), Helga Kraft's analysis focuses on basic probing questions about fascism and patriarchy. More specifically, she reads Langgässer's *Proserpina* as a counterstatement to the fascist trends and essentialist views of women's roles, of motherhood, and of the mother-daughter dyad, which continued to exist during the late 1920s and early 1930s despite emancipatory movements. The alienation of mother and daughter in a patriarchal society is the central focus of the two novels. The fascist tendencies of the fatherland have caused both writers to rethink one of the dominant myths, namely motherhood. While Langgässer deconstructs the myth of motherhood in an abstract sense, Edvardson faces, much more directly, the actual tyranny of fascism that destroyed her bond with her mother. She writes from her own experience as a concentration camp survivor. She had been separated from her mother when she was fourteen and was taken to Auschwitz by the Nazis because she was three-quarters Jewish. Of particular interest in both texts is the creation of multiple mother figures, which could suggest the vision of a "motherland," in which fascism might not be able to exist.

The section concludes with a chapter on the Nobel Prize-winning poet Nelly Sachs, which examines some of her poems as an answer to fascist persecution. Dinesen also provides some insight into Nelly Sachs's life in a completely assimilated well-to-do German-Jewish family in Berlin, her reactions to the Nazi takeover as well as her exile in Sweden.

With the National Socialists' accession to power in 1933 and their invasion of neighboring countries in 1939, an exodus of writers, artists, and intellectuals took place that was unprecedented in modern history (Stern). Many of these exiles found asylum in the United States. Guy Stern's chapter "Echoes of Exile . . ." attempts "to fathom the affinity between the exiles from Nazi Germany and the Anglo-American women writers who portrayed and often ennobled them." Stern sketches out various characterizations of German and Austrian exiles who were placed in roles of either victim, hero, or warner (pointing out the vulnerability of democracy, for example). This largely didactic literature was intended to alert Americans to the suffering, heroism, sacrifice, or leadership of the exiles. Women authors were drawn to this subject matter due to their empathy with pariah groups, and they—in Stern's words—"grasped the misery and grandeur of exile with even greater sensitivity" than the male authors.

Rather than exploring the works of established women writers such as Else Lasker-Schüler, Nelly Sachs, or Gertrud Kolmar, Dagmar Lorenz focuses on women who began to write in response to the traumatic events during the 1930s and the Holocaust. Lorenz reads this literature as Holocaust literature at large, but she also recognizes gender-specific aspects as a textual basis, such as women's socialization and their roles in pre-Nazi and Nazi Germany, in the concentration camps, and in postwar society. As Lorenz states: "Gender specific factors determined the ways in which women regarded themselves, how they conceived of their roles, and how they related to other people." Of particular interest with regard to our volume is Lorenz's analysis of Ruth Kluger's book *weiter leben* (1992). The Kluger text "Growing Up in the Eye of the Firestorm . . . ," which opens our volume, is an excerpt from *weiter leben*. Lorenz points out that Kluger not only describes how her past experiences affect her present views and lifestyle, but that her book demonstrates the long-range impact of the Holocaust on the survivors and the following generations. *weiter leben* bridges the gap between the different generations and genres of Holocaust literature in a unique way and asks questions about the past, which are particularly relevant in the light of recent political events in Germany. "Unified Germany torn by ethnic strife and xenophobia needs to hear the voices of the mothers and daughters of the Holocaust" (Lorenz).

Coming to terms with a past as horrendous and painful as National Socialism and Hitler's Third Reich, has occupied many writers, artists, and filmmakers during the last several decades. Some of the best-known contemporary women writers and filmmakers and their attempts to come to terms with this past (*Vergangenheitsbewältigung*) in their literary texts or films are discussed in the section "Women's Voices after 1945." Both chapters by Frederiksen and Ward focus on the problem of a moral dilemma for a writer. In the case of Ingeborg Drewitz the answer seems less difficult, since Ward recognizes parallels between the courage of Drewitz's protagonists and the author's own position. This is particularly true of Drewitz's little-known play about the concentration camps (1955), which was performed successfully years before Rolf Hochhuth and Peter Weiss were "hailed as the first to bring this difficult subject matter onto the German stage" (Ward). Luise Rinser on the other hand represents a more complex case, because of her silence about her apparent early enthusiasm for the Nazis, although she openly turned against them after 1937 and addresses the Nazi past in many of her texts.

While Rinser and Drewitz are writing primarily within a West German context, Christa Wolf is an East German voice who wrote *Patterns of Childhood* in the 1970s, at a time when the German Democratic Republic officially placed all blame for Germany's fascist past upon the western side (and world), ignoring the issues of

Vergangenheitsbewältigung, as well as the so-called Jewish question, and antisemitism. Wolf's text, however, reveals how it appropriated and transformed earlier discourses on fascism. Through the questioning of fact, the effect of imaginative and associative powers of fantasy, and the production of female subjectivity, Wolf offers a method for comprehending the fascist past and women's complicity with it, but the text also introduces readers to "sites and mechanisms of resistance" (Holub). Most importantly, Holub's chapter shows the reader that literary texts can play a role in political debates, and how political discussions can be transformed in a literary text.

Again connecting the past and the present, Elke Liebs sets her analysis of Grete Weil's *Meine Schwester Antigone* (1980) in the context of the late 1970s (the time in which the novel was written), the fascist past, and present-day, post-Wall Germany, where resistance to totalitarianism has once again become a topic of discussion. Central to the novel, which is partly autobiographical, is Weil's personal pain (persecution by the Nazis and her husband's death in a concentration camp), and her writing is directed "against the dulling of memory, against forgetting and against self-pity" (Liebs). Liebs examines the multifacetedness of resistance as well as the character of the mythological Antigone as a timeless symbol of resistance. The analogy between Antigone and Sophie Scholl is but one example—Grete Weil was one of the first to point that out.

Since our volume *Facing Fascism and Confronting the Past . . .* is concerned with cultural discourses, we have included an extensive chapter on "Film, Gender, and German History: Filmmaking by German Women Directors from Weimar to the Present," which provides "a general survey of filmmaking by women in Germany, with special emphasis on films that specifically address German fascism, antisemitism, or racism . . ." (McCormick). Richard McCormick includes in his discussions well-known films such as Sagan's *Mädchen in Uniform* (1931) (*Girls in Uniform*), Leni Riefenstahl's *Das blaue Licht* (1932) (*The Blue Light*), Helma Sanders-Brahm's *Deutschland, bleiche Mutter* (1979) (*Germany, Pale Mother*), Jutta Brückner's *Hungerjahre* (1980) (*Years of Hunger*), and finally Helke Sander's film *BeFreier und Befreite* (1992) (*Liberators Take Liberties*). *BeFreier und Befreite* focuses on the rape of German women at the end of World War II, especially by Soviet troops. It poses very sharply—as Lennox points out in the conclusion of this volume—the questions that this volume asks about women facing fascism and confronting the past. The film focuses on the victim/perpetrator dichotomy and on issues of complicity of German women with fascism; on patriarchal thinking, issues concerning sexuality, sexual violence, and gender in wartime; it connects the past and the present as it raises questions about historical context: for example, what about the atrocities committed against women in Bosnia in the most recent past?

Regarding the contributions by German women filmmakers to the New Cinema in general, McCormick concludes that they not only introduced but also used the long-ignored category of gender with sensitivity in their approach to the crimes of German history. In McCormick's opinion their films are "both more forthright and more political than what is generally to be found in films by the male auteurs of the German Cinema."

Since our volume opens with Ruth Kluger's discussion of women's experiences of the Holocaust, it seemed fitting to include some thoughts on the situation of German women after unification. Renate Möhrmann speaks from her own experience as a cultural-political representative of the CDU (Christlich-Demokratische Union; Christian Democratic Party) in the parliament of her state Nordrhein-Westfalen (North Rhine Westfalia). She speaks as a politician who is familiar with the misogynist world of parliament, but she focuses on positive as well as negative aspects concerning the situation of German women in post-Wall Germany. She takes a closer look at women's role in politics, discusses women and the family laws, and women's reactions to xenophobia in Germany.

This volume concludes with Sara Lennox's remarks on new scholarly perspectives and suggestions for further research regarding the topic of women facing fascism and confronting the past. She reiterates the importance of gender—femininity, masculinity, and their interrelationship—as "a potent factor at work in every area of cultural activity including literary representation." Lennox emphasizes the significance of connecting gender issues and the study of National Socialism and the Holocaust, which for scholars of German Studies must remain of central importance. In conclusion, she points out that the strong reactions of readers to literary texts such as Christa Wolf's *Patterns of Childhood* or the very critical and vocal reception of the film *BeFreier und Befreite* in Germany are evidence of the fact that the issues debated in this volume (representation, gender, and fascism) matter, not only inside the academy but also ouside of it.

Bibliography

Bock, Gisela. "Racism and Sexism in Nazi Germany: Motherhood, Compulsory Sterilization, and the State." In *When Biology Became Destiny: Women in Weimar and Nazi Germany*. Ed. Renate Bridenthal et al. New York: Monthly Review Press, 1984.

Bridenthal, Renate, Atina Grossmann, and Marion Kaplan, eds. *When Biology Became Destiny: Women in Weimar and Nazi Germany*. New York: Monthly Review Press, 1984.

Gättens, Marie-Luise. *Women Writers and Fascism: Reconstructing History*. Gainesville: University Press of Florida, 1995.

Kluger, Ruth. *weiter leben. Eine Jugend*. Göttingen: Wallstein, 1992.

Koonz, Claudia. *Mütter im Vaterland. Frauen im Dritten Reich*. Freiburg/Breisgau: Kore, 1991. Original American edition: Koonz, Claudia. *Mothers in the Fatherland. Women, the Family, and Nazi Politics*. New York: St. Martin's Press, 1987. The quote was taken from the preface of the German edition and translated into English by Elke Frederiksen.

Martin, Elaine, ed. *Gender, Patriarchy, and Fascism in the Third Reich. The Response of Women Writers*. Detroit: Wayne State University Press, 1993.

Owings, Alison. *Frauen: German Women Recall the Third Reich*. New Brunswick, N.J.: Rutgers University Press, 1993.

Ryan, Judith. *The Uncompleted Past. Postwar German Novels and the Third Reich*. Detroit: Wayne State University Press, 1983.

Stephan, Inge, Sabine Schilling, Sigrid Weigel. *Jüdische Kultur und Weiblichkeit in der Moderne*. Köln: Böhlau, 1994.

Stephenson, Jill. *Women in Nazi Society*. New York: Barnes & Noble, 1975.

———. *The Nazi Organization of Women*. New York: Barnes & Noble, 1980.

Thürmer-Rohr, Christina. "Aus der Täuschung in die Ent-Täuschung—Zur Mittäterschaft von Frauen." *beiträge zur feministischen theorie und praxis* 8 (1983): 11–26.

———. *Vagabonding. Feminist Thinking Cut Loose*. Translated by Lise Weil. Boston: Beacon Press, 1991.

TöchterFragen. NS-Frauen-Geschichte. Ed. Lerke Gravenhorst and Carmen Tatschmurat. Freiburg/Breisgau: Kore, 1990.

Weigel, Sigrid. *Bilder des kulturellen Gedächtnisses. Beiträge zur Gegenwartsliteratur*. Dülmen-Hiddingsel: tende, 1994.

Part I

Experiencing the Holocaust

1
Growing Up in the Eye of the Firestorm: A Jewish Childhood under the Nazis

Ruth Kluger

I.

The secret was death not sex and the grownups were sitting at the table whispering. I pretended that I couldn't fall asleep in my bed and begged that they'd let me sleep on the sofa in the living room, which we called *Salon*. Of course I didn't even intend to fall asleep, I wanted to get in on the forbidden news. Stories, horror stories, incomplete one and all. Some were about strangers, others about relatives, always about Jews. They'd talk about a cousin of my mother's, but much younger than she, I'll call him Hans, who had been discharged from a concentration camp. The voices at the table, women's voices, indistinct and barely audible, because I kept my head under the blanket, said K.Z., just the two letters. In German they make an ugly sound, they hiss, spit, and cough like this: *kah-tset*. Hans was scared, they had bullied him into not talking, and he hadn't talked, or perhaps he had, maybe just to his mother? They had tortured him, what is torture, how does one stand it, how is it done? But he was alive and back, knock on wood, let's be thankful, next question, how can we help him leave the country?

The author excerpted, translated, and adapted this text from her original German autobiography published in Germany under the German version of her name: Ruth Klüger, *weiter leben. Eine Jugend.* (Göttingen: Wallstein Verlag, 1992). A full translation of the original is forthcoming from the Feminist Press.

I was to meet Hans again in England, when I was no longer eight years old but the way I am now, impatient and absent-minded, prone to drop things intentionally or through clumsiness, even breakables, like dishes and love affairs, a woman who is perennially on the move, changing jobs and homes at the drop of a hat, and inventing the reasons while she is packing, a person who runs away as soon as she gets nervous, long before she smells danger. Because running away was the best thing I ever did, ever do. A favorite subject, you can be sure I'll return to it.

So there I was with Hans in England, in his home which he loved because he owned it. He was married to an Englishwoman, a Gentile, and his children were visiting, and I had come visiting from America, together with Heinz, another cousin on my mother's side, who had survived the war in Hungary with false papers that proved him an Aryan and a Catholic.

Hans was telling us indignantly how the rabbi hadn't wanted him to marry a Gentile and how he had left the rabbi and clung to his woman. I hadn't even thought of consulting a rabbi when I got married. Hans's father, killed in Auschwitz, had been the only observant Jew in the family. It was incongruous and therefore amusing, that his son, who had been the embodiment of my childhood's darkest secret, should concern himself, let alone get angry, decades after the fact, about some dumb English rabbi's objection to the woman of his choice. That was the best part. The rest was tea and cakes, and I was shifting in my seat, eager to get up, do something, go for a walk, anything to escape the enfolding envelope of boredom made of unremitting and senseless details of their everyday lives. Heinz, the other cousin, told me later, not without a touch of malice, that Hans had asked him if I suffered from hemorrhoids, because I wouldn't sit still for long.

But Hans wasn't your average English home owner: he had been tortured in Buchenwald when he was a teenager, while his little relation had kept her ears open under the blanket, determined to find out more about his experience. Not so much from sympathy as from curiosity, because he was the center of an exciting mystery, which concerned me too, in some nebulous way. Though no one would tell me about it because I was too young. And now?

Now I was better informed and could ask all I liked, whenever I liked, for those who had imposed the restriction were gone, dispersed, had died in gas chambers or in their beds, wherever. And I can't get rid of the prickly feeling that I am uncovering taboos, searching for indecencies, that I am not supposed to know about death and dying. As if there were anything else worth bothering about. The secret of the grownups who pretend that only grownups die because only they know how to cope with death. And yet on the street the Nazi boys were singing the song about the Jewish blood spurting from their knives, and they were carrying little knives as if to prove it.

So now I have a chance to ask Hans about the old secrets and I do. And the others in the confined space of the living room want to be left in peace: the children assure us that they were about to leave and had better go now, Heinz takes off his glasses, cleans them and wants to know whether we have to go through with this. Hans's Gentile wife leaves the room. She has heard all of this often enough and more than enough. This is manifestly true, but did she ever pay attention?

And Hans answers my questions and tells me his story. . . .

Why have I hardly ever visited this cousin? One reason is my indifference to family relations which it took me years to acknowledge. In Jewish circles it has become customary the world over to count the murder victims in our extended families, to insist that our children know these figures and to compare them with the remnant of the *mishpoche*. They are horrendous figures, huge collective graves in every family. "One hundred and five," says an uncle and the next one adds another dozen, while an aunt ticks off a few more names on her fingers. And for a long time I participated in this counting and accounting, and tried to persuade myself that I was in mourning for people of whom I had only the vaguest memory. But actually I was never nestled in such a *mishpoche*, mine went to pieces when I became conscious, not later.

But the real reason why I shy away from visiting relatives is my bad conscience. Hans's mother, my great-aunt, was one of the victims who died that most pitiful of all deaths, the infamous death in the gas chambers. And she was a relative I knew well, since we shared an apartment once. In my memory she remains the person who wouldn't let me drink water after eating cherries, a superstition undermining the authority of my absent father, who was the doctor in the family to whom nobody listened; she was the person who confiscated my collection of used streetcar tickets, claiming it was unhygienic; who insisted that I eat a revolting breakfast in the dark hours of the morning, before going to school, and who stood between my mother and me, keeping her at a safe distance so she wouldn't be bothered by her child. So what shall I say to her son who loved her when he asks me who hated her with a sharp, prickly aversion and can't forgive her even beyond her pathetic death?

After the war my mother walked away from my brother's death and hardly ever mentioned him again. There were no laments and there was no period of mourning. "Trauerarbeit," the labor of mourning Freud calls such a necessary period of remembering. She didn't do it, she just walked away. Not that she hadn't waited for him, for my father too. She searched the lists and she informed all the agencies that were bringing families together. So for a long time I fantasized that he was somewhere in the Communist world and didn't even know that we were still around. Even after I had come to this country, I sometimes dreamed that he would turn up and I wouldn't be able to recognize him because he had become an adult and perhaps he was prematurely bald or portly. I visualized him as someone I might know, not as the kid whom they shot in the dead of winter in a northern town. Freezing, he was naked.

You remember how some years back the TV news showed scenes of seal pups being clubbed to death by boys and men in Eastern Canada, and the boys' faces alive with innocent cruelty. What sticks in my mind is a seal mother who tried to protect her pup with great tenacity. Then she watched helplessly as it was clubbed and I believe she barked a little and then she walked away. Just like that. There was nothing more to be done. My mother took the loss like that seal, only she is no seal, and I don't know what happened to it in her picture-ridden mind.

My old mother tells me that my father used to say he had no elbows, he couldn't push. Of course she has a whole attic full of memories of him, and I who would give much to have more knowledge of him, stand outside the attic and have no key to it and don't know how to make her tell me more. I used to try, not just with her but with many people who had known him, all those friends, or supposed friends, and his relatives here in the United States. But nothing came of it. They either didn't understand the need of the orphan to know where she came from or maybe they resented this need, or they simply didn't know how to talk about him or how to tell something, anything. So I pick up snippets like the saying about the elbows. Out of the blue, this detail.

The reason I am so struck by it is the difficulty I have coming to terms with the gas chambers. For a long time after the war, for decades in fact, I fantasized that he had committed suicide. After all, he was a doctor, wouldn't he have known how to kill himself when the train from Drancy pulled into Auschwitz? I couldn't face having my father die in a gas chamber. I wrote poems in which he and his death figured. They had lines like, "My father drowned in every sea,/ Yet lifts his head at break of day/ Above the flood of memory . . . here in San Francisco Bay/ My father drowns in every sea."

But we know how they died in the gas chambers. The strong climbed on top of the weak in that last agony, as they choked to death. So the men were always on top when they pulled out the corpses and the women and children at the bottom.

That is what came to mind when I heard that he liked to say he had no elbows: that he trampled on those who were weaker. My father did this? On kids like me, when he died. But perhaps he didn't since he had no elbows? But do you have a choice, or haven't you reached the limits of freedom, when you are choking on poison gas? These are the questions I cannot answer and cannot shed.

We never did mourn. We walked away like the seal mother from the pup. Some of our children try to do this "Trauerarbeit" for us.

In 1940 when I was eight or nine the local movie theater showed Walt Disney's *Snow White*. I was a movie fan even then and wanted to go see it, but since I was Jewish I unfortunately wasn't permitted to go. I groused and bitched about this unfair situation until my mother proposed that I should go and forget about the sign that said "No Jews."

It was a Sunday, we were known in the neighborhood and to enter a movie house here was a challenge. My mother was convinced that no one would care whether one more child was watching, and she said I shouldn't think I was all that important and I should stop being a coward, because she was never a coward when she was my age. So of course I went, bought the most expensive type of ticket so as to be less noticeable and managed to sit down next to the nineteen-year-old baker's daughter from next door with her little siblings, enthusiastic Nazis one and all.

I sweated through the next ninety minutes and had no idea what happened on the screen. All I could think of was whether the baker's daughter was really looking at me angrily or whether I was only imagining it. The wicked queen of the film merged with my neighbor, her malice a poor imitation of the real thing, and it was I and no innocent princess who was out on a limb, twisting in the wind.

Why didn't I get up and walk out? Perhaps in order not to face my mother or because I thought that any move would attract attention, perhaps merely because one doesn't leave a theater before the film is over, or, most probably, because from sheer fright this solution didn't occur to me. I don't even know why my people didn't leave Vienna in time and perhaps there is a family resemblance between that question and why I stayed glued to my seat.

When the lights came on, I wanted to wait until the house had emptied out, but my enemy stood her ground and waited. She told her little brother to shush and fixed me sternly. There I was, in a trap, as I had surmised. It was pure terror. The baker's daughter put on her gloves and coat and finally addressed me.

Hadn't I seen the sign outside? Didn't I know what it meant? I could read, couldn't I? I had broken a law. She was using her best high German, no dialect for this patriotic occasion. If it happened once more she would go to the police. I was lucky she didn't go today.

The story of Snow White can be reduced to the question of who is entitled to inhabit the king's palace and who is the outsider. The baker's daughter and I followed this formula. She, in her own house, the magic mirror of her racial purity before her eyes, and I, also at home in this place, a native, but without permission and at this moment expelled and exposed. Even though I despised the law that excluded me, I still felt ashamed to have been found out. For shame comes about not through the commission of the shameful action but through discovery and exposure. If I had got away with my small illegality, I would have been proud of my daring. Yeats speaks of the "defiling and disfigured shape/ The mirror of malicious eyes casts upon his eyes until at last/ He thinks that shape must be his shape." My case exactly, and I might have felt better had I known the poem.

The usher, an older woman, helped me into my coat and handed me my purse, which I was about to leave on the seat. She was sorry for me and said a few soothing words. I nodded, incapable of answering because I was choking on my tears of humiliation, but grateful for that bit of kindness, alms for the poor.

I came home crying and furious, blaming my mother, for what seemed a near-catastrophe. She shrugged her shoulders. Who would think of bothering a child watching a fairy tale? Don't get upset. There are worse things. But that was the problem. Wasn't this bad enough? I had almost been arrested. What were the worse things? How should I know what was serious, and what wasn't? It was easy for my mother who presumably knew where you drown and where you can just barely tread water. But I didn't know a thing and wanted explanations. What was the worst and could it be something other than death? How could I surmise that my grownups didn't know much themselves, that they were entirely flummoxed by their situation and that, in fact, I was learning faster than they? I got the impression that I shouldn't trust my mother, that she had only bad advice for me. This impression was wrong. Like other people's advice, my mother's varies between good, bad, and indifferent. A couple of years later, when she happened to be right, my lack of confidence in her, dating from that afternoon at the movies, almost cost me my life.

II.

The other day I met a couple of likable students in Göttingen. I heard them talk about Auschwitz, but not, as is customary in Germany, as shorthand for the Holocaust but quite concretely as a place they seemed to know well. I started asking questions without telling them that I had been there before them, and learned that they had done their alternative service, their *Zivildienst* in the old concentration camp. Instead of serving in the military, they had whitewashed the fences in Auschwitz. I wondered aloud whether this made any sense. My doubts astonished them. Preservation was a form of restitution, they figured. Not that they liked the tourists (all those Americans!), and they were less than enthusiastic about the school children with their teachers. Nevertheless: the sites of suffering have to be preserved. And I ask myself: why?

Is it that the ghosts won't let go of us, and we expect that our unsolved questions will be answered, if we hang on to what is left, the place, the stones, the ashes? But it is not the dead we honor with these unattractive remnants of past crimes, we collect and keep them, because *we* need them in some obscure way. Violated taboos like child murder, mass murder, turn into ghosts for whom we provide a kind of home which they may haunt at will. Perhaps we are afraid they may leave the camps, and so we insist that their deaths were unique and must not be compared to any other losses and atrocities. Never again shall there be such a crime. The same thing doesn't happen twice anyway. Every event, like every human being, and even every dog, is unique. We would be condemned to isolation if we didn't use comparisons, for they are bridges from one unique life to another. Basically we all know that some aspects of what happened in the camps have been repeated elsewhere, today and yesterday and will find new forms tomorrow; and the camps too were only imitations (unique imitations, to be sure) of what occurred the day before yesterday.

There is a museum culture of the camps which is based on a deep superstition, that is, the belief that the ghosts can be met and kept where the living ceased to breathe. Or rather not a deep but a shallow superstition. A visitor who stands here and feels moved, even if it is only the kind of feeling that a haunted house conveys, will still be pleased by his own sensitivity. And so the visitor checks his reactions, examines his emotions, in other words, turns sentimental.

I once visited Dachau, because some American friends asked me to come along. Everything was clean and proper there, and it took more imagination than most people have to visualize the camp as it was forty years earlier. Stones, wood, barracks, central square. The wood smells good, and a fresh wind blows across the square. You can associate it with a youth hostel more easily than with tortured lives. And surely there are visitors who secretly figure they have had worse experiences than the prisoners in this orderly German camp. The missing ingredients are the odor of fear emanating from human bodies, the concentrated aggression, the reduced minds. I didn't see the ghosts of the men who dragged themselves through the long, evil hours, the so-called *Muselmänner*, who had lost the energy and the will to live. Sure, the signs and the documentation and the films help us understand. But the concentration camp as a memorial site? Landscape, seascape—there should be a word like "timescape" to indicate the nature of a place in time, at a certain time, not before and never again.

III.

Even today I don't like the looks of freight cars. Yet the problem with the transport from Theresienstadt to Auschwitz was not the type of car or wagon but that it was so overcrowded. It has become customary to say cattle cars, as if the proper way to transport animals is by torturing them. The doors were sealed, and air came through a small rectangle that served as window. Maybe there was a second rectangle in back of the car, but that was the place for the luggage. We had been told to take along everything we owned. (So that it could be more easily confiscated on our arrival, a kind of special delivery in which we unwittingly collaborated.) People who came from Theresienstadt didn't own much, but still too much for a freight car full of people, sixty or eighty. In fictional accounts, films or books of such transports, the hero often stands pensively at the little window or he holds up a child to see the landscape move by. But in reality only one person could stand in this privileged spot and he was not likely to give it up and was likely to be someone who knew how to use his elbows.

If I look at a map today, I see that the distance from Theresienstadt to Auschwitz is not very great. Yet it was the longest trip I have ever taken. The train stood around, it was summer, the temperature rose. The still air smelled of sweat, urine, excrement. An old woman who sat next to my mother slowly went crazy. She cried and whimpered, and I was impatient and angry with her, because here she was adding her private disintegration to the great collective evil which we shared. A defense reaction: I could not face or assimilate the sight of a grownup losing her mind in front of me. Finally the old woman pushed herself onto my mother's lap and urinated. And I still see the tense look of revulsion on my mother's face in the slanting twilight of the car and how she gently pushed the woman from her lap. Without malice, more like a nurse might free herself from a clinging patient. I thought my mother should have been indignant, but for her the situation was beyond anger and outrage.

I have just described a central event in my life, and yet I hardly ever get a chance to speak of it. It doesn't fit the framework of social discourse. For example, after I had written this in Germany, I visited friends and we talked about claustrophobia, and people mentioned incidents where they had got stuck and described feelings of panic or near panic. There was talk about the Chunnel and would the average person stand the confinement or flip? And there was a man who once couldn't get out of an elevator, and half the company remembered the air raid shelters of their childhood. And I didn't contribute my transport to Auschwitz, though it was on my mind, because if I had, it would have effectively shut up the rest of the company, they would have been bothered, troubled, sympathetic, and thoroughly uncomfortable. There would have been no further discussion of the way space affects us, which had been our subject. They would have resented me for spoiling the evening. My childhood falls into a black hole.

Sketches from Birkenau. A school teacher, whom I remember with some emotion but no respect. He would collect stalks of grass, of which there wasn't much, but he found what there was and patiently called the grasses by their respective names, and commented, "You see, even here in Auschwitz something can grow, there is life." But I knew better, and for me there was no comfort in the thought that the grass would outlast me.

Second sketch. The gas chambers as a subject of everyday banter. Two men are fighting in front of a barracks. "What are you yelling about," says one. "No point getting excited. The chimney burns for you as much as for me." He is not resigned, he is angry, he yells. There were discussions on whether it was technically possible to cremate as many people as rumor had it. The optimists thought that the crematoria, the "chimney" took care only of those who had died of more or less "natural" causes.

Third sketch. A German guard, on the other side of the barbed wire, preens with a walking stick that has a loaf of bread at the other end. What an idea to show the starving prisoners that one has the power to let bread spoil in the dirt. But I was used to hunger and don't particularly associate it with Auschwitz. My physical recollections of the camp are mostly of heat (the glaring sun during roll call, which often lasted for hours) and of the stench from the death machine that pervaded the camp, and of thirst.

Another sketch about a walking stick. This time it belonged to a naked two-year-old boy who paraded it in the washroom, and was happy because he had finally scared up a plaything. A man says to my mother, what a shame that a kid like that won't get a chance to grow up. "What did the man tell you?" I ask her. My mother repeats his words.

Two old women arguing. They stand in the glaring sun, gesticulating with emaciated fingers. A third woman joins them, a prisoner with some authority, and knocks their heads against each other, hard. The brutality of the scene hits me with full force, a sensation of deep terror: I am witnessing the dissolution of the social structure I had known at least sketchily. Later I used to think, I shouldn't have been so horrified, surely there are greater horrors. But today I think that I was not naive or simple-minded and that my reaction was not out of line. Old women in Auschwitz, their nakedness and helplessness, the needs of old people, their exposure. Old women on the mass latrines, where at least a dozen people at a time were dealing with their constipation or diarrhea, in full view of each other. The old don't take physical functions for granted as children and young women do. This holds true particularly for the generation I have in mind, the generation of my grandmother, who had been born in the nineteenth century with its notions of modesty.

And the naked corpses, heaped on trucks, piled up any which way, molested by flies, disfigured features that had faced the ultimate violence, the hair on their head disheveled, sparse pubic hair, all in the glaring sun. I stand and stare in fascination.

Selection, there was to be a selection, women between the ages of fifteen and forty-five were to be chosen for a transport to a labor camp, at a certain barracks at a certain time. There were those who argued that one should avoid the selection, stay away. My mother believed that no place could be worse than what we had here, but the word *Selektion* was not a good word in Auschwitz because it usually meant the gas chambers. One couldn't be sure that there was really a labor camp in sight, though it seemed reasonable, given the parameters of age. But then, reason was not a basic premise of this place.

Two SS men conducted the selection, both with their backs to the rear wall. They stood on parallel sides of the so-called chimney which divided the room. In front of each of them was a line of naked women, waiting to be judged. The one in whose line I stood had a round wicked mask of a face and was so tall that I had to crane my neck to look up to him. I told him my age, he turned me down, with a shake of his head, simply, just like that. Next to him the woman clerk, a prisoner too, was not to write down my number. As if I had stolen my life and had no right to keep it, as if my life were a book that an adult was taking from me because I had no right to read on.

My mother had been chosen, no wonder, she was the right age, a grownup woman. Her number had been written down, she would leave the camp in a short time. We stood on the street and argued. She tried to persuade me that I should try a second time, with the other SS man, in the other line.

This was in June 1944, and since it was very warm both the front and the rear doors of the barracks stood open. This back entrance was guarded, but the guard consisted of inmates, and my mother felt I could sneak by and take another turn. And this time please don't be a fool and don't tell them your real age of twelve years. I got angry and irritated and was half desperate. "I don't look older," I remonstrated. I felt she wanted to cause a great deal of trouble for me, like the time a few years ago when she had urged me to go to the movies, in spite of the legal prohibition. The difference between twelve and fifteen is enormous for a twelve-year-old. I was to add a quarter of my entire life. The lie which my mother proposed was so transparent: three years, where was I to find them?

I was troubled and frightened, but it was not the profound fear of death which overwhelmed me when I looked at the chimneys, the crematoria, spitting flames at night and smoke by day. That fear was like a disease, and the fear I felt now was more like the bearable fear of malicious grownups, a fear that one could cope with. And how would I stay in Birkenau without my mother? She prodded me by calling me a coward until I agreed but with the proviso that I would try thirteen, never fifteen.

The space I was trying to invade was guarded by a cordon, and I sneaked through as the two men who were responsible were in the process of calling to each other. I bent over a little to appear smaller and ran fast in the shadow of the wall and entered through the back gate, unobserved.

The room was still full of women. A kind of orderly chaos reigned which I associate with Auschwitz. The presumed Prussian perfection of the administration of the camps is a German invention. They were not well organized, or only superficially so, because there was nothing valuable to organize or retain. We were worthless, by definition. The selecting SS officers and their helpers stood with their back to me. I went unobtrusively to the front door, got rid of my clothes once more and took my place at the end of the line. I breathed a sigh of relief to have managed so far and so well. But I was the smallest and obviously the youngest in my line, undeveloped, undernourished, and nowhere near puberty.

I have read a lot about the selections since that time and all reports insist that the first decision was always the final one, that no prisoner who had been sent to one side and thus condemned to death ever made it to the other side. All right, I am the exception.

What happened next is loosely suspended from memory, as the world, before Copernicus, dangled on a thin chain from Heaven. It was an act that is always unique, no matter how often it may occur, an incomprehensible act of grace, or, put more modestly, a good deed. And yet the first term, an act of grace, is perhaps closer to the truth, even though it was caused by a human being, for it came out of the blue sky and was as undeserved as if its originator had been up in the clouds. I was saved by a young woman who was in just as helpless a situation as the rest of us and who cannot have wanted anything other than to help me. The more I think about the following scene the more astonished I am about its essence, that someone makes a free decision to save another person, in a place which promoted the instinct of self-preservation among prisoners to the point of crime and beyond. It was both unrivalled and exemplary. Simone Weil was suspicious of practically all literature, because literature tends to make good actions boring and evil interesting, thus reversing the truth, she argued. Perhaps women know more about what is good than men do, since men tend to trivialize it. Simone Weil was right, as I learned that day in Birkenau, the good is incomparable and inexplicable as well, because it doesn't have a proper cause outside of itself and because it doesn't reach for anything beyond itself.

I can't keep SS men apart, to me they are all the same uniformed wire puppet with polished boots, and when Eichmann was tried and executed I was embarrassingly indifferent to the whole process. These people were one single phenomenon, as far as I was concerned, and their differences in personality were irrelevant. Hannah Arendt offered the counterpart to Simone Weil's reflections on goodness, when she pointed to the simple fact that evil is committed in the spirit of mental dullness and narrow-minded conformity. Her reflections on evil caused much indignation among men, who understand, though perhaps not consciously, that this deromanticization of arbitrary violence was a challenge to the patriarchy. Perhaps women know more about evil than men, who like to demonize it.

The line moved toward an SS man who, unlike the first one, was in a good mood. His clerk was perhaps nineteen or twenty. When she saw me she left her post and almost within the hearing of her boss she asked me quickly and quietly and with an unforgettable smile of her irregularly shaped teeth: "How old are you?" "Thirteen," I said, as planned. And she, fixing me intently, whispered, "Tell him you are fifteen."

Two minutes later it was my turn, and I cast a sidelong look at the other line, afraid the other SS man might look up and recognize me as someone with whom he had already dealt. He didn't. When asked for my age I gave the decisive answer which I had rejected when my mother suggested it but accepted from the stranger. "I am fifteen."

"She seems small," the master over life and death remarked. Not unfriendly, rather the way one might evaluate cows and calves.

"But she is strong," the woman said, "look at the muscles in her legs, she can work."

She didn't know me, why did she do it. He agreed, why not? She made a note of my number, I had won an extension on life.

I didn't work in the munitions factory but usually in the open air. It was men's work. We cleared the forest and dug up and carried the trunks of trees and laid railroad tracks. Obviously something was supposed to go up in Groß-Rosen, but I was not interested in what it might be. It's in the nature of slave labor that the worker either ignores or hates the purpose and end product of his work. Marx would have enjoyed and, I hope, turned in his grave if he could have seen us apply his thesis. Sometimes our keepers lent some of us out to the civilian population, and then we would sit in some attic and string onions. That was better than the cold air. The villagers stared at us as if we were wild animals. (But I speak your language, I wanted to say.) Sometimes my friend Ditha and I had to work in the quarry, that was the worst of all, because no other place was so desolate and cold. We clung to each other, but that didn't help much. There was no protection against the cold, our clothes were too thin, and though we had wrapped our feet in newspapers, which was some help, I was still close to despair. We longed for the next rest period, for time to pass. Perhaps I can stay in the camp tomorrow as part of the cleaning crew. How can we go on this way and for how much longer? (About twelve years later I watch Ditha, who is like a sister to me as she plays with her small daughters in the sand. I hear her soothing, superior sounding voice, do this or don't do that, she says. Suddenly I see us as we were, Ditha's arm around me, the two of us crouching in the quarry in the cold wind. I turn away from her and the children, for the sand has solidified into Silesian granite and the children's game has become threatening. Why doesn't she go home with her children, all this sweetness is a lie.) I still dream of Silesian granite. It's a kind of wasteland, I look for warmth in that desolation, but there is none.

We women were the cheapest, poorest work force, most easy to replace and therefore least worthy of food. I marched to work with my eyes glued to the ground, hoping to find something edible on the road, because someone had once found a plum. I fantasized about an apple, it didn't have to be ripe and could be partly rotten. But there was never anything. Naturally not. We marched in columns and I was somewhere in the middle. Why should I be the one to find what others had overlooked?

In the forest we often had some contact with German civilians, for example foremen who directed our work. Once during a rest period I sat on tree trunk next to a fat, square man, who must have invited me to join him, for I would never have done it of my own accord. He was clearly curious; I probably didn't fit into his idea of forced laborers. A dark-haired emaciated child prisoner, a girl at that, who spoke flawless and presumably native German, unsuited for the work, a kid who belonged in school. He wanted to know my age. I wondered whether to tell him the truth, that I was thirteen or whether to continue the old lie, which had saved my life so far, and make out that I was three years older. What I really wanted was his lunch. He was eating a sandwich of lard on rye, a delicacy not to be found in the camp, and I wondered how I could get him to give it to me. To have obtained this bread with lard would have been an achievement, and I wanted it for this reason as much as from hunger. I wanted to share it with my mother and my friend Ditha who had become my foster sister. Ditha had contacts to some kitchen personnel and would occasionally produce some extra food, and I wanted to compete. I figured if I told the guy how young I really was, it might soften him up, but from the point of view of safety the lie that had saved my life was better, that is, that I was sixteen. I don't remember how I decided in the end, only that I didn't get his bread-and-lard. To give him his due, he cut off a large bite for me, but all one could do with that was eat it on the spot. He asked me a series of questions about myself which I answered with much reserve. Even if I had wanted to, I wouldn't have known what words to choose to describe what was happening to our people. But of course, I didn't want to anyway. Nothing could have been further from my mind than to take risks with a German.

The fat man on his part told me that German kids, too, didn't go to school anymore. They had gone to soldier, everyone. Did he want to persuade himself that all was fair and just in Christianstadt? He stuffed himself while telling me about the starving German people.

In today's Germany there are many well-meaning people about my age whose families employed forced laborers. ("Employed" is too good a word, let's say who "used" forced laborers.) They think back to these unpaid servants with pleasure, even affection. These Poles were well off in our household, they'll say, they used to play and laugh with us kids and they had enough to eat. They liked us. And I listen and ask myself, what about the alert reserve, the suspicion, the over- and underestimation of the enemy which must have occupied the minds of these deportees. Didn't you notice then, don't you remember now, shouldn't you revise your judgment? If the Germans who were children then haven't considered these questions, it is because no one sees himself as an enemy. The enemy is always the other, how can I be an enemy, when my parents love me and I am a friendly civil child. And so they never talk about forced laborers and they shrink visibly when I don't shy away from saying "slave labor."

I didn't want to be friends with the fat man, I wanted his food. And I wanted it not only for myself but to bring back to my mother and Ditha, and not only because I loved them but also to be able to say, Here. Look. I am good for something. Be that as it may, I didn't get his sandwich.

I imagine that in the mind of the fat man, if he is still around, I am a little Jewish girl who wasn't all that badly off, for she didn't tell any horror stories, though he encouraged her to be honest and to chat about her life. And she wasn't afraid, that was clear from the way she talked, therefore she had no reason to be afraid. Perhaps he uses this encounter as evidence the Jews were no worse off during the war than the "rest of us."

The first weeks of 1945, and by now there was so little to eat that you couldn't think of anything other than food. When I got my daily bread ration I stuffed it into my mouth as if I needed to eat it all in one swoop. Once in a great while I saw myself as I must have looked to someone else and was ashamed.

As the food grew worse, the social differences (and that is the only word for it) between the prisoners increased. Economic class distinctions, like everywhere else. The cooks and their children grew fat, actually fat. The less there was to eat, the more eagerly the keepers of the food ate it. Since they cooked not only for us but also for the guards they had access to whatever there was, and they helped themselves. When the winter clothes came (second-hand stuff that had been belonged to other victims), the cooks chose first and took what was best. I am standing in front of the central building, there is light in the kitchen, so I can look in the window, a cook shows off her plump daughter to another woman who is wearing worthless rags; she shows the ragwoman what a good skirt her daughter has on, and the daughter preens and poses as if this were a fashion show. Ragwoman admires the kitchen daughter in her new second-hand getup, because she is hoping for food, for a second helping.

One evening Ditha told me that the kitchen staff had some leftovers which they were saving for the children. I ran to the back entrance of the building, stood around for a while, a few more women who must have heard the same rumor joined me. I got impatient, perhaps these latecomers will push ahead, I was here first, and so I went up a few short stairs and then walked along the narrow well-lit hall to the back door of the kitchen. Suddenly a door to the right opened, a tall woman guard appeared, behind her an SS man I had never seen before. He calls to me with a strong Northern accent, using the polite form of address, I stand before him, my metal dish in hand, he asks what I want, I tell him I've heard there are leftovers, he says, "Now watch out." Idiot that I am I still think he'll let me pass, for why would he want to waste the leftovers, if indeed there are any, you don't throw away food when everyone is starving, do you now? And before I know it he has hit me in the face, full force so that I stumble backward all along the hallway and see stars. My wooden clogs fall off my feet, the dish falls from my hands, as I crash to the ground. When I recover my eyesight the other women have retreated, the SS man and his companion are gone, after some further verbal nastiness meant to send us packing. Ditha helps me get up, one or two of the others pick up my things with a bit of comforting tongue clucking. I feel that basically they feel that I provoked this scene, that it was my fault. Walking back to our barracks with Ditha I curse, "The pig actually used the polite form (er hat mich gesiezt)," as if that were adding insult to injury. My face still hurts and the chance for additional food has evaporated.

We return and tell our story. My mother claims that if she had been there, she would have hit back. "Why, then we were lucky that you weren't there," Ditha and I say in unison. She irritates me, because she stylizes herself at my expense, she is the potential heroine, unlikely as it may seem, and reduces me to poor-little-victim status. As if the humiliation of having been hit weren't enough, she has to add her superior pity.

But on that evening I recited one of my Auschwitz poems to my assembled roommates. In this poem the personified death machine proclaims that while it has consumed all who have come its way, it will in the end consume those who built it. I recited these verses with much verve and the secret thought, "You'll get your comeuppance, you creep who hit me, just wait." That was a comfort of sorts but of course it was nonsense, for we can be pretty sure that he didn't get his comeuppance. If he doesn't live in a luxury villa in South America, then perhaps he lives on retirement pay in Göttingen and he may even be the old pensioner whom I overheard talking to a young saleswoman in Schmidt's drugstore the other day. He was carrying on about foreigners, especially the ones from Poland. "They should all go into the gas chambers and the politicians can join them there," he said. I was about to choose between two tubes of toothpaste and almost dropped them at these words. I look at him, I guess his age, yes, homeboy is old enough, he knows the score. He notices my glance, and now it's his turn to look me up and down. "Did I hear what you said?" I ask. We look each other in the eye, a look of recognition. And with a sarcastic undertone, "You heard me correctly," he says.

Escape

We arrived in a small Bavarian town, as part of a trek of refugees from the East. I was still carried by a dizzy sense of happiness, the very opposite of what the genuine German refugees experienced. For they had lost everything, that is, all their property, while we hoped to have gained everything, that is, the rest of our lives. So this arrival in Straubing was for me sheer euphoria, and for the others a low point, a leave-taking from home. And here we were among free men and women who complained about this and that and were entitled to their complaints which would have been unimaginable during those other mass transports we had so recently experienced. We were fellow citizens and were treated as such. We got quarters in town, and the three of us ended up on a small farm at the edge of town, where we had a room for ourselves, sheer luxury.

But there is another side to this coin of triumph, and it is a sense of betrayal, not to say treason. Here are two examples, the first is comical. My mother made friends with the farm woman, who one evening looked deep into my mother's green eyes and asked how come one of my mother's daughters looked so Jewish. My mother, thinking how her two "daughters" didn't look one bit alike, figured this difference in appearance could best be explained through paternity. And so she confessed in sisterly confidence, as between two women who have seen a bit of the world, that she had once had an affair with a Jew, and begged the other woman not to talk about this weakness and sighed that it had caused her much grief and regret. It worked and in a sense it's a funny anecdote, but it's not quite the stuff of comedy and there is a bitter aftertaste in the retelling.

And here is the other example. I went shopping and suddenly the prisoners of an evacuated concentration camp occupied the street, guarded by SS men and their dogs. And I stood on the sidewalk. I had never seen "us" from the outside. What separated me from them was a matter of a few weeks, no more, after we had been together for years. They looked so tired, as if there were no place on earth left for them. The dogs looked alert, well fed, and purposeful. My previous comrades walked slowly and with all their strength gone, whereas I had acquired a firmer step in that short time. I had become a German girl, who occasionally went to church on Sunday, knew how to cross myself and helped out in the potato field. For the rest, I came and went as I pleased. And now here they were, my people. I stared at them with intense concentration and knew that they perceived me only as part of a hostile population.

That was an hour where the sense of having committed treason was not part of any comedy. Not that I wanted to be back with them, but that is the point. I wanted to remember seeing them, wanted to remember this one-sided meeting, yet I did not feel that I had to share their fate. Survivor guilt does not mean that you think you have no right to live. Speaking for myself, I never believed I should have died because others were killed. I hadn't done anything, why should I pay with my life? It's a question of debt rather than guilt, but the words are related as in the Lord's Prayer (forgive us our debts), and in German the one is *Schuld*, the other *Schulden*. One remains a debtor and doesn't quite know whom one owes. One would like to take from the victimizers to give to the dead, but one doesn't know how. For you owe me, I am a victim, but I owe them, for they are dead, more victim than I. One is debtor and creditor at the same time and is doomed to perform surrogate actions, alternating between giving and demanding, senseless actions in the light of reason.

That was my last contact with concentration camp inmates. They walked right through the middle of town, in broad daylight, and there were townspeople to my right and my left who looked away. Or closed their faces so that nothing could penetrate. We have our own troubles, kindly spare us yours. We waited on the sidewalk until the train of "subhumans" had passed. When a few weeks later the Americans occupied the city of Straubing, there was no one who had seen anything. And in a sense no one had. For you haven't seen what you haven't perceived and absorbed. In that sense only I had seen them. I still do.

Part II

From Weimar to National Socialism

2
The Primitive and the Modern: Gottfried Benn and Else Lasker-Schüler

Gisela Brinker-Gabler

Studies on the relationship between fascism and culture, especially those focusing on modernist authors' involvement with fascism or protofascism, have clearly shown the necessity of developing a very well-defined understanding of modernism with regard to both its revolutionary impulses and its fascist/protofascist tendencies.[1] It is important to keep in mind the problems of defining fascism, which as Richard Golsan points out, "extend beyond simply locating and classifying its regional and cultural variants" (xi). Therefore, to understand the complexities of any involvement with fascism/protofascism, which takes various forms, we need a detailed analysis of the specific circumstances of each case. In this chapter, I will investigate one of the specific circumstances that led to a fascist involvement for early German modernism (Expressionism)—that is, the new representation of woman as "primitive" that allows for regression and at the same time permits the masculinist assertion of domination and control.

In her essay, "'New Man', Eternal Woman: Expressionist Response to German Feminism," Barbara Wright demonstrates the extent to which the Expressionist concept of the "New Man" includes its logical companion: a counter-concept of woman. This concept of woman contributed to the Expressionist rebellion against civilization and against the superficiality of modern society, and helped to create a definition of self that was not human but, as Wright points out, male. "Through her traditional association with nature and matter, woman becomes identified with that lower level of being which the 'new man' is out to transform and dominate through the supposedly ineluctible power of his 'Geist' [spirit] and 'Wille' [will]" (587). I am particularly interested in the subject-position taken by the male artist as it relates to the representation of women to which Wright refers, as well as in the effects that this representation of women has had on the literary practice of Expressionist women writers. To take a closer look at this issue, we need a more precise description of the Expressionist (male) subject and how it defines itself. Of course, one could talk about the "traditional association of woman with nature and matter" (as Wright describes it) in its broadest sense. But I prefer to discuss the way this association of woman and nature happens at a specific historical moment. That requires a closer examination of two different aspects of Expressionism: first, its rejection of the representations of "nature" found in Impressionism, Jugendstil, and Naturalism; and second, its rejection of the materialism of modern science and its rebellion against civilization and bourgeois society. Taken together, these two factors create a propensity for both vitalism and primitivism. Out of the strange interaction between primitivism and modernity (which are considered opposing trends or trends that coincide in a specific way), new representations of woman emerge that modify or supercede existing representations of woman as "femme fatale," "femme fragile," or "undine" (water nymph). That does not mean that these images have disappeared. They continue to appear in the works of Expressionist authors. But my focus is the new representation of woman, its relationship to protofascism, and what it meant for women Expressionists.

Before I turn to Expressionist literature, I would like to mention early Expressionist art, which will help to illustrate the primitivistic tendency. In paintings by the artists of the "Brücke" group, primitivism emerges as a counter-image to modernity in different forms.[2] As Jill Lloyd explains in her fine study of primitivism in German Expressionist painting, there are a variety of bathing scenes that celebrate "a full blooded synthesis of man and nature," in which "woman in particular are merged in the surrounding vegetation," as e.g.in Kirchner's Moritzburg paintings (114). They differ from the asexual aspirations of Fidus's (alias Hugo Höppener) *Jugendstil* (Fig 2.1) illustrations, and their primitivist style sets them apart from the tradition of the nineteenth-century bathing scene. In Kirchner's work we also encounter urban imagery incorporated into the bathing scene (*Studio Scene*) (Fig 2.2). In the foreground we see an elegant urban couple, and in the middle ground the nude "bather," while in the background there is a schematic rendering of Kirchner's cabaret study, *The Tightrope Dance*. We find here, as Lloyd suggests, a characteristic pattern of contrast and analogy, the contrast between modernity and primitivism, but also the analogy of their vitalism, expressed by the relation of the urban imagery and the "primitivist" model. The same pattern of contrast and analogy can be seen in the painting *Seated Woman with Wood Sculpture* (Fig. 2.3). As Lloyd writes, the modern urban woman "is both different from and similar to her primitivist ambiance; she thus acts as a kind of interface between the 'primitive' and the modern" (155). This pattern of contrast and analogy disappears in Kirchner's later Berlin paintings. In the famous painting, *Five Women on the Street*, the modern and the primitive merge and coincide in a new way: "they become one and the same thing" (153). In this painting there is a merging of the prostitute and the primitive. In her essay on Benjamin's theory of culture, "The *Trauerspiel* of the Prostituted Body or Woman as Allegory of Modernity," Angelika Rauch points out that woman in the role of the prostitute "replaces the authentic experience of love, tied to a mythical past of feeling whole, with sexual experience heightened by the fantasy of a 'real' experience of the past and the lost object of love" (82). As prostitute and primitive, Woman becomes a wishful projection for a specific white, male subject, the vanguard artist, who, according to Carol Duncan, "protests modern bourgeois male-female relationships and asserts himself as a sexually demanding and controlling presence" (207).

Figure 2.1. Ernst Ludwig Kirchner. *Nudes Playing Under Trees* (*Spielende nackte Menschen unter Baum*), 1910. Oil on canvas 77×89cm. Artothek: Spezialarchiv für Gemäldefotografie, Peissenberg, Germany.

Figure 2.2. Ernst Ludwig Kirchner. *Studio Scene* (*Atelierszene*), ca. 1910–1911. Pen and Ink. 34.5×41.5cm. Kupferstichkabinett der Staatlichen Museen zu Berlin.

Figure 2.3. Ernst Ludwig Kirchner. *Seated Woman with Wood Sculpture* (*Sitzende Frau mit Holzplastik*), 1912. Oil on canvas 79×97cm. Virginia Museum of Fine Arts, Richmond. The Adolph D. and Wilkins C. Williams Fund. Copyright: Virginia Museum of Fine Arts.

As Marianna Torgovnick points out in her study *Gone Primitive: Savage Intellects, Modern Lives*, "Gender issues always inhibit Western versions of the primitive. Sooner or later those familiar tropes for primitives become the tropes conventionally used for women" (17). The projection of woman from a male subject-position as something analogous to nature and the primitive is characterized by antagonism and ambivalence. The natural and the primitive are both embraced and feared. As Hal Foster points out: "this ambivalence arises from a social contradiction—of the natural and the primitive privileged culturally precisely when endangered historically. (At the climax of the great industrial-imperial period, ca. 1914, how could the natural and the primitive not be ambivalently thought [of])" (63). Turning to the natural and the primitive—and Woman as its sign—therefore, is a "natural" (white male) response to social alienation, with the result that the abstract opposition of nature versus culture (and, in this context, Woman versus Man) leads to the mythologizing of both as absolute forces, forces of destiny. And so, as I explore the issue of women and the avant-garde, I must pay close attention to the male subject-position that identifies woman with nature and primitivism. How much leeway was there for real historical women in terms of their representation in art and literature, and what opportunities did they have to express their experiences and to embody their desires? I will address this question by discussing Gottfried Benn's poem "Expresstrain" (D-Zug) (published in the collection entitled *Sons*, dedicated to Else Lasker-Schüler), then a prose text by Benn, and finally a poem by Else Laser-Schüler addressed to Benn.

Expresstrain

Brown as cognac. Brown as leaves. Red-brown. Malayan yellow.
Express train Berlin-Trelleborg and the Baltic Sea resorts.

Flesh, that went naked.
Tanned to the very lips by the sea.
Deeply ripe, for Grecian pleasure.
And yearning for the scythe: how far the summer seems!
Almost the end of the ninth month already!

Stubble and the last almond thirst in us.
Unfoldings, the blood, the weariness,
The nearness of dahlias confuses us.

Man-brown hurls itself upon woman-brown:

A woman is something for a night.

And if it was good, for the next night too!
Oh, and then again this being by oneself!
These silences! This letting oneself drift!

A woman is something with fragrance.
Unspeakable. Dissolve. Reseda.
In her the south, shepherd and sea.
On every slope a pleasure lies.

Woman-light-brown reels towards man-dark-brown:

Hold me, dear; I'm falling.
I'm so weary at the neck.
Oh, this feverish sweet
Last fragrance blown from the gardens.
(Benn, *Primal Vision,* 221)[3]

(D-Zug

Braun wie Kognak. Braun wie Laub. Rotbraun. Malaiengelb.
D-Zug Berlin-Trelleborg und die Ostseebäder.

Fleisch, das nackt ging.
Bis in den Mund gebräunt vom Meer.
Reif gesenkt, zu griechischem Glück.
In Sichel-Sehnsucht: Wie weit der Sommer ist!
Vorletzter Tag des neunten Monats schon!

Stoppel und letzte Mandel lechzt in uns.
Entfaltungen, das Blut, die Müdigkeiten,
die Georginennähe macht uns wirr.

Männerbraun stürzt sich auf Frauenbraun.

Eine Frau ist etwas für eine Nacht.
Und wenn es schön war, noch für die nächste!
Oh! Und dann wieder dies Bei-sich-selbst-Sein!
Diese Stummheiten! Dies Getriebenwerden!

Eine Frau ist etwas mit Geruch.
Unsägliches! Stirb hin! Resede.
Darin ist Süden, Hirt und Meer.
An jedem Abhang lehnt ein Glück.

Frauenhellbraun taumelt an Männerdunkelbraun:
Halte mich! Du, ich falle!
Ich bin im Nacken so müde.
Oh, dieser fiebernde süße
letzte Geruch aus den Gärten.)
(Benn, Primal Vision, 220)

Benn's poem "Expresstrain" expresses the desire for a regression to nature and vegetation in the face of a modern, mechanized world. Regression offers the possibility of seeing the world in a new way. One after another, images are presented that express excitement and a sense of being driven, images that correspond to the view from the window of the Berlin-Trelleborg train. They originate in the exotic world of the south, and symbolize the longing for hot summer days and nights, instinctual nature, a return to Dionysian ecstasies. A lyrical male speaker speaks for a "we" (Wir) defined by gender ("The nearness of dahlias confuses us" [Die Georginennähe macht uns wirr]), and describes Woman as "something" (etwas), a nameless, faceless object, something that has to do with "fragrance" (Geruch)[4] and belongs to the vegetative world of gardens, like the mignonette, a strongly scented fall flower. The merging of the sexes becomes a union of "man" (with its masculine connotation) and nature, an archaic, anti-urban Mediterranean nature ("Süden, Hirt und Meer"), which allows for a recovery of some original undifferentiated unity. Woman as some*thing*, objectified and identified with nature, provides a temporary refuge and submits completely to man's sexually demanding and controlling presence. The last stanza allows her to speak, only to give expression to her self-annihilation.

The following passage from "The Conquest" (Die Eroberung), a prose sketch from Benn's Rönne cycle "Brains" (Gehirne), also describes regression to a more primitive state as a sought-after experience. The central figure, Rönne, is a manifestation of the Cartesian mind/body split, and demonstrates a new way to relate to the world, an ecstatic and visionary one. Rönne travels to a foreign place. "Out of long months of helplessness and exile after exile, I will possess this country, Rönne thought." (Aus der Ohnmacht langer Monate und unaufhörlicher Vertriebenheiten—: Dies Land will ich besetzen, dachte Rönne; *Werke,* 20). While in the foreign country he visits a bar one evening and watches women dancing:

> There one woman was dancing behind veils, with covered breasts, and with coral gums through which she laughed. Two stroked with flattering hands their bodies and drove fragrance and desire towards men. One thrust body and breasts forward, having unveiled. (*Primal Visions,* 219)

(Da tanzte eine hinter Schleiern, die Brüste gebunden, und ein Korallengaumen, aus dem sie lachte. Zwei wehten mit ihren Händen an ihren Leibern vorbei und trieben Geruch und Lust den Männern zu. Eine stieß Leib und Brüste hervor nach Enthüllungen.) (*Werke,* 26)

While watching this erotic spectacle, Rönne moves toward regression by having a primeval vision.

> But he felt all hands on his thighs, felt compelled to level himself to the ground, felt the throbbing, the confluence and fresh growth, and suddenly she stood there pregnant: broad heavy flesh, juices dripping from breast and body; a narrow, destitute skull under moist leafage, over a landscape of blood, over bellyings of animal tissue, evoked by an undoubting touch. (219)
>
> (Er aber spürte die Hände alle auf den Hüften, den Drang, sich abzuflachen auf die Erde, die Zuckungen, das Zusammenströmen und den Aufwuchs, und plötzlich stand vor ihm die Schwangere: breites, schweres Fleisch, triefend von Säften aus Brust und Leib; ein magerer, verarmter Schädel über feuchtem Blattwerk, über einer Landschaft aus Blut, über Schwellungen aus tierischen Geweben, hervorgerufen durch eine unzweifelhafte Berührung.) (26)

As is characteristic for Benn's early prose, the difference between inner reality (Rönne's vision) and outer reality collapses. The phantasm of nature and the primordial, as embodied in the archaic Woman, leads to a violent encounter with a woman, again as a temporary refuge. The ecstatic and violent surrender of self in sexuality alternates with sober rationality.

> Then he leaped at a woman, forced her open, bit to the bone that seemed his, drew screams which sounded as his own, and swooned over a thigh, strangeness storming all around him [I would prefer to translate this literally as: "taken by storm by a strange round"].
>
> Then morning rushed forward, red and victorious. Rönne walked through the waves of the dawn, through the sea that broke over the clouds.
>
> He saw the night behind him, pure and clear; now he took the path to the palm gardens on the edge of the town. (219)
>
> (Da sprang er eine an, brach sie auf, biß in Gebein, das wie seines war, entriß ihm Schreie, die wie seine klangen, und verging an einer Hüfte, erstürmt von einem fremden Rund. Dann stieß der Morgen hervor, rot und siegreich. Rönne schritt durch die Wellen der Frühe, durch das Meer, das über die Wolken brach.
>
> Rein und klar sah er hinter sich die Nacht, nun ging er den Weg zu den Palmengärten am Rande der Stadt.) (26)

Peter Uwe Hohendahl has pointed out the "tension between cerebration and hallucination, between rational consciousness and prerational wholeness" which is characteristic of Benn's early prose, and which, according to Hohendahl, "later found its release in Benn's commitment to German fascism" (90).[5]

The primal vision of Woman indicates a yearning for and yet fear of regression, instinctual nature, and death. It is created out of the Western crisis of identity, Western doubts about civilization. However, the attempt to overcome the alienation caused by modern rationality aligns itself inevitably to forceful virility and domination, although artistic control obliterates the evidence of aggression and oppression. Woman as life force is essentially different from man, alien, antagonistic, linked to a primal level of existence, seducing and threatening as a primitive mother-whore, inviting regression, violent masculine control, and exploitation at the same time. The body of Woman, primitive, vital, fertile, and nourishing, like the surrounding landscape, becomes identified with a landscape that has to be invaded, conquered, and appropriated. Thus, this attempt to solve the problem of the modern overcerebral man, by revaluation of the primitive as an alternative to civilization, is based on discourses of forceful masculinity, imperialism, and power.

Within the context of the Rönne sketches, the brain is no longer seen as the carrier of truth, but a mistake, leading to the destruction of feeling whole and being connected with nature. The contrast between a cerebral existence (Rönne) and a primitive existence (narrow, destitute skull) is transformed in the binary Man and Woman, in which Woman serves as the reminder of a prerational animalistic/vegetative existence promising vitality and the unity of life. What are the consequences for women of this representation of Woman? How can they resist representations that take on authority in speaking about them? According to Angelika Rauch in her essay, "Women as Allegory of Modernity," whenever the representation of "Woman" in the aesthetic realm is aimed at expressing what cannot be expressed in rational semantics it is not intended to produce knowledge of real women (78). The question is, however, who keeps apart Woman and woman? Otto Weininger, for example, in his famous study *Sex and Character* (1903) develops, as clearly indicated, a construct of Woman (Weib), representing the "a-logical," "a-moral," and matter and then later in his study continuously shifts from Woman to women.[6] In Benn's text, there are the same kinds of shifts from women (in the bar) to Woman and then back to woman again. How could women, reading and writing within the context of Expressionism, negotiate between the representation of Woman as a primitive form of existence, and their struggle with other conventional female concepts and roles? How were they able to find or create their own reality, sexuality, emotionality? I would like to discuss this in light of Lasker-Schüler's poem, "To the Barbarian" (Dem Barbaren), which is dedicated to Gottfried Benn.

To the Barbarian

I lie in the nights
Upon your countenance,

On the steppes of your body
Plant cedars and almond trees.

Ceaselessly I rummage in your breast
For the Pharaoh's golden joys.

But your lips are hard;
My miracles don't redeem them.

Please lift your snow-filled skies
From off my soul—

Your diamond dreams
Cut open my arteries.

I am Joseph and wear a sweet girdle
About my bright skin.

My seashells' frightened roar
Enraptures you.

But your heart lets no more oceans in
O you! (181)

(Dem Barbaren

Ich liege in den Nächten
Auf deinem Angesicht.

Auf deines Leibes Steppe
Pflanze ich Zedern und Mandelbäume.

Ich wühle in deiner Brust unermüdlich
Nach den goldenen Freuden Pharaos.

Aber deine Lippen sind schwer,
Meine Wunder erlösen sie nicht.

Hebe doch deine Schneehimmel
Von meiner Seele—

Deine diamantnen Träume
Schneiden meine Adern auf.

Ich bin Joseph und trage einen süßen Gürtel
Um meine bunte Haut.

Dich beglückt das erschrockene Rauschen
Meiner Muscheln.

Aber dein Herz läßt keine Meere mehr ein.
O du!) (180)

After reading Benn's "Expresstrain," with its feelings of being driven by natural urges, its ecstatic regression, we are struck by the much quieter tone of Lasker-Schüler's description of an attempted encounter. The man addressed as "Du" appears lifeless, cold, empty. The female speaker's restless, active urgings serve to bring him to life, not to experience a Dionysian ecstasy but just to feel closeness and experience boundlessness together. The description of the man's body, face, his chest and lips, pointing to his lack of vitality and life force, contrasts with the female speaker's imagination of herself as Joseph or the ocean. Both images express the woman's empowerment— "sweet girdle, bright [I would translate this as "colorful"] skin, seashells"—a summoning of magical forces that allow her to work wonders. The ecstatic excesses of a return to times of early civilization (Joseph), instead of primitivism, images of the fullness of life (cedar and almond trees), the identification of the woman with the origin of life (represented by the ocean)—all contrast with images of alienation and lifelessness. These images delineate a difference in gender politics and a change in the conception of the individual self and its relation to others. "My seashells' frightened roar/Enraptures you./But your heart lets no more oceans in." (Dich beglückt das erschrockene Rauschen/Meiner Muscheln. Aber Dein Herz läßt keine Meere mehr ein.) An encounter does ensue—with clear sexual connotations (Muscheln)—but it finds no echo in the man's heart. The man has other expectations than those of an encounter that will include love (Herz). There will be no "I-Thou" relationship, no real closeness: this painful recognition is expressed in the sad "O you!" (Ach Du!) If the encounter means merely sexual release, loneliness is all that each one is left with (loneliness is seen favorably in Benn's "Expresstrain" and the Rönne-cycle *Brain*). Although, in Lasker-Schüler's poem, Man and Woman are represented in contrasting images of lifelessness and fullness of life, which puts this poem in the context of Expressionism, there are no illusions about the nature of a temporary refuge provided by regression. To paraphrase Nietzsche, who was so important for Benn, it is the heart that drives the head to "go under" (*Untergang*) in a gesture of "going over" (*Übergang*), that allows one to transcend one's humanity. True liberation only comes when *Untergang* and *Übergang* are connected.[7] In contrast to the woman's gesture of resignation at the end, the man's desire for a regressive dreamlike state might be fatal: "Deine diamantnen Träume / schneiden meine Adern auf" (Your diamond dreams / Cut open my arteries). His longing for submersion of self in nature and instinctive primitive existence not only transforms others into objects, but creates the possibility of bloody encounters.

I find particular significance in the fact that immediately after the description of these "diamond dreams" the woman imagines herself as Joseph. Joseph was a visionary who was able to interpret the dreams of others—in this case the mythified "diamond dreams" of the Pharaoh. The identification with Joseph, who was a "chosen one," helps to empower the female speaker, and while it is a masculinization of the female speaker, at the same time, the figure of Joseph is feminized: "sweet girdle, colorful skin." Joseph, to use Sigrid Bauschinger's phrase about the Prince of Thebes, "is a figure beyond female and male" (118). Therefore, the static antagonism of Man/Woman (suggested by Benn) is transformed into something fluid; something fixed and eternal is transformed into something susceptible to change. For the Jewish poet Else Lasker-Schüler, Joseph stands for another way of seeing the world and Wo/man. The essence of this is the blurring of the distinction between masculine and feminine, resisting the transformation of women into Woman—envisioned as the static counterimage of Man, the embodiment of a prerational life force to which Man imagines he may regress.

Flight, ecstasy, and regression are, in Benn's writings, responses to the alienation and objectification of modern civilization. The experience of ecstasy and regression is only to be bought at the price of renewed objectification, the appropriation/disappropriation of another (a woman). Else Lasker-Schüler's poem expresses resistance to objectification and a static gender order, and shows their consequences: hopeless and painful loneliness that can be fatal. The discourse that primitivizes woman as a catalyst for a radical rupture, a regression into an undifferentiated totality, functions at the same time as the forceful assertion of a protofascist masculinity that holds on to the power of controlling and dominating a total submissive other. A more detailed account of the issues I have outlined has yet to be published. Such an account, written from a feminist perspective, would describe the relation of the subject-position of male Expressionists to representations of women and to the literary practice of women Expressionist writers. It would reveal to what extent the women Expressionists identified with certain representations of Woman and/or to what extent they expressed resistance to the (ab)use of such representations.

Notes

Translated by Elizabeth Naylor Endres.

1. One of the first informative studies to be published in German on this theme is the essay collection by Reinhold Grimm and Jost Hermand, *Faschismus und Avantgarde* (Königstein im Taunus: Athenäum Verlag, 1980).

2. For a recent study on Emil Nolde and primitivism see: Russell A. Berman.

3. Adapted by Michael Hamburger from the Lohner-Corman translation.

4. I prefer "odor" here as a translation of the German "Geruch."

5. In her essay "Ezra Pound und Gottfried Benn: Avantgarde, Faschismus und ästhetische Autonomie," Judith Ryan describes as cause for Benn's complex relationship with protofascism his "Vorstellung des Ich als eines grundsätzlich isolierten und in seinem damit einhergehenden Glauben an die Autonomie der Kunst" (25). For a recent discussion of Benn's case as example of "the dilemma of the historically detached and 'unpolitical' artist in a setting of political hooliganism" (70) see: Walter A. Strauss.

6. See for example: "Der Mann ist Form, das Weib Materie . . . Die Frauen sind die Materie, die jede Form annimmt. Jene Untersuchungen, welche für Mädchen eine bessere Erinnerung speziell an den Lehrstoff ergeben haben, als für die Knaben, können nur so erklärt werden: aus der Inanität und Nullität der Frauen, die mit allem Beliebigen imprägniert werden können" (394).

7. See Friedrich Nietzsche, *Also sprach Zarathustra*: "Ich liebe Den, der freien Geistes und freien Herzens ist: so ist sein Kopf nur das Eingeweide seines Herzens, sein Herz aber treibt ihn zum Untergang." *Sämtliche Werke. Kritische Studienausgabe in 15 Bänden*, ed. Giorgio Colli and Mazzino Montinari. Vol. 4. (Munich: Deutscher Taschenbuch Verlag [Berlin/New York: Walter de Gruyter], 1980), 18.

Bibliography

Benn, Gottfried. *Gesammelte Werke in vier Bänden*. Ed. Dieter Wellershoff. Vol. 2. *Prosa und Szenen*. Wiesbaden: Limes Verlag, 1958.

———. *Primal Vision: Selected Writings*. Ed. E. B. Ashton. [New York]: New Directions, [1960].

Bauschinger, Sigrid. *Else Lasker-Schüler: Ihr Werk und ihre Zeit*. Heidelberg: Lothar Stiehm Verlag, 1980.

Berman, Russell A. "German Primitivism/Primitive Germany: The Case of Emil Nolde." In *Fascism, Aesthetics, and Culture*. Ed. Richard J. Golsan. Hanover and London: University Press of New England, 1992, 56–66.

Duncan, Carol. "Virility and Domination in Early Twentieth-Century Vanguard Painting." In *Feminism and Art History: Questioning the Litany*. Ed. Norma Broude and Mary D. Garrard. New York: Harper & Row, 1982, 292–315.

Fascism, Aesthetics, and Culture. Ed. Richard J. Golsan. Hanover and London: University Press of New England, 1992.

Foster, Hal. "The Expressive Fallacy." In *Recodings—Art, Spectacle, Cultural Politics.* Post Townsend, Wash.: Bay Press, 1985, 59–73.

Hohendahl, Peter Uwe. "The Loss of Reality: Gottfried Benn's Early Prose." In *Modernity and the Text: Revisions of German Modernism.* Ed. Andreas Huyssen and David Bathrick. New York: Columbia University Press, 1989, 81–94.

Lasker-Schüler, Else. *Your Diamond Dreams Cut Open My Arteries.* Tr. and with an introd. Robert P. Newton. Chapel Hill: University of North Carolina Press, 1982.

Lloyd, Jill. *German Expressionism. Primitivism and Modernity.* New Haven/London: Yale University Press, 1991.

Rauch, Angelika. "The *Trauerspiel* of the Prostituted Body or Woman as an Allegory of Modernity." *Cultural Critique* (Fall 1987): 77–88.

Ryan, Judith. "Ezra Pound und Gottfried Benn: Avantgarde, Faschismus und ästhetische Autonomie." In *Faschismus und Avantgarde.* Ed. Reinhold Grimm und Jost Hermand. Königstein im Taunus: Athenäum Verlag, 1980, 20–34.

Strauss, Walter A. "Gottfried Benn: A Double Life in Uninhabitable Regions." In *Fascism, Aesthetics, and Culture.* Ed. Richard J. Golsan. Hanover and London: University Press of New England, 1992, 67–80.

Torgovnick, Marianna. *Gone Primitive: Savage Intellects, Modern Lives.* Chicago: University of Chicago Press, 1990.

Weininger, Otto. *Geschlecht und Charakter. Eine prinzipielle Untersuchung.* Munich: Matthes & Seitz, 1980. Rpt. Vienna 1903.

Wright, Barbara. "'New Man,' Eternal Woman: Expressionist Response to German Feminism." *German Quarterly* (Fall 1987): 582–599.

3
"This Number Is Not in Service:"
Destabilizing Identities in Irmgard Keun's Novels from Weimar and Exile

Ritta Jo Horsley

In her 1986 article "*Girlkultur* or Thoroughly Rationalized Female—A New Woman in Weimar Germany?" Atina Grossmann analyzed the position of economically and sexually independent women in the Weimar Republic, asserting in contrast to earlier views that the "New Woman was not merely a media myth or a demographer's paranoid fantasy, but a social reality that can be researched and documented" (64).[1] She called for scholars to take seriously the perception of a tremendous and unsettling change since 1914, to analyze why so much of that sense of rupture and change was "conceptualized and interpreted in terms of a New Woman."

Grossmann suggested that the image of the New Woman as threatening and contradictory represented the fear that the modern independent woman might no longer provide the "haven in a heartless world" so needed by a rapidly mechanizing society. The figure of the New Woman "embodied within her dual identity the conflicts aroused by rationalization and the ambivalence of modernity" (76), and it became the aim of social scientists and sex reformers to construct the synthesis of housewife, mother, and working woman that society needed, a woman who would be both "womanly" and "rationalized"—efficient and disciplined enough to perform all the tasks needed. This aim, requiring massive intervention of state support services in health and social welfare, was not fulfilled, and with the end of the Weimar Republic and the beginning of Nazi dictatorship came the demise of the New

Woman as a popular though ambivalent icon. Concluding her article, Grossmann wondered what dreams and ideals were held by the "younger sisters" of Weimar working women, who came of age at the close of the Weimar Republic and lived adult lives under National Socialism and its restrictive view of women's roles (77).

Since Grossmann's call to take the New Woman seriously, the portrait of the modern woman of Weimar as contradictory and ambivalent has begun to be traced in various disciplines, revealing a complex and mutually interactive field of discourses and socioeconomic conditions.[2] Concluding a recent *Signs* article in which she analyzes Weimar discourses around the female body as they affected and were in turn shaped by working women, historian Kathleen Canning points out:

> The discourses of the "new woman," sexual reform, eugenics, and the controversies over birth control and abortion, for example, focused the attention of a wide range of political and social groups on female sexuality. At the same time, however, this saturation of the social field created a social and discursive space in which women were encouraged and empowered to conceptualize their own sexuality. (396)

Canning shows the emergence of a counterdiscourse generated by the union women themselves, who insisted on their needs as "embodied," concretely suffering workers and who thereby reinscribed dominant natalist and universalizing class-based male discourses. Her study suggests that: "Weimar body politics was a particularly contested and fractured discursive domain, one that was particularly vulnerable to dispersal, resistance, and transformation"(396).

In this context of debate and change the New Woman emerged as a myth with powerful significance. The image of a self-assertive, sexually and financially independent female epitomized for many the drastically changed social and economic situation of Germany after World War I, and was frequently equated with the modern metropolis or with modernity itself.[3] Perceived as a threat to traditional bourgeois patriarchal values and hierarchies, the image of the New Woman was soon co-opted and domesticated to serve society's needs.[4] By the mid-twenties she had become a fixed cliché exploited by fashion and the popular media to enforce a style that imposed new norms even as it seemed to offer emancipation from traditional constraints. Sociologist Fritz Giese commented in his 1925 essay "Das Girl als Vorbild" (The Girl as Example/Model):

> An international feminine style evolved that erased all sociological differentiation. It was genuinely American in its uniformity, whether stenotypist, countess or factory worker. The short bobbed hair, the particular fashionable universal style, the particular fashionable "slim" figure, the athletic body without fat and erotic womanliness: that was the international feminine style around 1924.

(Es entwickelte sich ein internationaler Frauenstil mit Verschiebung aller soziologischer Differenzierung. Er war echt amerikanisch-uniform, ob er Stenotypistin, Gräfin oder Industriefrau blieb. Der Bubikopf, der bestimmte modische Universalschnitt, die bestimmte modische 'schlanke' Linie, der Sportkörper ohne Fett und erotische Fraulichkeit: das war der internationale Frauenstil um 1924.) (139)[5]

Popular journals reflected the image of the New Woman as employed and unmarried by choice, as a person interested in sport, film, travel and as a consumer of birth control products (Kübler, 3/42).[6]

By the late twenties and early thirties this myth of the modern independent woman had become subject to more intense criticism, and the return to more traditional images of femininity had begun. Popular magazines warned against female "bisexuality" and exhorted women to find their true femininity in subordination to their husbands or their role as mother; they featured more "feminine" fashions and articles on "the family in danger" (Petro, 119–127; Kübler, 42–55). Vicki Baum's sensationally popular student Helene Willfüer (in the novel of 1928) embodied this idealized, domesticated New Woman of late Weimar: in contrast to both the unfeminine student Gundula Rapp ("das Gulrapp") and the self-indulgent, libertinistic Yvonne Pastouri, the hard-working but sociable Helene represents "natural" femininity, maternal feeling and self-discipline, and eventually suspends her independence through marriage to her father-figure professor.[7] She would seem to fulfill the need referred to by Grossmann for a synthesis of new and old. Meanwhile, other women writers and artists expressed a sense of the New Woman as a figure still evolving, with inner discrepancies and an uncertain future; as Alice Rühle-Gerstel concluded her 1932 study of women's roles: "Today the female sex stands at a radical turning point of its development. The transition from the old to the new femininity does not follow a smooth, straight path and is occasionally dashed on the cliffs of masculinity." (Heute steht das weibliche Geschlecht an einer Umbruchstelle seiner Entwicklung. Der Übergang von der alten zur neuen Weiblichkeit vollzieht sich nicht geradlinig und scheitert zuweilen an den Klippen der Männlichkeit, 408–409).[8] With the banishing of the New Woman by Hitler a year later, her last words were dramatically fulfilled.

Of the authors tracing the fortunes of the modern woman at the close of the Weimar Republic, the novelist Irmgard Keun is among the most interesting.[9] *Gilgi, eine von uns* (1931) (*Gilgi, One of Us*) and *Das kunstseidene Mädchen* (1932) (*The Synthetic Silk Girl*) present two versions of the myth of the New Woman as she had evolved and survived in late Weimar culture: the "rationalized," self-sufficient, and ambitious typist Gilgi, prototype of the new class of Weimar white-collar workers, and the equally ambitious flapper Doris, who hopes to find fame and riches in the modern metropolis through her style and sex appeal. That Gilgi is intended as a typical representative of young women of her time is implied by the "one of us" of the title. And the tremendous—though also controversial—popularity of both novels suggests that they truly struck a nerve of the era. *Gilgi* was filmed by Paramount, translated into seven languages, and serialized in the Social Democratic journal *Vorwärts* (*Onward*) while *Das kunstseidene Mädchen* was published in the unheard-of first edition of 50,000 copies (Kreis, 97). The reviewer for *Die Frau* (*Woman*), journal of the bourgeois women's movement, reported that it was impossible to find *Das kunstseidene Mädchen* in any big city library, so popular was the book. Her review, entitled "Mädchen auf der Suche" (1932–33) ("Girls on a quest"), is typical in reading Keun's two books as successfully realistic representations of the efforts of young women to find their way among the conflicting roles and values of late Weimar society (Fließ, 172). According to another review, *Gilgi* commanded the interest of contemporary readers because it was "a document of the times" and because it dealt with one of the "most burning" problems of the era, "the conflict of the modern woman caught between her work and the love of her life" (Wedekind). Still another reviewer attributed Keun's "exceptional success" to her effectiveness "as a mouthpiece for those people of our time whose fates she describes" (als Sprachrohr jener Zeitschicksale, von denen sie zu berichten weiß; Weissinger, 5). Such comments reflect the predominant reception of Keun's first two novels as realistic representations, as literature portraying and addressing the new social class of Weimar women, "the armies of white collar workers" (die Heere der Angestellten; m.r. 6).

Unlike Baum's *stud. chem. Helene Willfüer*, however, *Gilgi* and *Das kunstseidene Mädchen* do not provide unified or affirmative portraits of the modern woman. Rather, they disclose contradictions that undermine the myth of the New Woman and reflect the growing uncertainty regarding women's roles in the late Weimar Republic. The open endings of both novels leave the futures of the New Women Gilgi and Doris in question and their stories subject to varying interpretation. In both cases Keun problematizes the popular images through developments on the plot level as well as through stylistic strategies. Disturbances in the authority and veracity of their speech reflect shifts and contradictions in the representation of the protagonists' identities. Keun's early novels both incarnate and destabilize the New Woman in her last phase as an icon of the Weimar Republic.

The underlying contradictions and instability of the New Woman in late Weimar may have made her demise under the Nazis seem all the more inevitable. In her subsequent writing, published in exile, Irmgard Keun reflects this social and political watershed: the New Woman and her struggles vanish from center stage, as the ambitious, independent protagonists of the early novels are replaced in the later books by young women of increasingly muted, passive, and even fearful cast, and by minor female characters showing stereotypical negative qualities such as narrow-mindedness and power-hungry bossiness (often implicitly or explicitly attributed to sexual frustration). But the spunky female does not disappear entirely, and the change in her character maintains continuities with her Weimar sisters. The first two books published in exile, while no longer treating the theme of the New Woman, still show traces of her independent spirit. The protagonist of *Das Mädchen, mit dem die Kinder nicht verkehren durften* (1936) (The Girl the Children were not allowed to associate with, translated as *The Bad Example*), is a lively, misbehaving tomboy who scorns the expectations of traditional feminine socialization and the idea of marriage.[10] *Nach Mitternacht* (1937) (*After Midnight*), a novel set in and satirizing the early years of the Third Reich is narrated from the perspective of Sanna, a simple and modest young woman without independent employment or ambition; she registers conditions and events with an innocent but critical eye and finally musters the insight and courage to leave the country to save her lover from the Nazis.[11]

With the timid character Lenchen of *D-Zug dritter Klasse* (1938) (*Express Train Third Class*), however, Keun presents a sharp departure from—almost a parody of—her earlier ambitious protagonists. Lenchen was interpreted by one reviewer of the time as an exposé of the ideal woman of Nazis and other reactionaries, as an embodiment of "the lovely maid, the feminine woman" (die holde Magd, die weibliche Frau; Blum, 120). Yet this interpretation reductively simplifies the situation and conceals continuities with the earlier portrayals. Themes of destabilizing language and identity encountered in the first three novels recur in the later ones, where the problems of (self-)deception and of woman's silencing come increasingly to the fore: the mother, Annchen, in *Kind aller Länder* (1938) (*Child of all Countries*), barely speaks, and in *Ferdinand* (1950), Keun's last completed novel, a *male* first-person narrator has replaced the female voice.

The elusive, often contradictory quality of Keun's protagonists as well as the disappearance of the female voice in her later works are reflected in the title she chose for the "life novel" she claimed to be writing at the end of her life, but of which no trace was found after her death in 1982: "Kein Anschluß unter dieser Nummer" ("This number is not in service," literally: "No connection under this number"). Like all Keun's titles, it is significant: an image of isolation and failed communication, it bespeaks the sense of alienation that had dogged her, particularly in the years of Adenauer, the economic miracle, the Cold War mentality and the restoration of conservative political values. She had herself been silent as a writer for the last twenty years of her life, and the unwritten life-novel is among other things a testimony to the difficulties of "confronting the past." Keun's tendency to fictionalize her own life bore fruit in her works but also resulted in the propagation of "errors" and exaggerations in the reconstruction of her biography, as when she told of being interrogated and forced to flee by the Gestapo (Kreis, 156–158). Questions of truth telling, lying, guilt, and anxiety recur in Keun's works, as do the themes of the inadequacy of language and the failure of communication. As a motto for her œuvre as a whole, "Kein Anschluß unter dieser Nummer" conveys a skepticism about linguistic authority and reliability and a resistance to being pinned down to a definitive statement, a particular "number." As such it is a fruitful perspective to investigate the shifting versions of female identities in the three novels that deal most explicitly with this topic: *Gilgi, eine von uns* (1931), *Das kunstseidene Mädchen* (1932), and *D-Zug dritter Klasse* (1938).

Gilgi initially appears to epitomize the "Girl" as described by Giese and featured in countless women's magazines: she is young, slim, and boyish and begins each day with calisthenics and a cold shower (*Gilgi*, 5). Although at the beginning of the book she still lives with her middle-class parents, Gilgi exhibits the modern woman's spirit of independence and self-sufficiency, as the first sentence indicates: "she holds it firmly in her hand, her little life" (Sie hält es fest in der Hand, ihr kleines Leben; 5) She rents a room of her own where she spends evenings practicing the foreign languages she is learning after hours to enhance her career opportunities. Adhering to a confident work ethic that corresponds in its own way to the rags-to-riches myth of many Weimar films, Gilgi is determined to climb to success through her own efforts, and looks with scorn on those who have given up or live only in the hope of a miracle, such as her fellow streetcar passengers on the way to work:

> The hopeless ones there in the streetcar—no, she doesn't have anything in common with them, she isn't one of them, doesn't want to be. They are gray and tired and indifferent. And if they're not indifferent, they're waiting for a miracle. Gilgi isn't indifferent and she doesn't believe in miracles. She believes only in what she accomplishes and earns.
>
> (Die Trostlosen da im Wagen—nein, sie hat nichts mit ihnen gemein, sie gehört nicht zu ihnen, will nicht zu ihnen gehören. Sie sind grau und müde und stumpf. Und wenn sie nicht stumpf sind, warten sie auf ein Wunder. Gilgi ist nicht stumpf und sie glaubt an kein Wunder. Sie glaubt nur an das, was sie schafft und erwirbt.) (11)

Gilgi's unsentimental, objective attitude to traditional values and pieties reflects the ideology of *Neue Sachlichkeit* (New Objectivity) and the emphasis of Weimar popular culture on both work and pleasure: "Work makes sense, and pleasure makes sense. Going with her mother to a coffee party would be neither pleasure nor work, but senselessly wasted time." (Arbeit hat Sinn, und Vergnügen hat Sinn. Mit der Mutter zur Kaffeeklatsch zu gehen, wäre weder Vergnügen noch Arbeit, sondern sinnlos verschwendete Zeit; 10). Gilgi applies a code of rationalized time apportionment to her every act: "Stick to your daily schedule. Don't depart from the system. Don't break down. Not in the tiniest detail." (Tagesplan einhalten. Nicht abweichen vom System. Nicht schlapp machen. In der kleinsten Kleinigkeit nicht; 5).[12]

Also characteristic of the New Woman of the twenties is Gilgi's initially pragmatic and unsentimental view of love and sex as belonging practically to the realm of entertainment. Two words that Gilgi abhors are "romanticism" (Romantik; 15) and "longing" (Sehnsucht; 47). In her experience romance— "a friendly in-love feeling ("ein freundlich verliebtes Gefühl; 71)—does not interfere with the more important goals of work and advancement. Moreover, Gilgi combines the New Woman's sexual freedom with the pragmatic rationalism of *Neue Sachlichkeit* in justifying her right to act on her feelings: "It's terribly immoral to wait, because it's so pointless" (Warten ist furchtbar unmoralisch, weil's so sinnlos ist; 67). Like many of her fictional and real contemporaries, Gilgi rules out marriage as a life goal: "except for marriage, being a movie star or beauty queen she's considering all the possibilities" (außer Ehe, Filmschauspielerin und Schönheitskönigin zieht sie jede Existenzmöglichkeit in Betracht; 16). Gilgi's two cousins, by contrast, are not in step with "the new era" (die neue Zeit; 42): already twenty-six and thirty, Irenchen and Gerdachen are ridiculed as useless and lazy, with no occupation or plans except an increasingly urgent search for a husband.

This portrait of Gilgi as stereotypical New Woman—independent, happily employed, sexually liberated, and dedicated to her own advancement—is soon challenged, however. The two friends Gilgi turns to for advice and support both criticize her way of life; the carefree, demimonde painter Olga chides her for being obsessed with her work and advancement, while the bitter socialist Pit condemns her lack of political awareness. The news that she had been adopted by her respectable middle-class family, finally, sets off an identity crisis on both the biological and the moral levels, and Gilgi begins reflecting about her assumed values and way of life. This process is symbolized and accompanied by her quest for her biological mother. Ultimately distancing herself from all three women who have served as "mothers" to her (the middle-class Frau Kron who raised her, the working-class seamstress Margarethe Trätschler, a temporary surrogate mother, and finally the wealthy socialite Magdalene Greiff, her biological mother), Gilgi represents the generation of young Weimar women for whom traditional class membership has become less important than the commonalities of her age group (Grossmann 1986, 65).[13] The search for her roots also undermines her original, rather smug belief in survival of the fittest—"People are where they belong" (Jeder ist da, wo er hingehört; 38)—and she begins to wonder whether she might not just as easily have become a prostitute such as one she talks with in a bar, had she not had the advantages provided by her adoptive parents (39).[14] Through Gilgi's evolving perspective the harsh realities of the Depression come into sharper focus, and the myth of the the self-made woman is questioned. By the end of the novel an ethic of solidarity and mutual responsibility has replaced individualistic striving: "I used to think it was enough to take care of yourself without getting help . . . but now I know that you have to help" (ich hab' mal gedacht, es genügte, sich allein durchzubringen und sich selbst nicht helfen zu lassen . . . aber jetzt weiß ich, daß man helfen muß; 139).

The modern, casual attitude of the stereotypical New Woman to sex and love is also questioned in this novel. Gilgi's passionate affair with Martin Bruck, an older, cultivated author and bohemian living off the inheritance from his upper middle-class family, disrupts her ordered, systematic life and takes her away from her friends and activities, her special private room and language study. Martin prefers to see Gilgi as a delightful toy and has little appreciation of her desire for autonomy and achievement. Soon dismissed from her job because of the worsening economy, Gilgi lets herself drift and gives up her previous goals. This relationship appears to give the lie to her originally cool, unsentimental assessment of romance and to demonstrate the impossibility for a woman to combine both career and love. As she tells her friend Pit: "I can't work when I'm together with him" (Ich kann nicht arbeiten, Pit—mit ihm zusammen; 168).

Moreover, the relationship with the more experienced and educated intellectual alienates Gilgi from her sense of her own identity as she tries to adapt herself to his interests and transforms herself into a glamorous lady of leisure: "Someone else turned me into this thing I see in the mirror" (Das, was ich im Spiegel seh', hat ein andrer aus mir gemacht; 90). In spite of its power in Gilgi's life the casualness of this "modern" romance also troubles her: she senses the impersonality of Martin's love and pays for her happiness with anxiety and pain (86), worrying because of their lack of common interests and values and the "loose, coincidental" nature of their relationship (87).

Additional contradictions in the new sexual freedom of the modern woman are also present. On the one hand Gilgi defends her right to guilt-free sexual pleasure against the conventional morality of her bourgeois family and leaves home when her parents question her behavior. And when she becomes pregnant she argues forcefully with a gynecologist who refuses to perform an abortion that it is the "ultimate immorality and absurdity" (das Unmoralischte und Absurdeste; 117) to force a woman to have a child she cannot feed or does not want. Contrasting such affirming positions, however, the narrative also reflects more problematic views of modern sexual mores. Sounding not unlike traditional warnings against unleashed female sexuality, Gilgi talks of her fear that her passion for Martin may turn her into a sex machine whose lust overshadows all else, including her love for him as an individual (114). The opposite message can be heard in the words of Gilgi's friend Hertha. Pregnant for the third time, the destitute mother speaks of her abhorrence of sex as "a terrible torment" (eine entsetzliche Qual; 137). Finally, eros, alcohol, and guilt combine in a deadly way to keep Gilgi from bringing promised help to her despairing friends Hans and Hertha. Befogged by whiskey and unnerved by a guilty conscience (she had concealed that she had once been involved with Hans), Gilgi is unable to explain the situation clearly to Martin and yields to his jealous desire that she stay with him. By the next morning her friends have committed suicide and Gilgi has real guilt to wrestle with. Here, "love" appears to stand in direct contradiction to ethical action and responsibility, thus adding a further dimension to the conflict between love and a self-determined identity.

The deconstruction of the stereotypical New Woman in this novel involves a continuing crisis in language and communication, which not only reflects the labile realities and conflicting discourses of late Weimar but is a recurrent thematic and stylistic characteristic of Keun's prose.[15] Gilgi's reflections about who and what she really is set off a new need to talk about herself. But she finds it almost impossible to articulate her questions, in part because she lacks the necessary words and concepts: "One really ought to talk with someone, but it wouldn't help. She has no words to express herself" (Man müßte mal reden mit einem, es hätte aber doch keinen Zweck. Sie hat ja keine Worte, um sich verständlich zu machen; 58). In part Gilgi's lack points to the limited education of the Weimar *Angestellten* and the technocratic horizon of modern culture; Gilgi has only "typewriter words and clockwork words" (Schreibmaschinenworte and Uhrwerkworte; 99) at her disposal. Moreover, her attempted dialogues with Martin and Pit reflect the unequal power constellation that exists between the female typist and the better educated males. This dynamic provides an important clue to the significance of the language problematics for Keun, whose female protagonists turn again and again to males to help them solve their problems. They are always misunderstood; there is a fundamental gap between what they try to communicate and the perceptions of the male "authority figures." The abstract political discourse of the socialist Pit is inaccessible to Gilgi, who complains, "that people who talk about politics always have to be so complicated and confusing" (daß Leute, die von Politik reden, das immer so ganz besonders kompliziert und verworren tun müssen; 40) Pit is also so caught up in his political philosophy that he dismisses her existential crisis: "Disgusting, how important you take yourself to be" (Ekelhaft, wie wichtig du dich nimmst; 40). Similarly, her intellectual lover Martin does not "hear" Gilgi or understand what really matters to her (91). The more Gilgi becomes preoccupied with the conflicts presented by her relationship, the more prominent are the themes of the impossibility of real communication and the inadequacy of their language: "One . . . doesn't have a single word that binds—one just catches words that are like soap bubbles (Man . . . hat kein einziges Wort, das bindet—fängt nur Worte, die Seifenblasen sind; 99).

Keun reveals here a distrust of language that recurs throughout her œuvre, a variation of the "Sprachskepsis" that has plagued twentieth-century authors since Hofmannsthal. Gilgi's confusion and anxiety regarding her future are exacerbated by her pregnancy and her fear of what it will mean for her relationship with Martin, but ultimately her dilemma points to a more fundamental crisis which cannot be so easily articulated:

> Why am I afraid? . . . Why don't I have any words—for Martin—or for me either? There are two layers in me—and the upper one, it dictates—everyday words, everyday actions . . . underneath the lower layer—always a desire, always a searching . . . no word can get at its depths.

> (Warum habe ich denn Angst? . . . Warum habe ich keine Worte—für Martin—und für mich auch nicht? Da sind zwei Schichten in mir—und die obere, die diktiert—alltägliche Worte, alltägliche Handlung . . . drunter die untere Schicht—immer ein Wollen, immer ein Suchen . . . kein Wort trifft zutiefst hinein.) (140–141)

With this conflict and linguistic confusion Keun reinserts the notion of Gilgi as "one of us," a typical young woman of her time caught between solidarity with her group and her love: "[She] is one like all the rest. . . . Self divided in two—self divided into a thousand pieces. Self—today's obligatory desire for the 'we'. Self—eternal cry for the 'you.'" (Das Mädchen . . . ist eine wie alle. . . . Zweigespaltenes Ich—tausendgespaltenes Ich. Ich—heutiger Pflichtwunsch nach dem Wir. Ich—ewiger Schrei nach dem Du; 141).

The novel closes with Gilgi's departure for Berlin to return to work and have her baby. But it leaves her future open and the conflicts in her identity unresolved. Shocked into action by her role in the deaths of her friends, she leaves Martin without a direct word, only a brief note that says nothing of her pregnancy. To be sure, the narrator interjects a prescription for the New Woman to have *both* love *and* an independent working life: "To be a human being means for you to be a human being and a woman and a worker and everything, everything . . . only that which one is able to give is demanded from a person." (Mensch sein heißt für dich Mensch sein und Frau sein und Arbeiter sein und alles, alles sein . . . wird von jedem nur das verlangt, was er geben kann; 219). But this rhetoric, which recalls the late Weimar ideal of the New Woman worker who must also fill roles of mother and wife, must be projected into a very uncertain future, since the novel has in fact exposed the impossible contradictions of this ideal in practice. The imagery of the conclusion further undermines a harmonizing interpretation. An orange rolls onto the railroad track before the powerful, onrushing locomotive which is to carry Gilgi to Berlin:

> "Clever, straight tracks—a big black locomotive—sensibly combined metal. Little wheels, large wheels—everything fitting together. A little orange . . . is lying unfortunately stupidly and without purpose between the straight, smooth, clever tracks.
>
> (Kluge, gerade Gleise—eine große, schwarze Lokomotive—sinnvoll zusammengefügtes Metall. Kleine Räder, große Räder—alles ineinander gehörig. Eine kleine Apfelsine . . . liegt unglücklich dumm und unzweckmäßig zwischen den geraden, glatten, klugen Schienen.) (171)

The image of masculine power, linear movement, rationality and modern technology contrasts sharply with that of the vulnerable, isolated, organic, circular "feminine" orange, which seems about to be destroyed—or at least overrun.[16] The reader is left to ponder the significance of this ambivalent conclusion, and the novel escapes or eludes a definitive reading of its "message," just as Gilgi has in effect escaped from the situations that might have limited and defined her identity and role: she eludes Martin and his efforts to remake her as she had fled her family and its middle-class expectations; she has left her job as a secretary, left behind her socialist friend Pit, her three mothers, and even the friends who committed suicide because her help did not arrive in time. Faced with social and psychological implications of her new roles, Keun's Gilgi leaves us with the ambivalences and unresolved contradictions of the New Woman in late Weimar society.[17]

Like Gilgi, Doris, "das kunstseidene Mädchen," initially embodies a particular feminine form of the Weimar myth of advancement and, like Gilgi, also goes through a process of disillusionment that relativizes this myth. In Doris's case too, her final position is paradoxical and contradictory; her very efforts to assert who and what she is bring her too to the point of not being able to say anything more about herself. Again Keun gives her novel a subtext that problematizes language and communication, weaving a web of misunderstandings, deceptions, and evasions that undermine the notion of reliable discourse.

Even more emphatically than Gilgi, Doris refuses to be pinned down to a traditional bourgeois identity and swears allegiance to her own version of the New Woman myth, the cinematic dream of finding fame and riches through glamour and sex appeal. From a poor family, ignorant of who her biological father is, equipped with a grade-school education, this secretary-turned-would-be-actress is determined to capitalize on her good looks and supposed expertise regarding men to advance herself. Doris believes in the "miracle" success story that filled many filmic and fictional dreams of Weimar "Angestellten": "Even Greta Garbo was once a sales clerk" (Auch Greta Garbo ist einmal Verkäuferin gewesen; *Gilgi*, 11). Convinced that she is an "unusual person" with special inner qualities that raise her above ordinary typists, Doris decides to write down her experiences, not as a diary but as a film scenario, since she views her life in such terms (*Das kunstseidene Mädchen*, 5–6). At the same time, her awareness of her social disadvantages and limited intellectual background also fuel her desire to become a glamorous star:

> I want to become a shining brilliance who's on top. . . . And people will really respect me because I'm a brilliance and then they'll find it wonderful if I don't know what eminence means and won't make fun of me like now . . . .
>
> (Ich will so ein Glanz werden, der oben ist. . . . Und die Leute achten mich hoch, weil ich ein Glanz bin, und werden es dann wunderbar finden, wenn ich nicht weiß, was eine Kapazität ist, und nicht runter lachen auf mich wie heute.) (29)

Doris becomes a a quasi-criminal and fugitive when she impulsively "exchanges" her own shabby raincoat for an elegant fur from a coatrack in the theater where she has walk-on parts. This act forces her to flee her home city for Berlin, the irresistible magnet for all who sought the excitement of social and cultural modernity in the 1920s and early 1930s. Here Doris experiences the vicissitudes of depending on male favor and protection. Like those of a modern female picaro, Doris's fortunes rapidly rise and fall as she moves from man to man, her zig-zag account itself an image of the chaos and instability of the last years of Weimar society.

As in *Gilgi*, the "modern" view of sex and love is presented in contradictory fashion in this novel. On the one hand, Doris's instrumentalization of her body and sexuality is a source of comic effect early in the novel, as when she placates her boss with sensual glances for every missing comma in the letters she has typed (6), or when she manipulates a cavalier into giving her a gold watch (9). She very consciously regards the activity of finding and manipulating men as her "work," her path to material success, as she indicates when she is fired from her secretarial job: "here I sit . . . without a new livelihood and just ask myself, now where is a man for my calamity." (jetzt sitze ich . . . ohne neue Existenz und frage mich nur, wo ist nun ein Mann für meine Notlage; 18). In the absolute devotion with which Doris has taken on this "Karriere" she appears to parody the vamp of the twenties. But the unintentionally comical elements of her self-presentation coexist with very serious levels of criticism and pain. Doris rails against bourgeois society for condemning women like her mother and herself who break its rules for women's sexual behavior (55). She realizes that the prostitute Hulla, who had committed suicide out of fear of her violent pimp, was a "good" person in spite of society's judgment of her (140). Increasingly, Doris's account reveals the darker sides of the glamorous ideal she has absorbed from popular film, magazines, and hit songs. Alienation of her own feelings and body (eventually she cannot bear to be touched by a man), the struggle for physical survival, loneliness, and fear that she may herself become a prostitute are the themes that predominate in the later parts of the book.[18]

In Doris's first-person account the problems of language, communication, deception, and evasion are once again an underlying element. Doris, like Gilgi, is often muted by the males with whom she tries to speak, and moreover, must try to take on whatever role, or identity they wish, as when she pretends to be Jewish, erroneously thinking this is what her intended cavalier desires (30). She readily fabricates exploits to impress possible mentors or rivals, as when she pretends to be having an affair with the theater director to improve her standing among the acting students (22). Indeed, Doris's whole way of life is a kind of pose, an effort to present herself as more sophisticated and glamorous than she is in reality. Her language, replete with neologisms and malapropisms, also reflects her desire to appear worldly.[19]

In her effort to define a place for herself she finds herself, as did Gilgi, in new territory, an outsider among the existing socioeconomic classes: "but that's just it, I have no one of my own kind. I belong absolutely nowhere at all." (aber das ist es ja eben, ich habe keine Meinesgleichen, ich gehöre überhaupt nirgends hin; 138). Even more than Gilgi, whom we last see on a train headed for Berlin, Doris leaves us with an unfinished story. With no train waiting to take her away, she will most likely return to her niche in the waiting room of the Berlin "Bahnhof Zoo." Like Gilgi, her original dream has not turned out as she expected; all her efforts have not brought her the wealth and fame she might have expected from popular movie scripts. In fact she has relativized this dream: "Maybe the fame and glamor are not so important after all." (Auf den Glanz kommt es nämlich vielleicht gar nicht so furchtbar an; 140). Penniless and exhausted, she debates her options, which she now recognizes include becoming a prostitute.

But this seemingly hopeless, inconclusive conclusion also prevents an easy verdict and reasserts Doris's resistance to classification, leaving us again with a sense of the contradictoriness of the new roles women were trying to live during this era. Doris expresses such an absence of clear answers when asked by her male protector to tell about herself: "What should I say? I don't know any words at all about myself now." (Was soll ich denn sagen? Ich weiß über mich jetzt gar keine Worte; 103). Like Gilgi, Doris runs away from the man she loves, "ein Besserer," an educated middle-class professional with whom she has lived for the last months. Always conscious of the social and educational difference between them, Doris had nevertheless allowed herself to fall in love with him and seemed about to let him impose his middle-class values on her way of life: she had agreed to return the beloved fur coat which had made her a fugitive in order to regain respectable status and get a regular job. But ultimately she cannot become the person he wishes, and leaves him abruptly as Gilgi had left Martin, without a word of farewell or explanation. As she says when offering him her diary, the chronicle of her life on the streets: "Doris is no worthless trash. I don't want to be some innocent thing, I want to be present as Doris and not as some foolish civilized fantasy of [this man]." (Doris ist doch kein Dreck. Ich will gar keine Unschuldige sein, ich will richtig als Doris hier sein und nicht als so alberne zivilisierte Einbildung vom [Mann]; 112). The only way Doris can resist his imposed naming and definition appears to be to leave him; her departure is thus an important gesture of resistance, of refusal to be pinned down to a male-defined, bourgeois identity.

Doris had decided to write her own story because she felt herself to be "an unusual person" (ein ungewöhnlicher Mensch; 6), different from the other girls at the office, and she writes in an original language free from the grammatical and stylistic restraints that were imposed on her as a secretary by her male boss. The very structure of her narrative departs radically from the traditional linear plots that enshrine the familiar female story of falling in love, overcoming conflicts, and finally achieving happiness in marriage and motherhood; her account is episodic, fragmentary, disconnected, and, as we have seen, open-ended and unresolved. Doris's story may thus be read as both the account of her largely unsuccessful attempt to find happiness according to the myth of the flapper, *and* as her undefeated resistance against definition by traditional gender roles.[20]

The novel *D-Zug dritter Klasse* (1938) (*Express Train Third Class*), written during Keun's exile, in the wake of her difficult relationship with Joseph Roth, offers a partial response to the question posed by Atina Grossmann concerning the younger sisters of Weimar's New Woman. After finding herself unable to publish in Germany because of her "un-German" treatment of sexual morality, Keun left the country for Ostende, Belgium, where she joined other emigré writers and intellectuals. After completing *Nach Mitternacht* (After Midnight), her 1937 novel on life in Nazi Germany, she was unable, as she later explained, to write any more about conditions in her native land for lack of first-hand knowledge (*Wenn . . .* , 153). Instead, she returned to the themes of feminine identity, male-female relations, and problematic communication of the Weimar novels, and with *D-Zug dritter Klasse* offered a brilliant analysis of an abusive relationship. At first blush this novel presents a very different feminine image from the initially ambitious and self-confident women of the earlier novels. In contrast to Gilgi and Doris, who choose uncertain independence over security and love that would trap them in false identities, Lenchen has allowed herself to become engaged to three men simultaneously out of sheer passivity and the need to be in a relationship, however damaging or unfulfilling. In Lenchen, Keun, like Marieluise Fleißer and later Ingeborg Bachmann, vividly presents a woman as she has been "damaged" by patriarchy. Yet despite the differences, *D-Zug* can be read as a further evolution of elements already present in the Weimar novels; in the setting of the late 1930s the destabilized identities of the New Woman are eroded still further, and the anxiety, guilt, and failed communication that attended the quests of Gilgi and Doris become the central focus in Lenchen's story.

Introduced as the passive victim of circumstances with her three unintended fiancés, Lenchen is a tragicomical variation of a woman psychologically trained by her society to powerlessness. Departing from the Weimar novels' use of modern popular culture as a means of constructing the identities of New Women (popular music, fashion magazines, film), Keun here employs more traditional expressions of German culture as influences shaping feminine character. As a girl Lenchen absorbed romantic fairy-tale images which led her to fantasize an unreal life filled with dreams of ethereal sentimentality:

> Everything that had to do with flowing gowns was beautiful, mysterious, good and noble. In fairy tales these gowns were worn by elves and good fairies, kings' daughters wore them and lovely brides. . . . Germanic maidens charged into battle in white flowing gowns, and slender ladies of castles stood clothed in flowing white at night on balconies to let their golden tresses blow in the wind and to be carried off by bold knights on white steeds.
>
> (Alles, was mit wallenden Gewändern zu tun hatte, war schön, geheimnisvoll, gut und edel. In Märchen wurden diese Gewänder von Elfen und gütigen Feen getragen, Königstöchter trugen sie und liebliche Bräute. . . . Germanenjungfrauen zogen

mit weißen, wallenden Gewändern in die Schlacht, und schlanke Burgfräulein standen weißwallend gekleidet nächtlich auf Altanen, um goldene Locken im Winde wehen zu lassen und von kühnen Rittern auf weißen Zeltern entführt zu werden.) (*D-Zug*, 13)

In the real world—Lenchen chooses a career in the theater, where she hopes to live out her fantasies—her lack of a strong self-concept leaves her vulnerable to overwhelming anxiety. "Her life continued to consist of anxiousness. She was afraid of the strange city, afraid of her landlady, afraid of waiters in a restaurant, afraid of her director, afraid of the audience." (Ihr Leben bestand auch weiterhin aus Angst. Sie hatte Angst vor der fremden Stadt, Angst vor der Zimmerwirtin, Angst vor Kellnern im Restaurant, Angst vor dem Regisseur, Angst vor dem Publikum; 17). With no ambition for herself, only the fear of disappointing others, particularly her parents (21), Lenchen has been socialized to please; appearance is more important than the reality of her own desires. She becomes involved with each of her lovers in turn out of weakness, because, as she says of the first, "together with him she wasn't afraid anymore, and was hardly homesick" (mit ihm zusammen hatte sie keine Angst mehr und kaum noch Heimweh; 18). From Berlin she writes to one man in South America and another in Stuttgart, constantly postponing the marriage dates and half-believing the comforting lies she writes. Not so easily put off is the drinker and bully Karl, who dictates her behavior and thoughts and torments her with mistrust and jealousy. Lenchen dreams of freeing herself from Karl, but again and again reverses herself or is simply unable to act. Her sense of self is not strong enough to oppose Karl's definitions of reality—he berates her for being inferior and immoral—and instead she escapes into sentimental fantasy. Particularly telling is Lenchen's recurrent daydream of a mysterious, comforting stranger and her admission that "she had never been in love with a real man" (In einen wirklichen Mann war sie nie verliebt gewesen; 66). Unlike Gilgi and Doris, Lenchen does not particularly enjoy sex, but goes along to please her partner (18). In order to avoid confrontation or acting on her own feelings, Lenchen constructs an ever more hopelessly entangled web of lies, telling Karl whatever will placate him and deceiving herself in the process. She becomes so caught up in her imagined stories that she can often no longer sort out truth from fiction, reality from fantasy in her own thoughts. In contrast to Doris, who manipulated the truth when it suited her needs even if it might get her into trouble, Lenchen's fabrications have become automatic, self-deceptive reactions.

The other significant, though virtually silent female figure of the novel, Aunt Camilla, is presented as a grotesque eccentric, and may be seen perhaps as an older, caricatured version of the once independent woman of the 1920s. Unmarried, an original inventor and thinker, she is considered to be either crazy (as most of her family has always believed) or as "perhaps old-maidish, as very talented, and otherwise as fully normal" (allenfalls . . . etwas altjüngferlich . . . sehr begabt und im übrigen . . . vollkommen normal; 45), by some in the family who are worried by the Nazi theories of inheritance of insanity (70). Her "technical abilities" are presented as absurdly useless: she works feverishly, destroying one thing to create something less valuable. She also writes, plays the piano, draws, and speaks foreign languages, representing, as it were, all the amateur talents such a modern "bluestocking" might have developed. There seems to be no possibility for her to earn an income; rather, she is dependent on her siblings for her livelihood. Camilla does not follow the normal rules of social behavior and polite conversation, she dresses in her own fashion and is stubborn. In the Third Reich such a woman, who is "different," whether truly mentally ill or not, presents a danger to the family as evidence of possible genetic "abnormality," and might be denounced by a hostile neighbor (47), and the family has decided she must be removed from Germany to a sister in Paris. Lenchen and Karl have agreed to accompany her, and are taking advantage of the journey to smuggle out of Germany money Karl has received as a gift.

The figure of Camilla and Lenchen's relationship to her can be viewed through more than one lens. On the one hand, Camilla's behavior is genuinely bizarre and is presented with a kind of black humor that seduces the reader into finding her comical. On the other hand, she symbolizes victimization by a society that has no place for those who deviate from its narrowly circumscribed norms, here for example those of marriage, submissiveness, and domesticity. In her lack of a husband or even the hint of interest in men, Camilla breaks the patriarchal "rules" of conventional society, particularly during the time of the Third Reich. In this she is, ironically, related to Lenchen, for Lenchen, with her three men, has also broken the rules. In spite of herself and precisely through her extreme manifestation of patriarchal socialization, Lenchen has turned the system of male domination on its head: each of her three fiancés sends money and letters, works and plans in order to make her his "own," believing in fact she is his own. Lenchen herself, however, lives most truly in the world of her fantasies, and is, with Camilla, both victim and unwitting rebel in her sexist and fascist society.

In addition to Karl's abusiveness and Lenchen's and Camilla's vulnerability, *D-Zug dritter Klasse* contains numerous examples of brutality against women. A young man tells how his mother, along with her children, is tyrannized by his penny-pinching father so that she is forced to lie to cover up small rebellions such as buying a pound of pears for her children (68). Again, the theme of a woman's lying is introduced; here even more clearly than in the case of Lenchen, it is a response of survival by the relatively powerless woman vis-à-vis a dominating male. Another character, a fruit dealer, recalls how he was virtually coerced, while intoxicated, into going to the room of a Berlin prostitute, where he was pressured for ever more money until, in desperation, he threw the woman out the window, as he now believes (58). The fruit dealer carries with him a pack of pornographic pictures, which he proudly displays; Lenchen cannot help but see one of the pictures: "A naked man was hitting a naked woman, who smiled in a polite and uninvolved way like a sales clerk who was wrapping up some soap for a customer, or a waitress serving a piece of cake." (Ein nackter Mann schlug eine nackte Frau, die dazu höflich und unbeteiligt lächelte wie eine Verkäuferin, die einem Kunden Seife einpackt oder wie ein Servierfräulein, das einem Gast Kuchen hinstellt; 77).

D-Zug dritter Klasse shows a world in which ominous undertones of violence, misogyny, and the pornographic image of women are part of everyday reality. It is a world in which the important female characters are stylized as either timid and dependent—"feminine"—or as desexed and eccentric, either caught in a spiral of deception and fantasy, or virtually silenced. It reflects a somber reduction in Keun's imagining of women's roles after the Nazi takeover. Where Gilgi and Doris were determined to advance themselves, Lenchen has only vague romantic fantasies. Where they had struggled to make themselves heard, she is virtually unable to speak for herself. Where they left limiting relationships, Lenchen can at best *imagine* herself trading one that is truly abusive for another that will be no more fulfilling. Yet even within this harsh world, the elusive figure of Camilla, who stages an unexpected early departure from the train taking all the money with her, and Lenchen, with her unquenchable fantasizing of ever new romantic scenarios, give us examples of female rebelliousness and resistance even among those defined as weak.

While her self-concept is most vulnerable, and her words have been shown to be most thoroughly unreliable and self-contradicting, Lenchen nonetheless represents a more extreme version of problems already seen in the New Women Gilgi and Doris. They too faltered linguistically at the points of trying to define and assert their identities. Communication with men, seen as sources of approval and enlightenment, proved frustrating and ultimately impossible. Faced with the authority of male voices and power, the women ultimately were silenced and withdrew from the relationship to avoid being defined and erased as individuals. The cultural myths of the New Woman as successful office worker or flapper also proved to be external definitions against which the protagonists measured themselves, often stammering in their uncertainty about how to fulfill contradictory or unrealistic models. The process of asserting their identity in the face of contradictory expectations was accompanied for Keun's Weimar women by anxiety and guilt feelings, by involvement in lies or the inability to communicate. By the time of Lenchen's story the New Woman has been banished, and the power of male domination has reached its zenith in Nazism. While it deals only peripherally with overtly political themes, *D-Zug* may be read as reflecting aspects of the psychological impact of the Nazi era, in which the partially masked problems of Weimar women became all too clear. The unresolved conflict between independence and intimacy experienced by Gilgi and Doris is here split into the two extremes of the dependent, anxious, fantasizing Lenchen and the grotesque figure of Camilla, whose pseudo-independence is achieved at the cost of being declared mad.

Irmgard Keun's representations of women shifted from late Weimar to the late 1930s, but her revelations of her culture's contradictions and their consequences for women persisted, even though they often eluded a definitive interpretation. In all three novels discussed, formulations of feminine identity are questioned and found to be a source of linguistic as well as conceptual uncertainty and disturbance. In their very instability and contradictoriness Keun's portrayals anticipate the shifting, dispersed subject of postmodern imagination. They also reflect their author's own captivating, capricious unpredictability. As she indicated in one of her last interviews, Keun resisted to the end being pinned down under one final "number": "Let me go somewhere else! Nothing holds me down!" (Woanders hin! Mich hält nichts fest!"; Keun, "Gespräch," 73).

Notes

The discussion of the 1938 novel *D-Zug dritter Klasse* (*Express Train Third Class*) represents a slightly revised version of part of my earlier article "Witness, Critic Victim." Unless otherwise indicated, quotations from the German are my own.

1. Calling for modification of earlier studies of Weimar women (Bridenthal and Koonz and Bridenthal, Grossmann, and Kaplan), Grossmann continues: "We now need to revise the 'revisionist' reading of Weimar women's history which forcefully punctured the myth of the 'emancipated woman of the roaring twenties'" (64). The concept "Neue Frau" (New Woman) existed prior to the Weimar Republic but signified a smaller elite of middle-class and artistic women seeking professional and social emancipation. See Sykora, "Alltagsmythos," 9–11.

2. For example, see the books by Petro, Soden and Schmidt, Sykora et al., and Vollmer-Heitmann, the book and article by Soltau.

3. For discussion see Petro, chapter 2, "Perceptions of Difference," and von Ankum "'Ich liebe Berlin mit einer Angst in den Knien,'" 370–371.

4. Grossmann (1983) shows how social scientists and sex reformers of Weimar endeavored to construct a feminine ideal that would combine the qualities of a "rationalized" working woman with those of wife and mother (156-159). See also Sykora, "Alltagsmythos," 9-24. Von Ankum (1995) traces such a transformation as a shift from the New Woman to the "New Mother," still a capable and independent worker but no longer threatening, since she now lives for her child and community rather than herself.

5. See also Sykora, "Alltagsmythos," 19.

6. Surveys of unionized female factory workers also revealed that the majority of them did not wish to marry, seeing married life as an end to their independence and the assumption of undesired burdens and drudgery (Grossmann, 1986, 68–69).

7. This reading is advanced by Kerstin Barndt, who also develops the racialist dimensions of this New Woman. See also von Ankum (1995).

8. This reading is advanced by Lynne Frame and by Kerstin Barndt (109–125), who also develops the racialist dimensions of this New Woman. See also von Ankum (1995).

9. As evidenced in recent articles of Krechel, Harrigan, Shafi, Horsley, Falk, Kosta, von Ankum, Rosenstein; in the published dissertations of Rosenstein, Jordan, and the dissertation in progress of Kerstin Barndt.

10. For a discussion of this book, see my "'Auf dem Trittbrett eines rasenden Zuges,'" 285–287.

11. For a discussion see Römhild, Sautermeister, and my article "Witness, Critic, Victim," 76–86.

12. For an analysis of Keun's Weimar novels in the context of New Objectivity, see Rosenstein 1995.

13. Barbara Kosta argues that the "maternal" plot lies at the center of this novel and its relevance to debates about the New Woman; for Kosta Gilgi's search for her mother suggests the modern woman's rootlessness (274).

14. In both the Weimar novels the line between "respectable" women and "prostitutes" is blurred. For example, prostitutes are described as looking like telephone company employees out of a job (*Gilgi*, 27); Doris constantly compares her situation to that of a prostitute and wonders if she will become one. The blurring of this distinction was characteristic of Weimar culture, as women's new roles brought them into public spaces previously off-limits to "respectable" women. (See also Sykora, "Alltagsmythos," 22, and von Ankum, "'Ich liebe Berlin mit einer Angst in den Knien,'" 372 *et passim*).

15. For a more detailed discussion of the problematics of language in Keun's early novels, see Horsley, "'Warum habe ich keine Worte?'"

16. The symbolism of train and machine versus circular feminine images recall the imagery of Walter Ruttmann's 1927 film, *Berlin, die Symphonie der Großstadt*. Hake interprets these as two sides of the modern metropolis in the film: linearity signifies control and circularity, associated with femininity, indicates loss of control and surrender to the attractions of the metropolis (137).

17. Von Ankum (1995) reads the conclusion of the novel as more clearly endorsing the ideal of the "New Mother."

18. Katharina von Ankum reads Doris as a would-be *flâneuse*, a feminine counterpart to the *flâneur* or modern urban idler; through her wanderings through the streets of Berlin Doris "discloses the basic patriarchal structure of modernity, in which the commodification of the female body becomes clearly evident" (entdeckt sie die patriarchalische Grundstruktur der Moderne, in der der Warencharakter des weiblichen Körpers unverhüllt zutage tritt; "Ich liebe Berlin mit einer Angst in den Knien,'" 369). Her article contrasting *Das kunstseidene Mädchen* with Anita Loos's *Gentlemen Prefer Blondes* emphasizes how Keun's novel shows disillusionment with major themes of Weimar culture and society: modernization, Americanism, consumer culture ("Material Girls," 161 *et passim*).

19. See Horsley, "'Warum habe ich keine Worte?'" 305–311.

20. I differ with von Ankum's conclusion that"[al]though Doris appears as narrator and author of her own story, she can ultimately represent herself only as the projection of the male gaze and define herself in reference to contemporary beauty ideals" ("Material Girls," 167).

Bibliography

Barndt, Kerstin. "Sentiment und Sachlichkeit. Schreib- und Leseweisen der Neuen Frau am Ende der Weimarer Republik." Diss. Freie Universitaet Berlin, 1999.

Blum, Klara. "Irmgard Keun." *Internationale Literatur. Deutsche Blätter.* 9. Jg., Heft 6 (1939). (Reviews of *Nach Mitternacht, D-Zug dritter Klasse, Kind aller Länder.*)

Bossinade, Johanna. "Haus und Front. Bilder des Faschismus in der Literatur von Exil- und Gegenwartsautorinnen. Am Beispiel Anna Seghers, Irmgard Keun, Christa Wolf, und Gerlind Reinshagen." *Neophilologus* 70 (1986): 92–118.

Brentano, Bernard. "Keine von uns." *Die Linkskurve* 4.10 (Oct. 1932): 27–28. (Review of *Gilgi*.).

Bridenthal, Renate, and Claudia Koonz. "Beyond 'Kinder, Küche, Kirche': Weimar Women in Politics and Work." In *Liberating Women's History.* Ed. Berenice A. Carroll. Urbana, Ill.: University of Illinois Press, 1976, 310–315.

Bridenthal, Renate, Atina Grossmann, and Marion Kaplan, eds. *When Biology Became Destiny; Women in Weimar and Nazi Germany*. New York: Monthly Review Press, 1984.

Bronsen, David. *Joseph Roth. Eine Biographie.* Cologne, 1974.

Canning, Kathleen. "History after the Linguistic Turn. Historicizing Discourse and Experience." *Signs* 19/2 (Winter 1994): 368–404.

Falk, Sabine. "Zum Frauenbild der 20er und 30er Jahre und seiner literarischen Bearbeitung durch Irmgard Keun." *Frauenalltag—Frauenforschung. Beiträge zur 2. Tagung der Kommission Frauenforschung in der Deutschen Gesellschaft für Volkskunde, Freiburg. 22.-25. Mai 1986.* Ed. Arbeitsgruppe Volkskundliche Frauenforschung Freiburg. Frankfurt am Main/Bern/New York/Paris: Peter Lang, 1988, 165–170.

Fließ, Elisabeth. "Mädchen auf der Suche." *Die Frau* 40 (1932/33): 172–178. (Review of *Gilgi, Das kunstseidene Mädchen*.)

Frame, Lynne. "Gretchen, Girl, Garçonne? Weimar Sciene and Popular Culture in Search of the Ideal New Woman, in: von Ankum (Ed.), *Women in the Metropolis, Gender and Modernity in Weimar Culture*. (Berkeley: UC, 1997), 12–40.

Grossmann, Atina. "*Girlkultur* or Thoroughly Rationalized Female. A New Woman in Weimar Germany?" In *Women in Culture and Politics.* Ed. Judith Friedlander. Bloomington: Indiana University Press, 1986, 62–80.

———. "The New Woman and the Rationalization of Sexuality in Weimar Germany." In *Powers of Desire: The Politics of Sexuality.* Ed. Ann Snitow, Christine Stansell, and Sharon Thompson. New York: Monthly Review Press, 1983, 153–171.

Hake, Sabine. "Urban Spectacle in Walter Ruttman's *Berlin, Symphony of the Big City.*" In *Dancing on the Volcano: Essays on the Culture of the Weimar Republic.* Ed. Thomas W. Kniesche and Stephen Brockmann. Columbia, S.C.: Camden, 1994, 127–137.

Harrigan, Renny. "Novellistic Representation of *die Berufstätige* during the Weimar Republic." *Women in German Yearbook 4.* Ed. Marianne Burkhard and Jeanette Clausen. Lanham, Md.: University Press of America, 1988, 95–124.

Horsley, Ritta Jo (Joey). "'Auf dem Trittbrett eines rasenden Zuges': Irmgard Keun zwischen Wahn und Wirklichkeit." In *WahnsinnsFrauen*. Ed. Sibylle Duda and Luise F. Pusch. Frankfurt am Main: Suhrkamp, 1992, 280–308.

———. "Irmgard Keun." In *Women Writers of Germany, Austria, and Switzerland. An Annotated Bio-Bibliographical Guide*. Ed. Elke Frederiksen. New York: Greenwood, 1989, 121–124.

———. "Irmgard Keun." *Dictionary of Literary Biography*. Vol. 69 of *Contemporary German Prose Fiction: 1945 to the Present*. Ed. Wolfgang D. Elfe and James Hardin. Detroit: Gale Research, 1988, 182–188.

———. "'Warum habe ich keine Worte? . . . Kein Wort trifft zutiefst hinein.' The Problematics of Language in the Early Novels of Irmgard Keun." *Colloquia Germanica* 23.3–4 (1990): 297–313.

———. "Witness, Critic, Victim: Irmgard Keun and the Years of National Socialism." In *Gender, Patriarchy, and Fascism in the Third Reich. The Response of Women Writers*. Ed. Elaine Martin. Detroit: Wayne State University Press, 1993, 65–117.

Jelinek, Elfriede. "'Weil sie heimlich weinen muß, lacht sie über Zeitgenossen.' Über Irmgard Keun." *die horen* 25 (Winter 1980): 221–225.

Jordan, Christa. *Zwischen Zerstreuung und Berauschung. Die Angestellten in der Erzählprosa am Ende der Weimarer Republik*. Frankfurt am Main/Bern/New York/Paris: Peter Lang, 1988.

Kesten, Hermann. "Irmgard Keun." In *Meine Freunde, die Poeten*. Munich: Desch, 1959, 423–434.

Keun, Irmgard. *Gilgi, eine von uns*. Berlin: Universitas, 1931. Rpt. Munich: dtv, 1989.

———. *Das kunstseidene Mädchen*. Berlin: Universitas, 1932. Rpt. Munich: dtv, 1989. Trans. by Basil Creighton as *The Artificial Silk Girl*. London: Chatto, 1933.

———. *Das Mädchen, mit dem die Kinder nicht verkehren durften*. Amsterdam: de Lange, 1936. Rpt. Munich: dtv, 1989. Trans. by Leila Berg and Ruth Baer as *The Bad Example*. New York: Harcourt, 1955.

———. *Nach Mitternacht*. Amsterdam: Querido, 1937. Munich: dtv, 1989. Trans. as *After Midnight*. Trans Anthea Bell. London: Gollancz, 1985. Trans. James Cleugh. New York: Knopf, 1938.

———. *D-Zug dritter Klasse*. Amsterdam: Querido, 1938. Rpt. Munich: dtv, 1990.

———. *Kind aller Länder*. Amsterdam: Querido, 1938. Rpt. Munich: dtv, 1989.

———. *Ferdinand, der Mann mit dem freundlichen Herzen*. Düsseldorf: Droste, 1950. Munich: dtv, 1990.

———. *Wenn wir alle gut wären: Kleine Begebenheiten, Erinnerungen, und Geschichten*. Düsseldorf: Fladung, 1954. Revised and enlarged edition. Ed. and with a "Nachwort" by Wilhelm Unger. Cologne: Kiepenhauer & Witsch, 1983. Rpt. Munich: dtv, 1993.

———. *Ich lebe in einem wilden Wirbel: Briefe an Arnold Strauss 1933–1947*. Selected and edited by Gabriele Kreis and Marjory S. Strauss. Düsseldorf: Claassen, 1988. Rpt. Munich: dtv, 1990.

———. "'Woanders hin! Mich hält nichts fest': Irmgard Keun im Gespräch mit Klaus Antes." *die horen* 27 (Spring 1982): 61–75.

King, Lynda. *Best-Sellers by Design. Vicki Baum and the House of Ullstein*. Detroit: Wayne State, 1988.

Klotz, Volker. "Forcierte Prosa: Stilbeobachtungen zu Bildern und Romanen der Neuen Sachlichkeit." In *Dialog: Festgabe für Josef Kunz*. Ed. Rainer Schönhaar. Berlin: Schmidt, 1973, 244–271.

Kosta, Barbara. "Unruly Daughters and Modernity: Irmgard Keun's *Gilgi, eine von uns*." *German Quarterly* 68.3 (1995): 271–286.

Krechel, Ursula. "Irmgard Keun: die Zerstörung der kalten Ordnung. Auch ein Versuch über das Vergessen weiblicher Kulturleistungen." *Literaturmagazin* 10 (1979): 103–128.

Kreis, Gabriele. *Frauen im Exil*. Düsseldorf: Claassen, 1984.

———. "'Schreiben aus eigener Erfahrung...' Drei Schriftstellerinnen im Exil: Lil Körber, Irmgard Keun, Adrienne Thomas." In *Zwischen Aufbruch und Verfolgung. Künstlerinnen der zwanziger und dreißiger Jahre*. Ed. Denny Hirschbach und Sonia Nowoselsky. Bremen: Zeichen und Spuren, 1993, 65–80.

———. *"Was man glaubt, gibt es." Das Leben der Irmgard Keun*. Zurich: Arche, 1991.

Kübler, Sabine. "Frauen zwischen Wandlung und Anpassung—Frauenbilder der *Frankfurter Illustrierten* von 1930 bis 1944." *Frauenalltag und Frauenbewegung im 20. Jahrhundert. Materialsammlung zu der Abteilung 20. Jahrhundert im Historischen Museum Frankfurt. Band III. Frauen im deutschen Faschismus 1933–1944*. Compiled and commented by Sabine Kübler, Anette Kuhn, Wilma Wirtz. Frankfurt am Main: Stadt Frankfurt, 1980, 41–89.

Lensing, Leo. "Cinema, Society and Literature in Irmgard Keun's *Das kunstseidene Mädchen*." *Germanic Review* 60 (Fall, 1985): 129–134.

Lorisika, Irene. *Frauendarstellungen bei Irmgard Keun und Anna Sehgers*. Frankfurt am Main: Haag + Herchen, 1985.

m. r. "Irmgard Keun: *Gilgi, Eine von uns*." *Die literarische Welt* 8.1 (1932): 6.

Mann, Klaus. "Deutsche Wirklichkeit." *Die neue Weltbühne* 17 (1937): 526–528. (Review of *Nach Mitternacht*.)

Petro, Patrice. *Joyless Streets. Women and Melodramatic Representation in Weimar Germany*. Princeton: Princeton University Press, 1989.

Roloff, Gerd. "Irmgard Keun—Vorläufiges zu Leben und Werk." *Amsterdamer Beiträge zur neueren Germanistik* 6 (1977): 45–68.

Römhild, Dorothee. "Weibliche Mittäterschaft und Faschismuskritik in Irmgard Keuns Roman *Nach Mitternacht*." *diskussion deutsch. Zeitschrift für Deutschlehrer aller Schulformen in Ausbildung und Praxis* 25.136 (1994): 105–113.

Rosenstein, Doris. *Irmgard Keun. Das Erzählwerk der dreißiger Jahre*. Frankfurt am Main: Peter Lang, 1991.

———. "'Mit der Wirklichkeit auf du und du'? Zu Irmgard Keun's Romanen *Gilgi, eine von uns* und *Das kunstseidene Mädchen.*" In *Neue Sachlichkeit im Roman. Neue Interpretationen zum Roman der Weimarer Republik.* Ed. Sabina Becker and Christoph Weiß. Stuttgart: Metzler, 1995, 273–290.

———. "'Nebenbei bemerkt.' Boheme-Gesten in Romanen Irmgard Keuns." In *Erkundungen. Beiträge zu einem erweiterten Literaturbegriff. Helmut Kreuzer zum 60. Geburtstag.* Ed. Jens Malte Fischer, Karl Prümm, and Helmut Scheuer. Göttingen: Vandenhoeck, 1987.

Rühle-Gerstel, Alice. *Das Frauenproblem der Gegenwart. Eine psychologische Bilanz.* (Leipzig, 1932) Rpt. as *Die Frau und der Kapitalismus.* Frankfurt am Main (= Archiv sozialistischer Literatur 19), 1972.

Sautermeister, Gert. "Irmgard Keuns Exilroman *Nach Mitternacht.*" *die horen* 27 (Spring 1982): 48–60.

Schank, Gerd. "*Das kunstseidene Mädchen* von Irmgard Keun. Skizze einer Frauensprache." In *Annäherungen, Studien zur deutschen Literaturwissenschaft im zwanzigsten Jahrhundert.* Ed. Hans Ester and Guillaume van Gemert. Amsterdam: Rodopi, 1985, 35–64.

Serke, Jürgen. "Irmgard Keun." In *Die verbrannten Dichter.* Weinheim: Beltz and Gelberg, 1977, 162–175.

Shafi, Monika. "'Aber das ist es ja eben, ich habe ja keine Meinesgleichen.' Identitätsprozeß und Zeitgeschichte in dem Roman *Das kunstseidene Mädchen* von Irmgard Keun." *Colloquia Germanica* 21 (1988): 314–25.

Soden, Kristine von, and Maruta Schmidt, eds. *Neue Frauen. Die zwanziger Jahre.* Berlin: Elefanten Press, 1988.

Soltau, Heide. "Die Anstrengungen des Aufbruchs. Romanautorinnen und ihre Heldinnen in der Weimarer Zeit." In *Deutsche Literatur von Frauen* Ed. Gisela Brinker-Gabler. Vol 2. Munich: Beck, 1988, 220–235.

———. *Trennungs-Spuren. Frauenliteratur der zwanziger Jahre.* Frankfurt am Main: extrabuch, 1984.

Steinbach, Dietrich. "Irmgard Keun." *Kritisches Lexikon zur deutschsprachigen Gegenwartsliteratur.* Munich: edition text und kritik, 1985, 19. Nachlieferung (19th Supplement).

Stern, Guy. "Die Nürnberger Rassengesetze im Spiegel der Exilliteratur." In *Exil. Forschung, Erkenntnisse, Ergebnisse. Sonderband I: Realismuskonzeptionen der Exilliteratur zwischen 1935 und 1940/41. Tagung der Hamburger Arbeitsstelle für deutsche Exilliteratur 1986.* Ed. Edita Koch and Frithjof Trapp. Maintal, 1987, 184–202.

Sykora, Katharina, Annette Dorgerloh, Doris Noell-Rumpeltes, Ada Raev, eds. *Die Neue Frau. Herausforderung für die Bildmedien der Zwanziger Jahre.* Marburg: Jonas, 1993.

Sykora, Katharina. "Die Neue Frau. Ein Alltagsmythos der Zwanziger Jahre." In *Die Neue Frau. Herausforderung für die Bildmedien der Zwanziger Jahre.* Eds. Katharina Sykora et al., 9–24.

Tucholsky, Kurt ("Peter Panter"). "Auf dem Nachttisch." *Die Weltbühne* 28. 5 (1932): 180. (Review of *Gilgi*.)

Vollmer-Heitmann, Hanna. *Wir sind von Kopf bis Fuß auf Liebe eingestellt. Die zwanziger Jahre.* Hamburg: Kabel, 1993.

von Ankum, Katharina. "'Ich liebe Berlin mit einer Angst in den Knien': Weibliche Stadterfahrung in Irmgard Keuns *Das kunstseidene Mädchen*." *GQ* 67/3 (1994): 369–388.

———. "Material Girls. Consumer culture and the 'New Woman' in Anita Loos's *Gentlemen Prefer Blondes* and Irmgard Keun's *Das kunstseidene Mädchen*." *Colloquia Germanica* 27.2 (1994): 159–172.

———. "Motherhood and the 'New Woman'": Vicki Baum's *stud. chem Helene Willfüer* and Irmgard Keun's *Gilgi—eine von uns*." *Women in German Yearbook* 11 (1995): 171–188.

Wedekind, Kadidja. (Rev. of *Gilgi*.) *Der Querschnitt* 12.1 (1932): 74.

Weissinger, Friedrich. "Irmgard Keun: Das kunstseidene Mädchen." *Die literarische Welt* 8.31 (1932): 5.

Wittman, Livia Z. "Erfolgschancen eines Gaukelspiels: Vergleichende Beobachtungen zu *Gentlemen Prefer Blondes* (Anita Loos) und *Das kunstseidene Mädchen* (Irmgard Keun)." *Carleton Germanic Papers* 11 (1983): 35–49.

———. "Der Stein des Anstoßes: Zu einem Problemkomplex in berühmten und gerühmten Romanen der Neuen Sachlichkeit." *Jahrbuch der internationalen Germanistik* 14.2 (1982): 56–78.

4

Victims or Perpetrators? Literary Responses to Women's Roles in National Socialism

Elaine Martin

Although the Holocaust and Nazi era emerged in the early postwar years as a topic in literature, film, and the media, scholarly research on the Third Reich was noticeably lacking until the 1960s. As Sybil Milton has noted, "Many scholars considered subjects [such as the Soviet Union, the world wars, and economic conditions] of greater significance and were uncomfortable with the barbarism of the Nazi period."[1] Research on the Nazi era, when it did appear, focused primarily on the activities of men, producing a scholarship in which women fell through "the historian's sieve, unclaimed by feminists and unnoticed by men," as Claudia Koonz observed (3).

Beginning in the late 1970s, however, a new kind of research—conducted for the most part by female scholars—began to appear which focused on women's activities and the roles they played throughout the Nazi years.[2] These studies dealt primarily with the activities of the mass of German women who were not victims, that is, they did not belong to one of the groups of women persecuted by the Nazis such as Jews, gypsies, prostitutes, or mental patients; rather, they belonged to the "aryan" group of those "not persecuted" (*nicht Verfolgte*) as Lerke Gravenhorst, Hanna Lauterbach, and others have termed them.[3]

In the 1980s a literature painfully articulated by victims and survivors (Jews, communists, resistance fighters) began to appear alongside the scholarly studies.[4]

An interesting blurring of the separation between primary and secondary literature often occurred in this period due to an increased focus on oral history narratives; this has resulted in numerous scholarly books and articles based on eyewitness accounts either of victims, perpetrators, or both.[5] Also important has been the continuous publication of a *Nachkriegsgeneration*-literature since the late 1970s, written by children "in search of" their Nazi parents. These texts range from Dörte von Westernhagen's *Die Kinder der Täter* (1987) (*The Children of the Perpetrators*) and Peter Sichrovsky's *Schuldig geboren* (1986) (*Born Guilty*), both based on interviews, to a wealth of fictional and autobiographical literary texts such as Elisabeth Plessen's *Mitteilung an den Adel* (1976) (*Message to the Aristocracy*), Ruth Rehmann's *Der Mann auf der Kanzel* (1979) (*Man in the Pulpit*), Barbara Bronnen's *Die Tochter* (1980) (*The Daughter*), and Elisabeth Reichart's *Februarschatten* (1984) (*February Shadows*).[6]

Developing out of the massive and enduring silence that enshrouded Germany in the immediate postwar years, but also developing out of the insistent, breaking-of-the-silence literature by the "children of the perpetrators" (Westernhagen), research in the late 1980s and 1990s entered a new phase. At its center stands a theoretical debate over terminology, women's roles, and specifically the relationship of feminist scholarship (and scholars) to research on National Socialism.[7] The initial impetus for this discussion came from several key publications representing different viewpoints. I am selecting three of these works as representative, beginning with Gisela Bock's *Zwangssterilisation im Nationalsozialismus. Studien zur Rassenpolitik und zur Frauenpolitik* (*Compulsory Sterilization in National Socialism. Studies on Racial Policies and Gender Policies*), published in 1986. In Bock's view, the victimization of certain groups of women and of Jews emanates from the same ideology of "unfit life" (*unwürdiges Leben*): "Like Jews, [millions of non-Jewish, inferior women and men] were seen as 'ballast' and 'parasites' to the 'body' of *Volk* and race, though Jews were seen as threatening this body from the outside, and other inferior beings were seen as threatening it from the inside" (Racism, 275–276). At the other pole, Claudia Koonz's *Mothers in the Fatherland*, published in the United States in 1987 clearly places the majority of German women in the category of perpetrators: "far from remaining untouched by Nazi evil, women operated at its very center" (6). Both of these positions have been criticized as has that of Christina Thürmer-Rohr, whose concept of co-perpetration (*Mittäterschaft*) in the early 1980s opposed the then-prevailing interpretation of women exclusively as victims. Many rounds of critique and countercritique (within as well as between groups) have taken place both at conferences in Germany and in print, a number of which have been summarized in the collection of essays *TöchterFragen NS-Frauen Geschichte* (*Daughters' Questions of N-S Womens's History*).

One might usefully view this debate as a kind of "Historikerinnenstreit" (women historians' debate): like their male counterparts who participated in the so-called *Historikerstreit* (historians' debate), the women scholars involved are interested in sociohistorical interpretations of the National Socialist era—but with some specifically feminist twists.[8] Whereas the *Historikerstreit* focused on broad questions of historical interpretation, the women scholars' debate has centered on three specific interrelated issues. The first concerns language and terminology, an example of which is Lerke Gravenhorst's reluctance to use the term "Germans" (*Deutsche*), as she explains, "I prefer to speak of 'people in and from Germany' than of 'Germans.' I do it especially in regard to women, because the expression 'German women' has a Nazi connotation" (Nehmen wir, 20).[9] Secondly, crucial questions of categorization are reflected in the plethora of symbolically laden terms used to refer to women in the Nazi era: *Täterin* (perpetrator; Ebbinghaus et al.), *Mittäterin* (co-perpetrator; Thürmer-Rohr), *Mitbeteiligte* (collaborator/co-participant; Brockhaus), *Belastete* (burdened/implicated; Westernhagen), *Unpolitische/Ignorantin* (apolitical, unknowing; Wiggershaus), *Mitläuferin* (supporter/hanger on; Westernhagen et al.), *Handlungskollektiv* (collective action; Gravenhorst). The third issue explores differing interpretations of women's relativized guilt in the Nazi era, summarized in the question: which was the predominant factor in National Socialist ideology, racism or sexism? Furthermore, what does this ideological focus mean for women's "historical-moral consciousness" (Gravenhorst, 20), a question that addresses particularly life in contemporary Germany and the issues of both personal and national responsibility.

Yet another difference between the two "gendered" debates has been numerous female scholars' insistence on personalization of their research in contrast to their male colleagues' formulation of the debate in largely theoretical realms. Lerke Gravenhorst and others have emphasized the importance of researchers identifying publicly their personal relationship to—and thus possible biases toward—National Socialism.[10] In the title of the volume co-edited by Gravenhorst and Carmen Tatschmurat, *TöchterFragen NS-Frauen Geschichte*, the word *Töchter* refers not to the daughters of former National Socialists as "objects" of research, rather to the identity of the researchers themselves, as prerequisite "subjects" of their scholarly inquiry.[11] Personalization of critical texts, an approach used effectively as early as the 1920s by Virgina Woolf, has been identified particularly with the Duke critics (e.g., Davidson, Tompkins, and Torgovnik) and more generally with new historicist readings, which, according to Anton Kaes, can be "unabashedly personal" (212).[12]

A final striking divergence between the men's and women's debates concerns their differing use of the historical concept of "continuity" (*Kontinuität*). In the *Historikerstreit*, this concept clearly represents a look *backward* to identify how the twelve years of National Socialism relate to earlier periods of German history. For many female scholars, by contrast, continuity concerns primarily the relationship of National Socialism to sociopolitical developments in Germany from 1945 *forward* to the present.[13] Karin Haubrich and Lerke Gravenhorst, commenting on the error of decoupling the personal element from National Socialist research, remark that impersonal theorizing permits a separation from history—especially from National

Socialist history—and reduces awareness of the parallels between the past and present (52). Dörte von Westernhagen, also interested in the postwar legacy of "guilty" parents to their inevitably "tainted" children, wonders what psychic traces Nazi crimes left on the persecutors, and what spiritual deformities this generation of parents unknowingly passed on to its children (87). She spells out the ways in which children of these parents were forced into a culpable complicity after 1945, noting that the parents' egos (*Selbstgefühl*) had been so shaken by the loss of the war and the revelations of war crimes, that their children had to help stabilize them. In order not to endanger their parents' caretaking abilities, the children learned not to probe vulnerable areas. Westernhagen believes that the adults' fear of their own weakness was all too justified. After all, they had seen in the Third Reich how the weak and helpless were destroyed; in many cases they had even participated in it. In their view, these sadistic expectations could easily be transmitted to the children (91).

The Germans whom both Gravenhorst and Westernhagen have in mind when they discuss the problem of a National Socialist legacy are the perpetrators. Westernhagen defines this group as "the guilty ones and participants of all shades," which includes "the masses ranging from enthusiastic supporters to those who cautiously approved" as well as "the group of rejectors, of spiritually distanced ones" (89). Gravenhorst, Windaus-Walser, and others insist all-inclusively that perpetrator means everyone who was not persecuted. The use of labels to characterize groups of people who participated in varying degrees in National Socialism concerns ideological postwar issues that are much more profound than mere wrangling over terminology. Rather, the use of these designations signals both specific interpretations of the past and public negotiation of a national history. This negotiation is extremely important because the version that emerges will be used as the basis for governmental decisions on domestic and foreign policy, including the payment of war reparations; it will determine the content of school books; it will promote certain power relationships in the economy and society; and it will regulate official interactions with foreign countries.

In following this debate, one is led to the conclusion that the majority of German women would indeed more accurately belong in a category of perpetrator (*Täterin*) than in one of victim (*Opfer*). For to view women exclusively as victims of National Socialist sexism shields the largest group from responsibility and guilt. These are precisely the women about whom Claudia Koonz wrote in 1987, when she said they had fallen through the historian's sieve. Despite the criticism of Christina Thürmer-Rohr's concept of *Mittäterschaft*, to the effect that she concentrates too much on the "Mit," (Co-), that is, on the context of patriarchy, rather than on "Täterschaft," (Perpetration), that is, on women's active role and consequent guilt, I find her term the most accurate of those proposed.[14] It reflects two simultaneously operative factors: on the one hand, women's active participation in National Socialism, and on the other, a patriarchal society and a National Socialist ideology, both of which were reductionist and hostile toward women. The emerging research on links between sexuality, violence, and war begun by Klaus Theweleit, Maria-Antonietta Macciocchi, and others in the 1970s further supports Thürmer-Rohr's equal weighting of the "Mit" and the "Täterschaft" as far as women's roles in National Socialism are concerned.

For me it was literature rather than history per se that revealed the lacuna left by the mass of German women who had been subsumed into a purged "passive participation" (*Mitläufertum*). My 1979 interview with Ingeborg Drewitz in Berlin led to the discovery of a group of texts in which women were experimenting with various ways of saying, "I was there; I was involved; thus I am guilty." This literature of *Mittäterschaft* has become increasingly important because of its potential contribution both to public negotiations of history and to personal struggles with issues of responsibility and continuity. The literary works I read at this time clearly contributed to a new way of approaching an ostensibly historical topic—an approach that anticipated by several years new-historicist interpretations, in which "it is precisely the fictive, make-believe form of plays, novels, films, and poetry that allows for ambiguity, complexity, and contradiction. Fictions can suggest, manipulate, and toy with solutions that, outside the institution of literature, would be dismissed as impractical, miraculous, criminal, or insane" (Kaes, 213).[15] Autobiography in particular is a fascinating venue for history and literature to meet and explore not only facts but also a personal examination (*Auseinandersetzung*) of those facts. The woman writer in this literature plays an unusually arduous and multilayered role: she stands interposed (as intermediary? as reporter? as interlocutor? as interpreter?) between historically based, autobiographically authenticated experience and its literary synthesis reified as cultural artifact.

I turn now to the ways in which several authors of autobiographical *(Mit)Täterin* literature (Zeller, Hannsmann, Wolf, Stern, Finckh, Maschmann) have dealt with the issues raised by historians and sociologists in the debate just described. In some respects these authors' works reflect concern with the same questions raised by academic scholars, but in others they go beyond the debate in treating subjects that have not yet been taken up by their historian and sociologist colleagues.

Of primary importance to all of these writers is the fact that participation in National Socialism was in no way neutral; rather, everyone was forced into making a public commitment either for or against it.[16] Christabel Bielenberg remarks in *The Past is Myself*, "In a regime such as Hitler's, there could be no standing on the sidelines, but there were also no rules to the game; each to his own conscience" (98). Women writers who were co-perpetrators are located at different points along the continuum. At one extreme is Melita Maschmann, who assumed a leadership role under the Nazis and underwent denazification after the war. After writing *Fazit* (1963) (*Sum Total*), she changed her name, went to India, and disappeared. Since then she has remained incommunicado, and according to her publisher, even her family is unaware of her whereabouts.[17] At the same end of the continuum, but less extreme, are Renate Finckh and Carola Stern, both of whom were enthusiastic BDM (Bund deutscher Mädel; German Girls' Organization) group leaders and believers in National Socialism until the agonizing end, in Finckh's case, even *after* the war. In the middle of this perpetrator-continuum, one might place Margarete Hannsmann, who, although she was a Nazi adherent throughout seven years of BDM indoctrination, underwent an awakening and change of heart around the age of sixteen. At the other end of the scales are the other *Mittäterinnen* who were neither Nazi activists nor opponents, such as Eva Zeller, Christa Wolf, Ingeborg Drewitz, and Ruth Rehmann.

The writers' personal interpretations of this *Mittäterschaft* range from Carola Stern, who said bluntly in our interview: "I didn't want to die without having said that I participated in it," to Eva Zeller, who claims: "I still have my unassailable alibi of tender years" (*Solange*, 186). With the exception of Maschmann, born in 1918 and thus already fifteen when the Nazis took power and twenty-eight at the war's end, all of the authors cited here were born between 1921 and 1929 and were thus children or adolescents throughout the Nazi period.[18] Theoretically then, they could all make use of Zeller's alibi, but in fact, it is a point of contention not only for individual writers examining their own consciences, but also *among* various writers, since many have read each other's works. In our interview, Margarete Hannsmann identified the age at which she—here as her protagonist, Ulrike—awakened to the evil of National Socialism and rejected it: "She realizes that it is leading to an evil end, but she cannot see it yet at twelve, thirteen, or fourteen. At the age of fifteen it begins, and by sixteen she has understood." Hannsmann said that other women writers of her cohort remained true to Hitler throughout and even past adolescence, and she commented, "I hold that against them. I said: You must have had a conscience. I had one at sixteen. Everyone must have had one. Everyone" (Interview).[19]

Even the authors who lean most heavily on their tender years as a justification, reveal moments of epiphany. At one point in our interview, for example, Eva Zeller reiterated the innocence of her protagonist "E," which she described as a state of "not yet able to know." But ten minutes later, she described in detail an experience of political awakening: "In the government work camp near Leipzig I became a 'victim' for the very first time. I was at the mercy of a woman, the camp director, who harassed me and had absolute power over me" (Interview). At the age of eighteen she began to think of the few people she knew who had suddenly disappeared. All at once she realized: "So that's how this happens. You have to experience it yourself. Until then it remains theoretical, abstract" (Interview).

Even the seemingly incorrigible Cornelia in Finckh's *Mit uns zieht die neue Zeit* (1979) (*The New Era Begins with Us*) admits that from a certain point on she knew the truth. When a schoolfriend says, nodding toward a group of assembled Jews, that they are being sent to Poland to be murdered, Cornelia shudders involuntarily and says, "From then on I knew" (155–156). Carola Stern reports that elderly men have stood up at the conclusion of her public readings and claimed, "We were at the front and we didn't know anything" (Interview). Her response is one of disbelief: "I cannot say to someone, 'You knew.' I'm amazed that I knew so much as a sixteen-year old girl, and they, as older officers didn't know a thing" (Interview).

Although these authors at one level simply describe both their belief in National Socialism and their participation in NS organizations, they also try to explain and understand the phenomenon. Most of them identify the sources of their youthful enthusiasm: idealism, the sense of belonging to a new era of historic proportions, feelings of importance and usefulness, freedom and independence—especially from the home and family—and the experience of peer acceptance. Zeller, who repeatedly refers to her protagonist "E" as a *Backfisch* (teenage girl)—a term also used by Stern—gives much greater emphasis to the justification of youth than the other authors, still writing about it in her second autobiographical novel, *Nein und Amen*: "We were young. A sentence that means everyone of my generation has two lives, one before 1945 and one after. And the second life is a constant justification and correction of the first, setting straight misunderstandings and removing misrepresentations" (163). Zeller concludes by saying, "That an entire generation has to deny its youth is without precedent, because never has a youth been promised so much and given so little" (*Nein*, 163). As this last sentence makes clear, Zeller assumes little personal responsibility for National Socialism, seeing it rather as something that happened to her and to her generation.[20] Although Carola Stern similarly said that National Socialism "happened to [her]" (Interview), she is more forthcoming than Zeller about her guilt: "I don't reproach myself that I wasn't in the resistance, because I didn't have that opportunity. I reproach myself because I failed as a human being" (Interview). She describes several instances in *In den Netzen der Erinnerung* (1986) (*In the Nets of Memory*) of personal "human failure" (*menschliches Versagen*), the most horrifying of which are scenes when she hears the screams of torture victims while working in a Hitler Youth center above the Gestapo headquarters and does nothing to intervene. Forty-two years later Stern writes of her protagonist, "The first time her humanity is tested, she fails. Instead of gaining insight, she loses vision. The memory tortures her. How sure can one be of oneself?" (201). In our interview, Stern said it was one of the most difficult passages in the book to write and added that she cried while writing it.

All of the authors cited recall extremely painful memories of human failure. For Zeller, it is failure to interact humanely with a prisoner on a train because of her own overriding fear. Two police officers ask her to accompany an "Eastern European worker" (*Ostarbeiterin*) to the toilet; once there, the woman repeats, "You, woman, please," imploring her to take a slip of paper (*Nein*, 232). Zeller describes the scene as a photograph, saying that after forty years, "the picture is completely overexposed" (*Nein*, 233). Tormented by thoughts that "she should have touched the woman, her face, her shoulder" (*Nein*, 233), she speculates on why she did not:

"[W]hat one calls the prevailing relations—these prevailing relations are oppressive. In what way could I have changed them? Perhaps in that I might have patted the tear-stained face? When will I finally dare to know what I already know? Well at least I took the slip of paper. Put it in my mouth. A reflex reaction. The chained dogs outside the door" (*Nein*, 233). Zeller frames this passage with reference to her pregnancy and the threat of the chained dogs outside the door as an exoneration of her cowardice—a justification belied by her confessional comment, "When will I finally dare to know, what I already know?" For Hannsmann, human failure is recorded in a series of small observations. Using rhetorical questions to indicate interpretive indecision, the narrator notes that Ulrike enthusiastically participated in a book burning in Salzburg, and speculates on whether her later efforts to rescue banned books being readied for destruction are an act of compensation: "Could Ulrike have thought: atonement?" (227). For Finckh, like Zeller, the test comes in the form of a personal, physical, albeit more violent confrontation. The farmer's wife for whom Cornelia works commands her to beat the Polish cowherd, saying, "[O]ne cannot go easy on Poles. . . . A Pole is just like a swine" (147). She gathers her courage and strikes the boy with a stick, but his hate-filled look haunts her for days. The narrator concludes from this experience: "That's how I personally learned how quite ordinary people can become mutes and bullies (literally, beaters). Why not also murderers?" (148). The larger underlying question of what "quite ordinary people" are capable of doing—and under what conditions—has concerned numerous women writers.

One becomes acutely aware in reading prison diaries and concentration camp accounts of the fragility of civilization. Christa Wolf's protagonist, Nelly, as an eighteen-year-old, discusses with her father the question "whether one can make an animal out of any person" (*A Model Childhood*, 43). Her father tends to believe, yes, that it is possible, because he has seen too much in his life. The narrator's own daughter, Lenka, in turn finds her parents' explanation of the Nazi era incomprehensible: "[H]ow one could simultaneously have been there and not been there, the dreadful secret of people in this century" (42). Luise Rinser's *Gefängnistagebuch* (1946)(*A Woman's Prison Journal*, 1987), depicts prisoners' traumatization and provides a concrete and detailed description of the deliberate process of dehumanization she experienced:

> Here in prison you turn out the very opposite of what you ought to become. You become anti-social. . . . You become familiar with a wicked, furtive hatred of your oppressors, you become a hypocrite, you learn to steal, if you hadn't learned it already. You learn malicious revenge, you carry out a hundred petty acts of revenge, and gradually you lose your awareness of human dignity and turn into a beaten, malevolent, servile, dulled animal. You need vast spiritual reserves to remain a human being here. Only in prison do you get to know your evil instincts. (48–49)

Like Carola Stern, for whom describing the NS torture scene reactivated the original agony and suffering, most of the women writers who fall into the co-perpetrator category, suffered both emotionally (Stern, Hannsmann, Rehmann) and physically (Wolf, Zeller) while writing about the Nazi era. The emotional and physical toll came from reliving brutal or anguishing experiences but also from the painful admission of one's own acts of inhumanity or moral failure.

Although contemporary readers are drawn—through observations on universal human behavior, references to contemporary events, and devices such as rhetorical questions—into a dialogue with these texts, many of us, as members of the postwar generation, are distanced from the events by time, and American readers in particular are distanced by culture and geography as well. But the writers themselves do not have the advantage of such distancing; in fact the intervening years since their childhood have in many ways become an obstacle. Margarete Hannsmann clearly marks the problem of narrative perspective that is a decision all authors of autobiographical books about childhood must face: should she put on paper the "sheer, painful kitsch" (114) of those years as revealed by the carefully preserved papers in her old suitcase? Or should she retell the story in new words, control it through reformulation, and shape it stylistically? Zeller shares Hannsmann's concern, questioning whether it is permissable for her, armed as she is with her present consciousness, to describe how it was using her voice from the earlier times (*Nein*, 14). Writers, unlike readers, are also subject to self-exposure, as Christa Wolf observes: "Woe to our time, which forces the writer to exhibit the wound of his own crime before he is allowed to describe other people's wounds" (*A Model Childhood*, 171). In order to be capable of writing anything at all, these writers, with the exception of Maschmann, all distance themselves by ascribing names to their protagonists: Zeller's "E" or "E-M," Finckh's Cornelia, Sterns's Eka, Wolf's Nelly, Drewitz's Gabriele, and Hannsmann's Ulrike, although authors such as Wolf and Hannsmann openly play with overlapping identities of author, narrator, and protagonist. Hannsmann writes early in her book: "I, Margarete, who is named Ulrike here, so that it is easier for me to tell about myself" (16). Ruth Rehmann, whose *Der Mann auf der Kanzel* (1979) (*The Man in the Pulpit*) is clearly autobiographical but in terms of focus is essentially a "father book," refers to her protagonist simply as "the child."[21] Considering herself a "self-conscious witness," she remarks that such witnesses have the problem of guilt being so close to them that it does not appear in a pure form, rather in opaque combinations that defy clear division. The more precisely one tries to cut, the more deeply and painfully one cuts into one's own flesh, and the more difficult the separation becomes not only between good and evil, but also between oneself and those in the Nazi era (181). The kind of guilt Rehmann refers to here parallels the guilty co-responsibility ascribed to families of alcoholics, who aid and abet the drinkers, shielding them from critical outside players (friends, neighbors, colleagues, the extended family) and from reality. This is precisely the collaborative role Rehmann's protagonist plays vis-à-vis her willfully ignorant pastor-father.

This was emphasized in a discussion with students at the University of Alabama in 1995, who vehemently rejected the conclusion of Rehmann's *Der Mann auf der Kanzel*. They objected because the author could not reach a decision about her father's culpability, thus rendering her guilty of the same failure of which she accused her father: she seemed unprepared to admit certain truths (in this case her father's guilt). In part though, the students were manifesting their own discomfort that the father's guilt was undecided, that there was no clear judgment from which the correct interpretation could be drawn. This is more than the usual discomfort and dismay caused by an open-ended text. Rather, a singularly intense, almost palpable, uneasiness arises both in reading about and writing about the Nazi era.

A tentative explanation for this phenomenon is suggested by the nature of prejudice itself. In the first of a three-part series on obesity published recently in the *New York Times*, Natalie Angier addressed the question of prejudice against obese people:

> [M]any people of normal weight fear the fat person because obesity embodies in the most graphic way possible the terrible potential they see lurking in themselves. For many, a fat person variously symbolizes loss of control, a reversion to infantile desires, failure, self-loathing, sloth, passivity and gluttony. . . .
>
> "The fat person represents the part of us that has gone to seed, has morally disintegrated," said Dr.Susan C. Wooley . . .
>
> And while many people manage to keep their anxieties and insecurities tucked safely inside, beyond the scrutiny of others, some see the fat as their own neuroses made flesh, forcing them to confront their own imperfections.

In the same way many of us—both readers and writers—experience anxiety and fear about the general loss of control and the moral disintegration which we associate with National Socialism. Marguerite Duras, writing about the war, cites the multilayered identification and anxiety of recognizing one's own potential to torture: "Thérèse is me. The person who tortures is me. So also is the one who feels like making love to Ter, the member of the Militia. Me. I give you the torturer along with the rest of the texts" (115). An essential inexplicability—an irrationality—seems to underlie the Third Reich when it is reduced to questions of human potential and behavior.[22] The darker topics that women writers collectively have addressed are in many cases interrelated: behaviors centered around the survival instinct, including dehumanization and bestiality; a militarist world view; fascist aspects of sexuality as they relate to dominance and aggression; racism; and an overall tolerance for violence.

In our interviews, several authors mentioned the Nazi emphasis on spectacle with mass gatherings and torchlight parades, and they compared the mood, especially in the early years to a Mardi Gras (*Karneval*) atmosphere.[23] During such rallies and political gatherings heavy drinking occurred, many played hooky from work and school, and one increasingly had the sense of normal rules having been suspended. In Christa Wolf's *Kassandra* (1983) (*Cassandra*, 1984), Trojan King Priam tells his priestess daughter: "[I]n war everything that would apply in peace was rescinded" (84). For many, social ranks were also reversed: those who had been on the bottom rungs of society suddenly had authority over those who had previously been their social superiors. In a similar reversal, certain prohibited behaviors now obtained social sanction. Ruth Waldeck makes this point in a unique essay that "reads" Wolf's *Kindheitsmuster* (1979) (*A Model Childhood*) not as literature or autobiography but as a sociohistorical text.[24] Noting examples of "pleasure in cruelty," "violent fantasies," and "pleasure in viewing others' suffering" in *Kindheitsmuster*, Waldeck bares the symbiotic relationship between National Socialist ideology and the world view of its adherents. She argues that the National Socialist rituals in which Nelly actively participated absorbed her conflicted feelings and unprocessed experiences like a giant mixing machine and reshaped them. According to Waldeck's interpretation, the impure and disgusting aspects of sexuality were transferred to the pimply Jewish boy so that Nelly could mature in purity as a member of the Hitler youth: "Nelly is indebted to National Socialism because she needs it. It guarantees her a conflict-free acting out of her raging desire and relief from her disturbing sexual impulses" (303).

In *Kassandra*, published seven years after *Kindheitsmuster*, Wolf pursues more intently and overtly the links between a militarist mentality, bestial behaviors, and sexual lust. Although these three factors merge in various configurations, Wolf ultimately locates them in a single Greek warrior whom she repeatedly identifies—imitating Homer's formulaic epithets—as "Achilles the beast." When Achilles desecrates the temple to murder the defenseless Troilos, Kassandra is a horrified witness: "In what role was his enemy approaching my brother? As a murderer? As a seducer? Could such a thing be—the voluptiousness of the murderer and the lover in one?" (74). Kassandra reads in Achilles' face lust: "naked, hideous male gratification" (74), and concludes, "if that exists, everything is possible" (74). Wolf taps into many readers' and writers' deepest anxieties by exploring both the violent underside of sexuality and the sexual underside of violence, especially of the organized and socially sanctioned violence called war.

Wolf has not been the first to identify these connections. Klaus Theweleit, who has been taken to task by numerous reviewers for his free-associative approach in the two-volume *Männerphantasien* (1977–78) (*Male Fantasies*, 1987–89), explicitly draws the connection between sexuality and violence among the roving bands of *Freikorps* men after World War I, from which the Nazis drew their first members.[25] Despite possible methodological shortcomings, Theweleit has identified an important and insufficiently explored connection. He amasses 858 pages of verbal and visual images in support of his thesis, which links male fear of female (sexual) engulfment with a deep lust for violence. Barbara Ehrenreich's lucid introduction to the English edition makes the reader's task somewhat easier by distilling out arguments basic to Theweleit's position. "As a theory of fascism," she writes, "*Male Fantasies* sets forth the jarring—and ultimately horrifying—proposition that the fascist is not doing 'something else,' but doing what he wants to do" (xi). In the chilling words of a Freikorpsman himself: "People told us that the War was over. That made us laugh. We ourselves are the War. Its flame burns strongly in us. It envelops our whole being and fascinates us with the enticing urge to destroy" (x). Theweleit's interpretation of war, and specifically the battlefield, as a male response to women's encroachments on traditional male territory is an argument Sandra Gilbert also puts forward in her essay about World War I, "Soldier's Heart." Similarly, Theweleit's identification of the sexual subtext of fascism has been explored by the Italian scholar Antonietta-Maria Macciocchi in revealing new ways that link not only sexuality with violence and war but also religion and cults of death.[26]

For a number of women writers, fascism and sexuality are linked in the person of the father, giving rise early in their lives to what I term "father trouble." Eva Zeller's father, her "beloved enemy" (*Lieblingsfeind*), hates Hitler but ironically duplicates the role of dictator within the structure of his own family. The narrator says that her father is "the lord over wives, children, colleagues, who are all supposed to worship him" (*Nein*, 224).[27] His power rests partially in a sexual dominance that borders on terrorization. Living with his fourth wife, he still sends pornographic pictures to his first wife, and carries on numerous affairs. It turns out that at the same time he forced Eva's mother into an unwanted abortion, he impregnated her cousin, "the beautiful Ruth," who later committed suicide. This man may sound like a wholly unscrupulous social outcast, but we learn that quite the contrary, he is a respected pillar of society and a noted scholar; this of course raises the larger question of socially acceptable male behavior. If this contempt for women is accepted—perhaps even admired—peacetime behavior, what would one expect of such a man in a war situation? In Zeller's case the question remains unanswered since her father did not serve in the military, but Roger Cook, in his essay on the film *Deutschland, bleiche Mutter* (*Germany, Pale Mother*), suggests a possible answer: "In times of war, when society legitimizes the male warrior instincts, women are likely to become victims of such terror" (115).

Ulrike Knecht's father in Margarete Hannsmann's *Der helle Tag bricht an; Ein Kind wird Nazi* (1982) (*The New Day Dawns: A Child becomes Nazi*) manifests even more clearly the will to sexual dominance inherent to fascist ideology in his perverted relationship with his daughter. Hannsmann renames her hometown "Albheim" as a spinoff on *Alptraum* (nightmare), and in our interview she said forcefully, "My father was a devil." Gotthilf Knecht, his weakness already intimated in these names given him by his author-daughter (Gotthilf = God help, Knecht = servant), is a slightly built and severely crippled veteran of World War I, who can barely walk. He represents if anything the exact opposite of the Nazi ideal of manhood. By contrast, his pubescent daughter Ulrike is sexually precocious and extremely attractive to men of all ages.

The stark opposition of these two figures recalls the two photos from World War I that initially appeared on facing pages of Sandra Gilbert's essay "Soldier's Heart."[28] One depicts five healthy, smiling, robust, young women leaning in unconstrained "masculine" postures against a fence, and the other shows seven men seated stiffly in a line. All of the men are war amputees; this lineup of torsos in suits and ties is quite shocking visually. The extreme nature of this contrast is reproduced in the relationship of Ulrike Knecht to her father. The emasculated father, in love with his daughter and admiring but fearing her wildness, cannot accept the freedom (from him) that her developing sexuality represents. His attempts to contain and control her sexuality disintegrate into repeated scenarios of punishment in which he whips her with a cat-o-nine-tails. Sex, lust, pain, and domination become entangled in the whippings, which always occur in the bathroom behind closed doors where she must voluntarily remove her underpants and present her buttocks. What ensues clearly indicates the twisted nature of this father/daughter relationship: she is obliged to request his forgiveness. In this perverse reversal, the victim is held guilty for her own victimization. As a result, Ulrike learns to associate sexual pleasure exclusively with pain and death; she experiences a single, recurring fantasy of sexual pleasure: an execution. When I asked Hannsmann whether she contemplated writing about her father again in the future, she replied, "I will not descend into this cellar again" (Interview).

The fear of female sexuality and the corresponding need to circumscribe and control it, as suggested by Theweleit, Macciocchi, and others, and documented autobiographically by numerous women writers appears inherent to the fascist concept of manhood. The acting out of sexual desire in general represents disorderliness and a sense of being out of control—behaviors that would have undermined the National Socialist/fascist world view which brooked no challenge to its controlled ideology and carefully elaborated hierarchies of power. John Hubner gets at the heart of this fear when he writes in *Bottom Feeders*, his book about two pornographer brothers:

> [T]here is something deeply subversive about the explicit display of sex. Sex strips away identities it takes a lifetime to build. A naked aroused man is not a brain surgeon or a university president or a Methodist bishop. He is an animal with an erection.[29]

The levelling effect of sexual expression suggested here would obviously have been intolerable to men who subscribed to an ideology keen on establishing difference and maintaining myths of its own adherents' superiority. Gudrun Brockhaus, summarizing work done by Dorothea Schmidt, Margot Koman, Godele v. d. Decken, and others, opens another, as yet largely unexplored connection: a comparison of National Socialist women's fantasies with those of men. She notes that this research exhibits in many places striking similarities to Theweleit's work on male fantasies, for example the mixing of sexuality and violence, the fascination with intoxication, and the fearful search for limits. Basing her interpretation on an essay by Luce d'Eramo, Brockhaus shows how an exaggerated warrior mythos (male) compensated National Socialist men for their total obedience (female) to the party; this explains the fascist public emphasis on a cult of virility.

Women writers such as Zeller and Hannsmann have made an initial attempt to describe the fascism/sexuality link as it took shape in individual women's lives during the Nazi era. These efforts may potentially raise as many questions as they answer, particularly in light of recent research on the nature of desire. The act of questioning may, however, be subversive and revolutionary in and of itself—an interpretation suggested by the fact that this activity was so vehemently suppressed under National Socialism.[30] Melita Maschmann says of her adolescence, that just as they reached the age when they could have learned to think . . . the era began in which thinking was considered an activity of degenerate brains (83). In retrospect most of these writers would likely agree that thinking critically (questioning) constitutes the first step in the development of resistance. The asking of questions as a methodology is certainly not new, but in the present series of demystifying questions being posed by women about the Nazi era, two differences are noticeable: first, they are able to pose questions that have both the present and the future as their framework, that is, an examination of the past in terms of a broad historical continuity, and second, rather than anticipate answers, the writers privilege the questions themselves. This reaction can be seen as a development from their adolescent experience of National Socialism, as Eva Zeller explains:

> Even the best school in greater Germany could not teach one thing: independent thinking, which in practical terms would have meant asking questions, plying ourselves and our teachers with questions, questions that wanted more than ready-made answers. There were no questions, only answers upon answers. (*Solange*, 240)

Disciplines such as history, sociology, and literature have overlapped in the 1980s and 1990s in various areas of research on women in the Nazi era. This overlapping has been mutually enriching because of the different ways that similar questions have been addressed. Common concerns have centered on language, responsibility, guilt, morality, racism, sexism, and continuity. Future research on women in the Nazi era may develop most fruitfully in two directions: autobiography and memory. While autobiography provides an interdisciplinary context in which significant progress in thinking through the Nazi era can occur, progress on understanding the nature and function of memory is being made in fields as divergent as psychology, history, medicine, and literature.

Scholars of oral history have noted the unusual "relationship between memory and the future" (Passerini, 12), which reflects the concern of many scholars of the Nazi era with postwar continuity. Luisa Passerini notes, "It is not by chance that the issue of generations, biological as well as political, and of transmission of memory between them is such a crucial one" (12). For the "middle generation," in the wake of societal collapse in 1945, "[a] sense of responsibility for their children, and the knowledge that half of their life still lay in front of them motivated them to seek for modes of continuity in their biographies and memories" (Passerini, 12). Thus, memory—its shortcomings, selectivity, unreliability—has become more important in the work of both social scientists (Tröger et al.) and literary writers (Wolf, Zeller, Finckh). There is reason to believe that the public negotiation of memory has historically helped sustain patriarchal attitudes that reproduce fascism. But memory work is also crucial to personal reconciliation with a difficult past. In this respect, it is equally applicable to all of the writers discussed in this essay. It binds them, both to one another and to scholars of the Nazi era, in a mutual undertaking.

Notes

I would like to thank my colleagues Ute Winston, Thomas Kovach, O. Kimball Armayor, and Richard Anderson for their various contributions to this chapter.

This chapter was originally presented as a paper entitled "Victim, Collaborator, Resister, Perpetrator? Women Writers Respond to National Socialism," at the Symposium, "German Women Writers from Weimar to the Present," at the University of Maryland, February 25–28, 1993. It has been reconceptualized and extensively rewritten to focus on the category of collaboration/perpetration.

1. Milton discusses at greater length this research, which she says "can be classified in three ways: —Research conducted by historians in various European countries that chronicles their nations' suffering under German occupation. —Research focused on specific aspects of the Nazi regime—such as biographies of Hitler and other leading Nazis; the diplomatic, military, economic, and administrative history of Nazi Germany; and the electorate that voted for or against Hitler. . . . —Research on the Nazi crimes against the Jews" (A52).

2. I refer here to work by Jill Stephenson, Leila Rupp, Renate Bridenthal, Richard Evans, Rita Thalman, and others.

3. "Mit den 'nicht-verfolgten' meine ich alle Deutschen, die weder der Leib und Leben bedrohenden rassistischen, eugenischen oder homophoben Verfolgung im NS-Staat ausgesetzt waren, noch sich selbst durch Hilfe für die Bedrohten oder durch politischen Widerstand der Verfolgung aussetzten" (Hanna Lauterbach, "Verbrecherinnen," 141).

4. The bulk of this new literature fell into one of two categories: life stories of Jewish concentration camp survivors, and life stories of resistance fighters in the Nazi era, or of opponents of National Socialism (*Gegnerinnen*), who either were not part of an organized resistance movement or were involved peripherally through their families/husbands (Staden,

Maltzan, Yorck von Wartenburg, Bielenberg). To name only a few of the survivor-authors: Lisa Scheuer, Isabella Leitner, Gisella Perl, Hanna Lévy-Hass. Accounts by women survivors of the Holocaust began to appear as early as the 1950s, including notable texts such as Gerda Klein's *All But My Life* (1957), Charlotte Delbo's *Aucun de nous ne reviendra* (1965) (also other works by Delbo spanning the sixties and seventies), and Fania Fenelon's *Playing for Time* (1977). The 1980s, however, saw an increase in both autobiographies/primary texts and scholarly work on Holocaust survivor narratives. For a discussion of the literary aspects of these texts see Marlene Heinemann, *Gender and Destiny; Women Writers and the Holocaust*. Of the many examples of accounts by resistance fighters, one could mention three, all of whom were communists: Lore Wolf, Anni Wadle, Lina Haag.

5. See for example, Zorn/Meyer 1984, Schüddekopf 1982, Ebbinghaus 1987, Tröger 1987, Szepansky 1983, 1986, Kerschbaumer 1980.

6. For a discussion of Rehmann's and Bronnen's novels, as well as of Monika Köhler's *Die Früchte vom Machandelbaum* (1980), see Susan Figge's essay, "Fathers, Daughters, and the Nazi Past: Father Literature and Its (Resisting) Readers," and for a comparison of Reichart's two novels (*Komm Über den See* and *Februarschatten*) with Brigitte Schwaiger's *Lange Abwesenheit* (1982), see Maria-Regina Kecht's "Resisting Silence: Brigitte Schwaiger and Elisabeth Reichart Attempt to Confront the Past"; both essays are in *Gender, Patriarchy, and Fascism in the Third Reich*, ed. Elaine Martin.

7. Lerke Gravenhorst dates this public discussion to 1986, summarizing important stages in *Töchter Fragen NS-Frauen Geschichte*: "Kristallisationspunkte der veränderten Aufmerksamkeit sind Tagungen ebenso wie Veröffentlichungen. Zu den hier relevanten Tagungen gehören die Soziologinnentage im Juni 1986 an der FU Berlin; eine Arbeitstagung in der Heimvolkshochschule Glienecke in Berlin 'Frauen als Opfer des Nationalsozialismus' 1989; und die Tutzinger Friedenstage an der Evangelischen Akademie Tutzing mit dem Seminar 'Zur Diskussion des Nationalsozialismus in der neueren Frauenforschung' (1989). Entsprechende Veröffentlichungen stammen u. a. von Angelika Ebbinghaus (1986), Dorothea Schmidt (1987), Karin Windaus-Walser (1988, 1989a), Frigga Haug (1988) und Annette Kuhn (1989)" ("Nehmen wir," 23, note).

8. Both historians and sociologists have participated in this discussion, which has primarily taken place among "feministischen Intellektuellen und Wissenschaftlerinnen in und aus Deutschland," as Lerke Gravenhorst describes them ("Nehmen wir," 27). Some of the main contributors to the discussion to date have been Karin Windaus-Walser, Gisela Bock, Annette Kuhn, Lerke Gravenhorst, Frigga Haug, Claudia Koonz, Christina Thürmer-Rohr, Annemarie Tröger, Dorothea Schmidt, Marianne Lehker, and Angelika Ebbinghaus. The original *Historikerstreit*, a public debate held in Germany in 1986 and initially carried out in newspapers and magazines, concerned how National Socialism and its genocidal policies should be understood: as an aberration (*Sonderweg* thesis), or as an inevitability in German historical development (continuity thesis). For a lucid summary of the key players and positions within a historical context, see Geoff Eley, "Nazism, Politics, and the Image of the Past: Thoughts on the West German Historikerstreit 1986–1987," *Past and Present* 121 (1988): 171–208. For the primary texts, see *"Historikerstreit" Die Dokumentation der Kontroverse um die Einzigartigkeit der nationalsozialistischen Judenvernichtung* (Munich: Piper, 1987).

9. All translations from the German in this essay are mine with the exception of Wolf's *Kindheitsmuster*, for which I have used the translation indicated.

10. See also "Don't Forget: Fragments of a Negative Tradition," by Renate Siebert, in *Memory and Totalitarianism*, ed. Luisa Passerini.

11. Other scholars have also attempted to address the personal aspects of scholarship, both individually and in experimental collaborative efforts. For example, the editors of *Lingua Franca*, who recently published excerpts of Alice Kaplan's memoir, *French Lessons*, noted that it "examines the way personal history feeds scholarly obsession. It is an intimate account of Kaplan's intellectual coming of age, an experiment in autobiography composed for the Duke University writing group in which she, along with English professors Cathy Davidson, Jane Tompkins, and Marianna Torgovnick, tried out subjective approaches to academic prose" (34). See Kaplan, "Out of the Past." For a summary of the Duke critics interested in "autobiographical scholarship," see "The I's have it; Duke's 'Moi' Critics Expose Themselves," by Adam Begley, *Lingua Franca* (March/April 1994): 54–59.

12. For a discussion of Virginia Woolf's analysis of fascism in *Three Guineas* and its link with works by contemporary German women writers, see *Women Writers and Fascism: Reconstructing History* by Marie-Luise Gättens.

13. The concept *Kontinuität* is also used by individual researchers in more specialized contexts that correspond to neither of these usages. For example, Dagmar Reese and Carola Sachse, in a critique of Gisela Bock's work on *Sterilisationspolitik* use "Kontinuität" to refer to conditions of women's employment that carried over from pre-Nazi (Weimar) years into the Nazi era (Reese/Sachse, "Frauenforschung," 94).

14. Lerke Gravenhorst argues: ". . . ich [halte] die Bewertung von 'Täterschaft' in dem Begriff für wichtiger als die Bewertung des 'Mit-', das wiederum für Christina Thürmer-Rohr im Mittelpunkt steht. Angesichts der NS-Untaten scheint mir doch das Wissen um 'Täterschaft' unmittelbar wichtiger zu sein als das Wissen um die Tatsache, daß es eine patriarchal strukturierte und abhängige Täterschaft, eben Mittäterschaft war" (Nehmen wir, 30).

15. This belief that literature can transcend facts to render larger truths has existed in various forms for centuries. Aristotle writes in the Poetics: "The difference between a historian and a poet is not that one writes in prose and the other in verse . . . . The real difference is this, that one tells what happened and the other what might happen. For this reason poetry is something more scientific and serious than history, because poetry tends to give general truths while history gives particular facts" (VIII. 4-IX. 5). *Loeb Classic Aristotle*, v. 23, The Poetics, ed. W. Hamilton Fyfe. (London/Cambridge, Mass: Harvard University Press, 1973).

16. Renate Finckh writes in *Mit uns zieht die neue Zeit* about the *Jungmädelgruppe* of which she is a leader: "Dienst hatte man Donnerstag und Samstag nachmittags, und er war für alle Pflicht. Wir hatten die Befugnis, ein Mädel, das dreimal unentschuldigt fernblieb, von der Polizei holen zu lassen" (118).

17. Personal communication of Lutz-W. Wolff, an editor at DTV in Munich, in May 1988.

18. Maschmann (b.1918), Hannsmann (b.1921), Rehmann (b.1922), Zeller (b.1923), Drewitz (b.1923), Stern (b.1925), Finckh (b.1926), Wolf (b.1929).

19. Hannsmann referred in her remarks here particularly to Carola Stern, Melita Maschmann, and Renate Finckh, all of whom remained believers in National Socialism until the final collapse of the Third Reich. Renate Finckh, in an interview with Heike

Mundzeck, said: "Ich war damals 16 Jahre alt, also eigentlich schon ein junger Mensch, von dem man eigenes Nachdenken erwarten kann. Aber ich hatte bereits ein 'Ersatzgewissen' und ausreichende Ersatzargumente. Ich wollte und konnte nicht nachdenken. Ich sagte mir: Jetzt mögen viele schlimme Dinge passieren, aber das muß wohl so sein, wir haben Krieg und kämpfen für eine bessere Zukunft" (in *Der Alltägliche Faschismus; Frauen im Dritten Reich*, ed. Charles Schüddekopf, 75).

20. Sociologist Annemarie Tröger's research, based on interviews with numerous women who lived through the Nazi era and World War II, reveals an interesting phenomenon that is pertinent here:

> "The notion of being a victim permeates nearly all the war accounts of the women interviewed. . . .
>
> The religious and popular symbol of the victim absolves the victim of responsibility and guilt. A victim of the war cannot be responsible for it. In the postwar German understanding, this notion is carried even further: as a victim one cannot be held responsible for fascism. This is certainly one reason that interviewees brought up the war as soon as the uncomfortable issue of National Socialism was raised in the interview. Suffering shields Germans from the threatening and guilt-provoking questions surrounding the issues of fascism, concentration camps, and the Nazis' treatment of Jews. (298–299)

21. See Susan Figge's work on father literature by daughters, for example her essay "Fathers, Daughters, and the Nazi Past: Father Literature and Its (Resisting) Readers," in *Gender, Patriarchy, and Fascism in the Third Reich*, ed. by Elaine Martin.

22. Barbara Ehrenreich writes in her foreword to Theweleit's first volume of *Male Fantasies*: "In the sociological or Marxist worldview, fascist murder appears either as an instrumentality—the terrorist spectacle required to maintain absolute authority—or as an intrusion of the 'irrational,' which, for most social scientists, is also the unknowable. Then there are the psychoanalytic theories of fascism, which at least have the merit of addressing the 'irrational' as a subject of inquiry. The problem here is that, too often, fascism tends to become representational, symbolic" (xi).

23. In our interview (November 1986), Ingeborg Lauterstein, author of *Vienna Girl* and *The Water Castle*, represented Vienna following the *Anschluß* in these terms. She also used the image of a rock concert.

24. Waldeck describes her unique, nonliterary perspective on *Kindheitsmuster* thus: "Mein Interesse richtet sich also nicht auf die Geschichte der Autorin als Individuum, sondern auf die in diesem Roman entfaltete gesellschaftlich bedeutsame Problematik: auf das Verhältnis von Nationalsozialismus und Weiblichkeit" (294).

25. See for example William Doty's review in the *South Atlantic Review* (53.2, 1988) in which he refers to volume 1 as "Theweleit's diffuse, disorganized tome," and concludes that his "own sympathies with the book, especially with its feminist and revisionist psychoanalytic perspectives, are not strong enough to overcome [his] dismay that so important a theme would be so carelessly presented."

26. See Macciocchi's essay "Female Sexuality in Fascist Ideology," and my own discussion of Macciocchi in "Autobiography, Gender, and the Third Reich," (especially pages 184–189) in *Gender, Patriarchy, and Fascism in the Third Reich*, ed. Elaine Martin.

27. For a more detailed discussion of this father/daughter relationship, see my essay, "Patriarchy, Memory, and the Third Reich in the Autobiographical Novels of Eva Zeller," *Women in German Yearbook* 6 (1991): 47–62.

28. Connecting visual and literary/linguistic images seems to have rich potential. Sybil Milton commented that "most history books and courses . . . neglect recent research that focuses on new ways to utilize old sources. For example, I have studied photographs of the Holocaust to obtain new insights into the uses of propaganda and ideology in camouflaging persecution" ("Re-Examining").

29. Cited by D. Keith Mano in "Pornographers' Progress," his review of *Bottom Feeders*, *New York Times Book Review*, February 14, 1993, p. 13.

30. The use of questioning as a methodology is an important legacy of the Frankfurt School, as George Marcus and Michael Fischer summarize in *Anthropology as Cultural Critique*:

> The most exciting tool wielded by the Frankfurt School was their demystifying series of questions about the ways culture and psychology might be manipulated by political and economic processes. In probing why the highly cultured bourgeois societies of Western Europe should allow themselves to fall into mass dictatorships, . . . Horkheimer and Adorno asked if the psychodynamics of identity formation in the family was not changing in a manner that made authoritarianism increasingly natural. Secondly, they questioned if the industrial production of culture was not working to reinforce such authoritarian trends. Although Horkheimer and Adorno gave overly pessimistic answers to these questions, in part because of the looming threat of fascism, their mode of formulating questions remains important for cultural critique up to the present. (120)

Bibliography

Angier, Nathalie. "Why So Many Are Prejudiced Against the Obese." *New York Times*, November 22, 1992.

Bernardoni, Claudia. "Ohne Schuld und Sühne? Der moralische Diskurs über die feministische Auseinandersetzung mit dem Nationalsozialismus." In *Töchter Fragen NS-Frauen Geschichte*. Ed. Lerke Gravenhorst and Carmen Tatschmurat. Freiburg: Kore, 1990, 127–134.

Bock, Gisela. "Racism and Sexism in Nazi Germany: Motherhood, Compulsory Sterilization, and the State." In *When Biology Became Destiny*. Ed. Renate Bridenthal et al. 1984, 271–296.

———. *Zwangssterilisation im Nationalsozialismus. Studien zur Rassenpolitik und zur Frauenpolitik*. Schriften des Zentralinstituts für sozialwissenschaftliche Forschung, FU Berlin 48. Wiesbaden: Westdeutscher Verlag, 1986.

Bridenthal, Renate, Atina Grossmann, and Marion Kaplan. *When Biology Became Destiny: Women in Weimar and Nazi Germany*. New York: Monthly Review Press, 1984.

Brockhaus, Gudrun. "Opfer, Täterin, Mitbeteiligte. Zur Diskussion um die Rolle der Frauen im Nationalsozialismus." In *Töchter Fragen NS-Frauen Geschichte*. Ed. Lerke Gravenhorst and Carmen Tatschmurat. 1990.

Cook, Roger F. "Melodrama or Cinematic Folktale? Story and History in *Deutschland, bleiche Mutter*." *The Germanic Review* 66.3 (1991): 113–121.

Duras, Marguerite. *The War: A Memoir*. Trans. Barbara Bray. New York: Pantheon, 1986. [*La Douleur*, Paris: P.O.L. éditeur, 1985].

Eley, Geoff. "Nazism, Politics and the Image of the Past: Thoughts on the West German *Historikerstreit* 1986–1987." *Past and Present* 121 (Nov. 1988): 171–208.

Figge, Susan. "Fathers, Daughters, and the Nazi Past: Father Literature and Its (Resisting) Readers." In *Gender, Patriarchy, and Fascism in the Third Reich*. Ed. Elaine Martin. Detroit: Wayne State University Press, 1993, 274–302.

Finckh, Renate. *Mit uns zieht die neue Zeit*. Baden-Baden: Signal, 1978.

Gättens, Marie-Luise. *Women Writers and Fascism: Reconstructing History*. Gainesville: Florida University Press, 1995.

Gilbert, Sandra. "Soldier's Heart: Literary Men, Literary Women, and the Great War." *Signs* 8.3 (1983): 422–450.

Gravenhorst, Lerke. "Nehmen wir Nationalsozialismus und Auschwitz ausreichen als unser Eigentum in Anspruch? Zu Problemen im feministisch-sozialwissenschaftlichen Diskurs in der Bundesrepublik Deutschland." In *Töchter Fragen NS-Frauen Geschichte*. Ed. Lerke Gravenhorst and Carmen Tatschmurat. Freiburg: Kore, 1990, 17–38.

Gravenhorst, Lerke, and Carmen Tatschmurat, eds. *Töchter Fragen NS-Frauen Geschichte*. Freiburg: Kore, 1990.

Haag, Lina. *Eine Handvoll Staub*. Frankfurt: Röderberg, 1977.

Hannsmann, Margarete. *Der helle Tag bricht an; Ein Kind wird Nazi*. 1982. Munich: dtv, 1984.

———. Personal interview. Stuttgart, May 28, 1991. Unpublished manuscript.

Haubrich, Karin, and Lerke Gravenhorst. "Wie stellen wir heute moralische Wirklichkeiten von Frauen im Nationalsozialismus her? Titel im Blickfeld." In *Töchter Fragen NS-Frauen Geschichte*. Ed. Lerke Gravenhorst and Carmen Tatschmurat. Freiburg: Kore, 1990, 39–58.

Heinemann, Marlene. *Gender and Destiny: Women Writers and the Holocaust*. Westport, Conn.: Greenwood, 1986.

Kaes, Anton. "New Historicism and the Study of German Literature." *The German Quarterly* 62.2 (1989): 210–219.

Kaplan, Alice. "Out of the Past: Encounters With a French Collaborationist." *Lingua Franca* (September/October 1993): 34–40.

Kerschbaumer, Marie-Thérèse. *Der weibliche Name des Widerstands: Sieben Berichte*. Munich: dtv, 1982.

Koonz, Claudia. *Mothers in the Fatherland*. New York: St. Martin's Press, 1987.

Lauterbach, Hanna. "'Aber dann hätten wir ja nur noch Verbrecherinnen . . .' Kommentar zur "Diskussion über den Anteil am 'Handlungskollektiv Deutschland.'" In *Töchter Fragen NS-Frauen Geschichte*. Ed. Lerke Gravenhorst and Carmen Tatschmurat. Freiburg: Kore, 1990, 141–148.

Leitner, Isabella. *Fragments of Isabella: A Memoir of Auschwitz*. Ed. Irving A. Leitner. New York: Crowell, 1978.

Lévy-Haas, Hanna. *Vielleicht war das alles erst der Anfang. Tagebuch aus dem KZ Bergen-Belsen*. Berlin: Rotbuch Verlag, 1979.

Macciocchi, Maria-Antonietta. "Female Sexuality in Fascist Ideology." Trans. and ed. Michèle Barrett et al. *Feminist Review* 1 (1979): 67–82.

Marcus, George E., and Michael M. J. Fischer. *Anthropology as Cultural Critique*. Chicago: University of Chicago Press, 1986.

Martin, Elaine, ed. *Patriarchy, Gender, and Fascism in the Third Reich; The Response of Women Writers*. Detroit: Wayne State University Press, 1993.

———. "Patriarchy, Memory, and the Third Reich in the Autobiographical Novels of Eva Zeller." *Women in German Yearbook* 6 (1991): 47–62.

Maschmann, Melita. *Fazit; Mein Weg in der Hitler-Jugend*. Munich: dtv, 1979.

Meyer, Birgit. "Brief an Lerke Gravenhorst." In *Töchter Fragen NS-Frauen Geschichte*. Ed. Lerke Gravenhorst and Carmen Tatschmurat. Freiburg: Kore, 1990, 135–140.

Milton, Sybil. "Re-Examining Scholarship on the Holocaust." *The Chronicle of Higher Education* 21 (April 1993): A52.

Mundzeck, Heike. "Renate Finckh im Gespräch mit Heike Mundzeck." In *Der alltägliche Faschismus*. Ed. Charles Schüddekopf. Bonn: Dietz, 1982, 68–79.

Passerini, Luisa, ed. *Memory and Totalitarianism*. International Yearbook of Oral History and Life Stories. V. 1. New York: Oxford University Press, 1992.

Perl, Gisella. *I Was a Doctor in Auschwitz*. New York: Ayer, 1984.

Reese, Dagmar, and Carola Sachse. "Frauenforschung und Nationalsozialismus. Eine Bilanz." In *Töchter Fragen NS-Frauen Geschichte*. Ed. Lerke Gravenhorst and Carmen Tatschmurat. Freiburg: Kore, 1990, 73–107.

Rehmann, Ruth. *Der Mann auf der Kanzel; Fragen an einen Vater*. Munich: dtv, 1981.

Rinser, Luise. *Gefängnistagebuch*. Frankfurt: Fischer, 1973 [Munich: Zinnen-Verlag Kurt Desch, 1946].

———. *A Woman's Prison Journal: Germany, 1944*. Trans. Michael Hulse. New York: Pantheon, 1987.

Scheuer, Lisa. *Vom Tode, der nicht stattfand*. Reinbek: Rowohlt, 1983.

Schüddekopf, Charles. *Der alltägliche Faschismus; Frauen im Dritten Reich*. Bonn: Dietz, 1982.

Stern, Carola. *In den Netzen der Erinnerung*. Reinbek: Rowohlt, 1986.

———. Personal interview. Cologne, June 11, 1988. Unpublished manuscript.

Szepansky, Gerda. *Frauen leisten Widerstand: 1933–1945*. Frankfurt: Fischer, 1983.

———.. *'Blitzmädel', 'Heldenmutter', 'Kriegerwitwe': Frauenleben im Zweiten Weltkrieg*. Frankfurt: Fischer, 1986.

Theweleit, Klaus. *Male Fantasies*. V. 1 and 2. Minneapolis: University of Minnesota Press, 1987, 1989.

Thürmer-Rohr, Christina. "Aus der Täuschung in die Ent-Täuschung—Zur Mittäterschaft von Frauen." *beiträge zur feministischen theorie und praxis* 8 (1983): 11–26.

———. "Mittäterschaft der Frau—Analyse zwischen Mitgefühl und Kälte." *Studienschwerpunkt 'Frauenforschung': Mittäterschaft und Entdeckungslust* published by Institut für Sozialpädagogik der TU Berlin, Berlin 1989.

Tröger, Annemarie. "German Women's Memories of World War II." In *Behind the Lines; Gender and the Two World Wars*. Ed. Margaret Higonnet, Jane Jenson, Sonya Michel, Margaret Weitz. New Haven: Yale University Press, 1987, 285–99.

Wadle, Anni. *Mutti, warum lachst du nie?* Drensteinfurt: Huba, 1988.

Waldeck, Ruth. "'Heikel bis heute'—Frauen und Nationalsozialismus. Überlegungen zur weiblichen Selbstdefinition als Opfer anhand von Christa Wolfs Roman *Kindheitsmuster*." In *Töchter Fragen NS-Frauen Geschichte*. Ed. Lerke Gravenhorst and Carmen Tatschmurat. Freiburg, Kore, 1990, 293–308.

Westernhagen, Dörte von. *Die Kinder der Täter: Das Dritte Reich und die Generation danach*. Munich: dtv, 1991.

Wiggershaus, Renate. *Frauen unterm Nationalsozialismus*. Wuppertal: Hammer, 1984.

Windaus-Walser, Karin. "Frauen im Nationalsozialismus. Eine Herausforderung für feministische Theoriebildung." In *Töchter Fragen NS-Frauen Geschichte*. Ed. Lerke Gravenhorst and Carmen Tatschmurat. Freiburg: Kore, 1990, 59–72.

Wolf, Christa. *Kassandra*. Darmstadt: Luchterhand, 1983.

———. *Cassandra. A Novel and Four Essays*. New York: Farrar, Straus & Giroux, 1984.

———. *Kindheitsmuster*. Darmstadt: Luchterhand, 1979.

———. *A Model Childhood*. New York: Farrar, Straus & Giroux, 1980.

Wolf, Lore. *Ich habe das Leben lieb; Tagebuchblätter aus dem Zuchthaus Ziegenhain*. Dortmund: Weltkreis, 1983.

———. *Ein Leben ist viel zuwenig*. Berlin: Verlag Neues Leben, 1973.

Zeller, Eva. *Nein und Amen*. Stuttgart: DVA, 1986.

———. *Solange ich denken kann*. Stuttgart: DVA, 1981.

———. Personal Interview, Munich, May 15, 1986. Unpublished manuscript.

Zorn, Gerda, and Gertrud Meyer. *Frauen gegen Hitler: Berichte aus dem Widerstand 1933-45*. Berlin: Elefanten Press, 1984.

Part III

Individual Women's Voices against Fascism

5
Literary Antifascism: Anna Seghers's Exile Writings 1936 to 1949

Gertraud Gutzmann

In October 1942, *The Seventh Cross*, a novel by the German writer Anna Seghers, became the choice of American critics as the "Book of the Month." The selection of this particular novel must have come as a surprise to North American readers for whom Seghers was hardly a familiar literary figure. Most critics, however, regarded her as a major European writer, comparable in literary status to prominent exiles such as Thomas Mann or Hermann Broch.[1] The enthusiastic reception of *The Seventh Cross* on the American book market was all the more surprising, since it is a novel about daily life in Nazi Germany around 1936, with the escape of seven captives from a concentration camp as its main plot, and many such stories had been published in the United States ever since the arrival of refugees from Nazi Germany in the early thirties. The senior editors of Little, Brown and Company of Boston, Seghers's publishers, understood quite well that American readers had lost interest in fictional accounts of life in the Third Reich. After extended debate about the wisdom of publishing yet another concentration camp story, Little, Brown nevertheless decided to promote the Seghers novel. They recognized its difference from other such stories, in particular its political potential for the American war effort. Angus Cameron, one of the senior editors, endorsed the publication of *The Seventh Cross* with these arguments: "We feel that it plays a central role in clarifying to the American people at a very crucial time the real nature of things German; its role in making it clear that the President is right when he says that there is a difference between the German people and the Nazis."[2]

It seems ironic that *The Seventh Cross* was expected to inspire Americans to fight Nazism, for Seghers had written the novel during her years of exile in France, when she was still hopeful that a strong resistance movement against the Hitler state would develop in her home country. Popular opposition to National Socialist rule, however, failed to materialize in Germany. Yet the expectation that literature could have an impact on political processes, a view expressed in Cameron's letter, corresponded to Seghers's initial conception of the social function of art. As early as 1931, she declared in her "Kleiner Bericht aus meiner Werkstatt" ("Report from my Workshop"), her first formal statement on committed literature: "Denn wir schreiben ja nicht, um zu beschreiben, sondern um beschreibend zu verändern" (We do not just write for the sake of describing reality, but rather to bring about change; 15). Seghers hoped to counteract National Socialist propaganda, in particular its emphasis on war and violence as adventures, a message that had captured the imagination of vast numbers of young, unemployed Germans in the final years of the crisis-ridden Weimar Republic. Her essay "Was wissen wir von Jugend-Cliquen?" "(What Do We Know about Youth Gangs?"), written in 1931 for the women's magazine *Der Weg der Frau*,[3] deals with young people's longing for action and for an opportunity to prove themselves. Such longings had been manipulated by Nazi propaganda more effectively than by the German left which had failed to win the support of working-class people. Seghers dealt with this failure in all of her major exile writings. Novels such as *Der Weg durch den Februar* (1934) (*The Way through February*), *Die Rettung* (1936) (*The Rescue*), as well as *Das siebte Kreuz* (1943) (*The Seventh Cross*) present Seghers's critical views of her own party's past political strategies. In addition, they give expression to her concept of politically committed art, one that insists on formal experimentation and on freedom from political dogma and prescriptive theory. More importantly, Seghers establishes in these stories and novels a striking analogy between the freedom and spontaneity of aesthetic imagination and artistic creation and the process of immediate experience and political learning of her protagonists, most of them men and women of the working classes.

In the late thirties, the debates on realism and on political art, especially the charged exchanges between Georg Lukács, Bertolt Brecht, Hanns Eisler, and Ernst Bloch, posed a challenge to Seghers's stance on literature and politics. In two letters to Lukács she challenged his insistence on a narrowly and dogmatically defined concept of realism, based on a traditional literary canon and on an allegedly scientific construction of reality. She pleaded instead for a realism that was open-ended, informed by national histories, indigenous cultural traditions, and responsive to different geographic settings. Seghers also questioned Lukács's criteria for determining what constituted exemplary antifascist literature. Behind the disputes over realism and the fight against National Socialism lay differing orientations toward the Marxist heritage as well as different plans for the kind of society they hoped to help establish after the overthrow of Nazi rule. Seghers's exile writings show a closer affinity to the views of leftist writers such as Ernst Bloch, Walter Benjamin, and Bertolt Brecht than to those of her Hungarian friend and mentor Lukács.

In contrast to some of these leftist thinkers, though, Seghers claimed for her own writing traditional aspects of literature, especially its use as a form of storytelling. She conceived of the writer as a chronicler of contemporary history for future readers in her native German. Walter Benjamin was the first to recognize the political significance of Seghers's narrative experiments in transforming into art the experiences of her times. In his review of *Die Rettung* (*The Rescue*), a novel about the economic crisis in a German mining town in the late twenties and the gravitation of working-class people toward National Socialism, Benjamin emphasized Seghers's reverting to earlier narrative traditions of recording the common people's history: the chronicle or the almanac.[4] He stressed the significance of Seghers's modifications of the traditional novel, especially the dissolution of a major plot into multiple stories, told not from the perspective of an omniscient narrator but from the perspective of the oppressed. Inspired by Benjamin's reading of her novel, and by his essay "The Storyteller"[5] of 1936, Seghers continued her literary experiments in the attempt to work through the chaos and political violence of her times. In so doing, she ascribed her readers an active role in envisioning a future society freed from Nazi dictatorship.

In his essay, Benjamin introduces his readers to the nineteenth-century Russian writer Leskov as one of the last great storytellers. As he traces the development of storytelling in earlier times, he pays equal attention to its disappearance in the modern world. Benjamin is not merely concerned with the loss of a cultural craft, but rather with the loss of insight and understanding, transmitted from the community of storytellers. He calls such communities places of wisdom from which vital impulses are transmitted to the body politic. Convinced that the diminished role of the storyteller as human counsellor was related to the loss of the ability to transmit experience, Benjamin writes in his exile in France: "If today 'having counsel' is beginning to have an old-fashioned ring, this is because the communicability of experience is decreasing. . . . After all, counsel is less an answer to a question than a proposal concerning the continuation of a story just unfolding. To seek this counsel one would first have to tell the story . . . counsel woven into the fabric of real life is wisdom" (Benjamin, 83). He attributed the dissolution of story and storytelling to the rise of the bourgeois novel and to the development of modern mass media. "The birthplace of the novel is the solitary individual," he writes, one "who is no longer able to express himself by giving examples of his most important concerns, is himself uncounseled and cannot counsel others" (86–87). To give counsel is, however, the function that Seghers seeks to restore to her prose fiction, an aim explicitly stated in novels *The Seventh Cross* and *Transit*, and in the short story "The Excursion of the Dead Girls" (1946).

In *Transit* (1944), Seghers's novel of flight from Nazi occupied Europe and of the experience of exile, Benjamin's reflections are woven into a dialogical model of narration, directed toward a fictive listener, a configuration of the author's readers whom she, for the time being, was unable to reach. She therefore assumes the task of chronicling events and experiences in contemporary history that Nazi propaganda kept from the German people, especially from the country's youth. "A no-man's land was to be established between the generations," Seghers's narrator warns in *The Seventh Cross*, a void that "old experiences would not be able to traverse" (140). *Transit,* along with her exile writings, attempts to reclaim that "no-man's land," and to settle it with storytellers who count on informing with their stories the building of a future society.

At the opening of the novel, an anonymous young worker, a fugitive from Nazi Germany, is sitting in a Marseille harbor café in the spring of 1941. He tells his anonymous listener the experiences of displaced people from all parts of Europe. They are trapped in Marseille, one of the last free ports of the European continent. Caught in a nightmarish world of red tape, visas, functionaries, and consulates, they spend their days in the effort of procuring their passages for countries of overseas exile. In contrast to these refugees, the exiled young German does not plan on leaving Europe. His friends, working-class people of Marseille, urge him to stay and to defend with them their home region.

The young German exile, as narrator of the novel, combines into a kaleidoscopic whole the life stories entrusted to him. The anonymous listener whom he addresses incessantly is a configuration of Seghers's future reader. He is asked to share the task of working through the unsettling experiences and the violent history that the young exiled worker narrates, and to conceive of a different future. In a key passage, Seghers has her narrator articulate such a role when he states programmatically: "If something had to be invented, if this patched-up life grew too paltry and mean, I myself would want to be the inventor, but not on paper" (*Transit*, 117).

Anna Seghers envisioned the building of a future German society as a democratic process, a development that would allow and sustain contradictory positions, even opposition (". . . eine Entwicklung durch Widersprüche").[6] In such a process, writers, or literature, would play an important part, but not the role of educator of the masses to serve the interests of a repressive poltical system.[7]

German women's history in the twentieth century has a place in all of Seghers's writings, but it is her explicit critical enterprise in the "The Excursion of the Dead Girls," Seghers's most autobiographical story. It can be read as her fictional articulation of literature's function in postwar Germany. In a series of essays, especially in "Aufgaben der Kunst" (1944) ("The Task of Art," 1949) she reflects on the role that art and literature might play in the reconstruction of German society, especially in the reeducation of the country's youth.[8] With a striking degree of realism she raises the question: "Where and what shall we reeducate, if brothers and fathers have been led by 'national' motives to slaughter Jews and prisoners en masse? The noblest work of art can scarcely 'reeducate' a brain that has undergone such training. But in transforming a people, a book or play can be useful if it places before the younger generation some lost concepts, some long-falsified ideas" ("The Task of Art," 9). Recalling the defeat of the German left in the fight against National Socialism in the late twenties, she points to the difficulty of finding the right "points of attack" in the effort to combat fascist ideology in postwar Germany. "Generations of artists will have to teach the brutalized German people what the indivisible inviolable individual means," is her sober conclusion.[9] "The Excursion of the Dead Girls" is a contribution to such an educative effort.[10]

Set in Mexico near the end of World War II, the story begins with Netty, its first-person narrator, an exiled German woman writer who is walking through the desolate, arid countryside, determined to find a white wall that she had seen in the distance. The wall turns out to be part of a deserted ranch. As Netty steps through an open gate, the scenery changes and she finds herself back in the lush, green, Rhine countryside near her native city of Mainz around 1913. As narrator, Netty moves back and forth between past and present, artfully intertwining different time frames. It is clear from the start that the schoolgirls, as the title suggests, are no longer alive. Yet in the narrator's visionary return to that special day of her youth, shortly before the outbreak of World War I, the dead girls are resurrected out of her need to understand and to communicate both the meaning and the futility of their lives.

As Netty brings forward each of her schoolmates in their youthful promise in the idyllic setting on the Rhine, she interrupts her descriptions with incessant comment on their later lives and fates in Hitler's Germany around 1943. On identifying her two closest friends Leni and Marianne, for example, Netty observes: "At each end of the seesaw sat a girl; they were my two best friends from school. Leni was pushing vigorously with her big feet, wearing angular button shoes." At this point, reflection and comment impact on the idyllic scene. "I remember," Netty tells her readers, that Leni "always inherited the shoes of an older brother. However, her brother had already been killed in action during World War I in the autumn of 1914" (40). "At the same time, I was surprised," Netty continues in her remembering, "that Leni's face showed no traces of the grim events that had spoiled her life, not the slightest sign of the blows that the Gestapo had inflicted upon her at the time of arrest when she refused to give away information about her husband" (40). Leni is the embodiment of steadfast antifascism, of loyalty to a cause and a partner.

In this particular figure, the author pays tribute to women as part of communist-led resistance to National Socialism.

At the same time, Seghers refrains from portraying women as mere victims of Nazi propaganda and of violent intrusions into their daily lives. Many of her former school friends, such as Marianne, Nora, and Ida, had become ardent supporters of the Nazi state. "Marianne would choose a new relationship with a certain Gustaf Liebig," Netty remembers, "a man who later became a leader of the SS Storm Troopers of our city" (45). As Liebig's wife, Marianne refused to prevent the placement of Leni's little daughter in a Nazi reform school. "Every penny spent on Leni and her family would be wasted." (41).

Marianne's betrayal of her former close friend is juxtaposed with the vision of the two young girls' loving embrace on the day of the school excursion, with Marianne putting her arm around Leni's neck, "gently pulling some straw out of her friend's hair" (41). Narrative juxtapositions such as these are maintained throughout the story. In describing the meeting of a boys' class from Mainz with the schoolgirls in the garden restaurant on the Rhine, for example, Netty points out a boy by the name of "Walter" who would later on became an "exceedingly good-looking SS man" (47). In that capacity, he was appointed to lead a transport of Nazi opponents that would "take away forever Leni's husband." On the excursion day, however, Leni is shown standing near the boy "Walter," "without suspecting," the narrator interjects, "by how many future enemies she was surrounded in the garden" (47).

But it is not only communist resistance against Nazism that Seghers commemorates in "The Excursion." She also presents examples of women's refusal to become accomplices of the violent intrusions of the National Socialists into the private lives of ordinary citizens. One such example is Gerda, a teacher, who commits suicide at the realization that her husband, out of fear of losing his job, had joined ranks with the Nazis. Lore, another former classmate, violates the "racial laws" of the Hitler state in continuing her relationship with a Jewish man. She takes poison upon learning that a Nazi admirer whose advances she had rejected has turned her in to the Gestapo. Miss Mees, one of the schoolgirls' teachers, stands out for her steadfastness as a member of the German Confessing Church. Women figures such as these serve as counterimages to the representation of German women as enthusiastic, emotionally charged, and devout supporters of Hitler and the Nazi state.[11]

Central to Seghers's fictional exploration of the intersections between life stories and historical developments is her Jewish heritage and its systematic destruction in the Third Reich. Seghers restores this heritage in two key figures of her story, that of the German teacher Miss Sichel and of Netty's mother, and reclaims their importance for her own formation as writer and political activist. When bringing into relief Miss Sichel on the day of the school excursion, Netty reports with a chronicler's close attention to detail that her teacher, on the excursion day, "was dressed just like her students in fresh bright colors," and that she was admired and loved by her pupils. Nora, for example, "poured coffee for her favorite teacher." In her eagerness to please her, she "had even decorated Miss Sichel's place quickly with a few jasmine branches" (42). At this point, a break occurs, which is characteristic of the entire story, as Netty contrasts the idyllic picture with a report of Nora's ultimate betrayal of her once beloved mentor. As a leading figure in the local National Socialist Women's Organization, Nora would "rudely chase that same teacher, then trembling from old age, off a bench along the Rhine," Netty had learned from friends. She wanted to sit "on a bench that was free of Jews" (43).

Netty as narrator does not provide answers to the unsettling questions she raises about the changes that took place in these women's lives and in the political culture of their country, changes that ruptured the bonds of friendship and the emotional ties of the girls to their former teacher. The destruction of individual lives in this story is echoed in the fragmented syntax of Netty's narration. Seghers leaves these fragments to her readers' reflections and meditations. They are the ones to search for answers to the question why all the girls sitting around the restaurant table on the Rhine on the day of their school excursion, pleased to have their young teacher so close (41), would some day make her the object of their racial hatred and betrayal. None of them came to their teacher's aid when she was deported to the death camps in Poland. All that Netty has to offer her readers are uncertainties, hypothetical half questions, incomplete wishes, imagined alternatives to actual happenings. Her recollections glide into these perspectives consistently while keeping the historical certainties firmly embedded in the structure of her narrative.[12] It is left to her future readers to look into the circumstances under which individual human beings, groups, or an entire people became accomplices in acts of denunciation and betrayal, and of the persecution of others in their midst.[13] While Netty, the writer and political activist, had escaped such a fate, other women figures, Miss Sichel, Sophie, and the narrator's (and author's) mothers were annihilated in the death camps.

The weight of that knowledge bears down heavily on the narrative in "The Excursion of the Dead Girls," in particular in its closing passage. Netty, in faraway Mexico, on the way back to her place of refuge, wonders how she should spend the time "today, tomorrow, here and there," because she now felt "an immeasurable stream of time, unconquerable like the air" (52). At this moment of existential dislocation she remembers the task that her Jewish German teacher, Miss Sichel, had assigned her on the return from her school outing. Suddenly she recalls her teacher's instruction that she should describe carefully the school excursion for the next German lesson. "I intended to do the assignment right away," Netty resolves, "tomorrow even this evening, after my wariness had gone away" (52). "The

Excursion" is the essay that Miss Sichel had assigned the girl Netty. She had fostered in her student a love for reading literature and for writing essays and stories. As Netty's German teacher, she embodies both Jewish and German cultural traditions, integral parts of Seghers's own formation. Furthermore, through this figure and her role in the schoolgirls' lives, Seghers affirms the Jewish presence as central to German culture, a narrative countergesture to the one-sided portrayal of Jews as victims of persecution and annihilation in German history.[14]

Miss Sichel's admonition is a metaphor for Seghers's understanding of her social responsibility as a writer. Her narrator Netty speaks of a "higher duty," of the need "to remember forever the most minute details" (43). She arrives at this insight at a point when she is describing Miss Sichel in her youthfulness on the day in the country. "Suddenly, as I was sitting close to her . . . it occurred to me . . . ," Netty states, that "Miss Sichel's hair had not always been white, that at the time of our excursion it was fluffy and brown" (43). The teacher's white hair is, however, not only a sign of old age. It draws instead attention to the historical changes and their devastating effects on individual lives. The mention of Sophie, a former classmate, and of her traumatic experiences at the height of Nazi rule in Germany makes this connection explicit. "Not only the hair of the teacher," Netty reminds us, "but also the hair of the pupil Sophie, now still black as ebony . . . would be completely white when they were deported together to Poland by the Nazis, in a freight car crammed full and sealed. Sophie was even all shriveled up and old when she died unexpectedly in the arms of Miss Sichel like a sister of the same age" (47).

Memory shards such as these express the author's groping efforts to find a language for the enormity of the annihilation of German and other European Jews in the death camps in Poland, the news of which gradually began to reach exile communities in the Americas. Seghers's narrator seems to resist the need to name the actual destination of the "freight trains" and the lethal fate of their human "cargo." "Deportation to Poland" or the mention of a "painful, cruel end in a remote village" to which Netty's (and the author's) mother had been "banished by Hitler" (51) are oblique references to sites of terror that the world came to the associate with the names of Auschwitz, Treblinka, Maidanek, or Lublin.[15] Even the author's commemorative efforts cannot restore wholeness to her peoples' shattered lives nor the culture of which they were once an integral part.

The weight of that knowledge seems to bring Seghers's narrator close to a breakdown. As she, in her visionary return from the school excursion, arrives at her home in Baufhof Street, she sees her mother waving and smiling at her from the family's balcony amidst boxes of geraniums (51). Embedded in Netty's narrative restoration of her mother to the wholeness of younger years is, however, an epitaph that leaves no doubt about her actual fate. "She stood there, cheerful and erect," it reads, "destined for a busy family life with the usual joys and burdens of the everyday, not for a painful, cruel end in a remote village, where she was to be banished by Hitler" (51). Even if the epitaph does juxtapose all that has become "irrevocably lost," with its "undestroyed, indestructible" presence in Netty's visionary return home (40), it leaves no doubt about her mother's annihilation in one of the death camps. Netty's visionary attempts to reach or retrieve her mother's figure are in vain. She is "much too tired" to climb the stairs that would bring her close to her mother. A "gray-blue fog of fatigue" seems to envelop everything. Even though she forces herself up the staircase, steps that are "unreachably high" and "unconquerably steep" (51), she fails to reach the top. Overcome by anxiety and pain at the realization that "fate could prevent her" from ever seeing her mother again, she is about to experience a breakdown.[16] At this point, a shift in scenery occurs and Netty finds herself back in the arid, barren Mexican countryside. She resolves to conquer the state of intense grief, displacement, and the weight of empty time by writing the school essay that her teacher had assigned her.

"The Excursion of the Dead Girls" is the very essay that Netty decides to prepare for the next "German lesson," for political learning in postwar Germany. The lessons to be learned, however, are not mediated by an omniscient authorial presence, but are to be deciphered instead in a collaborative effort by writers and readers. "Der Autor und der Leser sind im Bunde: sie versuchen zusammen auf die Wahrheit zu kommen," Seghers wrote in 1947, shortly after her return from exile (Author and reader collaborate in the search for truth).[17] At that time, she also published an article on Mexican mural painting in which she pays tribute to such artists as Diego Rivera, Xavier Guerrero, David Orozco, and others.[18] Seghers had studied their works with close attention to the political potential of their aesthetic choices. "The Excursion of the Dead Girls" and her novel *Die Toten bleiben jung* (1949) (*The Dead Stay Young*) show the influence of these artists' conceptions of popular art on her own understanding of the role of art and literature in the social and political reconstruction of her country.

The white wall that Seghers's narrator Netty had set out to explore at the opening of "The Excursion" serves as a canvas for the author's artistic experiment. Seghers populates this empty space with shadowy figures whose outlines she extracts from her fragmented memory and history's scenes of rubble. The canvas suggests not only new reading material, but also a new way of reading recent German history, directed especially at the country's youth whom the narrator in *The Seventh Cross* views as "lads and girls out there, once they had gone through the Hitler Youth, the work service, and the army would be like the fable children nurtured by animals who finally tore their own mothers to pieces" (140). In a series of essays with a German theme that Seghers wrote about the same time as she completed "The Excursion," she repeatedly addressed the prospects for reeducating Germans after the military defeat of the Nazi state. Among the themes she considers central to such "reeducation" is the image of women in Nazi ideology, which she contrasts with their actual roles and duties in the Third Reich. In her essay "Volk und Schriftsteller" (1941) ("Writers and Their People"), Seghers asserts: "Regardless of what Hitler has done with the 'mothers,' no matter how often German women were praised on mother's days, or distinguished with 'mother crosses' for having borne sons to fight in this vilest of wars: the true meaning of 'mother' has not been obliteratred; for it is one of those concepts that each human being, each minute renews through her or his own experience."[19]

In "The Excursion of the Dead Girls," however, almost all of the women perish at the hands of the Third Reich, whether they ardently supported the Hitler state or refused to embrace its ideology.[20] Seghers's story presents an idealized counter-image to such a fate. Instead of being swept away by the "stream of history," for which rivers frequently figure in her writings, Seghers shows the schoolgirls travelling upstream, back to Mainz, on the day of the excursion. They are seen linking arms with one another "in a bond that was part of the large bond of everything natural under the sun" (48). As she evokes this image, the narrator declares in a reproachful tone: "Nobody ever, while there was still time for it, reminded us of this trip together. No matter how many essays were written about our country, . . . it was never mentioned that our swarm of girls, in particular, sitting close to each other going upstream in the slanting afternoon light belonged to our country" (49). Seghers reiterates here the social responsibility of art to confront Nazi ideology among Germany's youth in the process of rebuilding the country.

"The Excursion" attempts to meet that responsibility by unmasking with didactic subtlety a number of myths that had been at the core of Nazi ideology, among them that of women as "mothers of the Volk." In search of effective "Angriffspunkte" (points of attack), as Seghers stated in her essay "Aufgaben der Kunst" (198), she reworks in her story the biblical myth of the wise and foolish maidens, in particular its configuration in medieval cathedral architecture. Her manner of introducing each of the former schoolgirls is reminiscent of the role of an art guide as she identifies each woman figure, describes her youthful appearance, and then comments on her later development. Netty, the narrator, goes as far as to refer explicitely to the motif of the wise and foolish maidens, when she compares, for example, Marianne's exquisite beauty and Leni's "naïve" trust in her fellow students to the "figures out of stone from the Middle Ages in the cathedral of Marburg" (41).[21] Miss Sichel, the Jewish teacher, and Miss Mees, the schoolgirls' Christian mentor—the chain with a cross that she wore around her neck is mentioned repeatedly—could be seen as representations of the two allegorical figures of synagoga and ecclesia that were placed above the sculptures of the wise and the foolish maidens. Synagoga, shown as a blindfolded, shrivelled-up woman, stood for the Old Testament, or the Jewish religion; Ecclesia with her insignia of crown and cross, represented the New Testament, the Christian faith, and a "new bond" between church and state, from which "synagoga" and the "foolish maidens" were excluded.[22] Seghers, however, breaks down the division of her schoolgirls in groups of "wise or foolish maidens." The fortunes that her women figures experience temporarily, as well as their violent deaths, are not the results of "wise" or "foolish" choices. In the author's view, the Third Reich was a dead-end street for all of them, with the exception of Miss Mees, the older teacher, Netty, the exiled writer, and Leni's child who had been placed in a Nazi reform school. As survivors of the Third Reich, they represent three generations of German women to whom the story turns with the appeal to free themselves from the entrapment in lethal myths, and to take an active part in the political and cultural reconstruction of their country. Seghers repeatedly expressed the hope that her story about the "dead girls" would figure prominently among the "reconstruction and educational materials" in postwar Germany.[23]

Anna Seghers had good reason to think that she would have a part in the reconstruction of her country. A telegram from the Basic News Division of the United States Office of War Information, sent to the author on May 10, 1945, makes clear that the Americans had plans for using Seghers in the "psychological warfare" amongst the German population. In that telegram, Theodore Kagan, Chief of the Basic News Division Office, writes: "STATEMENT SHOULD BE IN A FORM YOU FEEL WILL BE HELPFUL IN CONVINCING THE GERMAN PEOPLE OF THE TRUTH FROM WHICH THEY HAVE SO LONG BEEN INSULATED AND SHOULD BE ADDRESSED DIRECTLY TO THEM."[24] The telegram appears as a paraphrase of the central theme of Seghers's exile writings: the "no-man's land between the generations" through which "old experiences would not be able to traverse" (*The Seventh Cross*, 140).

It comes as no surprise that Seghers should have quoted these lines in her essay for the Division of Psychological Warfare in Europe. It is unclear, however, whether or not the essay ever reached the office of that division. It is equally uncertain that Seghers's message was ever broadcast to German audiences in the American zone of occupation. The essay is nonetheless important for it makes a distinction between Nazis and other Germans, as do her earlier essays and her prose fiction written in exile. In this respect, it differs, as Alexander Stephan rightly points out, from the position upheld by the movement "Free Germany" that all Germans were Nazis, a stance that caused the State Department to view the movement as "pro-Soviet."[25] Even though Seghers does not shy away from addressing Nazi violence, war crimes, the responsibilities of perpetrators and fellow travelers, she ends her essay with a plea for the young generation. Hidden in cellars and air-raid shelters in the end phase of the Third Reich, they should have a right to live on "free ground" as "free people" (Stephan, 175). She expressed a similar appeal in 1950 before her audiences at the Second Congress of Writers in East

Berlin. Speaking of Germany's youth, she insists: "Innocent of Auschwitz, innocent of Lidice, innocent of the Warsaw Ghetto! May these children never become guilty!" Writers and artists are once again assigned the role of humanist mentors to the country's youth.[26]

In 1950, the division of Germany had been completed, the former allied victorious armies over Nazism had become enemies of the "Cold War," and the two Germanys had turned into its central battleground. By that time, Anna Seghers, who had left her Mexican exile in 1947, had settled in East Berlin where she was accorded a prominent position in the country's cultural life. At the same time, she found herself frequently in conflict with political and cultural policies advanced by hard-line Stalinists, such as Walter Ulbricht, Alfred Kurella, and Alexander Abusch, with whom she had differed in regard to art and party politics as early as the mid-thirties. In the emerging socialist state in East Germany, there was little room for a reader-writer dialogue, a shared search for "truth," a view that she expressed as late as 1947 in the preface to the first German publication of her novel *Die Rettung*. The prospects for a democratic reconstruction of the country, a process in which differences and contradictions could be dealt with openly and publically were equally dim by that time. It comes as no surprise, then, that Seghers's novels and stories, which are open-ended and promote self-generated political learning, chief among them *Transit* and the "Excursion of the Dead Girls," were basically ignored in the early years of the GDR's existence. It was not until 1962 with the publication of an essay by Hans Mayer that "The Excursion" received any critical attention. *Transit* experienced a similar fate. Christa Wolf rescued it from oblivion, however, with her creative response to this most modern of Seghers's novels. "The Excursion of the Dead Girls" and *Transit* provided Wolf with theoretical and aesthetic resolutions to issues that she faced in two novels about her own generation's experiences in the Third Reich, *Nachdenken über Christa T.* (1968) (*The Quest for Christa T.*, 1971) and *Kindheitsmuster* (1976) (*Patterns of Childhood*, 1984).

The East German government, shortly after the founding of the German Democratic Republic, had called on the returning exiles to write about the building of socialism instead of continuing to dwell on the National Socialist past. Seghers and other former exiles insisted, however, that writers of her generation could not turn to the new era without including the recent past.[27] As early as the summer of 1945, a time when she was still in Mexico, Seghers took note of the fact that even in the eastern zone of occupation a "time limit" was to be placed on dealing with the Nazi past. In a letter to her friend Jürgen Kuczynski in London she emphasizes that it would take years for the German people to work through that past.[28] In the GDR's official discourse on the Third Reich, the annihilation of European Jews received scant mention while antifascism, in particular the role of Communists in opposition to National Socialism, received privileged treatment.

It is not surprising that Anna Seghers's story "The Excursion of the Dead Girls" has received renewed attention after German unification. The news of widespread surveillance and denunciation among ordinary citizens in the service of the former GDR state seems to have caused Fritz Rudolf Fries, a writer with a complex past in that society, to refer to the "Excursion" as a startlingly relevant text. "Read in the end phase of the GDR," he wrote in 1990, "this story seems to talk about us, about our cowardice and our compromises, our sadness and about our modest hope that the solidarity of the simple people could be achieved with simple means; but that would require, above all, the overcoming of our fear" (In den späten Jahren der DDR gelesen, wird diese Erzählung ein Stück von uns, von unserer Feigheit, unseren Kompromissen, unserer Traurigkeit und der kleinen Hoffnung, daß sich die Solidarität der einfachen Leute herstellen läßt mit ganz einfachen Mitteln, zu denen freilich die Überwindung der Angst gehört; "Fritz Rudolf Fries," 11).[29] Even if Seghers herself, in her later life a prominent figure of the GDR, was not free from fear of power of the state, a major theme of her novel *The Seventh Cross*, her exile writings merit continued reading; for they ask for truths in human history that archives and documents seldom hold.

Notes

1. Clement Greenberg, "Anna Seghers; 'The Seventh Cross,'" 388.

2. A letter from Angus Cameron to Anna Seghers of February 18, 1943. I am grateful to Little, Brown and Company for a copy of this letter.

3. Anna Seghers, "Was wissen wir von Jugend-Cliquen?" 175–176.

4. Walter Benjamin, "Eine Chronik der deutschen Arbeitslosen. Zu Anna Seghers's Roman 'Die Rettung,'" 537.

5. Walter Benjamin, "The Storyteller," 83.

6. Anna Seghers, "Aufgaben der Kunst," 199.

7. It is important to note here that Anna Seghers did not publically distance herself from the German Communist party, its political objectives and practices. She nevertheless found herself repeatedly in conflict with the party, especially with its views on art and literature in the fight against fascism. The same is true of her views on the role that party leaders, artists, or intellectuals should play in the process of raising "common people's" consciousness and to influence their political actions. In a forthcoming article, I intend to discuss these issues in greater detail.

8. In Alexander Stephan's book *Anna Seghers im Exil: Essays, Texte, Dokumente* (Bonn: Bouvier, 1994) there is a note by the author in which she speaks of her plans for a film version of "The Excursion," and that she hoped it would be used for the reeducation of young Germans. I have dealt with this aspect of Seghers's story in greater detail in an essay of 1982, entitled "Anna Seghers's 'Ausflug der toten Mädchen' als ein Beitrag der Literatur zur

Neugestaltung Deutschlands," in Donald G. Daviau and Ludwig Fischer, eds., *Das Exilerlebnis:Verhandlungen des vierten Symposiums über deutsche und österreichische Exilliteratur* (Columbia, S.C.: Camden House, 1982), 476–487.

9. Even if Seghers insists in this essay on one of the core concepts of humanism, the coherence of the subject and its dignity, a concept central to antifascism, her story, with its discontinuous narrative presents its readers with a fragmented history and destroyed bodies.

10. In the following, all references to the story are from Anna Seghers, "The Excursion of the Dead Girls," in: Elisabeth Rütschi Herrmann and Edna Huttenmaier Spitz, eds., *German Women Women Writers of the Twentieth Century* (New York: Pergamon, 1978), 39–52.

11. Seghers presents in her story a broad spectrum of reading women's history during the Nazi era. That she did so as early as 1944 is remarkable; for in historical discourse since the end of WW II, the focus has shifted from women as slavish supporters of the Nazi state to that of women as victims of patriarchy, Nazi ideology in particular. Recent studies focus on women's roles as accomplices and perpetrators in the Third Reich, actions and positions and dispositions that Seghers reflects upon in "The Excursion of the Dead Girls."

12. Alexander Stephan also comments on this narrative feature of "The Excursion" in his study *Anna Seghers im Exil*, 50–51.

13. For an instructive and incisive discussion of these issues, see Sigrid Weigel's "Erinnerung vor Gericht. Zum Opfer-Täter-Diskurs über den Nationalsozialismus in Helga Schuberts 'Judasfrauen' und ihren Gerichts-Quellen," 198–231. For earlier historiography on women as ardent supporters of the Third Reich, see Hermann Rauschning, *Hitler Speaks. A Series of Political Conversations with Adolf Hitler on his Real Aims* (London: T. Butterworth, 1939), 259 ff.; also Joachim Fest, *The Face of the Third Reich* (Hammondsworth: Penguin, 1972), 401 ff. See furthermore Richard Grunberger, *A Social History of the Third Reich* (Hammondsworth: Penguin, 1974), 177 ff.

14. Fritz Pohle arrives at a similar reading of this figure in his essay "Vorbereitung für die nächste Deutschstunde und mehr: 'Der Ausflug der toten Mädchen (1943/44)," *Argonautenschiff: Jahrbuch der Anna-Seghers-Gesellschaft* 1 (1992): 41–49.

15. Friedrich Schütz has researched Seghers's Jewish background. He reports that on March 30, 1942, Seghers's mother, Hedwig Reiling, together with nine hundred and ninety other Jewish citizens from Hessia, was deported to Piaski near Lublin where she was killed. See Friedrich Schütz, "Die Familie Seghers-Reiling und das jüdische Mainz," 169. Alexander Stephan cites from Seghers's letters to friends and relatives, documents he found in the FBI files on the author, in which she reports about her efforts to rescue her mother, that she had obtained a Mexican visa and a Swiss visa as well. But the Nazis would no longer permit her mother to leave Germany. Alexander Stephan, *Anna Seghers im Exil*, 29.

16. In one of the letters that Alexander Stephan cites, Seghers writes the following about the loss of her mother: "Sometimes I read the five, six letters which I have received from my mother and each time I fall into an indescribable state of rage and grief, but there is nothing to be gained by sustaining it" (29).

17. Anna Seghers, "Vorwort zum Roman *Die Rettung*," 17.

18. Anna Seghers, "Die gemalte Zeit. Mexikanische Fresken," 69–73. Judith Ryan has pointed out Seghers's indebtedness to the frescos of Diego Rivera in her attempt to "depict people from different generations and from a range of social classes," in the hopes "to address the non-elitist reader without sacrificing subtlety of form" (*The Uncompleted Past*, 37).

19. Anna Seghers, "Volk und Schriftsteller," 192.

20. Hans Mayer, "Anmerkungen zu einer Erzählung von Anna Seghers," 117–26.

21. "Marburg" is misleading; for these groups of sculptures are not to be found in Marburg churches. The cathedral of Magdeburg, however, is famous for sets of sculptures of the wise and foolish maidens, as is the Straßburg cathedral. Anna Seghers, who held a doctorate in art history refers to the "Straßburger Münster" in her essay "Woher sie kommen, wohin sie gehen" ("What was Their Origin? Where are they Headed?") (199).

22. For a detailed discussion of these practises, see Alfred Weis, "Ekklesia und Synagoge," *Reallexikon zur deutschen Kunstgeschichte* (1958), 1189–1215. See also Lilli Burger, "Die ursprüngliche Aufstellung der Magdeburger klugen und törichten Jungfrauen," *Jahrbuch für Kunstwissenschaft* 1930, 1–17. Burger quotes from a dissertation by W. Lehmann of 1916 about the parable of the foolish and wise maidens. Lehmann was Seghers's doctoral adviser; under his guidance she completed in 1924 her dissertation on the theme of "Jude und Judentum im Werke Rembrandts," ("Jew and Judaism in the Works of Rembrandt").

23. Alexander Stephan, *Anna Seghers im Exil*, 161.

24. Stephan, 176. The materials that Stephan unearthed from the files of the FBI and of the military secret services are invaluable to Seghers scholarship. My own earlier readings of Seghers's story, in particular its usefulness as material for reeducation programs in postwar Germany, can now rely on documents in which the author expressly states such a purpose.

25. Stephan, 177.

26. Anna Seghers, "Rede auf dem II. Deutschen Schriftstellerkongreß 1950," 80.

27. Ibid., 81.

28. Jürgen Kuczynski, "Nachrichten von mittendrin," 159–165.

29. My translation.

Bibliography

Benjamin, Walter. "Eine Chronik der deutschen Arbeitslosen. Zu Anna Seghers's-Roman 'Die Rettung." In *Schriften III*. Ed. Hella Tiedemann-Bartels. Frankfurt: Suhrkamp, 1972, 530–538.

———. "The Storyteller: Reflections on the Works of Nikolai Leskov." In *Illuminations*. Trans. Harry Zohn. Ed. and with an introduction by Hannah Arendt. New York: Schocken Books, 1969, 83–109.

Burger, Lilli. "Die ursprüngliche Aufstellung der Magdeburger klugen und törichten Jungfrauen. In *Jahrbuch für Kunstwissenschaft*. Ed. Ernst Pall. Berlin: Kleinhardt und Biermann, 1930, 1–13.

Cameron, Angus. "A letter to Anna Seghers." February 18, 1943. Archives of Little, Brown and Company, Boston.

"Fritz Rudolf Fries." *Argonautenschiff: Jahrbuch der Anna-Seghers-Gesellschaft* 1 (1992): 9–11.

Greenberg, Clement. "Anna Seghers; 'The Seventh Cross.'" 155. 16. (Oct. 17, 1942): 388–390.

Kuczynski, Jürgen. "Nachrichten von mittendrin." *Neue Deutsche Literatur* 39.11 (1991): 159–165.

Mayer, Hans. "Anmerkungen zu einer Erzählung von Anna Seghers." *Sinn und Form* 4.1–3 (1962): 117–125.

Ryan, Judith. *The Uncompleted Past*. Detroit: Wayne State University Press, 1983.

Schütz, Friedrich. "Die Familie Seghers-Reiling und das jüdische Mainz." *Jahrbuch der Anna-Seghers-Gesellschaft* 2 (1992): 151–173.

Seghers, Anna. "Aufgaben der Kunst." In *Über Kunstwerk und Wirklichkeit I: Die Tendenz in der reinen Kunst*. Ed. and introduction Sigrid Bock. Berlin: Akademie-Verlag, 1971, 197–201.

———. "Die gemalte Zeit. Mexikanische Fresken." In *Über Kunstwerk und Wirklichkeit II: Erlebnis und Gestaltung*. Ed. Sigrid Bock. Berlin: Akademie-Verlag, 1971, 69–73.

———. "[Rede auf dem II. Deutschen Schriftstellerkongreß 1950]." In *Über Kunstwerk und Wirklichkeit I*, 76–84.

———. "The Excursion of the Dead Girls." In *German Women Writers of the Twentieth Century*. Ed. Elisabeth Rütschi Herrmann and Edna Huttenmaier Spitz. New York: Pergamon, 39–52.

———. *The Seventh Cross*. Trans. James A. Galston. Boston: Little, Brown and Company, 1942.

———. "The Task of Art." *Mainstream-New Masses* (Dec. 19, 1949): 9–11.

———. *Transit*. Trans. James A. Galston. Boston: Little, Brown and Company, 1944.

———. "Volk und Schriftsteller." In *Über Kunstwerk und Wirklichkeiti: Die Tendenz in der reinen Kunst*. Ed. Sigrid Bock. Berlin: Akademie-Verlag, 1971, 192–197.

———. "[Vorwort zu dem Roman *Die Rettung*]." In *Über Kunstwerk und Wirklichkeit II*, 16–17.

———. "Was wissen wir von Jugendcliquen?" In *Aufsätze, Ansprachen, Essays 1927–1953*. Berlin: Aufbau, 1980, 14–16.

———. "Woher sie kommen, wohin sie gehen: Über den Ursprung und die Weiterentwicklung einiger Romangestalten Dostojewskis, besonders über ihre Beziehungen zu Gestalten Schillers." In *Über Kunstwerk und Wirklichkeit II*, 181–217.

Stephan, Alexander. *Anna Seghers im Exil: Essays, Texte, Dokumente*. Bonn: Bouvier, 1993.

Weigel, Sigrid. "Erinnerung vor Gericht: Zum Opfer-Täter-Diskurs über den Nationalsozialismus in Helga Schuberts 'Judasfrauen' und ihre Gerichtsquellen." In *Bilder des kulturellen Gedächtnisses: Beiträge zur Gegenwartsliteratur*. Dülmen-Hiddingsel: tende, 1994, 198–321.

Weis, Adolf. "Ekklesia und Synagoge." In *Reallexikon zur deutschen Kunstgeschichte: Band IV*. Hg. Ernst Gall und L. H. Heydenreich. Stuttgart: Alfred Druckenmüller, 1958. 1189–1215.

6

Turning The Gaze Inward: Gertrud Kolmar's *Briefe an die Schwester Hilde 1938–1943*

Monika Shafi

In December 1994, the 100th anniversary of the poet Gertrud Kolmar was commemorated in an exhibition in Berlin.[1] *Orte* (Places), the exhibition's title, aptly denotes Kolmar's life-long search for spaces outside the bourgeois order. Kolmar's quest was for the most part a journey into the inner realms of her imagination, where she could create exotic islands, bizarre landscapes, and celebrate the vast *Welten* (Worlds) of lost or long-forgotten continents and times.[2] It was essentially a pre-modern world and world view that informed Kolmar's poetic vision, and the ensuing gender dichotomy seemed only to confirm her rather traditional outlook. Thematically and structurally indebted to nineteenth-century poetic traditions, Kolmar's lyrics appear at first glance to be ill at ease with the genesis of modernism at the beginning of the twentieth century. Not surprisingly, Kolmar frequently referred to herself as a poet whose voice would not be heard: "Ich bin ein Kontinent, der eines Tages stumm im Meere / versinkt" (I am a continent that one day soon will sink without a / sound into the sea; Smith, 60–61).

Gertrud Kolmar's reception until the 1980s certainly confirms this melancholic outlook. The bulk of her poetry as well as her prose and dramatic works did not appear during her lifetime, and she remained throughout her artistic pursuits in essence a writer without an audience.

In 1983, the critic Manfred Durzak noted that the striking difference between the literary fame and reputation the Jewish poets Else Lasker-Schüler and Nelly Sachs enjoyed in postwar West Germany, and the almost obscure status to which Kolmar was relegated, had less to do with the intrinsic quality of Kolmar's work than with the fact that she was a *victim*, not a survivor of the Holocaust. Analyzing the life and works of a murdered Jewish author, however, made any "Vergangenheitsbewältigung" a lot more difficult and guilt-ridden (528). This silence surrounding Kolmar is part of the *Nachgeschichte* (post-history), which presents itself partly as an overt, partly as a covert fight over memories ("Vorwort," X). Despite the fact that Kolmar's poetry and prose continued to be published, Durzak's view was more than justified, as the dearth of scholarly articles indicated.

Since the late 1980s Kolmar's oeuvre has enjoyed a rediscovery, which can be attributed mainly to the growing strength and diversity of feminist literary criticism.[3] Initially, even feminist scholars shied away from this author because her embrace of traditional gender division, particularly her celebration of motherhood, did not lend itself to a feminist critique of patriarchal norms. However, a more differentiated approach, which focused on the complex interplay of defiance and compliance in women's writing, aided in recognizing the subversive stance Kolmar entertained toward her society.[4]

Subversion and resistance also characterize Kolmar's correspondence with her sister Hilde Wenzel, who in March 1938 had fled to Switzerland. Kolmar was the only one of the four siblings who remained in Germany with her ailing father. In September 1942 her father was deported to Theresienstadt, and Kolmar was murdered in Auschwitz in 1943. From September 1938 until her deportation in February 1943, Kolmar corresponded with Hilde, and she also addressed numerous letters to Hilde Wenzel's five-year-old daughter Sabine. While the letters from Hilde Wenzel to Gertrud Kolmar have been lost, Kolmar's correspondence, which comprises a total of eighty-eight letters and postcards, was published by Johanna Zeitler in 1970 as *Briefe an die Schwester Hilde 1938–1943* (*Letters to the Sister Hilde 1938–1943*).

These letters are the only documents revealing Kolmar's private life. No other records, such as diaries, or extensive correspondences with different relatives or authors, have survived.[5] Since Kolmar is known as an extremely reclusive author, who created her work in the isolation of her home and who during the time of the Weimar Republic shunned Berlin's lively literary scene, these messages become the window onto a self otherwise strictly guarded and hidden. Kolmar apparently hardly ever talked about her writing, and she did not share information about creative projects and challenges or her own identity as a poet. Precisely these subjects, however, become a major topic of her epistolary dialogue with Hilde.

Besides its relevance for Kolmar scholarship, this correspondence is also of unique documentary value for studying both Jewish life inside Germany during

World War II and the history of the Holocaust. The letters indirectly chronicle the various stages of the Nazi persecution leading to the "Final Solution." Even though the letters were written under strict censorship—whose effects can be seen in the careful encoding of crucial news and events—they reveal nevertheless a chronology of the important decrees and police actions governing the fate of Germany's Jewish citizens (Zeitler, 219).

While still living in Germany, Kolmar thus witnessed its transformation from a place denoting home into a place that signified complete alienation. Not only did she lose all material possessions, all civil and human rights, including the right to publish, but the *Heimat* ceased to exist. It became a *terra incognita*. Her frequent descriptions of estrangement, whether spatial, temporal, or linguistic, suggest that she experienced a profound exile *inside* Germany. One could thus classify the letters as "exile literature," written, however, within Germany's borders. In fact, this "exile in the homeland"[6] dichotomy profoundly shaped Kolmar's perception of her self and of her Berlin environment.

For the most part *Briefe an die Schwester Hilde* has been read as an important autobiographical source that has helped explain Kolmar's personality and oeuvre, rather than as an integral part of her work. A first classification was provided by Johanna Zeitler who characterized the correspondence as a "loosely arranged autobiography" (218), and Lawrence L. Langer subsequently referred to it as a "spiritual autobiography" (1978, 247). Yet neither of them addresses the complex issue of genre qualities, that is, the construction and representation of the self that is at the center of all autobiographical discourse. Precisely this perspective informs the present article, in which I attempt to show that Gertrud Kolmar's *Briefe an die Schwester Hilde,* while resonating with dominant themes of her oeuvre, develops these in a specific genre context, the epistolary autobiography. Instead of viewing *Briefe* as an important, but ultimately ancillary document, I propose a reading of the correspondence as a literary text, thus shifting the emphasis from its relevance as a collection of personal data and material to its textual and genre qualities.

One has to bear in mind, of course, that Kolmar did not compose a literary correspondence. *Briefe* is very much an unmediated text and in that sense it differs sharply from her other work. An analysis within the proposed genre context reveals, however, the extent to which Kolmar, faced with persecution, violence, and ultimately destruction, developed a particular persona in order to resist Nazi ideology and violence. Kolmar responded to Nazi terror by forging a self that would be able to resist the onslaught on her subjectivity. Peter Haidu has emphasized that one of the main elements of genocide and the Holocaust is "the radical desubjectification of the individual as part of the collective from which individual subjectivity derives" (296). A close reading of Kolmar's letters reveals that her fight against this desubjectification resulted in a "conscious posture of self-affirmation" (Lixl-Purnell,

5). The dialogue with her sister enabled her to articulate traditional and unconventional modes of self that helped her to both endure and defy her oppressors. Viewing the correspondence within the context of the epistolary autobiography—for which numerous precedents exist within the literature of nineteenth-century women writers—thus yields a more comprehensive understanding of the self-exploration and resistance Kolmar displayed in these letters.

The hybrid genre "epistolary autobiography" has been of particular importance to women writers since the eighteenth century because it has lent itself to a multifaceted discourse of subjectivity while simultaneously permitting the incorporation of external reality. The unique flexibility of the letter, which is both a presentation of the self and an exchange with the other, was ideally suited to articulate the complicated and often thwarted identity processes of women authors.

In her groundbreaking study *Dis/Closures: Women's Autobiography in Germany Between 1790 and 1914* (1986), Katherine Goodman explored both the empirical as well as the discursive patterns that distinguished women writers' autobiographies from those of their male counterparts. For generations women were wedged between the domesticity ascribed to them by traditional gender politics and the male arena from which they were barred by lack of education and social acceptance. Goodman argues that women could not avail themselves of the dominant autobiographical model, the unified, representative self epitomized by Johann Wolfgang von Goethe in *Dichtung und Wahrheit*. Excluded from the public sphere, women writers were unable to generate this mastery of world and self. Conscious of their limited choices, it became necessary for them to develop a "self in conflict in order *not* to identify totally either with an alienated, conventional self or with an uncomplicated vision of a single repressed self" (1988, 317).

Their particular position of exclusion led women writers to emphasize the inner realm, the private sanctuary of emotions that is often shared with the partner in the epistolary dialogue. While Goodman recognizes the importance of the "nonidentical self" (1988, 317) for women's autobiographies, she nevertheless guards against a postmodern dispersed subject, for "the concept of 'self' is essential if we are not to remain fatalistic and without a sense of choice" (1986, xvi). Goodman's notion of a 'self in conflict' is particularly useful for an interpretation of the Kolmar correspondence, because it helps explain not only the contemporaneity of traditional and nonconventional modes of self but also the strains of self-affirmation under extreme, life-threatening circumstances.

"The published letter is always a paradox" (Nickisch, 107), stated the scholar Paul Raabe, and this dictum seems particularly apt with regard to Kolmar's letters. In fact, Kolmar often complains about the awkward, unpolished style of her letters, her inability to write "natural letters" (*Briefe*, 32).[7] Also, a strict censorship influenced the correspondence both stylistically and thematically, for camouflage and allusion were needed in addressing important events and developments. Kolmar refers, for example, to her own immigration plans as "the English matter" (*Briefe*, 15). After her father's deportation, she signals Hilde her concerns in a role play in which "Käthe" (Kolmar's second name) awaits news from her recently divorced "husband," that is, Kolmar's father (*Briefe*, 173).

Literary issues, on the other hand, as well as the unprecedented disclosure of very intimate thoughts and memories, were some of the few subject matters Kolmar could openly write about. More importantly, these discussions seemed to provide her with spiritual support and allowed her to find meaning in an existence that became increasingly void of any means of control. One can in fact trace this process of self-inscription in the correspondence, which developed from a more or less conventional exchange of regards into extensive, intimate confessions. What had started as an avenue for short messages and greetings produced a far-reaching and complex representation of Kolmar's personality, artistic vocation, and her resistance to National Socialism.

In the immediate months following Hilde's departure, Kolmar added only a few lines at the end of cards or letters written by her father. But the first long letter, dated September 13, 1938, displays a broad self-analysis. Kolmar is responding to her sister's complaint about being unable to find adequate work and her ensuing lack of self-esteem. While addressing her sister's problems, Kolmar simultaneously describes her own experiences:

> Though I can imagine a so to speak "absolute" love for a profession which has nothing to do with husband and child, I can't share it. . . . I have to confess that for many years of my life I would have been less unhappy, if I myself would have had such a "male" attitude . . . and not regarded my profession only as a kind of substitute. . . . Well, that's how things are . . . and if you think that I did not get stuck in the first beginnings, then I must add that I have paid a very, very high price for this perfection. (*Briefe*, 9–19)

This revelation is striking both in its exceptional frankness as well as in Kolmar's critical assessment of her own artistic endeavors. She is hinting at the ambivalent relationship between her creative and her personal fulfillment and self-confidently assesses her achievements. The novelty of this confession is also signalled by a remark at the end of the letter: "Daddy would certainly also like to add something, but I don't want to show this letter to him" (*Briefe*, 11).

Yet, despite the far-reaching statements about her own personality and views, Kolmar did not turn this correspondence into a self-centered introspection. On the contrary, she never lost sight of Hilde's concerns and frequently expressed her sisterly sympathy, love, and support. But given Kolmar's reclusive personality and lifestyle and the lack of a previous intimate relationship with Hilde, it seems that the geographical distance presupposed the emotional closeness, as if both separation and hardship enabled Kolmar to reveal her inner self in this unparalleled way. The letters thus do not fit the general classification of correspondences as being either predominantly dialogic, partner-oriented, or more monologic, focusing on introspection and soul-searching (Nickisch, 61). Instead, this exchange seems to equally combine both approaches. Kolmar pays close attention to events or problems in Hilde's life and often takes them as a lead for describing her own personality and beliefs. As a result, the correspondence encompasses a fairly detailed account of Kolmar's everyday existence as well as the transcendence of her factual life by numerous and lengthy discussions about literature. Kolmar's concrete and creative self thus formed a highly ambivalent relationship, which was characterized by the tension between the reality of Nazi Germany surrounding her and the intellectual and spiritual forces she tried to mount against it.

In November 1938, after the "Kristallnacht," Kolmar and her father were forced to sell their spacious home in Finkenkrug, a rural suburb of Berlin, and they moved into one of the so-called "Jew's houses" in the inner city. Kolmar's extensive descriptions of the mundane aspects of her current life such as walking long distances or constantly moving furniture in the apartment, which she and her father had to share with other Jews, functioned as a kind of "double-voiced" discourse. These descriptions simultaneously disguised (to the censor) and disclosed (to her sister Hilde) the displacement and the profound estrangement she suffered. Kolmar not only mentions the lack of privacy and solitude brought about by the constant—and to her mostly annoying—presence of the other tenants, but she also indicates her complete inability to establish a relationship with her new environment. Walking along the roads, she realizes

> somewhat stupefied that—in contrast to my previous habits—I did not really perceive the buildings, the shops and the people I passed. "You have to watch out, pay attention," I gave an order to myself. Fine. Five minutes later my vision seized again; it was as if my gaze had turned around to the inside, like that of a dreamy, inattentive schoolchild. Soon, we will have been here for half a year, and I just can't seem to be able to come to terms—bearable or unbearable—with this neighborhood; I am as strange to this place as I was on the first day. (*Briefe*, 23–24)[8]

This lack of spatial orientation is paralleled by her loss of temporal orientation. In a letter dated July 2, 1941, she gives a comprehensive summary of her withdrawal from the present:

> And I feel a closeness only between myself and the past; what happens to me *now* is unreal, distant. I don't really dream, but I am also not awake; I walk so to speak in an intermediate world, which takes no interest in me and in which I take no interest (*Briefe*, 98)

The American critic Betty Bergland had suggested that M. M. Bakhtin's concept of the chronotope or time-space dimension is particularly useful in examining the autobiographical female subject because it reveals the different spatial and temporal choices of subjects who are outside the dominant cultural traditions and paradigms. According to Bergland the attractiveness of the chronotope stems from its implicit use of "noncognitive approaches," since these "visualize the consequences of discursive practices on the speaking subjects" (135). Although Bergland focuses in her study on the autobiographies of women of different ethnic and racial backgrounds and their relationship to dominant patterns of time/space configurations, I find this approach equally useful for analyzing Kolmar's situation in Germany. A chronotopic analysis reveals how Kolmar consciously selected other spaces, other times, and other self-representations than those either forced upon her by the Nazi regime or chosen by the *other Jews* in her environment. As the various passages from *Briefe* disclose, a key factor in Kolmar's chronotopic representation was the distance she created between herself, her fellow Jews, and the Nazi order. In all her pursuits Kolmar differed distinctly from her Jewish neighbors and coworkers, a difference she frequently discussed with her sister.

In almost every other letter written between Fall 1942 and her deportation in February 1943, Kolmar complained and sharply criticized the Jewish people, particularly the women with whom she was forced to live and work. In fact, only in these portrayals does her tone become angry, even scathing: "I see and hear only the unnecessary, the foolish, the unpleasant, the bad" (*Briefe*, 164). She scolds them for dealing with their fate by nostalgically remembering their privileged lives as members of Berlin's Jewish elite, and she compares them to the French Royalists returning after Napoleon's fall from power "who had learned nothing and had forgotten nothing" (*Briefe*, 196). Kolmar regrets that her peers, including her father, look only to a German, not to a Jewish past and that they are completely unable to develop the kind of "positive attitude" (*Briefe*, 193) she herself is striving for. She admits to finally understanding why "for the past twenty years I felt so little at home, yes, so unhappy" (*Briefe*, 195) because she never shared their desire for complete assimilation. Instead, Kolmar insists on the importance of the Jewish history and heritage. She is learning Hebrew, even attempts to write poems in it, and recommends authors such as Martin Buber or Edzard Schaper to her sister. The letters clearly demonstrate that Kolmar abandoned her class and its way of thinking. Her critique of Jewish assimilation is, however, appreciated neither by her father nor by her peers. The ensuing lack of tolerance she experiences stigmatizes her once again as the "other woman," the role Kolmar so often explored in her poetry and prose.

In this situation Kolmar is seeking for other women who share her resistance through withdrawal. She describes, for example, a gypsy woman whom she noticed one day at work as the embodiment of the self she is searching for. She characterizes the forlorn expression on the woman's face as

> an impenetrable isolation, a silence, a distance, which could not be reached by any word, by any look directed at her from the outside world. . . . And I realized: That was exactly what I always wanted to possess and yet could never fully attain; because if I had it, nothing and nobody from the outside could do me any harm. But I am getting there and it makes me glad . . . (*Briefe*, 114)

By associating herself with a subject far lower in social rank and status than herself, Kolmar dismisses not only the norms of her own class, but she also subverts the prevailing Nazi race discourse. A human being deemed inferior and unworthy to live is chosen to symbolize self-reliance and spiritual resistance. Kolmar's portrait strikes me as having an almost emblematic quality, signifying both the loss and the mastery of the loss she is trying to achieve. Reading the gypsy woman as a chronotopic configuration shows Kolmar's deliberate choice of non-German and non-bourgeois models, which is echoed in other passages of the correspondence. She refers, for example, to herself "as a kind of would-be Asian" (*Briefe*, 25), and confesses her longing for the East, which denotes both Asia and Israel.[9] Withdrawal and complete self-reliance were, however, not unknown to Kolmar. She points out that her personality as well as her desires had prepared her for the kind of autonomy that was now needed. In a letter written in July 1942, she states:

> The earlier decades in which we were "doing very well," were not for me. They required abilities mostly of the social, the gregarious kind which I lacked for the most part; but what the present times demand that I certainly have. I measure up to the today. Already as a child I would have liked to be a Spartan woman, later on I wanted to become in any case a heroic woman. . . . Today I can be . . . an "original hero" (without attracting any unwelcome attention). (*Briefe*, 160)

I have argued elsewhere that the heroic persona that Kolmar casts here for herself is one of the dominant poetic paradigms in her oeuvre, reflecting her wish to transcend the boundaries of the contemporary social order and of her private world in order *to act* in the public realm.[10] Kolmar's self-description shows, however, that she was now recreating a poetic persona, the heroic woman, as an empirical mode. What had so far governed a fictive, a literary self, was rapidly being transformed into concrete reality. The path leading from the Spartan to the Gypsy woman thus delineates an autobiographical and poetic development whereby modes of fictive selfhood employed to transgress social, historical, and gender borders were altered in order to survive the desubjectification imposed on her. The heroic persona born out of Kolmar's profound desire to critique and poetically defy the present had, after all, always been a fictive script, powerful yet limited to imagination and texts. Now Kolmar tested its validity as an empirical practise, since it had become the only viable alternative to the helplessness and passive nostalgia she witnessed among many Jews of her own class.

Another crucial element of Kolmar's self-representation and one that again shows her complete defiance of bourgeois norms is the "bitter-sweet love story" (*Briefe*, 122) the author describes in great detail in the last third of the correspondence. The letters chronicling the relationship between the then forty-seven-year-old poet and a factory co-worker who is in his early twenties acquire an almost diary-like quality. Kolmar shares with her sister not only the entire development of this relationship, including various conversations and encounters, but also her own interpretations of this romance. In these letters Kolmar comes across very much as a woman in love who is experiencing a fleeting moment of joy, knowing that her lover will soon leave her. This pattern of hope, happiness, and loss characterizes most of Kolmar's numerous love poems. Again, Kolmar transforms a fictive persona and paradigm, the abandoned woman, into an empirical reality. It seems as if this love affair was prefigured in her writing and that she shaped it according to the persona she had developed in her poems.

These thematic correspondences between art and life find an equivalent in the narrative terminology Kolmar uses for the encounter. Story, hero, plot, novel, sequel—the nomenclature indicates that the author is fashioning the romantic episode following literary modes. Kolmar is literally writing her own life as a script, so that her correspondence becomes in a way a final supplement to her work. While her oeuvre is shaped by a strong autobiographical element, creating literature from experience, her last letters almost follow the opposite path by creating experience as literature.

Through these personas and paradigms Kolmar tried to shield herself from the Nazi terror. She also derived spiritual strength from what she called the "eternal events" (*Briefe*, 30), which could denote love, nature, religion, or art. She valued, for example, literature only if it was written *sub specie aeternitatis*, and her descriptions of the artistic process all employ an organic, nature vocabulary, which underlines the cyclical nature of existence. She reminds her sister that though Goethe and Schiller had experienced the French Revolution and Napoleon, these contemporary events had hardly left any traces in their works (*Briefe*, 33). Kolmar feels that she has followed a similar course, by creating "that what remains, animal and plant, eternally returning, enduring in passing and growing"(*Briefe*, 31).[11] Summing up her own creative mission in the statement, "I am a woman poet, yes I know that, but I would never like to be woman writer" (*Briefe*, 106), she stresses that her art continues the legacy of classic German literature and philosophy. The same legacy had also shaped the heroic persona which toward the end of her life acquired, however, an increasingly martyr-like quality. In a letter written on November 25, 1941, Kolmar describes an emphatic embrace of her destiny, "Amor fati: love of destiny" (*Briefe*, 196), as her credo, and in December 1942, she communicates the following resolution to her sister:

> That's the way I want to encounter fate, be it as high as a tower, be it black and looming as a cloud. Even if I don't know my fate: I have accepted it in advance; I have opened myself up to it in advance, and therefore I know that it won't crush me, that it won't consider me too small. (*Briefe*, 187)

Yet, it is precisely this heroism and martyrdom that are so difficult to assess, for Kolmar posits a self that gains its strength from accepting its impending destruction. For Langer this heroism is a very courageous and admirable, but ultimately naive stance, because its inherent humanist values were rendered meaningless in the face of the Auschwitz horrors. He therefore warns against idealizing this kind of martyrdom, which, in praising the human will to triumph, overlooks that the very foundations of this spirit were eroded by the Holocaust (Langer 1982, 206). Similarly, Joan Ringelheim in her article on "Women and the Holocaust" cautions against the "mystification" of spiritual resistance and survival (760). While these concerns are certainly justified, they seem to me not to invalidate Kolmar's position, but rather point to the epistemological dilemma any Holocaust discourse is faced with. Kolmar, as Langer himself noted, was not aware of the inferno awaiting her. She was thus describing a pre-Auschwitz situation, but we can judge her stance only from a post-Auschwitz point of view, thereby inevitably inserting the terror we know about into her own self-assessment. The "issue of representation" (Geyer and Hansen, 177), which has dominated much of the recent discussion on the Holocaust, becomes the lens through which we also look at Kolmar's faith and trust in words and spiritual growth. But does a critique of Kolmar's heroism not seem to almost negate her extraordinary strength and courage? After all, Kolmar had, for whatever reason, decided to stay in Germany, and the only part of her existence she could actively control was her inner life and self. To her, this was the only way of defying her oppressor. In my reading of the correspondence, Kolmar resembles an Antigone-like figure who defies her oppressors, but who pays with her own life. Kolmar was finally able to *live* the heroic destiny she had always longed for, but it was a heroism devoid of public actions and impact. Moreover, it was a heroism turned onto itself. It guided Kolmar through the last years of her life, helping her to cope with fear, fatigue, and profound loneliness as well as enabling her to find meaning and a sense of purpose in her existence. Despite the tremendous physical and mental pressures, Kolmar made every effort to keep writing to her sister, thus fighting until the very end against the silencing imposed on her. Under these circumstances, any form of writing became an act of defiance, since it entailed an affirmation of the self.

In her analysis of written reports of concentration camp survivors, Ellen S. Fine described resistance strategies that were especially crucial for women in combating the inferno of the camps. She mentions sharing memories, bonding with other women, and seeking support in the world of literature and ideas, techniques that can also be observed in Kolmar's correspondence. Fine singles out literature as the most powerful element of spiritual resistance. As an example she cites the poem "Written in Pencil in the Sealed Freight Car" by the Israeli author Dan Pagis, for it shows that: "At such a critical moment, the mere attempt to write suggests a faith in the permanence of words. The literary act can be an act of resistance" (80).

The attempt to write can also express hope and a belief in the future. Nowhere in the correspondence does this connection to the future become more apparent than in the numerous and lengthy letters Kolmar wrote to her niece Sabine. These letters, I believe, provided her with a different, but equally important source of strength. Both Zeitler and Langer paid no attention to this particular group of letters, in which Kolmar was utterly absorbed in her role as aunt. The notes show her completely attuned to the mind and world of a little girl, and they reveal nothing of her own oppression. Instead, she recounts memories of her own childhood, envisions Sabine as a beautiful and famous ballerina, or invents fairy tales. In creating these narratives for Sabine, Kolmar could in a different way also resist and transcend the Nazi rule. Through these letters and stories she could create memory and thus guard against a desubjectification which was, after all, aimed not only at (her) physical destruction but ultimately at the complete erasure of the individual and collective Jewish memory.

Echoing with many of the themes and paradigms of Kolmar's oeuvre, *Briefe an die Schwester Hilde* reveal how a deliberate choice of other spaces and times enabled the author to create a different persona, a kind of "second self," which made it possible for her to write and to resist the displacement and silence imposed on her. In that sense, the letters carry the "mission of memory" (Fine, 94). Ultimately, the recollection of Kolmar's life story, like that of millions of other victims, ends abruptly, without closure. Living with this rupture and preserving the memory of voices like Kolmar's continues to be our legacy.

Notes

1. Marion Brandt, ed., *Orte* (Berlin: Kontext, 1994).
2. "Welten" is the title of a short lyrical cycle which Kolmar composed in 1937.
3. See Shafi (14–19) for an overview of literary criticism, including feminist approaches, to Kolmar.

4. See Shafi, 32–73.

5. Johanna Woltmann lists a few other Kolmar letters in her excellent exhibition catalogue (Marbacher Magazin), most notably the two letters Kolmar addressed to her cousin Walter Benjamin (61–63).

6. I borrowed this title from: Joan L. Brown, ed., *Women Writers of Contemporary Spain: Exiles in the Homeland* (Newark: University of Delaware Press, 1991).

7. Unless otherwise stated all translations from *Briefe an die Schwester* are my own.

8. I wish to acknowledge the help Manuel Kraus provided with translating some of Kolmar's *Briefe*.

9. The cycle "Welten" (worlds) contains numerous poems expressing the poetic persona's desire for the East, most notably the poem "Asien" (Asia).

10. Shafi, 28–31.

11. Even in the cycle "Das Wort der Stummen" ("The Word of the Silenced"), her most direct and astute accusation of the Nazi terror, Kolmar does not view the physical, but the spiritual survival as the ultimate goal.

Bibliography

Bergland, Betty. "Postmodernism and the Autobiographical Subject: Reconstructing the "Other." In *Autobiography and Post-modernism*. Ed. Kathleen Ashley, Leigh Gilmore, and Gerald Peters. Amherst: University of Massachusetts Press, 1994, 130–166.

Brandt, Marion, ed. *Gertrud Kolmar: Orte*. Berlin: Kontext, 1994.

Brown, Joan L., ed. *Women Writers of Contemporary Spain: Exiles in the Homeland*. Newark: University of Delaware Press, 1991.

Durzak, Manfred. "Im Exil." In *Geschichte der deutschen Lyrik vom Mittelalter bis zur Gegenwart*. Ed. Walter Hinderer. Stuttgart: Reclam, 1993, 502–505.

Fine, Ellen S. "Women Writers and the Holocaust: Strategies for Survival." In *Reflections of the Holocaust in Art and Literature*. Ed. Randolph L. Braham. New York: Columbia University Press, 1990, 79–95.

Geyer, Michael, and Miriam Hansen. "German-Jewish Memory and National Consciousness." *In Holocaust Remembrance: The Shapes of Memory*. Ed. Geoffrey Hartman. Oxford: Blackwell, 1994, 175–190.

Goodman, Katherine. *Dis/Closures: Women's Autobiographies in Germany Between 1790 and 1914*. New York Ottendorfer Series Neue Folge, Vol. 24. New York: Peter Lang, 1986.

———. "Elisabeth to Meta: Epistolary Autobiography and the Postulation of the Self." In *Life/Lines: Theorizing Women's Autobiography*. Eds. Bella Brodzki and Celeste Schenck. Ithaca and London: Cornell University Press, 1988, 306–319.

Haidu, Peter. "The Dialectics of Unspeakability: Language, Silence, and the Narratives of Desubjectification." In *Probing the Limits of Representation: Nazism and the "Final Solution"*Ed. Saul Friedländer. Cambridge: Harvard University Press, 1992, 277–299.

Langer, Lawrence L. "Gertrud Kolmar and Nelly Sachs: Bright Visions and Songs of Lamentation." In *Versions of Survival: The Holocaust And The Human Spirit*. Albany: State University of New York Press, 1982, 191–250.

———. "Survival Through Art: The Career of Gertrud Kolmar." Publications of the Leo Baeck Institute. *Year Book XXIII*. 1978. 247–256.

Lixl-Purnell, Andreas. "Introduction. Women of Exile: Isolation as Identity." In *Women of Exile: German-Jewish Autobiographies since 1933*. Ed. Andreas Lixl-Purnell. New York: Greenwood,1988, 1–9.

Marbacher Magazin 63/1993. Gertrud Kolmar. Bearbeitet von Johanna Woltmann.

Nickisch, Reinhard M. G. *Brief*. Stuttgart: Metzler, 1991.

Ringelheim, Joan. "Women and the Holocaust: A Reconsideration of Research." *Signs* 10.4 (1985): 741–761.

Shafi, Monika. *Gertrud Kolmar: Eine Einführung in das Werk*. München: iudicium, 1995.

Smith, Henry A. *Dark Soliloquy: The Selected Poems of Gertrud Kolmar*. New York: The Seabury Press, 1975.

"Vorwort." In *Fünfzig Jahre danach: Zur Nachgeschichte des Nationalsozialismus*. Ed. Sigrid Weigel and Birgit Erdle. Zürich: vdf Hochschulverlag, 1996, IX–XII.

Zeitler, Johanna, ed. Gertrud Kolmar. *Briefe an die Schwester Hilde 1938–1943*. München: Kösel, 1970.

7

Reconstructing Mother—The Myth and the Real: Autobiographical Texts by Elisabeth Langgässer and Cordelia Edvardson

Helga Kraft

The tragic relationship of the writer Elisabeth Langgässer and her daughter Cordelia Edvardson is scarred by a mother/daughter conflict of historic dimension. Both wrote autobiographical works that in very different ways take a position against the mystification of the mother image during the Hitler era. Their works reflect both the cultural trends and the effects of the social and political conditions of the time on the fate of the individual.

There has always existed a connection between mother/daughter relationships and the fatherland, in the past as much as today. The notion that fascist elements lurk in democracies and the realization that gender plays a role in producing and reproducing collaborators in crime has expanded into a special discourse.[1] Shortly before the unification of Germany in 1990, Christa Wolf viewed the situation in the German Democratic Republic by explicity referring to gender:

> Now politicians and economists are dominant. The political parties are once more powerful. . . . Granted, all of them, politicians, business managers, and party functionaries, need a fatherland for their enterprises. So far, a motherland is not in sight."

> (Das Wort haben jetzt die Politiker und die Wirtschaftsleute. Das Wort haben wieder die Parteien. . . . Sie alle—Politiker, Wirtschaftsmanager, Parteifunktionäre—brauchen für ihre Unternehmungen ein Vaterland, das sehe ich ein. Ein Mutterland ist, wie bisher, nicht in Sicht.) (*Im Dialog*, 16–17)[2]

Wolf uses "fatherland" as a negative term. It becomes a gendered concept shaped by the usual alliance of politics and economics from which women are excluded. Women as historical subjects and participants have also been remarkably absent in the two recent debates about the German past in the Federal Republic: the West German *Historikerstreit* (German historian's controversy), which erupted in 1986, and the current debate about the GDR's legacy of National Socialism. In the public debates political systems and gender are separated; the latter usually appears under the rubric of "women's problems." Many women seem to have internalized this division as well: there is little action by women in the political arena or in the media to address such one-sidedness.

Change occurs at a snail's pace. Virginia Woolf had already noted in 1936 that systematic exclusion of women from the cultural, political, and economic institutions makes even a democratic society such as Britain profoundly undemocratic for women (*Three Guineas*). Woolf noted that the middle-class family reproduces gendered subjects within the family structure as well as through the power structure of the public world. Both women and men collaborate to perpetuate this system. Women usually do so either because they have consciously or unconsciously internalized their assigned role for security's sake or because their voices are not heard. For Woolf it is this family situation that is of prime importance for the development of fascism. It should be noted that Woolf's findings were not meant to obfuscate the particularly pernicious form that fascism assumed in Germany and that brought suffering to Langgässer and Edvardson. Yet, we must be vigilant about other potential fascisms now and in the future. Woolf's argument that fascism vitally depends on a patriarchal notion of gender is still very much ignored.

What then is the "motherland" Christa Wolf is looking for? At this point it is a utopian concept that Wolf explores in her writings which is still very much a *Kein Ort Nirgends* (*No Place Nowhere*), to borrow the title of one of her texts. But more women's voices are being heard today, and a new discourse on gender and the fatherland as well as an exploration of the power and weakness of mothers in the fatherland is growing, at least among writers. Women writers of this century are asking related questions in an individualized manner. Often, these questions are dealt with in autobiographical or semi-autobiographical texts that either question the father or look for a mother. This can be an individual mother, a universal, primeval mother, or a mother who is not like the patriarchal collaborative one. The latter constitutes a new model of a mother who can convey identity to a daughter alienated from her fatherland. However, she faces a dilemma: either she continues to find herself excluded, or if she is included, she becomes a collaborator.

The first of the two texts under discussion attempts an analysis of the concept of the primeval mother. The second shows a daughter caught up in the maelstrom of fascist consequences, and, after losing a fatherland, attempting to come to terms with the conflicting images of her own mother.

Elisabeth Langgässer (1899–1950) and her daughter Cordelia Edvardson (1929–) authored autobiographical texts which enter a new mother-daughter discourse that admits conflict. Langgässer's text, *Proserpina* (1933), is directed against a narrow, constricting mother image prevelant in the dominant discourse during both the Weimar Republic and the Hitler era. Edvardson's *Gebranntes Kind sucht das Feuer* (1989) (*Burnt Child Seeks out the Fire*) shows a daughter whose societal values have been shattered together with her mother image, and who attempts to come to terms with the consequences of that loss. In a shocking way their works reflect the influence of social and political circumstances on the fate of individual women.

Langgässer's novel was completed around 1929, the year her daughter was born. At that time women professionals had made progress: there were 2,500 women physicians, 300 women lawyers, and even a few dozen women professors and judges in Germany (Koonz, 45). The "New Woman" wanted to realize her potential by working outside the house and by discarding Wilhelminean strictures regarding sexuality. However, as critic Claudia Koonz reminds us in her book *Mothers in the Fatherland* (1987), no widespread change took place and a majority of women regarded the new images with skepticism and continued to emulate traditional models.

Langgässer, however, like many women artists of her time, belonged to the avant-garde. Partially due to her multiethnic background—her mother was Jewish but she grew up Catholic—she had become alerted to a crisis in the traditional systems of belief. Her Catholicism was always a very personal one. As a school teacher she had entered professional life very early; but because she gave birth to an illegitimate child, Cordelia (whose Jewish father was married to someone else), she lost her position as a teacher. As a nontraditional mother she was censured immediately. She then moved from her home town in the Rhine area (Rheinzabern, close to Alzey) to the center of action, Berlin, in 1929. As a self-employed writer she belonged to the periphery of a group of women authors who were expressing and publicizing emancipatory ideas. Langgässer had barely turned twenty when women were granted the vote and thus felt comfortable being an emancipated woman.

Although motherhood was not rejected in novels written by emancipated women writers of the time, their reevaluation of women's roles and potentials spelled danger for the conservative and fascist models that followed. The basis of these models was to socialize girls first and foremost for their task as mothers. The prevalent resistance to a new image of women in the late twenties and thirties can be illustrated by a study published in 1938 by Irmgard Schüttrumpf about the mother-child problem in the German women's novel during the time of the women's movement. Schüttrumpf makes an ideologically motivated attack against emancipated women writers, thereby reflecting the philosophy of the Third Reich. Her study focuses on novels written between 1880 and 1920 by authors close to the women's movement. The idea of an independent mother who raises her daughters independently for a new and freer society—as Langgässer did—is criticized and contrasted with a natural "timeless, eternal womanhood" (zeitloses, ewiges Frauentum). Without giving any sources or explanations, Schüttrumpf argues in terms of this conventional essentialism—which does not have to be proven—in favor of a universal womanhood representing the "genuine nature" (das echte Wesen) of women. Needless to say, it includes all traditional feminine characterists, such as natural readiness for service and passivity. The avant-garde writers are reproached for not including this true essence of womanhood in their novels. Consequently, "aesthetic failure" (dichterisches Versagen; 8) is attributed to them, a judgment indicative of totalitarian political procedure, which values artistic production according to the prevailing ideology. It also becomes obvious that the powers of the patriarchy are based on gender differences: for instance, Schüttrumpf concludes that the right to work, demanded by "modern" woman, presents a conflict with "motherhood." She further criticizes that the women in these novels problematize their own existence (10). Writers such as Clara Viebig, Gabriele Reuter, Ilse Frapan, Helene Böhlau are accused of falsifying womanhood because, supposedly, their feminine blood is secretly fighting the emancipatory movement. Contrary to the perception of these writers, Schüttrumpf claims that women have a "yearning for dedication and self-sacrifice" (zu Hingabe und Selbstaufgabe drängen; 20). The aim of such an ideology is transparent. There are two standards: one privileging men and one denying rights to women. When Schüttrumpf speaks of "the ill-fated power of the intellect, which destroys feeling" (der unseligen Macht des gefühlszerstörenden Intellektes), she insidiously applies it only to women. And among people who desire choices in building their identity, it is only the woman who "does not notice that in reality she is a slave of her own personality illusion" (merkt nicht, daß sie in Wirklichkeit Sklavin ihres Persönlichkeitswahnes ist). A few of the authors are even reproached for favoring "a perversion of feminine life and feminine soul" (Entartung weiblichen Lebens und weiblicher Seele; 37) in their works. It does not surprise us that the study finds this kind of literary trend especially among Jewish women writers. Schüttrumpf uses unsubstantiated essentialism as a racist and sexist weapon.

The tendencies of the women's movement and the countertendencies of fascism intersected as Langgässer wrote *Proserpina*, in which she reflected on her own childhood. In 1929, three generations of women—her mother, herself, and her illegitimate daughter—lived together. Before her brother took over as provider, Langgässer earned a living for all of them as an instructor of pedagogy and methodology at a *soziale Frauenschule* (social women's school). She also produced literary works and advertising texts. Juggling her artistic interests, her profession, the demands of her little daughter, and her strong-minded mother, the lifestyle of this single mother ran counter to the political ideologies discussed above.

The new, uncertain circumstances of Langgässer as modern daughter invite questions that a mother representing the patriarchal model cannot answer. Thus, Langgässer the writer creates a modern version of the ancient Persephone/Demeter myth, describing it in a dark, romantically enriched, surrealistic dream language—a difficult medium for modern readers. Tapping into the Roman heritage of her native Rhein area she uses the Roman name Proserpina for the primeval mythical daughter. But, she also puts Jung's archetypes onto a modern stage decorated with Christian symbols. The acting figures of the novel change in a protean fashion and the events have the quality of a Freudian dream, dreamt by the protagonist. The author sends a new Proserpina in search of a missing mother. The novel makes it clear that Langgässer, like many other contemporary writers, suffered from the mechanistic life style in the industrial age where the concept of "mother" had become a stereotype. She wrote within the framework of the modernist tradition as she attempted to revitalize empty myths through which women might again be a part of a larger collective existence. While her equation mother = nature leads her into an essentializing trap, she never falls into it, because she links the concepts she explores to women's potentials rather than essentials.

Langgässer incorporates her own childhood memories symbolically. Proserpina, the cosmic daughter, feels motherless, cut off from her origins. With her fertile, creative mind, she finds that her own birth mother, who has internalized the humdrum existence of everyday life, cannot be a role model. Not even her mother's milk agrees with the child. She was ill during most of her early childhood and compensated for real experiences with stories and fantasies. The writer seems to examine the resulting emotional deficit by exploring possibilities of a stronger and more encompassing mother image. The recreation of her own childhood yields a rich imagery because her home environment in the Rhine River area is endowed with layers of ancient artifacts and memories. After all, Romans lived there at the time when the original Proserpina was worshipped. History is never past, it lies underfoot, underground, in the unconscious. Time and space constraints disappear in Langgässer's narrative style. History is no longer linear. The temporal, surface level of order in the child's environment and its societal dictates are challenged. The novel also reflects the post–World War I mentality of many Germans who mourned the destruction of their value systems and questioned progress. As nature, culture, and history merge, the novel shows that the past still exerts a powerful influence on the present.

When Proserpina is finally permitted to leave her bed and go out at least into the house garden, she experiences real nature as threatening. Her imagination populates the environment with nature spirits, which become embodied. They merge with real people around her who become larger than life and in turn grow into mythical and Christian symbols. The girl feels lured into the depth of "Mother Nature" by way of a seemingly cultivated garden, a location that hides the realm of death, opulent and terrifying. Her inner and the outer world merge. It is doubtless her name that prompts the child to internalize the Roman myth of Proserpina, the eternal daughter, and her mother Ceres, also worshipped as Mother Nature, and to relive it in a new way. This kind of historical and ahistorical simultaneity prevents the development of a plot line. Through the sacrifice of such a narrative Langgässer succeeds in stylistically exploring those hidden areas of women's separate existence that would be destroyed by a linear story.

Contrary to the ancient myth, Langgässer creates a Proserpina who is not protected by her mother. A frightening side of the mother's power is expressed when the narrator laconically asserts that "all the mother goddesses are at the same time rulers of the underworld" (die Muttergöttinnen sind alle zugleich Herrscherinnen der Unterwelt; 22).[3] In the late Greek version of the myth, Proserpina's predesessor, Persephone, is the daughter of Zeus and Demeter (also called Mother Earth). With the consent of her father, Zeus, Persephone is raped by her own uncle, the god Hades, and abducted by him to the underworld. This happens as Persephone is about to pick a flower in a meadow. Since this flower is a narcissus the myth implies that the girl is about to develop a subjective identity based on her own reflection. Yet, this mustn't take place in a patriarchy where women remain objects, and thus the male gods interfere by taking Persephone to the "other" world, the underworld. Only when Demeter, in her raging pain, devastes all life on earth is Zeus forced to return the daughter. Yet the mother cannot get her back completely because she ate of a pomegranate in Hades. This is an early parallel to Eve's eating the apple. The Persephone myth confirms that the sexuality of women was already seen in connection with the dark forces (which in Christianity became sin), despite the fact that the girl was a rape victim. This early version is even more unsettling than the biblical one because Persephone was not warned about eating of the pomegranate and did not know the consequences. Nevertheless, she is being sent to death again and again for part of the year. Only through the sacrifice of the innocent daughter can life continue on earth.

The allusion to this myth lends Langgässer's novel a subtext that implies the daughter's role as victim. She rewrites this element of the myth in an individualistic and modernist way to express the daughter's powerlessness, as she attempts to deal with her own inner drives of early adolescence, and as she yearns to participate in the motherly powers of nature to satisfy those undefined desires.

Langgässer tentatively examines a symbolism imbued with patriarchial overtones in which the power of the mother is connected with the dark, destructive forces of nature and not to a *philotas*, that is, the tenderness of a humanizing eros, which the feminist Irigaray found in ancient mother-daughter myths. Langgässer's vision of the mythical mother touches on the concept of the "große Mutter" (great mother), one of Eric Neumann's and Carl Jung's archetypes, whose negative powers, according to these psychologists, are threatening the individual and collective psyche of the Western world. Langgässer's novel boldly questions the truth-value of such allegations.

The narrator constructs a collage of a super-mother-triad which combines erotic, reproductive, and nurturing elements, and which rules over life and death. This construction takes place in the imagination of the daughter and constitutes a new variant of Demeter, who represented the triad of young woman, mother, and old crone in early myth. Langgässer uncovers deep layers of that complex and elusive image of "mother" and adds Christian spirituality as well as aspects of real women's lives. She multiplies this triad so that each entity fans out into three additional mythical women: Eve/Aphrodite/Selene, Ceres/Maria/Hecate, Witch/Wise Woman/Mother Nature. All three are connected to birth, love, and death. Together they are powerful. Earlier mother myths, in which goddesses were drawn with positive and life-giving traits, flow into Langgässer's novel—for instance the prepatriarchal myths rediscovered by Bachofen and later by feminists such as Adrienne Rich, Nancy Chodorow, and Heide Göttner-Abendroth. In some contemporary feminist discourses Demeter is recognized as a primeval goddess who later on incorporated other goddesses celebrated in the Eleusinan mysteries which were inaugurated between 1400 and 1100 B.C. Adrienne Rich notes: "The real meaning of the mysteries was this reintegration of death and birth, at a time, when patriarchal splitting may have seemed to sever them entirely" (238–239). After two thousand years of such division the daughter in Langgässer's novel must piece together a fragmented mother image.

On the surface level the three multiple mother figures are real women who populate the daily life of the child. In the girl's imagination they grow in complexity. The first mother, her birth mother, extends care to the daughter in a physical sense. For the girl she becomes Ceres, symbol of societal morals and guardian of the family. She also appears to her as the Catholic Mary, the intermediary bringing salvation, and Selene, heathen moon and birth goddess. These three images conflate in this mother image of the child's vision; but she develops no deeper tie to her birth mother. The presence of the sober housewife does not satisfy the imagination of the child, and she develops a feeling of abandonment. On this level of civilized existence in the house of her mother she feels as if she were in the underworld, which to her means "the winter sleep of obedience, which would have saved her in cold and darkness from death" (der Winterschlaf des Gehorsams, der sie in Kälte und Finsternis vor dem Tode bewahrt hätte; 98). However, she opts for disobedience and thus escapes this type of underworld constituted by a pre-programmed existence.

The second real mother figure is a beautiful woman, a young servant who takes care of the girl in the mother's absence. Through her she learns about the effect of physical attraction. Aphrodite is personified in her. Inspired by this image, the novel's Proserpina eats a pomegranate just like her mythical predecessor, and for the first time she is able to differentiate between what her culture calls "good" and "evil" (98). The underworld is here represented by the frightening first erotic sensations, which irrationally seek to find expression and liberation in uncomprehended desires but clash with society's taboos. The tenderness of Aphrodite of which Irigaray speaks and which humanizes Eros, is evident in the interaction of the girl and the second mother figure. Yet for the women Irigaray's *philotas* is destroyed by the superior place man has in the story and in the patriarchy.

The third mother figure is an old, wise woman, a witch-like gardener, whom the child visits often, and who seems to control the powers of nature. She personifies the old crone, the witch, Hecate, or Mother Nature. This mother image teaches Proserpina that power can be exercised through an individual strong will, through action, intuition, and imagination. Thus, a link between woman's potential for physical as well as mental reproduction is recognized. In her creative powers, the wise woman seems to be the narrator's model for her own creative writing. The realm of the mighty, magical mother is depicted as the dangerous underworld where patriarchal conscience is absent, and where power over life and death can be used at will. This is the area Langgässer seems to be most interested in as an emancipated woman; it is also the area closed to women and guarded by patriarchal taboos, which are expressed by symbols of Catholicism with which Langgässer struggles here but later turns to increasingly.

In the second, revised version of the novel *Proserpina, Welt eines Kindes* (1933) (*Proserpina, World of a Child*, published before the original version), the mother image is toned down in its terrifying features. Perhaps it was a necessary procedure to assure publication at a time when a stereotypical ideal mother was dominating the media. Langgässer's explorations of mother-daughter power are in opposition to the image of the idealized, highly decorated mother with seven children promoted by the National Socialists. In the original version of 1929, which was published first in 1949 with the subtitle *Eine Kindheitsmythe* (*A Childhood Myth*), the mother image contains a destructive, even death-bringing component, as well as aspects of witchcraft, elements from the realm of ghosts, and magic. Also, the real mother is more often present, and as a consequence, the conflict is more sharply delineated. Heidy Margrit Müller's study of the differences between the two versions is quite revealing in this respect. As Langgässer conceded later, she preferred the first version, which she was able to publish only after the downfall of the Third Reich. During the years of Nazi rule she had been forbidden to publish any of her works or to write at all.

In the first version of the book Proserpina dares to practice her newly discovered power for the first time when a young male gardener, who appears to her as Pan, awakens her sensuality and at the same time her feelings of jealousy and revenge. The girl "plays" the role of the terrible mother herself; she becomes the goddess of the underworld who is caught in destructive chaos. Brutally she dismembers her doll, which resembles her beautiful and envied rival in love. The death of a cat seems to be her doing as well. These images convey a vitality of the individual that diminishes the negative aspects of her groping attempts to handle power for her own desires. The daughter must seek an affirmation of her own identity, no matter what the consequences might be.

The three motherly images created by Langgässer redefine motherhood radically. It is no longer expressed by the glorified image of a "self-less" housewife and mother collaborating with the patriarchy but by the enormous power resting in all women and consisting of the ability to desire, produce, and destroy. Langgässer not only goes beyond draping psychological processes with mythical images: she explores the role of language as well. The child Proserpina not only experiences unknown motherly powers through the enticement of nature around her, the narrator notices a second entrapment: "however, a second rapture was more dangerous and much deeper, because it fell unnoticed through non-violent language" (doch war eine zweite Entrückung gefährlicher und auch tiefer, weil es unbemerkt durch die gewaltlose Sprache fiel; 74). By entrapment she refers to the lure of the other, the mother's realm. Human language "born of water and spirit" (aus Wasser und Geist geboren; 95), she maintains, belongs to the world of the father, but since the father of the story, in his incarnation as Evoe, turns out to be a god of the underworld and a messenger of Proserpina's mother, language and spirit are emanating from the motherly forces as well. Langgässer is here clearly undermining the Freudian concept of the "phallic woman" who threatens but is always part of the patriarchal system. In *Proserpina*, on the other hand, the spiritual father is nothing but an emissary of a matriarchal system. Since Langgässer is deeply positioned in Christian alternatives, she has the daughter eventually blame herself for the death of her beloved father, although he dies of an incurable illness toward the end of the novel. This self-blame reflects one of

Freud's early observations that the daughter must be sacrificed if the father is to live, that is, if patriarchy is to continue.[4] The girl blames herself because she should have died, not he. Langgässer, one of the writers trying to look beyond dualism, touches upon the question what impact the death of the father and the reemergence of the matriarchal goddesses might have on her time. But she cannot come to a conclusion, since her society is still a very traditional one. The narrator tells us that mother and daughter disappear to an unknown place after the death of the father as if they, too, have ceased to exist as individuals. Is the combined disappearance of mother and daughter from time and space to be understood as an interpersonal fulfillment, in which conflicts have disappeared? Or is it no longer possible to continue the search through language, the instrument of the father? The author leaves this question open.

Langgässer felt the pulse of her times, in which the true essence of origin was still accepted without question and new myths backed up these claims (Hitler's *Mein Kampf*, "justifying" inhumanity to achieve Aryan purity, had already been written). The bipolar division of spirit and nature, which had prevailed up to then in the Western world, had given way to a carefully chosen undefined mixture, which exploited individual feeling and thought for political purposes. The modern Proserpina is a daughter, whose sacrifice for a male society is absurd. Actually, there is nothing to save any more.

While Langgässer's story stops at puberty, the main part of her daughter's novel *Gebranntes Kind sucht das Feuer* (1986) (*Burnt Child Seeks out the Fire*) begins at this time. The two novels, written before and after World War II, frame the worst time in German history. Edvardson who experienced true abandonment wrote her book out of a need to reconstruct the image of a mother and in so doing achieve a more secure identity. The plot is quickly summarized. The fourteen-year-old Cordelia is torn from her parents by the Nazis, forced to work as a nurse and later taken to Auschwitz. At the end of the war she is released to Sweden, where she recovers only slowly from a severe illness. She lives there with foster parents, later marries and raises children of her own. The last, brief paragraph of her book deals with her emigration to Israel. Unlike her mother, she uses real names in her recollections, but distances herself, just as Langgässer did, from her own childhood identity by choosing to write in the third person singular. In a retrospective view of her early childhood Cordelia vividly remembers a certain feeling of being different, a knowledge about a special task she had to perform for her mother. The name Proserpina had always been familiar to her. She describes a symbiotic existence, in which the roles of mother and daughter were inverted at times. The child seeks protection in the arms of her mother,

> and the mother is in the arms of the child, because the guiltless, innocent child is the refuge of the mother, her salvation and her sacrificial lamb. Who nursed whom? Who

> sent Proserpina out to pick flowers which drew their vital powers from the earth of the realm of the dead?
>
> (und die Mutter an der Brust des Kindes, denn das schuldlose, unschuldige Kind ist the Zuflucht der Mutter, ihre Rettung, und ihr Opferlamm. Wer stillte wen? Wer sandte Proserpina aus, Blumen zu pflücken, die ihre Lebenskraft aus der Erde des Totenreichs sogen?) (58)

Cordelia tells her readers that she had never read her mother's Proserpina novel. It hadn't been necessary, the narrator states, as the message for the daughter had been received much earlier. For her, the topic of the "great mother" is no longer an intellectual game, as it was for her mother, but it becomes reality. The grown-up narrator of *Gebranntes Kind sucht das Feuer* (*Burnt Child Seeks out the Fire*) reflects that it had always been understood that she, as daughter, had to sacrifice herself. As a fourteen-year-old she was ready to save her mother. Without a second thought she rendered a fatal signature, which assured her mother's freedom but precipitated her own transport into Hitler's death camps. The deportation of the child was ordered because Cordelia was three-quarters Jewish. Her mother, who was only half-Jewish and was now married to a non-Jew, and her younger children from this marriage, were safe from the clutches of Hitler's race police. In an attempt to protect her eldest daughter, Langgässer had arranged an adoption by a non-Jewish couple. This was a punishable act and was discovered. The Nazi officials assailed the bond of trust between mother and daughter by manipulating young Cordelia with the threat that her mother would be incarcerated for her felony if she, Cordelia, would not wear the yellow star identifying her as Jewish. Cordelia signed without hesitation, thus abdicating her rights as a citizen.[5] She had internalized the mythic lesson of the primeval Proserpina; she must sacrifice herself for her mother. When she is together with her mother, life and death are one and the same for her: "Oh yes, to be allowed to sleep, protected, gently, in the womb of death, of my mother" (O ja, schlafen zu dürfen, geborgen und sanft, im Schoß des Todes, der Mutter; 17).

Edvardson's book explores the consequences of her childhood socialization in a hostile, racist environment. She reports that she spent the beginning of her childhood without a father, and in a close symbiosis with her mother whom she practically deified. She whimsically considered a father as dispensable as owning an elephant or swallowing cod liver oil. Early on she had been conscious of her special status. She knew, she would never wear "the crown of a blue eyed princess but the crown of thorns of suffering." She had absorbed the amalgam of her mother's myths early: she was Proserpina and she was also the child Jesus. Her mother merged with the queen of heaven. When the threatening danger of a Nazi visit had once again passed, the child felt as if

> the Mother of God (had) . . . hidden her under her sky blue coat, decorated with stars, or perhaps it had been the mother of the girl after all, who, with her magic powers, had thrown a cloak of invisibility over the daughter . . .
>
> (Die Mutter Gottes (hatte) . . . sie unter ihrem himmelblauen, sternenbesetzten Mantel verborgen, oder vielleicht war es ja die Mutter des Mädchens gewesen, die mit ihren Zauberkünsten eine Tarnkappe über die Tochter . . . geworfen hatte . . .) (58)

In the proximity of her mother she didn't fear anything, not even the Nazi threat: "As long as the girl stayed inside the protective jurisdiction of her mother's magic, there was no real danger. Death no longer frightened her." (Solange sich das Mädchen im schützenden Bannkreis der Beschwörungen ihrer Mutter hielt, drohte ihr keine ernste Gefahr. Der Tod schreckte sie nicht länger; 33). She was ready to do everything for her mother. As an eight- or nine-year-old she had heard the speech of a *BDM*-leader[6] and, as a consequence, she internalized Hitler's program for women. In this talk, she says, "Above all, it probably was the admonition for self-sacrifice, which had touched her deepest instincts" (Vor allem war es wohl die Mahnung zur Aufopferung, die sich an ihre tiefsten Instinkte wandte; 37–38). An uneasiness invaded her when she noticed that her mother did not express the same instincts in return. When the girl had to render that signature in a life-and-death decision, she felt abandoned by her mother: "Uncertain, the daughter looked at her mother, and her eyes met a white mask, in which the extremely red mouth glowed like a wound. She couldn't expect any support from her mother at that moment. This much the girl understood instantly" (Unsicher sah die Tochter die Mutter an, und ihr Blick traf auf eine weiße Maske, worin der allzu rote Mund wie eine Wunde glühte. Von der Mutter war im Augenblick keine Unterstützung zu erwarten, das wurde dem Mädchen sofort klar; 67). The mother goddess shrivels here to a cold mask of fear, an illusion that cannot offer protection.

The young girl realized

> nothing had to be said, there was no choice, there had never been a choice; she was Cordelia, who kept her pledge of loyalty; she was also Proserpina, she was the chosen one, and never had she been closer to the heart of her mother.
>
> (nichts brauchte gesagt zu werden, es gab keine Wahl, hatte nie eine gegeben, sie war Cordelia, die ihr Treuegelöbnis hielt, sie war auch Proserpina, sie war die Auserwählte, und nie hatte sie dem Herzen ihrer Mutter nähergestanden.) (68)

But she could not help relating her feelings to the sufferings of Christ, and she asked in a gender reversal: "Mother, why did you abandon me?" (Mutter, warum hast du mich verlassen? 74). As the mythical Proserpina, she was being sent into the Orcus by her mother. She became an assistant to the infamous Dr. Mengele in the concentration camp of Auschwitz. There she had to make two lists: one with the names of prisoners condemned to die in the gas chambers, the other with the names of those who would be allowed to live a little longer. Is there a more fitting image of a modern Proserpina, who is forced to stand next to the incarnation of supreme evil in the realm of death, against her will, in order to save her mother?

Cordelia rejects the style her mother had selected for her life and for her literary productions. Yet she admits that remembering her childhood myths gave her the power to survive under deadly conditions. She herself replaces mystification and private aestheticism with sober, deconstructive analysis and an active participation in the community. This is her way of coming to terms with her own identity. The difference is reflected in the clarity of her prose, which contrasts strikingly with the ambiguous dark probings of her mother's novel *Proserpina*. Sweden, her postwar homeland, was a suitable, neutral place to find herself. She eventually embraced her Jewish heritage and went to Israel, where she actively participated in the development of that country. Instead of replacing, as Langgässer had done in *Proserpina*, her own mother with a mythical, motherly power that could compensate for her abandonment, she added to her German birth mother, Elisabeth Langgässer, two other women who supported her during her life in a motherly fashion: Stefi Pedersen of Stockholm and Sylvia Krown of Jerusalem; they became her mothers as well, and she dedicated her book to all three of them. Not until long after her release from the concentration camp did she visit her mother (a single brief visit in 1949). At her request, she placed at her mother's disposal facts and dates of her journey of suffering from Theresienstadt to Auschwitz for literary use. However, Langgässer's transformation of these materials did not bring mother and daughter closer together. Cordelia cannot understand her mother, who reworked her life into a poetic myth in which the daughter couldn't recognize herself. Edvardson belongs to a generation that can no longer condone an aesthetic cloaking of real, terrifying experiences.

In another book, *Die Welt zusammenfügen* (1988) (*Putting the World Together*), Cordelia Edvardson wrote, forty years after the death of Elisabeth Langgässer, about her conflict with her mother, which was still troubling her:

> I have been pregnant with you for sixty years. . . . Again and again I believed the hour had come. . . . Every time the labor pains stopped, you were the fruit of my womb. . . .
>
> You nourished me and choked me at the same time. . . .
>
> "You must not have strange gods before me," you said and left very little room, for me, and the men in my life and my own children, your grandchildren.
>
> I became one of those women, and we are many, who could never be quite mothers to our children, especially to our daughters; our mothers did not permit it. . . .

> What will be left of me after I have given birth to you and have severed the umbilical cord? And what is to become of you? And when you will no longer own my life, how will you find peace in your grave, in which you are have been resting for forty years? Beloved, hated mother! I am afraid of you. I fear your revenge.
>
> (Fast sechzig Jahre bin ich mit Dir schwanger gegangen. . . . Wieder und wieder glaubte ich, meine Stunde sei gekommen . . . . Jedesmal hörten die Wehen auf, du warst meine Leibesfrucht. . . .
>
> Du hast mich genährt und gleichzeitig erstickt. . . .
>
> "Du sollst nicht andere Götter haben neben mir", befahlst Du und ließest mir sehr wenig Raum, mir und den Männern in meinem Leben und meinen eigenen Kindern, Deinen Enkeln. Ich wurde eine dieser Frauen, und wir sind viele, die unseren Kindern nie ganz Mütter sein konnten, vor allem nicht unseren Töchtern; unsere Mütter ließen es nicht zu . . . . Was bleibt von mir, wenn ich Dich geboren und die Nabelschnur durchtrennt habe? Und was wird aus Dir? Wie findest Du Ruhe im Grab, in dem Du schon fast vierzig Jahre liegst, wenn Du nicht länger mein Leben besitzt? Geliebte, gehaßte Mutter! Ich habe Angst vor Dir. Angst vor Deiner Rache.) (134–136)

This text mirrors a powerful connection between mother and daughter and a dependence that haunts the daughter's life. At the same time, Edvardson is aware that the terrible mother is, in the final analysis "her dream" (ihr Traum), and she intends to make the attempt to "free herself" (sich freizusprechen) from her mother, because she knows of the "responsibility of human beings for their own dreams" (Verantwortung des Menschen für seine Träume; 134). But her road of suffering shows that this image of an admired ideal, with which the daughter grew up, is untenable: the image of a loving mother who protects her daughter and guarantees her a happy life. In a generational reversal, daughters need to give birth to their mothers by reconstructing their image through autobiographical texts. Edvardson asks: what are mothers, when they know that their daughters don't need them anymore? We might add, what fills the gap, when the symbiotic constellation of Demeter, Ceres, and Proserpina is no longer serving patriarchy through a prescribed sacrifice?

This alienation of mother and daughter in a patriarchal society is the central focus of the two novels. The fascist tendencies of the fatherland caused the two writers to rethink one of the dominant myths. In *Proserpina,* Langgässer searches for emancipation and deconstructs the myth of universal motherhood that stands against the individual desires of the daughter. Yet, her attempts come too early, she breaks off her novel inconclusively. Edvardson, on the other hand, goes beyond mere reflection. She faces squarely the actual tyranny of fascism that destroyed her bond with her mother. Both women become daughters without mothers, one in an abstract, the other in a concrete sense. At the same time they become alienated from their "fatherland." In this tenuous position, the traditional dyad of mother and daughter is lost, without something new having taken its place. The loss is painful, but for both women in a different sense new options open up, for Edvardson more clearly than for Langgässer. The wish of both writers, to choose many women as mothers, is a step toward a "motherland" in which fascism might not have a chance.[7]

Notes

1. For instance, see the book by Gättens, *Women Writers and Fascism. Reconstructing History.*

2. This translation, like all subsequent translations of German texts, is my own.

3. All quotations in the text are from *Proserpina* (Frankfurt am Main/Berlin/Vienna: Ullstein, 1982).

4. See Freud's essay "Das Motiv der Kästchenwahl" (The Motive of the Choice of Box)(24–37) and Treusch-Dieter's discussion of it (161–183).

5. Lately, Langgässer has been criticized for her attempts to fit into an Aryan environment by pleading with the NS government. In her book, *Wotans Rabe. Elisabeth Langgässer, ihre Tochter Cordelia und die Feuer von Auschwitz* (1997) *(Wotan's Raven. Elisabeth Langgässer, her daughter Cordelia, and the Fires of Auschwitz)*, Ursula El-Akramy notes that Langgässer would gladly have come out of her inner immigration if she had been allowed to do so. For instance, she wrote a letter to Reichskulturwalter (national minister of culture) Hinkel on August 17, 1937, in which she makes the following revealing statement: "Meinen künstlerischen Beruf kann ich auf die rein arische Linie meiner mütterlichen Vorfahren [. . .] zurückführen. Ausserdem habe ich einen arischen Halbbruder [. . .] ich bin mit einem Mann von rein arischer Herkunft verheiratet [. . . .] (My artistic profession goes back directly to the purely Aryan lineage of my maternal predecessors. Moreover, I have an Aryan half-brother. I am married to a man of pure Aryan descent;114).

In a 1997article on Langgässer's 1936 novel *Der Gang durch das Ried (The Walk through the Bog)* Cathy Gelbin notes that rather "than representing an indifferent stance toward the Hitlerian state in this novel, the author attempts to write the hybrid Aladin (who is the protagonist) and thus Langgässer herself, back into the fascist notion of the German Volk" (Gelbin, 155). In analyzing the novel Gelbin comes to the conclusion that the writer "merely changes the negative connotations of older discourses around the Jew and the hybrid into positive ones, while leaving the stereotype intact" (Gelbin,158–159).

I neither wish to psychologize Langgässer's wish to write herself into the Nazi discourse as a German during the threatening times, nor can I speculate about possible guilt on her part concerning the fate of her daughter. I rely on the known facts, according to which she did her utmost to save her child. Both were victims of unbearable circumstances.

6. BDM = Bund deutscher Mädel (League of German Girls), the female version of the Hitler youth for fourteen- to eighteen-year-old girls.

7. An earlier version of this chapter appeared in German as "Verlassene Töchter und die Asche des Muttermythos," in Helga Kraft and Elke Liebs, eds., *Mütter—Töchter—Frauen. Weiblichkeitsbilder in der Literatur* (Stuttgart/Weimar: J. B. Metzler, 1993), 193–214.

Bibliography

Allen, Ann Taylor. *Feminism and Motherhood in Germany, 1800–1914*. New Brunswick, N. J.: Rutgers University Press. 1991.

Bahr, Ehrhard. Geschichte und Allegorie: "Möglichkeiten des allegorischen Romans zur Zeit des NS Regimes: Elisabeth Langgässer und Thomas Mann." In Deutsche Exilliteratur. Literatur im Dritten Reich. Ed. Wolfgang Elfe, James Hardin, and Gunther Holst. Bern: Lang, 1979, 103–110.

Edvardson, Cordelia. *Gebranntes Kind sucht das Feuer*. Munich: Deutscher Taschenbuch Verlag, 1989.

———. *Die Welt zusammenfügen*. Munich: Deutscher Taschenbuchverlag, 1989.

El-Akramy, Ursula. *Wotans Rabe. Elisabeth Langgässer, ihre Tochter Cordelia und die Feuer von Auschwitz*. Frankfurt am Main: Verlag Neue Kritik, 1997.

Frühwald, Wolfgang. "Das 'Eckhaus im Norden Berlins': Zu Elisabeth Langgässers und Cordelia Edvardsons Deutung des Judentums." In *Hinter dem schwarzen Vorhang: Die Katastrophe und die epische Tradition*. Ed. Friedrich Gaede, Patrick O'Neill, Ulrich Scheck. Tübingen, Francke, 1994, 209–216.

Freud, Siegmund. "Das Motiv der Kästchenwahl." *Werke aus den Jahren 1913–1917*. Vol. 10 of *Gesammelte Werke*. Imago Publishing Company Ltd.: London, 1946, 24–37.

Gelbin, Cathy. "In Quest for a Unified Self: Race, Hybridity, and Identity in Elisabeth Langgässer's Der Gang durch das Ried." *New German Critique* 68 (1997): 141–160.

Gättens, Marie-Luise. Women Writers and Fascism. Reconstructing History. Gainesville: University of Florida Press, 1995.

Heidmann-Vischer, Ute. "La Fonction de lémprunt mythologique dans Proserpina, recit d'enfance d'Elisabeth Langgässer." *Cahiers d'Études Germaniques* 26 (1994): 85–98.

Hitler, Adolf. *Mein Kampf*. Munich: F. Eher Nachf., 1936.

Irigaray, Luce. *Le Temps de la différance*. Paris: Librairie Général Francaise, 1989.

Kraft, Helga, and Liebs, Elke, eds. *Mütter—Töchter—Frauen. Weiblichkeitsbilder in der Literatur.* Stuttgart: J. B. Metzler, 1993.

Koonz, Claudia. *Mothers in the Fatherland: Women, the Family, and Nazi Politics*. New York: St. Martin's Press, 1987.

Langgässer Elisabeth. *Der Gang durch das Ried*. Ein Roman. Leipzig: Hegner, 1936.

———. *Proserpina. Welt eines Kindes*. Leipzig: Hesse & Becker, 1933.

———. *Proserpina. Eine Kindheitsmythe*. Hamburg: Claassen & Goverts, 1949.

———. *Proserpina*. Frankfurt am Main/Berlin/Vienna: Ullstein, 1982.

Müller, Karlheinz. *Elisabeth Langgässer*: Eine biographische Skizze. Darmstadt: Gesellschaft hessischer Literaturfreunde, 1990.

Müller, Heidy Margrit. *Töchter und Mütter in deutschsprachiger Erzählprosa von 1885* bis *1935*. Munich: iudicium, 1991.

Rich, Adrienne. *Of Woman Born. Motherhood as Experience and Institution.* Tenth Anniversary Edition. New York/London: W. W. Norton & Company, 1986.

Schüttrumpf, Irmgard. *Das Mutter-Kind-Problem im deutschen Frauenroman zur Zeit der Frauenbewegung.* Dresden: M. Dittert & Co., 1938.

Gerburg, Treusch-Dieter. "Das Kästchenproblem. Zum Psyche-Mythos bei Freud." In *Mütter und Töchter: Über die Schwierigkeiten einer Beziehung und die Bildung weiblicher Identität.* Ed. Eveline Valtrink. Hofgeismarer Protokolle. Tagungsbeiträge aus der Arbeit der evangelischen Akademie 124. Evangelische Akademie: Hofgeismar, 1987, 161–183.

Wolf, Christa. *Im Dialog,* Aktuelle Texte. Frankfurt am Main: Luchterhand, 1990.

———. *Kein Ort. Nirgends.* Frankfurt am Main: Luchterhand, 1979.

Woolf, Virginia. *Three Guineas.* New York: Harcourt Brace, 1938.

8
At Home in Exile—Nelly Sachs: Flight and Metamorphosis

Ruth Dinesen

Nelly Sachs (1891–1970) began to write poetry as a young girl after an unhappy love affair but did not consider herself a professional author until, as a German Jew, separated from her cultural milieu by the Nazi laws, she found herself a participant in the social arrangements of the Jewish Cultural Association (*Jüdischer Kulturbund*) in the late thirties. In May 1940 she escaped with her mother to Sweden, where she stayed for the rest of her life. In 1966 she was awarded the Nobel Prize (together with Shmuel J. Agnon).

Nelly Sachs was basically a religious personality, hardly suited to oppose Nazi terror politically. Her reaction to National Socialist ideology and its consequences took place on a different level. One of her reactions to threatening violence was direct and physical. For example, when in the presence of both her and her mother, their Berlin apartment was looted by SA men, accompanied by their wives, she suffered paralysis of the larynx that made speaking impossible for five days. Or when Israel's existence was threatened by the Israeli-British-French attack on Egypt, she suffered a heart attack (*Briefe*, 175). Such strong reactions of a sensitive person are of course signs of a deep inner concern, but they are not viable answers to political threat.

Nelly Sachs's contribution to the resistance against the Nazi regime is of a linguistic nature. Since her childhood she had composed small poems and prose texts.

On the basis of this long experience, it was possible for her to oppose the manipulated and perverted Nazi language with an only apparently naive but in reality embattled, yet healing poetic language.

Massive propaganda was present at the beginning as the basis of the Nazi regime. Before every application of force, there was always a goal-oriented misuse of words such as *Volk* (people or nation) or *Jude* (Jew), a strategy that contained a germ of later genocide.

Nelly Sachs dealt with this perversion of language in her poem "Völker der Erde" (1950) (Peoples of the Earth):

> O that no one means death when he says life—
> and not blood when he speaks cradle—
> (*O The Chimneys*, 93)

> (O dass nicht Einer Tod meine, wenn er Leben sagt —
> / und nicht Einer Blut, wenn er Wiege spricht—)
> (*Fahrt ins Staublose*, 152) (Journey into the Dustless)

When she fled, Nelly Sachs was able to take nothing but her inherited German language. In untiring work, she performed the linguistic means to make her poems believable witnesses for resistance against inhumanity and a place of new metaphors and ever-new variations of continuing themes and motifs, in which she tried to resolve rememberance for the victims. She also struggled to use language as a means of deriving meaning from life and suffering. Here her mystical religiosity becomes evident; with the perpetual riddle of good and evil and of our cosmic existence.

The religious interpretation of resistance as exile, which is here examined, appears in this connection as existential resistance against fascist perversion of language and against contempt for basic human value concepts.

In her exile poetry, her own situation as one of thousands of refugees becomes a metaphor of fleeing as a basic condition of human life: the never-ceasing flight through metamorphoses. This essential insight appeared to her as an experience of epiphany, which resulted in a series of poems written in 1957–58, with a concentrated effort during the spring of 1958. With the words,

> I hold instead of a homeland
> The metamorphoses of the world—
> (*O The Chimneys* 145)

> (An Stelle von Heimat/halte ich die Verwandlungen der Welt—) (*Fahrt ins Staublose* 262), which she chose as an epigraph for the poems in her book *Flucht und Verwandlung* (Flight and Metamorphosis), published in 1959, she describes one of her main themes of this period: the coincidence of "home" (Heimat) and "exile" (in der Fremde sein).

Nelly Sachs was born and educated in Berlin. As an adult she lived in comfortable circumstances as an unmarried only daughter in a quiet district of the city. By 1940 circumstances in Berlin had become so menacing that she was forced to flee the country. Stockholm, where her small and humble dwelling was part of an apartment block in a district of workers and *petits bourgeois*, would never become a home in the sense of a place of warmth and security, full of memories of childhood—good and bad—of experiences with friends, with teachers, with shopkeepers. She would never come to the point of knowing the feelings and habits of her neighbors, which enables a native to interpret events with somnambulistic security and act adequately in relations with people. She would always have to translate into the context of her own experiences in order to understand and would never get rid of the unstable feeling of being a foreigner.

Left alone by the death of her mother in 1950, Nelly Sachs sat at the edge of her bed with her old-fashioned typewriter placed on a little round table in front of her and wrote thousands of letters and some hundred poems, the main part of these dealing with the ability of language to grasp the conditions of life, only now and then giving expression to an extreme feeling of being abroad. Once in the month of March, with the frozen sea under her windows and the cold sky above, heavy with gray clouds, she "suddenly" remembered the early morning walks in April with her father in the Tiergarten park in Berlin, when the trees were blooming.[1] In a letter to Peter Hamm, dated 15 February 1958, she puts it as follows: "It is a rough climate to be in exile! Believe me, Peter, it demands courage, courage again and again"[2] (Peter, es ist ein hartes Klima, in der Fremde zu sein! Glaub es mir. Es gehört Mut, immer wieder Mut dazu; *Briefe*, 186). When Nelly Sachs nevertheless declares exile a homeland, it is obvious that this cannot be meant in the sense of a return to the house of her childhood. The poet's vision of exile is less concrete; it means a home, not only for herself, but for all restless refugees, a place for the homeless people of the world.[3] The definition of exile as a condition of life depends on a religious attitude, articulated in the texts as a cosmic dimension.

In 1957 Heinrich Ellermann published Nelly Sachs' s volume *Und niemand weiss weiter* (*And No One Knows How to Go On*). This large and heterogeneous volume of poetry was well received and signified a breakthrough for Nelly Sachs into the official literary world of Western Germany. Not only was she elected to membership in several literary academies,[4] she began corresponding with the younger generation of German poets—a fact that meant even more to her than the official honors.[5] In her letters from the years 1957 and 1958 a new approach to the meeting of humantity and nature can be found, which leads to a poetic eruption in the spring of 1958. The poems of this period show a rare homogeneneity in language and image, with themes ranging from specific problems of refugees to universal visions of nature's energy, all of them dealing with the question of humanity and nature as historical and cosmic manifestations:

Redeemed
from sleep
the great darknesses
of the coal forests
will
leap up
shedding
the glittering leaves
of light-years
and reveal their souls—

Naked
worshipper
of lightning
and song of fire
kneeling
thrusting again
with antlers of being-beside-oneself
at the cliffs of beginning
with the wave-mother's
world-encircling music.
(*O the Chimneys*, 185)

(Erlöste/ aus Schlaf/ werden die grossen Dunkelheiten/ der Steinkohlenwälder/ auffahren/ abwerfen/ das glitzernde Laub/ der Lichterjahre/ und ihre Seele aufdecken—/ / Beter/ nackend/ aus Blitzen und Gesang aus Feuer/ kniend/ stossend/ mit Geweihen des Ausser-sich-Seins/ wieder an den Klippen des Anfangs/ bei der Wogenmütter/ Welt einrollender Musik) (*Fahrt ins Staublose*, 326)

Exemplifying "the metamorphoses of the world" the poem focuses upon the conditions of life, not only of human life, but of the life of our planet. The "heaviness" of this life is logically represented by the stone (omitted in the English translation of

"Steinkohlenwälder" as coal forests, line four). The expression *coal forests* of line four contains the transformation of living forests into stone. The dark forests, once captured by sleep and banned to the merely mineral existence of coal, will wake up, the coal will demonstrate the essence of their lives, the very kernel of its own being, which is light. Under the weight of the soil the wood was crystallized, now the trees will return with leaves of living light. These "glittering leaves" carry the memory of the long years of darkness, antithetically named "light-years" as a notion of uncountable numbers of years, a measure generally used by astronomers for cosmic distances of stars. The years of darkness carried an enigmatic meaning, comprised in this contrast. Through the slow growth of coal, darkness has been transformed into light. But even this revelation of light is not the last step in the visionary expression of the inner dynamics of the seemingly dead *materia*. The trees of darkness shed their leaves, like ordinary trees in autumn, thus unveiling their structures. They become "naked," stripped of their flesh, their souls become visible, they "reveal their souls" (line ten).

As the word *soul* signifies, this is no simple restoration of a former situation, it is a return on a spiritual level. Spiritual to Nelly Sachs does not mean fantastic or less realistic, spiritual means the very essence of this special living being. In the poem, "In einer Landschaft aus Musik" (1957) (In a landscape of music, *O the Chimneys*, 107), she uses the fragrance of the sandal tree as a word for the essence of this sort of wood. In our poem the essence of the forests transformed into coal consists of flashes of lightning, accompanied by the roaring of the fire, like a thunderstorm or—in this context more adequately—like a volcanic eruption. The expression *leap up* in line six of the poem has already signalled the brisk and powerful upward movement, caused by the enormous forces concentrated in the depths of the coal forests. The German word here used for essence is *Seele*. The translators put it in the plural: "souls". This may be grammatically correct, but it transforms the meaning of "Seele" from core of existence into some sort of beings like dryads (wood nymphs) and complicates the understanding of the next verse-group.

The soul, which is the dynamic essence of the coal, is portrayed in personal terms of praying, kneeling, thrusting in ecstasy at the representative of divine creation, "the cliffs of beginning" (line eighteen). This second verse-group might seem like a description of some sort of Pentecostal service, the worshipper being-beside-himself (line seventeen), thus gaining the power to break open the divine hiding place, accompanied by the worldwide music of the sea, "the wave-mother's world-encircling music" (lines nineteen to twenty). This cosmic service is opened by the light, accompanied by the fire in a meeting with the stones of the cliffs and the waters of the sea: the four elements of the mystic concentrated in one great effort to restore an open access to the sphere of the creator or the "beginning" (line eighteen).[6]

The hardest, the most inanimate of the elements, the stone has set free its soul, which appears to be ether—or light—and fire, the nearest to God, the most spiritual of the four elements, fire being emblematic of the Holy Ghost. So this service appears as a great reunion of the elements of the visible world, signalling the possibility of a new beginning out of the waters of chaos.

Here the poem sets an extraordinary and bold contrast to the biblical tradition. According to the first chapter of Genesis, God "in the beginning created the heavens and the earth. And the earth was without form, and void; and darkness was upon the face of the deep. And the Spirit of God moved upon the face of the waters. And God said, 'Let there be light'" (King James version). The poem's notion of "the cliffs of beginning" (line eighteen) alludes to the biblical myth of creation, but the creative power of this first beginning seems to be petrified. Consequently the process of a new creation is not described as a manifestation of the almighty father-word, but as an act of the mothers.[7]

Instead of the translators' "encircling" in the last line of the poem, the orginal German text uses the word *einrollend*. That means clearly that the waves roll "the world" like a stone or like a piece of amber up onto the beach. "Einrollen" in German is also used for putting a stone into play again, or for rolling the puck in ice hockey back again onto the playing surface. This would be an adequate picture for an outworn world, given a new chance to take part in the play of life. The notion of "wave-mothers" is associated with mothers giving birth, so the picture would be that of a mother rolling her baby up into the light of the world, giving the child a possibility of living. The "world" receives a new chance for life, but—it may be assumed—life in a new sense.

This new sense of life is expressed as "music." In her previous volume of poetry, Nelly Sachs had used the picture of "the stone dancing / changes its dust to music" (*O the Chimneys*, 111) (und der Stein seinen Staub/ tanzend in Musik verwandelt; *Fahrt ins Staublose* 181) and contained in it her longing for a new life, where the hard and heavy material of the world would be changed into mere essence. At other times the poet would express her longing as a vision of a new language, mute, with no need for words. This central poetological concern of hers was signalled earlier in our poem by the wordless prayers and songs of fire, a sort of nature's own language, unafflicted by the words of humans.[8] Whereas the language of nature certainly belongs to this material life, music will be the language of an essentially new life. The poem "Redeemed from Sleep" (Erlöste aus Schlaf) offers an insight into the implications of "the metamorphosis of the world," the transition—through an enormous effort of the dynamics of living nature: ether, fire, stone, and water—into a new beginning. This is the never-ceasing movement, which Nelly Sachs in the epigraph of the volume *Flucht und Verwandlung* (Flight and Metamorphosis) chooses as her "homeland."

The poem under discussion evokes a cosmic nature without animals or human beings; earth as a "star" left alone to redeem itself. The "song" (line fourteen) and the "music" (line twenty) of elementary nature are pre- and post-language phenomena and do not implicate any creative or restorative word. Only the poet witnesses the transition of nature into a new status. She is not present as an "I" in the poem, invisibly she lends words to a report about a waste planet caught in a changing process of nonhuman dimensions. How can she elect this landscape to be her "homeland?" In the epigraph the poet spoke for herself when she said: "I hold instead of a homeland / the metamorphoses of the world." In the following poem she choses a figure to represent the artist:

Dancer
like a bride
you conceive
from blind space
the sprouting longing
of distant days of creation—

With the streets of your body's music
you feed upon the air
there
where the globe of earth
seeks new access
to birth.

Through
night-lava
like
eyelids opening gently
the first cry of the creative volcano
blinks.

In the branches of your limbs
the premonitions
build their twittering nests.

Like a milkmaid
at dusk
your fingertips pull
at the hidden sources

of light
until you, pierced by the
torment of evening,
surrender your eyes
to the moon for her vigil.

Dancer
woman in childbirth
you alone
carry on the hidden navel-string
of your body
the identical god-given jewels
of death and birth.
(*O the Chimneys*, 147)

(Tänzerin/ bräutlich/ aus Blindenraum/ empfängst du/ ferner Schöpfungstage,/ spriessende Sehnsucht—// Mit deines Leibes Musikstrassen/ weidest du die Luft ab/ dort/ wo der Erdball/ neuen Eingang sucht/ zur Geburt.// Durch Nachtlava/ wie leise sich lösende/ Augenlider/ blinzelt der Schöpfungsvulkane/ Erstlingsschrei.// Im Gezweige deiner Glieder/ bauen die Ahnungen/ ihre zwitschernden Nester.// Wie eine Melkerin/ in der Dämmerung/ ziehen deine Fingerspitzen/ an den verborgenen Quellen/ des Lichtes/ bis du durchstochen von der/ Marter des Abends/ dem Mond deine Augen/ zur Nachtwache auslieferst.// Tänzerin/ kreissende Wöchnerin/ du allein/ trägst an verborgerner Nabelschnur/ an deinem Leib/ den Gott vererbten Zwillingsschmuck/ von Tod und Geburt) (*Fahrt ins Staublose*, 263–264)

The dancer had always been the poet's favorite artist. Not only biographically, but especially in her literary works dancing represents the highest form of artistic life.[9] The dancer stands for the highest spirituality, simply because, as it is expressed in our poem, in her body music has become flesh (line seven) and the radiance of a spiritual dimension becomes visible. Her artistic work involves music, which is the wordless language of the poet's vision.

With thirty-seven lines this relatively long poem describes a progress through time. The situation at the end is different from the situation at the beginning. The dancer of the first stanza is a bride. She does not merely resemble a bride—as one might presume from the second line, "like a bride"—she is posed in the situation of a bride, the "blind space" being her bridegroom, from whom she conceives, as it were, the fruit of their love—"the sprouting longing," words suggesting the growth of the child in the mother's womb. The lines of the last stanza then describe the birth of the divine child ("god-given," line 36), not yet released from the navel cord, therefore still dependent on nourishment from the mother's body. That is to say, this poem expresses the process of pregnancy, something very concrete occurring in the body of the pregnant woman, who must care for adequate food while her womb takes on form around the fetus, all of this signalled in the second stanza by the focus on the feeding of the dancer's body and by naming the roundness of the being-to-be-born. The third stanza anticipates the "gentle opening" of the "eyelids" of the newly born and its first cry. According to the logic of the poem the definition of the dreams and fantasies of the pregnant woman as "premonitions" follows in the fourth stanza, whereas the fifth stanza associates the mother's milk with the pains and sorrows of pregnancy and childbirth. The "torment of evening" points to the moment of fear and pain, which is expressed by the German words "kreissende Wöchnerin" ("woman in childbirth," line 32).

With this idea of a bride, Nelly Sachs has sculptured not only the most realistic, but at the same time the most feminine hero one could imagine, fulfilling her quest through pregnancy and childbirth, whereas the bridegroom remains mysterious. What reminds the reader of a wedding is a sort of distant meeting across the borders of the cosmos with a transcendent dimension without name. The "blind space" can be associated with the utmost darkness behind the light and fire of creation, which is supposed to surround the unseen and unknown God of the *Zohar* (Scholem, 31). This impersonal highest Being is called "blind," it has no qualities, neither the quality of sight, nor its equivalent of giving light. If this association to the highest, hidden Being of the *Zohar* had some relevance for the first stanza, this might be confirmed by the reference in the sixth line to the "distant days of creation." It is as if creation has not yet begun, as if the world were still waiting to appear, which corresponds to the "blindness" of the creative *nihil*, the darkness brooding over the waters of chaos.

Unlike the preceding poem, this one does not mention any waters, although lines ten to eighteen, with the globe seeking "new access to birth" and the picture of a volcanic eruption resembling that of the coal forests' awakening in fire and lightning, thus hammering "at the cliffs of beginning" ("Redeemed" line eighteen), suggest the force of water. Although it focuses on the "first cry" and the "eyelids opening" of the newborn, this second poem deals with a less elementary, more spiritual dimension of redemption. This spiritual dimension is signalled in the verses framing the volcanic eruption. Lines seven to eight present a picture of the dancer feeding "upon the air," as if she were seeking her food on fields close to the borders of transcendence, or at least in the spheres of the cosmos: the German word *Musikstrassen* (music streets) is as an analogy to *Sternenstrassen* (star streets). Like the poet seeking the point of revelation, the possibility of epiphany, with the words of the language her alter ego uses the wordless music in her quest for a new beginning. The "twittering nests" of line 21 correspond to "music." Here the "music of" her "body" has already generated nests full of young birds, lending music a material existence, all of it a picture used for the vision of a new sort of life as formulated in the word *premonitions* (Ahnungen) (line 20). So these framing lines formally reproduce the impression of the pregnant dancer's body, surrounding the "globe of earth" as if it were a fetus in growth, at the same time maintaining the spirituality of the drama.

The fifth stanza or verse-group gives the impression of its being too much or even superfluous. If it were omitted, the poem would present a beautiful composition, beginning and ending with the dancer, in the first stanza as a bride, in the last one as a woman in childbirth. Then as a second circle the lines 7–8 and 19–21 mentioned above focus on the body of the dancer framing the new earth seeking birth. The fifth stanza does not fit into this structure. What then is its function? At first it might be seen simply as a necessary delay of the birth, designating the long months of pregnancy, containing a description of the stress of the situation, the never-ceasing attention of the pregnant woman ending with the sacrifice of her intent eyes.

Indeed, this is no ordinary pregnancy. The dancer carries the conditions of a new cosmic life "on the hidden navel-string" (line 34) of her body. Presenting an unmistakable feature of this exceptional task, the fifth stanza pictures her as a cosmic milkmaid, who spreads the light from hidden sources over the earth, like streams of milk, until nightfall. She goes out in the morning like the sun of Psalm 19, who does not only make it possible to see but from whom nothing on earth can hide. Giving light and looking are undivided components of this picture. This is the background for the last lines of this group, lines 29–30, where the dancer surrenders her eyes to the moon to shine and to watch. The allusion to the Bible is not fortuitous. The dancer of this poem is a hero entrusted with a task in our tradition otherwise left to Christ. The words used for her quest remind us of the passion of Christ, who surrendered during the vigil on the Mount of Olives, who was tormented, whose side was pierced open, all this in accordance with his task of redemption. This equivalent explains the dancer's access to the "hidden sources of"—divine or creative—"light" (lines 25–26). In the text of Psalm 19 the sun is compared with a bridegroom, appearing from his dwelling in the morning. It might be assumed that this picture inspired Nelly Sachs to display her own dancer-hero in the position of a bride—once more the poet's choice of a female protagonist is emphasized.

Nelly Sachs had been brought up "in a good Christian family," as she is said to have occasionally expressed it.[10] Thus, references to Christ or to the Bible as a whole are not unexpected. She had to learn how to be a Jew. It became a task of her whole life to be able to stand the dichotomy of German and Jewish. The Nazi propaganda against those Germans now classified as Jewish kindled latent antisemitism and demanded ethnic cleansing actions against these "intruders" among the Germans. Through oral presentations, presentations in print, in cartoons and in films, in which Jews were shown as rats and vermin, violent fellow travellers were agitated to attack their Jewish fellow citizens. From this the later officially conducted genocide developed. "To say yes to being Jewish" ("Ja-Sagen zum Judentum;" Weltsch) was not easy, but accepting a Jewish identity was the only means of resistance against lingering death. However, Nelly Sachs did not succeed in forging a connection to a genuine Jewish tradition in the face of imminent danger (Dinesen, "Suche," 1).

But having been forced to flee by the Nazis, she sought, in the years of exile, for elements of Jewish tradition that could both correlate with the faith she had been brought up with and further her artistic creativity. So she was happy to find the picturesque cosmos of Hasidic myths through Martin Buber[11]—the same exotic world of eastern Jewry which fascinated Chagall—and, in addition to these naive legends, the mystical theology of the Spanish Kabbalah of the *Zohar*.[12] Because Nelly Sachs discovered this literary statement of Jewish mysticism during the years preceding this poem, we would do well to look at its bridal dancer-hero as a modification of the Shekinah. To the Kabbalists the utmost cause of all being, the *en-sof*, has no qualities and does not communicate; this God is hidden and unknown, but the dark place of His is surrounded by a radiance, from which rays of light emanate through different levels, until they reach the virginal womb of the Shekinah like a seed, and creation takes place. Therefore Shekinah often appears as a bride, who represents the female creative power of the hidden, unknown God. At the same time the divine radiance is filtered through her, in a way that makes the light tolerable and visible to humanity. The milkmaid in this poem could be interpreted as a symbol of this idea.

During the long history of the idea of Shekinah, at some times a "negative" side of the femaleness of the Shekinah was emphasized. As a merely receptive part of divinity she was then described as a wasteland, a well dependent on the waters of springs, or, purely, as a reflection of light, that is to say as a moon (Scholem, 171). This moon-picture may have inspired Nelly Sachs to the picture of the dancer in the fifth stanza rendering her eyes to the moon, although the feminine I of the poem functions as the only active part in the events, and the femaleness has no negative aspects here.

As a part of divinity, Shekinah is in exile, caught and hidden in every bit of the living world. In every human being, in every animal, tree, even every stone and raindrop, sparkles of divinity are enclosed. This imprisoned divine fire is longing for a reunion with the creator. Shekinah—as the personification of this longing for fulfillment—resembles a bride longing for her bridegroom. This longing of Shekinah is no vegetating passivity, it is a dynamic passion, which will some day break open the doors of Heaven. The "dust-crowned Shekinah," only once mentioned in a poem of Nelly Sachs, "Immer hinter den Rändern der Welt" (For ever beyond the bounds of the world; *Fahrt ins Staublose* 194–195), is in exile, separated from her origin, and she functions at times as a picture of a world alien to the divine sphere, but with a memory of and a longing for reunion with this same divinity; this reunion would, according to the poet's belief, be like a redemption. The creative power of femininity in her dancer has a quest to embark on and complete, with consequence for the living world as well as for the hidden God, because they would both be freed.

Consequently it may be presumed that this fifth stanza is necessary, for the poet as well as for her reader, to make quite clear the unique position of the dancer-hero of this poem and to make possible the transition to the concluding last stanza. As the birth of a new earth is not accomplished, the poem has an open ending. The dancer remains in the status of a "woman in childbirth" carrying not one child but two, who are still dependent on the nourishment of her body. The German word "Zwillingsschmuck," in the English translation "identical jewels," includes the notion of "twins," which conveys the complementary duplicity "of death and birth." This "jewel" rendered to the dancer by God ("god-given") or in reverse, to God by the dancer—the German expression *Gott vererbt* at least allowing both interpretations—does not designate the longed-for new beginning, but the return of metamorphoses, death and birth passed on through new generations of cosmic life.

The poem did not lead to a transcendent homeland, as one might expect, considering the unmistakable religious note of its language and its pictures. On the contrary, it is an apotheosis of a human being, which is entrusted with the task of holding alive the never-ceasing movement of the metamorphoses of the world, and who fits totally into this unsteady homeland of the cosmos through the movements of her dance. Even more: she seems to be the new redeemer of a world that cannot reach, with its own strength, the longed-for "new access to birth," a new and better beginning. The last and most dangerous task of this female redeemer—only suggested through the work of the milkmaid and the notion of the "god-given jewels" (line 36)—is to open the eyes of divine nothingness, to let the creative light of a divine dimension fall upon the longing creature, thus annihilating the painful border between cosmos and transcendence.

As suggested at the beginning of the interpretation of this last poem, I understand the dancer as representing the poet, as an ideal of her own. This interpretation elaborates the statement of Nelly Sachs, quoted at the beginning of this chapter.

Fleeing,
what a great reception
on the way—

Wrapped
in the wind's shawl
feet in the prayer of sand
which can never say amen
compelled
from fin to wing
and further—

The sick butterfly
will soon learn again of the sea—
This stone
with the fly's inscription
gave itself into my hand—
I hold instead of a homeland
the metamorphoses of the world—
(O the Chimneys,145)

(In der Flucht/ welch grosser Empfang/ unterwegs—// Eingehüllt/ in der Winde Tuch/ Füsse im Gebet des Sandes/ der niemals Amen sagen kann/ denn er muss/ von der Flosse in den Flügel/ und weiter—// Der kranke Schmetterling/ weiss bald wieder vom Meer—// Dieser Stein/ mit der Inschrift der Fliege/ hat sich mir in die Hand gegeben—// An Stelle von Heimat/ halte ich die Verwandlungen der Welt—) (*Fahrt ins Staublose*, 262)

As if it summarized the previous texts, this central poem of the volume *Flight and Metamorphosis* speaks of the dynamic flight of the elements through metamorphoses, and of a stone "with the fly's inscription." This reminds us of the forests turned into stone in the first poem. The writing poet—like the dancer of the second poem, but with the means of poetry—has been entrusted with the task of releasing the sleeping creature.

The poems here interpreted give examples of and demonstrate the complex reaction of the poet to the National Socialist terror. On the level of language she reacted to the perversion of the German language with an untainted genuine form of expression, which she used in memory of and in mourning for the victims during her exile years. This poetic language was applied with ever-increasing intensity as a means of recognition of basic human and cosmic conditions of life. She considered this task to be one imposed on her by nature, as can be seen in the words about the stone placed in the hand of the speaker in the last poem.

The National Socialist ideology usurped the place of a religion through the liturgy of mass demonstrations and the intoxication of the "Führer" cult, through the idea of a thousand-year Aryan Reich free of Jews. It is amazing how Nelly Sachs took on the term *Jewish*, which had been used as an insulting and threatening term, as a challenge to become aquainted with the Jewish tradition, and to convert the suffering she had to endure in exile into a positive metaphor. Through the Old Testament and the Christian tradition she came into contact with late Jewish mysticism of the Kabbala Chassidism where she discovered images and ideas for a search for God of a different kind. Leaving the empty pseudo-religion of the Third Reich far behind her, she surmounted all known religious traditions with her cosmic mysticism. The reversal of the relationship of God and world is particularly striking: Nelly Sachs seeks energies of redemption in human beings and in the cosmos. Her poetic vision of a cosmos that is progressing toward a divine sphere through ever-new metamorphoses does not fit into any orthodoxy.

The distinctly feminine dimension in the work of Nelly Sachs is seen as a positive element in the poems here interpreted. Creative and redeeming qualities emanate from a maternal element that is equally indebted to nature and spirit. Only the similarity between the suffering of the dancer and the passion of Christ points toward the tendency of the poet to equate the feminine with suffering.

Nelly Sachs confronts herself and her readers with historical reality, without, however, interpreting it politically. Before the backdrop of her religious cognitive horizon the National Socialist regime appears as the incarnation of evil per se. Against such evil she sets a vision of her own creation, one based albeit on a traditional understanding of the creative possibilities of poetic language. For her, reverting to a biblically derived mysticism of the word means a revelation of her own capabilities, and entails a responsibility for and an emphasis upon ensuring the truth-bearing function of the word. Focusing so strongly on this aspect of the word, she is all the more able to recognize the source of the historical form of inhumanity in the perversion of language. With the language of her new poetry, the language of integrity, she engages in resistance against the fateful misuse of words. This remythologizing of the word in the work of Nelly Sachs functions as a counterbalance to dehumanized political fanaticism.

Notes

1. Unpublished letter to Otto Scheurmann, Berlin, 3 March 1954.
2. My translation.

3. A similar idea can be found in Jean Améry, *Jenseits von Schuld und Sühne. Bewältigungsversuche eines Überwältigten* (Stuttgart: Klett-Cotta, 1977), which states the impossibility for the persecuted Jew to find a basis anywhere but in the acceptance of his situation as a foreigner (149).

4. Member of the "Deutsche Akademie für Sprache und Dichtung in Darmstadt" (1957), of the "Freie Akademie der Künste", Hamburg (1961), of the "Bayrische Akademie der schönen Künste," München (1963).

5. 1957: Alfred Andersch, Ingeborg Bachmann, Elisabeth Borchers, Paul Celan, Peter Hamm; 1958: Hans Magnus Enzensberger, Hans Rudolf Hilty; 1959: Rudolf Peyer, Werner Reinert; 1960: Hilde Domin.

6. It is a characteristic feature of Nelly Sachs's poems to include the whole of existence by enumerating the four elements, e.g., the early poem "Die Kerze" (*Fahrt ins Staublose, 23*) (The candle), in which ether, fire, water, and dust, summarized as "the elements," form the enigma of the bridegroom.

7. In the German text "Wogenmütter" is plural: wave-mothers.

8. Such a poetics of falling silent is defined by Dorothee Ostmeier in her work on the scenic literary works, *Sprache des Dramas—Drama der Sprache. Zur Poetik der Nelly Sachs* (*Language of Drama, Drama of Language. On the Poetics of Nelly Sachs*), as part of her interpretation of the linguistic realization of the dramas as an expression of being exiled from the German, and in the final analysis, from any language; this is not only expressed in silent gestures, but also thematically (3).

9. So we have to understand the poem "Die Tänzerin. D.H." (*Fahrt ins Staublose*, 37) as an epitaph for Dora Horwitz, an early friend of hers. Although Dora Horwitz was a painter in her real life, the text honors her by portraying her as dancer.

10. According to Dorothee Zimmermann.

11. Among the books of the Nelly-Sachs-archive, Stockholm: *Die Erzählungen der Chassidim* (Zürich: Manesse, 1949, with a dedication from Oktober 1959), *Die Geschichten des Rabbi Nachman, ihm nacherzählt von Martin Buber* (Frankfurt am Main: Fischer Bücherei, 1955), *Die Legende des Baalschem* (Zürich: Manesse, 1955). According to her own testimony and that of Anneliese Neff, an early friend of hers, these relatively late copies were preceded by the reading of the legends in Berlin in the 1930s.

12. Gershom Scholem, *Die Geheimnisse der Schöpfung. Ein Kapitel aus dem Sohar* (Berlin: Schocken Verlag, 1935), in the archive shows numerous marks and comments in Nelly Sachs's handwriting.

Bibliography

Bower, Kathrin Maria. "In the Name of the M(Other? Articulation of Memory in the Post-Holocaust Poetry of Nelly Sachs and Rose Ausländer." Diss. U. of Michigan, Ann Arbor, 1995.

Cassagnau, Lauren. "Utopie et dialogue dans la poésie de Nelly Sachs." Contacts: Sér.3, Études et document.24. Frankfurt am Main/Bern/New York: Peter Lang, 1993.

Dinesen, Ruth. "Nelly Sachs (1891-1970): Gedichte aus dem Irrenhaus." In *Wahnsinns-Frauen* (sic) 2. Ed. Sybille Duda and Luise F. Pusch. Frankfurt am Main: Suhrkamp, 1996, 223–54.

———. "Die Suche nach Identität—Das Jüdische bei Nelly Sachs." *Exil* 12 (1992): 19–29.

———. *Nelly Sachs. Eine Biographie.* Frankfurt am Main: Suhrkamp, 1992.

———. *Briefe der Nelly Sachs.* Ed. Ruth Dinesen and Helmut Müssener. Frankfurt am Main: Suhrkamp, 1984.

Fleischer, Burga. *Gebärde der Versöhnung: die dramatische Dichtung der Nelly Sachs.* Eitorf: Gata, 1996.

Kessler, Michael, and Jürgen Wertheimer, ed.s *Nelly Sachs: Neue Interpretationen.* Staufenburg—Colloquium 30. Tübingen: Stauffenburg Verlag, 1994.

Ostmeier, Dorothee. *Sprache des Dramas—Drama der Sprache. Zur Poetik der Nelly Sachs.* Tübingen: Niemeyer, 1997.

Rudnick, Ursula. *Post-Shoa Religious Metaphors: the Image of God in the Poetry of Nelly Sachs.* Frankfurt am Main/Bern/New York: Peter Lang, 1995.

Sachs, Nelly. *Fahrt ins Staublose. Die Gedichte der Nelly Sachs.* Frankfurt am Main: Suhrkamp, 1961.

———. *Flucht und Verwandlung.* Stuttgart: Deutsche Verlags-Anstalt, 1959.

———. "Leben unter Bedrohung." In Walter A. Berendsohn. *Nelly Sachs. Einführung in das Werk der Dichterin jüdischen Schicksals.* Darmstadt: Agora, 1974, 9–12.

———. *O The Chimneys. Selected Poems, Including the Verse Play, Eli.* Trans. Michael Hamburger, Christopher Holme, Ruth and Matthew Mead, and Michael Roloff. New York: Farrar, Straus and Giroux, 1967.

———. *Und niemand weiss weiter.* Hamburg and München: Heinrich Ellermann, 1957.

Scholem, Gershom. *Von der mystischen Gestalt der Gottheit. Studien zu Grundbegriffen der Kabbala.* Frankfurt am Main: suhrkamp taschenbuch wissenschaft 209, 1977.

Weltsch, Robert. *Ja-Sagen zum Judentum. Eine Aufsatzreihe der "Jüdischen Rundschau" zur Lage der deutschen Juden.* Berlin: Verlag der "Jüdischen Rundschau," 1933.

Wiedemann, Barbara. "Stumme Schreie. Zu einem Gedicht von Nelly Sachs." In *Hermeneutik. Literarische und geisteswissenschaftliche Beiträge zu Ehren von Peter Horst Neumann.* Ed. Holger Helbig, Bettina Knauer, and Gunnar Och. Berlin: Königshausen & Neumann, 1997.

Part IV

Exile and the Holocaust

9

Echoes of Exile: The Literary Response to the Exiles by American Women Writers

Guy Stern

I am not an American soldier walking through Colorado canyons
Towards a glass of Scotch and the tune I want in the jukebox, and the woman
I want in my arms.
I am one of an army of lost men who follow a point of the compass
In common. We will not be single, undetermined men walking
alone again.
Until our feet are breaking through the snows of home.

—Kay Boyle, *American Citizen, Naturalized in Leadville, Colorado*

With the National Socialists' accession to power in 1933 and their invasion of neighboring countries, beginning in 1939, an exodus of writers, intellectuals, and artists took place that was unprecedented in modern history. Many of these refugees from Germany, Austria, Poland, Czechoslovakia, and Hungary found asylum in the United States. " By 30 June 1944, the staggering number of 279,649 persons from the Third Reich had found either temporary or permanent refuge in America. . . " (Pfanner, 14).

Liberal American intellectuals, and particularly the women among them, were among the strongest supporters of the new arrivals. Dorothy Thompson, then one of America's most prominent journalists, was one of the first to expose Nazi brutality, and at the 1939 meeting of the International PEN Club in New York, she coupled a denunciation of Fascism with a warm greeting to the new arrivals.[1] Agnes B. Meyer, another well-known American journalist and the wife of the publisher of the *Washington Post*, was instrumental in bringing Thomas Mann to the United States and remained his most loyal American supporter.[2] Eva Gottbeck, translator (and wife of the composer Marc Blitzstein), "deserves credit as an important [American] translator and early proponent of Brecht's works" (Lyon, 37).

The presence of the exiles in the United States was similarly registered and frequently extolled by America's creative writers. To be sure, the initial echoes of exile in American literature were faint, audible at first only in the writing of American expatriates who had heard the first claps of the gathering thunderstorm. They could be heard in the works of Kay Boyle and Christopher Isherwood, in the words of such occasional visitors to Europe as Lillian Hellman and Ben Hecht, and in those of active supporters of the refugees. They reverberated in the fictionalized or dramatized accounts of the rise of National Socialism in which the exiles, escaping or just escaped, inevitably formed part of the *dramatis personae*.

But no matter what the author's relationship with the new outcasts from Germany and Austria may have been, he or she tended to allot to them one of three archetypal structural roles, that of victim, hero, or warner. And the writers' intentions were clear and unambiguous: to alert an indifferent America to the suffering or heroism, to the sacrifices or leadership of the exiles. Indeed, the authors wanted to awaken the democratic world to the dangers posed by a murderous enemy and, frequently, to the need to strike him down before he could devour the New World. The exiles, often ennobled beyond credibility, were meant to serve as America's role models, while the United States inched its way, under the prodding of Franklin Roosevelt, from neutrality to intervention.

It was inevitable that such texts would be illustrative, exemplary, in the sense that Cervantes labelled his stories *novellas ejemplares* and that, in consequence, such texts would bear a great deal of similarity to one another. In the years following World War II, by way of contrast, the literary functions assigned to the exile figures would become infinitely more varied and complex. Certainly texts of disparate quality appeared in the post–World War II period, but the authors' ambition, if not always realized, was "to write literature." But in those earlier years the overriding intent had been didactic, if not polemical. Although not inevitable, the result was to have the aesthetic or "entertainment" aspects of a work serve as a sometimes roughly running vehicle for the message. Even well-established writers occasionally subordinated aesthetics to ethics.

It is not surprising that numerous works, serving a once topical cause, would prove to be ephemeral. It appears far more surprising that so many proved to be enduring. And it should be noted that many of these early works emanated from women writers such as Kay Boyle, Lillian Hellman, and Edna St. Vincent Millay, a group that at that time formed a clear minority on the American Parnassus. They seized upon the subject from the very first. From a feminist perspective it is not difficult to see why this should be so. Far from enjoying total acceptance and often considered and/or considering themselves as outsiders, American women writers before mid-century could empathize with pariah groups, both male and female, and they found in the exiles—in their quandaries and efforts at self-assertion in times of adversity—a ready symbol for their own relegation and their need to confront and conquer it. These motivations emerge clearly from Ellin Mackay Berlin's novel, *Land I Have Chosen* (1944), its woman protagonist a characteristic prototype of the persecuted exile.[3]

Berlin (1903–1988) had to muster considerable self-assertiveness against a dominating father who, a scion of society, tried every conceivable means to prevent her marriage to the Russian-Jewish immigrant Irving Berlin and would then disinherit her after her elopement. But another very personal psychological incentive lifted her from writing magazine pieces for *Variety* and *The New Yorker* to composing a powerful anti-Nazi novel, featuring an exile heroine, and to take to the streets and airways to propagate her convictions. In 1940, when she first conceived of her novel (Bergreen, 382), she and her husband—as their daughter would later chronicle—were driven by the fear that Hitler could win the war and coerce the United States into following his racist policies, with disastrous results for their "half-Jewish" children (Barrett, 186). This presentiment caused her to go on the stump against U.S. isolationism, to join the Committee to Defend America by Aiding the Allies, and to denounce Anne Morrow Lindbergh for having been deceived by Nazi propaganda: "The Nazis have disguised old-fashioned tyranny to look like something new. They have touched the heart of a poet like Mrs. Lindbergh" (Bergen, 384). Her courage becomes all the more remarkable as we learn that each public speech made her physically ill (Barrett, 189).

When Berlin added the writing of fiction to her activism, she chose the theater as one of her settings and an actress as her heroine. It was a world she had come to know intimately through her husband's unceasing work for stage and film.

Berlin portrays a German actress who rejects the Nazi ideology and decides to stay in the United States during a guest tour and divorces her husband, who had become a Nazi sympathizer. But she thereby endangers her "non-Aryan" mother, left behind in Germany. A German agent, active in New York, now begins an elaborate game of psychological warfare in order to extort a large sum of money from her which her mother had been able to deposit in New York. The Nazi agent succeeds, of course, and worse still, the German government knows that the mother, deprived of many essentials, is close to death. Berlin manages to depict physical and psychological maltreatment to equal effect. The novel sold nearly a half-million copies and the movie option (never exercised) sold for a record sum of $150,000.

In those early years, specifically the years before and during World War II, every genre of literature that appeared promising in dramatizing the fate of the millions of persecuted and in celebrating the minimal victory gained by the few exiles who managed to escape was marshalled against the Nazi horror. Even the then relatively new form of the radio play was harnessed to that purpose because it seemed best suited to bestir the American public. But no matter what the genre, the early heroizing of the exiles took two essential forms: leading German refugee personalities were invoked and lifted onto lofty pedestals, and fictional characters were created to perform valorous deeds. Thomas Mann and Albert Einstein, for example, appear in novels, plays, and poems long before they would reappear in fictional guises after the war. One of the women writers, Phyllis Bottome (pseud. for Forbes-Dennis, 1884–1963), reached for a more subtle approach. In her best-selling novel *The Mortal Storm* (1937), she called attention to the fact that one of her protagonists, Dr. Johann Roth, was ideologically fashioned after the psychiatrist Alfred Adler by dedicating the work to his memory and by her admitting in her autobiography that his death spurred her toward completing the novel (*The Goal*, 288). As a future biographer of the psychiatrist, she endowed Dr. Roth with the humanistic and humanitarian qualities of her model. Even when facing certain death in a concentration camp, he counsels his daughter: "I had always the desire to find all mankind my brothers. . . ."[4]

Phyllis Bottome was, to be sure, a less likely candidate for fighting Hitler by word and deed than Ellin Berlin. She felt no personal threat. Yet she and her husband returned to England from the safety of America during the height of the Battle of Britain as an affirmation of loyalty. The autobiography of her early years (up to age eighteen), entitled *Search for a Soul*, provides clues, however, about her abhorrence of injustice and tyranny.

Daughter of a clergyman—gentrified despite his being born in America—she was shaped by both letters and life. Her autobiography abounds with fictional and real victimized characters with which she identifies: Dickens's Little Nell, Harriet Beecher Stowe's slaves, Captain Dreyfus during the time of his trial, and Oskar Wilde during his imprisonment . Witnessing the plight of a poor New York family, turned away by rich Dutch neighbors after their hut had burned down, appears to have left a permanent mark on her (Bottome, *Search*, 104–105). Hence it seems only logical that she would abhor the Nazis and preface her autobiography with a ringing declaration of freedom: "A tyrant is incapable of controlling his own heart and mind. A coward has chosen to be the prey of tyrants so that he may escape the duties and obligations of freedom" (Bottome, *Search*, xii).

Her indictment of Nazism became even stronger as the war progressed. "Hitler's long tireless shadow pursued us. We were miserably anxious about the friends whom we had left behind us in Munich" (*The Goal*, 207). In her novel *Survival* she again chooses an exile, this time a "half-Jewish" psychoanalyst from Austria, as protagonist and narrator. But in telling of his mental travails before and after his escape to England and his rehabilitation through the ministrations of the British woman he loves, she foregoes the subtleties of *The Mortal Storm*. With some justification most reviewers, while conceding her undiminished narrative skills, faulted her numerous references to Adler and her didactic editorializing (e.g., Ulrich, 19). Toward the end of the novel Rudi, the Austrian Jew, intermingles a declaration of love with an essayistic credo:

> As I see it, we have to get rid of this top-dog world out of which murder springs! Russians, Americans, Chinese, we ourselves! We must prove ourselves the spiritual enemies of the Nazis. This sense of superiority is the dead tissue of the cancer cell that must be cut away from us, before victory comes, or else a new cancer will form itself. When we are fighting side by side as brothers, to win a world that belongs equally to all of us—then we shall win the war; if enough of us do not want this new world—then we shall lose the war and with it human brotherhood. (Bottome, *Survival*, 338)

Here, too, an understandable moral fervor by a thoroughly decent writer would come at the expense of aesthetic finesse.

The fictionalized heroic exiles of that early period tend to resemble each other. The prefatory poem to this chapter celebrates such a heroic exile, modelled on Kay Boyle's third husband.[5] But she, like several other American authors, at first stopped short of heroization; a deliberate eschewal of any ties to the hated dictators or their puppets seemed to suffice before America's entry into the war. In one of her novels, *Primer for Combat* (1942),[6] written in the form of a diary, the American heroine-diarist, living with her husband in occupied France, has fallen in love with a maimed ski instructor from Austria. But she breaks off their affair when he reveals his narcissistic and spineless nature by making his accommodation to the Petain government. Her new ideal becomes another Austrian, hitherto a minor character, who refuses to return to Austria (222) but also rejects the alternative of staying in occupied France. In a scene borrowed from the rescue of her future husband—the whole novel has been called a "roman à clef" (Mellen, 262)—she helps him to escape to Switzerland (361). The title *Primer for Combat* suggests that he will continue to fight fascism.

Beyond its didactic message Boyle's narrative strategy—switching protagonists in midstream—rings in a highly useful variant on structuralist archetypes.[7] The "hero" is reduced to insignificance; his "supporter" ultimately is elevated to his role. A hero who caves in under adversity must be replaced; the structure reinforces that message.

It may well be that the autobiographical elements lend additional strength to the story; with complete justice Joan Mellen has subtitled her Boyle biography *Author of Herself.* Similarly, Boyle attributes the roots of her rebellious, often tempestuous life to the history of her ancestors. Their example propelled her from an average Midwestern background to the battles against fascism, against discrimination in the United States, the Vietnam War, and in her last years, to the espousal of Amnesty International. In her essay "Farewell to Europe" (*Words That Must Somehow Be Said*, 93–95), she speaks of an ancestor, a general in Washington's army, an aunt "the official cartoonist of the National Woman's Party and a staunch fighter for the franchise," and a mother who supported the protesters of "the Children's Crusade":

> In the years I lived abroad my grandmother, my mother, and the others were somehow there with me in explanation and justification of the things I said about America. They were present when Europe looked to us for liberation from the Nazi armies, and they were there when that liberation came. They went with me, these ardent believers in the spirit of free inquiry, into the political prisons of Franco's Spain and into the processing centers of Western Germany, where refugees from the East waited for asylum. Indeed, it would perhaps be more accurate to say that I went to these places because my forebears were with me and that it was they who led me there. (*Words*, 95)

Thus, her own life fell in step with that of her ancestors. She was an expatriate in France, Austria, and postwar West Germany. It was a wise choice that Marc Robinson included her in his anthology *Altogether Elsewhere: Writers on Exile*. Her prose piece "Frankfurt in Our Blood," half fiction, half reportage, is one of the most moving pieces of the return of an elderly refugee woman to her beloved and dreaded hometown (Robinson, 313–318). Briefly deceived by the false promises of the Nazis in the early thirties, Boyle, in short order, became their implacable enemy. "From the beginning of her literary career, she has used her voice to make known the cries of the socially, emotionally and politically voiceless" (Bell, xiii).

The prototypical hagiography of an exile in these prewar and wartime texts occurs in the drama *Watch on the Rhine* (1942), by Lillian Hellman (1905–1984).[8] The play's unswerving commitment to the overthrow of fascism was of course predicated on Hellman's entire political past, but her unmistakable admiration for the German resistance fighters may stem from her observations during the Spanish Civil War and other encounters during her European travels.[9] Hence, she casts a German underground anti-Nazi, Kurt Müller, as her hero. Married to an American woman, he arrives with her and their children in the house of his mother-in-law. The dialogue between the Americans and the Germans reveals the United States' naiveté in regards to the dangers of Fascism. "Are you a radical?" his mother-in-law asks Kurt, the resistance fighter, shortly after his arrival (Hellman, *Four Plays*, 276). In the end, Kurt, having killed a would-be informer, returns to his resistance work in Germany. But even without this somewhat melodramatic motivation it is clear that Müller can do no less than continue his fight against Fascism despite the promise of a relatively secure life in the haven of a family ready to accept him. But it is Müller's impact on the American family that Hellman wants the American audience to share. "We're shaken out of the magnolias, eh?"—so the hero's mother-in-law summarizes the results of the dramatic events (*Four Plays*, 276). And the moral of *Watch on the Rhine* is unmistakable: Americans must emulate the exemplary exile-hero, at least in spirit.[10]

As noted above Lillian Hellman's "trek to the Rhine" was prompted, as with so many other American writers, by a synthesis of widespread reactions to world events and highly individual motivations. Hellman, the daughter of upper-middle-class Jewish parents, born in New Orleans, rebelled early against racism in the South. Her biographer tells of her pulling her black nursemaid, over her protest, into the front part of a public bus: "[She] professed the politics of the oppressed and was for all sorts of radical and liberal causes. She was for the Spanish loyalists, labor unions, environmentalists, and against Franco, big corporations, the FBI, and Richard Nixon" (Rollyson, 17 and 2).

Her hatred of Hitler was even more vehement. She was among the early warners; her "premature anti-Fascism"—plus her previous leanings toward communism—would later earn her a summons before the House Un-American Activities Committee. She, too, traced the genesis of *Watch on the Rhine* to her experiences during the Spanish Civil War—genuine enough, even if they are (as Martha Gellhorn and others have pointed out)—embroidered and at times inaccurate. In Spain she had met exiles such as Gustav Regler and Otto Simon (a.k.a. Otto Katz) and had come to admire them; in the United States she also encountered refugees, both the idealists and the victims as well as some opportunists. She had been to a Nazi rally in Finland and had watched the ineffectuality of American liberals:

> I had no right, from my safe place, to feel bitter about such people, but I did and, of course, by 1938 I had been through the life and death of my friend Julia, and had been to Spain during the Civil War, and had been moved by men willing to die for what they believed in.
>
> I wanted to write a play about nice, liberal Americans whose lives would be shaken up by Europeans, by a world the new Fascists had won because the old values had long been dead. (*Pentimento*, 488)

Lillian Hellman was, if on a more modest scale, an activist like her hero, Kurt Müller. Her famous story of Julia, the American underground heroine in wartime Austria, was in all likelihood an amalgam of poetry and truth; her own smuggling of funds to the anti-Nazi underground was probably authentic (*Pentimento*, 401–452; Rollyson, 526–528). Hellman was a fundraiser for her causes, participated in anti-Fascist benefits, and gave readings from her works at U.S. Army bases.

Curiously enough the last-named activity does not appear in her autobiographies nor in scholarly accounts of her life and work. Yet she must have repeatedly spoken to U.S. soldiers, as she did toward the end of 1943 at Fort Hamilton, New York, shortly before our departure (i.e., of Military Intelligence Personnel) for England aboard an antiquated Australian steamer, the *Rangitata*. What sticks in my mind is the forcefulness of her reading from dramas-in-progress and political essays and the way she responded to questions. She did not treat them as a quest for knowledge on the part of her soldier-audience, but interpreted them as a rebuttal or challenge. We, on the way to Europe—and therefore a bit deferred to by civilians—were taken aback by her combativeness and frequently caustic replies. But then she had already been to the places for which we were just starting out.

Time and again this literature reflects the ideological struggle between democracy and autocracy by confronting the advocates of these two systems of government. Obviously, exiled characters were not necessary for such a confrontation; occasionally the role of the villain could be assigned to homegrown demagogues. Real-life models were not lacking. More often, however, especially as the war progressed, the fictional voices for fascism were quickly silenced by affirmative, even aggressive defenders of democracy. American playwrights fell into a "pattern of affirmation,"[11] an imaginary overcoming of fascism by adherents of democracy. When exiles were introduced as authorial voices, they served to point out the vulnerability of democracies; they were to draw the parallels between the frailty of the Weimar Republic and the chinks in the armor of other democracies. One of the most eloquent texts was, to be sure, written by a male dramatist, Elmer Rice (1892–1967), but he joins the issue most directly by means of two astute female protagonists. His 1940 saga of the troubled flight of a Pan-Am Clipper from Lisbon to New York, the drama *Flight to the West*, which juxtaposes, in a ship-of-fools fashion, various nationals and representatives for different ideals, also features a German-Jewish exile woman. The following dialogue between her and an American woman summarizes her paradigmatic warning:

> **FRAU ROSENTHAL:** To us, we thought, nothing can happen; like peasants who build their villages on the sides of a volcano, where smoke comes out of the top. Then one day, comes not only smoke, but fire and boiling lava that flows over the houses and burns the sleeping people alive.
>
> **HOPE:** Yes, I know. But I just can't believe it will ever be like that in America.

FRAU ROSENTHAL: Who knows what will be in five years or ten years? Ten years ago in Germany, we laughed at Hitler. We said he is a foolish fellow with a Napoleon complex, that only stupid shopkeepers can take seriously.

HOPE: Well, if a Hitler ever did come to life in America, I'm sure only the worst elements would listen to him.

FRAU ROSENTHAL: It was these elements in Germany that became the storm troopers and made Hitler Chancellor. And then the others followed—the educated and the respectable people, they followed—even the artists! My husband, for years, gave help to young German artists. When they asked for advice or assistance he never refused. But after Hitler, it was different! They denounced him as an enemy of German culture. (Rice, 88)

Frau Rosenthal represents the voice of pessimism in the chorus of the in-flight passengers, but her voice appears to be drowned out, ultimately, by the paean to democracy and to a more roseate future proclaimed by the appropriately named (and pregnant) Hope. But the dark eloquence of Frau Rosenthal's warnings nonetheless marks them as being close to the authorial voice.

The forties were the time for the sounding of a last alert for America and one of America's best-known female poets responded. In 1943, Edna St. Vincent Millay (1892–1950), in the least lyric of her poems, would tell of "The Murder of Lidice" that ended with the Cassandra-like outcry that American towns might very well suffer a similar fate of pillage and selective destruction at the hands of a victorious German army.[12] Millay's clarion call had emerged over time. Her social consciousness had reached its first apogee as a protester against the conviction of Sacco and Vancetti in 1927, when she—with many others—was arrested for demonstrating in front of the State House in Boston. Initially a pacifist, she became an ardent foe of the Axis powers even before World War II, causing her to write propaganda poems under the aegis of the Writers War Board. "The Murder of Lidice" is one of these texts. While it is anything but good poetry, it has the virtue of being good propaganda and a moral response to utter immorality. More often than not, exiles, even when they were only minor characters, would lend authority to such warnings. Whether fictional exile characters or their prototypes, they commanded respect. And when paying them that respect American antifascists, such as America's Pulitzer-Prize winning poet Stephen Vincent Benét, often singled out women. In a preface to a collection of anti-Nazi essays, which included a contribution by Erika Mann, Benét specifically focused on exiles like her as the warning voices needed in America: "Her chief concern seems to be with certain very practical things—the essential defenses of freedom against the forces that would destroy it."[13]

One other typical and possibly final motif appears in prewar and wartime American literature. There are a few texts—unfortunately very few—in which the victimization of the exiles leads to an appeal for their rescue. One of the truly stirring exhortations came from one of the most impressive writers I was privileged to meet. Written in a spirit of protest against the do-nothing attitude of governments, Martha Gellhorn's novel, *A Stricken Field* (1940), on the fate of Czechoslovakia, shows the journalist-heroine befriending a German exile couple in Prague. Gellhorn (1908–) tries to help them by enlisting British, French, and Czech officials in her vain struggle to win a stay of extradition for all refugees.[14] In an afterword to a new edition, Gellhorn discloses that this fictional attempt at intercession was based on her own actions. Quoting from a letter she wrote at that time, she explains what impelled her to this action. "The League High Commissioner for Refugees, one Sir Neill Malcolm, showed up for two days in Prague and didn't see a single refugee but I had seen them, all of them, all over the place and I was sick at heart and very angry" (*A Stricken Field*, 184). In retrospect she concedes, probably thinking of her fictional alter ego as well as of herself, that "[n]ovels can't accomplish anything" (184). But the grudging concession of a reviewer may have come closer to assessing Gellhorn's or her heroine's acts of altruism: "I cannot see that this novel can accomplish anything unless it gives some of us a greater sympathy with the refugees whom we encounter—as who does not these days " (Gellhorn, 312). Greater sympathy, one might answer, could have been a start-up toward a rescue action.[15] In the final assessment of her novel Gellhorn says: "Despite its faults . . . I am proud of it" (Gellhorn, 312).[16] To have written this work in behalf of the exiles, when so many officials and bureaucrats turned their backs on them, entirely justifies her pride.

Most of the texts cited so far, documenting the appearance of exiles in texts during the early years of Nazism, were obviously meant as a form of *littérature engagé*. Nowhere, however, does a purpose emerge as clearly as in a set of radio plays that "were written for and are dedicated to the war effort."[17] They crystallize once more the themes, motifs, and issues of these early echoes of exile. First broadcast over the Blue Network as "The Free World Theater," then anthologized, the series was sent on its way with a preface written by Thomas Mann. He was utterly candid as to its propagandistic purpose:

> Indeed it has come to a point where one uses the word propaganda for the purpose of deprecating ideas which one dislikes. The public utterance of opinions which one does not share one calls propaganda; but one would highly resent having one's own convictions thus described.
>
> Now then the great advantage of this book is that the propaganda which it offers cannot and will not be so described by anyone in a hostile sense. Its propaganda

> is so free of partisanship, offense and challenge, it is so natural and pro-human that hardly anyone will be tempted to utter the disapproving cry: "Propaganda!"
>
> It is good propaganda in so far as it is effective, absorbing and entertaining. And it is good propaganda in so far as it awakes our hearts which are so much inclined to drowse in indifference and summon them to hate evil and to believe in a better world as the fruit of victory, (Mann, ix–x)

Whenever the exiles are mentioned or appear as characters in this series they often gain superhuman dimensions. Thomas Mann emerges as a cultural hero when two GIs, separated by social class, exchange memories of their common home town in Budd Schulberg and Jerome Lawrence's radio play *Tomorrow*. One GI muses: "When you figure a guy like that was run out of Germany, it kind of gives you a better idea of what we're out here fighting for" (*Tomorrow*, 26). In a final and improbable bit of symbolism a heavy tome of Mann's essays serves as an improvised splint when one of the soldiers is wounded.

In short, these radio plays constitute, in their aggregate, a kind of paean to the exiled characters represented. But it was left to the sole woman contributor to the broadcasting series to bring to life the suffering and unsung heroism of children in wartime. Celebrating, throughout most of her play, the valor of the children of Stalingrad and deploring their plight, Fanya Foss Lawrence—one of her stories became a starring vehicle for Bette Davis and the exiled actress Elisabeth Bergner—ends her script with an embrace of all the children persecuted by the Nazis:

> Children of France, Spain, Greece
> Here [in this song] is your bread and meat.
> Children of Norway and Holland
> This is your milk and honey.
> It will smash the ghetto walls of Poland.
> It will crack the concentration camps and prisons.
> (*The Fountain of Dancing*, 98)

It is fair to ask, by way of an epilogue, what became of this mimesis of exile experience, so auspiciously launched by these American women writers. What started as a mild snowslide during the early years of Nazi rule became an avalanche. Virtually no aspect of the lives and accomplishments of the exiles was left unexplored. And while it can be argued that their male colleagues also addressed the subject consistently, it is equally true that women writers often grasped the misery and grandeur of exile with even greater sensitivity. Of course, not all reached the pellucid psychological understanding and intuitive empathy for the exiles of Anita Brookner's *Latecomers* (1988),[18] particularly her portrayal of two lifelong friends and business partners living harmoniously in London, separated only by their totally different reactions to a brief visit to the Federal Republic.

Few prose works have evoked as eloquently the tragedy of a German-Jewish exile breaking down and dying under the strain of having to adjust to the demands placed upon him by a small-time business and the restrictions of his orthodox piety as Florence Channock Cohen's short stories in *My Name Aloud* (1969).[19] But even where their prose or poetry falls short of such artistry, the texts of Anglo-American women writers produced strands of exilic experiences that, in the aggregate, became an encompassing tapestry. Elaine Feinstein, in her novel *The Border* (1984)[20] portrays the German intellectual at bay through her snapshot of Walter Benjamin, while Alice Goodman, the librettist of the opera *Nixon in China*, conjures up a sadistic Henry Kissinger.[21] Susan Sontag enriches her short stories by interspersing some of her fiction with the wisdom of Hermann Broch's aphorisms.[22]

The tension between a Jewish couple, he German-born, she American, surfaces in Norma Rosen's fiction *Green* (1963).[23] The wife is unable to understand her husband's post-Holocaust belief in God and lack of repulsion for everything German. Grace Paley, in her short story, "*Dreamer in a Dead Language*" (1986),[24] pillories the restrictive American immigration policies affecting persecuted asylum seekers.

Or on a note less grim, but indicative of the exile's pervasive impact on America's writers, April Bernard's novel *Pirate Jenny* (1990)[25] tells the hilarious picaresca of a small-town American go-getter who breaks into New York's fast track by pretending to be the daughter of Lotte Lenya and Kurt Weill. Even more telling is the fact that women writers, familiar with the plight of the exiles from Nazi Germany, used it as a trope for the "lonely crowd" of the twentieth century. In a poem "Now and Then" (1963) by Babette Deutsch, deploring the abyss between a child's and an adult's world, and the latter's inability to return to that lost paradise, she has recourse to a startling metaphor:

> The shabby treasures of an exile's trunk
> Include no passport to that wonderland. (Deutsch, 87)[26]

Currently, American women writers, beyond the many subjects they have explored previously, are adressing themselves to the exiles' death and legacy. In 1992, a drama by the playright Sybille Pearson (1937–) opened at the Mark Taber Forum in Los Angeles to superb reviews, somewhat attentuated by those in New York. Entitled *Unfinished Stories*, it focuses precisely on the death of an exile and the spiritual legacy he leaves behind.[27] It captures the last day in the life of Walter, an eighty-year-old physician from Berlin. At age thirteen, he had run away from home to join Erich Mühsam and his group of revolutionaries in their fight for social justice; he may even be the student to whom Mühsam, at the cost of his own life, yielded his exit railroad ticket from Germany. Now, after a lifetime of perservering in his struggle for Mühsam's ideals, he is dying of cancer and, like many exiles before him, commits suicide. But his daughter-in-law has caught his spirit and his grandson, in a symbolic act, pockets his grandfather's notes about Mühsam as the curtain falls. No doubt Sybille Pearson, born Sybille Weiss in Czechoslovakia in the pre-invasion year 1937, added her own personal involvement to the poignant scenes played out by her characters.

This chapter attempts to fathom the affinity between the exiles from Nazi Germany and the Anglo-American women writers who portrayed and often ennobled them. But the last word on this relationship should be left to the exiles themselves, by registering—via one example—the exiles' reception of *their* reception in American creative literature. Erika and Klaus Mann not only used a quote from Dorothy Thompson as the motto for their collected essays, they also singled out one work, the above-mentioned novel by Phyllis Bottome, as a noteworthy example of American literature going to war against fascism and of taking note of the exiles:

> The sympathy for, the understanding of the situation, material and spiritual, of the German exiles has found literary expression. . . . Various impressive stories, written by American authors, tell about the sinister circumstances which forced so many decent Germans to leave their country. One of the most exciting, most truthful epic descriptions of Nazi horror is Phyllis Bottome's novel, *The Mortal Storm*. (*Escape to Life*, 329–330)[28]

And they might have added, if they could have known it at the time, that women writers such as Phyllis Bottome, would—through their poems, dramas, and fiction—bestow on the exiles a measure of immortality.

Notes

1. "Writers of World Asked to Condemn the 'Mystics of Violence': Romain Demands End of Neutrality; Tells Writers It Is Time for the Pen to Fight the Sword in World Delegates from Thirty Countries," *New York Times*, May 9, 1939, Part I, p. 18. See also Carol Paul Merritt, "Die Rezeption deutscher Exilautoren durch die liberale amerikanische Presse während der Jahre 1933–1945," in John M. Spalek and Joseph Strelka, eds., *Deutschsprachige Exilliteratur seit 1933*. II (New York, Bern: Francke Verlag, 1989), 1470–1492.

2. The support that Agnes Meyer lent Thomas Mann is detailed in Vaget's article "Schlechtes Wetter, gutes Klima: Thomas Mann in Amerika," in Helmut Koopmann, ed., *Thomas-Mann-Handbuch*. (Regensburg: Alfred Kröner Verlag. 1990), 68–77.

3. Berlin, *Land I Have Chosen* (New York: Doubleday, Doran, 1944).

4. Phyllis Bottome, *The Mortal Storm,* American ed. (Boston: Little, Brown & Co., 1937), 313. The film was made by MGM in 1940.

5. See Sandra Whiple Spanier, *Kay Boyle: Artist and Activist* (Carbondale and Edwardsville: Southern Illinois University Press, 1986), 165: "Two of her most serious works of the forties were inspired by her husband's [Baron Joseph von Franckenstein's] experiences, while training for the United States ski troops in the Colorado Rockies. In 1944, the same year in which *Avalanche* appeared, she published *American Citizen Naturalized in Leadville, Colorado. . . .*"

6. Kay Boyle, *Primer for Combat* (New York: Simon and Schuster, 1942).

7. I am drawing here on V. I. Propp's seven "spheres of action" in narratives, as summarized in Terence Hawkes, *Structuralism and Semiotics* (Berkeley and Los Angeles: Univ. of California Press, 1977), 91.

8. See Lillian Hellman, *Four Plays, With an Introduction by the Author* (New York: The Modern Library, 1942).

9. Even though Hellman's stay in Spain was short—only two weeks—she did meet exiles such as Gustav Regler and Otto Simon. See Carl Rollyson, *Lillian Hellman: Her Legend and Her Legacy* (New York: St. Martin's Press, 1986), 113. Otto Simon, also known as André Simon and by his real name Otto Katz, was born in Prague, worked as a journalist in Berlin, and fought for Communist causes in various parts of the world. For a short biography see Arnold Lustiger, *Schalom Libertad, Juden im spanischen Bürgerkrieg* (Cologne: Kiepenheuer & Witsch, 1991), 292–293.

10. Hellman admits to this didactic intent in her "Introduction" to her *Four Plays,* vii.

11. The term "patterns of affirmation" was coined by Chester E. Eisinger in his *Fiction of the Forties* (Chicago and London: University of Chicago Press, 1963), 44–61, by which he means both novels affirming the war effort and those that "go in quest of value rather than to deny its existence or validity" (60).

12. Edna St. Vincent Millay, *The Murder of Lidice* (New York, London: Harper and Brothers, 1942), 32.

13. See Stephen Vincent Benét, "Six of us talking," a preface to *Zero Hour: A Summons to the Free* (New York, Toronto: Farrar and Rinehart, 1940), 8.

14. Martha Gellhorn, *A Stricken Field* (New York: Penguin, 1986), 184. For a close analysis of the autobiographical elements in the novel, see Carl Rollyson, *Nothing Ever Happens to the Brave: The Story of Martha Gellhorn* (New York: St. Martin's Press, 1990), 129–134.

15. The reviewer's quote appears in Gellhorn's "Afterword" to *A Stricken Field* (312). She names the Boston *Transcript* as a source but doesn't identify the reviewer.

16. Gellhorn, "Afterword," *A Stricken Field,* 312–314.

17. Arch Oboler and Stephen Longstreet, *Free World Theater: Nineteen New Radio Plays* (New York: Random House, 1944), subsequently abbreviated as FWT.

18. Anita Brookner (New York: Pantheon, 1988). For a review also lauding the novel's understanding of the exiles' state of mind, see David Leavitt, "Look, We Have Come Through," *New York Times Book Review,* April 2, 1989, 3.

19. Cohen, "The Promise," *My Name Aloud,* in Harold U. Ribelow, ed., *Jewish Stories by Jewish Writers* (South Brunswick, New York, London: Thomas Yoselaff, 1969), 49–63.

20. Feinstein, *The Border* (New York: St. Martin/Marek, 1984).

21. See John Adams (composer) and Alice Goodman (librettist), *Nixon in China* (Houston: Hart Graphics, 1987).

22. See Susan Sontag, "Project for a Trip to China," in *I, etcetera* (New York: Ferrar, Strauss and Giroux, 1978), 21–22.

23. Rosen, "What Must I Say to You?" in *Green. A Novella and Eight Stories* (New York: Harcourt, Brace & World, 1967), 203. According to an introductory note to the text, "[this] short story . . . first appeared in the *New Yorker Magazine*, October 26, 1963."

24. Paley's story in her collection *Later the Same Day* (New York: Farrar, Strauss and Giroux, 1985) 11–36. The powerful impact of this story is also attested to in a superb review. See Rita D. Jacobs, [Review of *Later the Same Day*], *World Literature Today* 60 (Spring 1986): 310–311.

25. Bernard, *Pirate Jenny* (New York, London: W. W. Norton, 1990).

26. Deutsch's closeness to the German exile experience may perhaps be explained by the fact that she also excelled as a translator of German poetry. See Deutsch and Avrahm Yarmolinsky, *Contemporary German Poetry* (New York: Harcourt Brace, 1923).

27. The author and William Morris Agency kindly supplied me with an MS of the drama. A slightly edited version has recently been published. See Sybille Pearson, Unfinished Stories, American Theatre 9 (January 1993), special section following p. 24, 19 pp., unpagin.

28. Erika and Klaus Mann, *Escape to Life* (Boston: Houghton Mifflin, 1939), 329–330.

Bibliography

Adams, John, and Alice Goodman. *Nixon in China*. Houston: Hart Graphics, 1987.

Altogether Elsewhere: Writers on Exile. Ed. Marc Robinson. Winchester, Mass: Faber and Faber, 1994.

Barrett, Mary Ellin. *Irving Berlin: A Daughter's Memoir.* New York, London: Simon and Schuster, 1994.

Bell, Elizabeth S. "Introduction." In Grace Paley. *Words that Must Somehow be Said. Selected Essays, 1927–1984*. Ed. Elizabeth S. Bell. San Francisco: North Point Press, 1985, i–xiv.

Benét, Stephen Vincent. Preface: "Six of us talking." In *Zero Hour: A Summons to the Free*. New York, Toronto: Farrar and Rinehart, 1940, 3–10.

Bergreen, Laurence. *As Thousands Cheer: The Life of Irving Berlin.* New York: Viking, 1990.

Berlin, Ellin. *Land I have Chosen*. New York: Doubleday, Doran, 1944.

Bernard, April. *Pirate Jenny*. New York, London: W. W. Norton, 1990.

Bottome, Phyllis. *The Goal.* London: Faber and Faber, 1962.

———. *The Mortal Storm*. American ed. Boston: Little, Brown & Co., 1937.

———. *Search for a Soul.* New York: Reynal and Hitchcock, 1948.

———. *Survival*. Boston: Little, Brown and Company, 1943.

Boyle, Kay. *American Citizen Naturalized in Leadville, Colorado. A Poem*. New York: Simon and Schuster, 1944.

———. *Primer for Combat*. New York: Simon and Schuster, 1942.

———. *Words That Must Be Said: Selected Essays of Kay Boyle, 1927–1984*. San Francisco: North Point, 1985.

Brookner, Anita. *Latecomers*. New York: Pantheon, 1988.

Cohen, Florence Channock. "The Promise." In *My Name Aloud. Jewish Stories by Jewish Writers*. Ed. Harold U. Ribelow. South Brunswick, New York, London: Thomas Yoselaff, 1969, 49–63.

Deutsch, Babette. "Then and Now." In *Collected Poems, 1919–1962*. Bloomington: Indiana University Press, 1963.

Deutsch, Babette, and Avrahm Yarmolinsky. *Contemporary German Poetry*. New York: Harcourt Brace, 1923.

Eisinger, Chester. *Fiction of the Forties*. Chicago and London: University of Chicago Press, 1963.

Feinstein, Elaine. *The Border*. New York: St. Martin/Marek, 1984.

Gellhorn, Martha. *A Stricken Field*. New York: Penguin, 1986.

Gellhorn, Martha. Afterword. In *A Stricken Field*. New York: Penguin, 1986.

Hawkes, Terence. *Structuralism and Semiotics*. Berkeley and Los Angeles: University of California Press, 1977.

Hellman, Lillian. *Four Plays, With an Introduction by the Author*. New York: The Modern Library, 1942.

———. *Three: An Unfinished Woman. Pentimento. Scoundrel Time*. Boston and Toronto: Little, Brown and Co., 1979.

Jacobs, Rita D. [Review of *Later the Same Day*.] *World Literature Today* 60 (Spring 1986): 310–311.

Lawrence, Fanya Foss. "The Fountain of Dancing." In *Free World Theater: Nineteen New Radio Plays*. New York: Random House, 1944, 85–99.

Leavitt, David. "Look, We Have Come Through." *New York Times Book Review*. April 2, 1989, 3.

Longstreet, Stephen, and Arch Oboler. *Free World Theater: Nineteen New Radio Plays*. New York: Random House, 1944.

Lustiger, Arnold. *Schalom Libertad, Juden im spanischen Bürgerkrieg* [Schalom Libertad, Jews in the Spanish Civil War]. Cologne: Kiepenheuer & Witsch, 1991.

Lyon, James K. *Bertolt Brecht in America*. Princeton: University Press, 1980.

Mann, Erika and Klaus. *Escape to Life*. Boston: Houghton Mifflin, 1939.

Mann, Thomas. Introduction. In Stephen Longstreet and Arch Oboler. *Free World Theater: Nineteen New Radio Plays*. New York: Random House, 1944.

Mellen, Joan. *Kay Boyle: Author of Herself*. New York: Farrar, Strauss and Giroux, 1994.

Paley, Grace. "Dreamer in a Dead Language." In *Later the Same Day*. New York: Farrar, Strauss and Giroux, 1985.

Paul Merritt, Carol. "Die Rezeption Deutscher Exilautoren durch die liberale amerikanische Presse während der Jahre 1933–1945" [The reception of German exile authors in the liberal American press during the years 1933–1945]. In *Deutschsprachige Exilliteratur seit 1933*. [German language exile literature]. Vol. 2. New York. Ed. John M. Spalek and Joseph Strelka. Bern: Francke Verlag, 1989, 1470–1492.

Pearson, Sybille. *Unfinished Stories, American Theatre.* January 9, 1993: 24, 19 pp., unpagin.

Pfanner, Helmut F. *Exile in New York. German and Austrian Writers after 1933.* Detroit: Wayne State University Press, 1983.

Rice, Elmer. *Flight to the West: A Play in Seven Scenes*. New York: Coward McCann, 1941.

Rollyson, Carl. *Lillian Hellman: Her Legend and Her Legacy*. New York: St. Martin's Press, 1986.

———. *Nothing Ever Happens to the Brave: The Story of Martha Gellhorn*. New York: St. Martin's Press, 1990.

Rosen, Norma. "What Must I Say to You?" In *Green, A Novella and Eight Stories*. New York: Harcourt, Brace & World, 1967, 192–205.

St. Vincent Millay, Edna. *The Murder of Lidice*. New York, London: Harper and Brothers, 1942.

Sontag, Susan. "Project for a Trip to China." In *I, etcetera*. New York: Farrar, Straus and Giroux, 1978, 21–22.

Ulrich, Mabel S. "Key to Endurance. [Review of] Phyllis Bottome *Survival*," *Saturday Review of Literature* 26 (18 Sept. 1943): 18–19.

Vaget, H. R. "Schlechtes Wetter, gutes Klima: Thomas Mann in Amerika" [Bad weather, good climate: Thomas Mann in America]. In *Thomas Mann Handbuch*. Ed. Helmut Koopmann, Regensburg: Alfred Kröner Verlag, 1990, 68–77.

Whiple Spanier, Sandra. *Kay Boyle: Artist and Activist*. Carbondale and Edwardsville: Southern Illinois University Press, 1986.

10

The Interchange between Experience and Literature: German-Jewish Women Writers of the Holocaust

Dagmar C. G. Lorenz

In Nazi Germany and in Austria after the so-called *Anschluss* of 1938 persons classified as Jews faced persecution and deportation. Faced with constant threat and social isolation many of them explored avenues of self-expression that they might not have considered under normal circumstances. They kept notes and diaries, wrote letters, or experimented with literary forms, most frequently lyric poetry and prose.

Following the Nazis' rise to power, the passing of the Nuremberg Laws (1935), the *Kristallnacht* (1938), and the introduction of the Yellow Star mark the escalation of terror. Other hardships imposed on Jews included forced labor, incarceration, the loss of citizenship, and deportation. Jews under Nazi rule witnessed how their friends and family members disappeared. Aware of the deportations to ghettos and death camps, many individuals went into hiding or exile. These experiences had a profound impact on the writing of already established authors such as Else Lasker-Schüler, Gertrud Kolmar, and Nelly Sachs. Moreover, women without prior writing experience turned to writing as a survival strategy. Their texts often reveal a process of individuation: as their writing becomes increasingly sophisticated, they also develop more appropriate strategies to cope with reality (Reiter, 24–26). It is the kind of development that Arnost Lustig depicts in *The Unloved.*

Rather than exploring authors who were already established before 1933, I shall focus on women who wrote in response to Nazi rule and the Holocaust. I shall highlight three aspects: the search for an adequate mode of expression to cope with the unforeseen chaos and a world that according to Ruth Angress felt "like a crater of the moon, a place only peripherally connected with the human world" (Angress, 250), the limited usefulness of conventional literary patterns for framing the Holocaust experience, and the creation of new forms of expression.

The majority of Jewish women whose unpublished manuscripts are preserved in archives came from a middle-class background. So did the authors whose texts were published. Their autobiographies, fiction, and poetry had a significant influence on the emergence of a new German Jewish literature as defined by Gilman and Remmler. At the German *Gymnasium* (high school with a university preparatory curriculum), these authors had absorbed the literary and philosophical canon of the *Bildungsbürgertum* (educated middle class). Although they write about unprecedented experiences for which their homes and schools had not prepared them, most of them are surprisingly conservative as far as the form and ideology of their works are concerned.

The structural and stylistic ideals of German nineteenth-century literature, after which most of these authors modelled their texts, stood in the way of developing textual strategies appropriate to the external reality and states of mind with which they had to cope. In particular the patter of the *Bildungsroman* had shaped their notion of plot and character development. Even in the camps they filtered their experiences through Enlightenment or Idealist philosophy and classical literature. Aware of their limitations in terms of language and conceptualization, many writers lamented that their words did not express their thoughts and feelings—and fell silent. Others attempted over and over again to articulate their concerns, but ultimately failed because they were unable to change their mode of writing.

In addition to factual information, memoirs trace emotional reactions to life in Nazi Germany and the ghetto and concentration camp experience. Contemporary readers may often be struck by the narrators' seemingly eccentric ways of coping with disaster. Cultural activities or the lack thereof and attempts to maintain the decorum of a bourgeois life style even in ghettos and concentration camps are concerns in many memoirs. They must be understood in light of the pre–World War I Central European education. In his essay "The Ignored Lesson of Anne Frank," Bruno Bettelheim took issue with the reactions of educated, family-oriented Jews, because he considered them counterproductive (Bettelheim, 246–257). He contended that their rigid bourgeois values proved to be a straight jacket.

The same applies to the aesthetic ideals to which many of the authors aspired. Johann Wolfgang Goethe's *Wilhelm Meister* and Gustav Freytag's *Soll und Haben* (*Credit and Debit*) had established a narrative pattern according to which a young protagonist goes on a quest prior to establishing himself as a useful citizen. Through various encounters he achieves maturity and acceptance by society. Clearly, this pattern clashes with the stories of Holocaust survivors. Their "quest" is involuntary, the "educational" episodes take place in concentration camps or in secret hiding places. Holocaust accounts do not usually end with the narrator's integration into German middle-class society. Likewise, stories about the immigration experience and life in a new country are ambivalent.

Women authors face the dilemma that the hero of the traditional educational novel is a non-Jewish male. Nonetheless, even Jewish women writers followed the established pattern. Their chosen genre caused them to reproduce, even to endorse the hierarchical structures of German and Austrian society. The values of the Wilhelminian and Franz Josephinian era—they overlapped with those of the Victorian era—had shaped the attitudes of Jewish women who experienced the Nazi takeover as adults. Although they had nothing to gain from intellectual elitism and German nationalism, embedded in which were antisemitism and misogyny, they did not recognize the threat posed to them by the tenets of their own class. Although they were the declared targets of National Socialism, they participated in the discourses that were used against them.

Since the late eighteenth century Jewish writers had wrestled with the problems associated with adapting the German language to their own experience. Rahel Varnhagen, Fanny Lewald, and Franz Kafka wrote in a language lacking the register to express the Jewish experience. In *Kafka, Toward a Minor Literature*, Deleuze and Guattari characterize Kafka's language as "deterritorialized" and maintain that he "appropriated [the German language] for strange and minor uses" (Deleuze and Guattari, 17). These observations apply also to Jewish women writing about the Holocaust. Some of them succeeded in reconfiguring their native German to express the "unspeakable." Most memoir writers, however, did not transcend the limits of their language. Their memoirs, although they fulfilled an important function for the writer at the time of writing, are documents of the fateful interdependence of language, perception, and conceptualization. Theodor Adorno's statement that after Auschwitz poetry was no longer an option is applicable to the situation of writers whose language has been overtaken by history; it does not signify that their attempts to write about the Holocaust were inadmissable or wrong (Adorno, 30). The literary genres and the language available to them were not appropriate to communicating the Holocaust experience, and in some cases the influence of the Nazi media is obvious in the respective text.

Some of the most creative Holocaust memoirs were written by very young authors with little formal education. By contrast, texts by experienced educated women often disappoint the readers' expectations. One such example is the unpublished memoir "Stärker als das Schwert! Den Märtyrern von Theresienstadt zum Gedächtnis" (1946) ("Stronger than the Sword! In Memory of the Martyrs of Terezin") by Klara Caro, a social worker and a rabbi's wife. Caro reveals her disorientation at the time of the Nazi takeover, her uncertainty as to how to respond. In her account, astute insights clash with rigid conservatism. Contrary to many middle-class women, Caro does not share the optimism and patriotism of other memoir writers. Perhaps as a result of her and her husband's professional dealings with the Nazi authorities, she seems more aware of the dangers the Nazis posed than many of the housewives who took up writing. In impressive detail Caro, who was deported to Theresienstadt, describes her life in the ghetto and her relationships with other prisoners. Herself a victim of discrimination, Caro nonetheless expresses the ethnocentric and class prejudices characteristic of the larger society. She sets herself and her friends apart from certain groups and individuals and stereotypes her fellow prisoners according to their gender, ethnicity, religion, and class. Her bias toward children of mixed background show that she agrees with the concept of racial and ethnic purity. Her assertion that pure-blooded Jews take part in criminal activities less frequently than so-called *Mischlinge*, half-castes (Caro, 18), suggests that she endorses some of the rules and regulations underlying the ghetto structure and does not fully realize the criminal character of that institution. The memoir reveals that a victim of National Socialism could subscribe to beliefs similar to her victimizers'. Caro's education and her social aspirations proved stronger than her experience. Absorbing the views of the larger society prevented Caro from experiencing her plight as an injustice that she shared with all the other prisoners.

Another memoir writer displaying similarly rigid authoritarian beliefs is Erna Low, an Austrian woman who survived Auschwitz. After the liberation Low left Germany. Her memoir, entitled "I was in Oswiecim," is written in English. In a heroic posture not uncommon in Holocaust writing, as Marlene Heinemann points out in *Gender and Destiny*, Low casts herself as a valiant woman reminiscent of some of the exemplary German female literary heroines. Low frequently stresses her courage and her somewhat privileged position in the camp hierarchy. She attributes great importance to her relatively minor acts of sabotage in the storage facilities in Auschwitz and showcases them as acts of exceptional bravery. One such episode is Low's encounter with Rudolf Hoess, the camp's commandant. Low describes her defiant behavior toward him to illustrate her boldness (Low, 40).

Like Caro, Low also clings to the ideology with which she was raised. Through it she affirms her identity in a hostile environment and proves that to a certain extent she is in control. Yet, inadvertently, the Hoess episode also suggests that the Nazi commandant and Low, the privileged Jewish woman prisoner, speak the same language: he respects her bravery and treats her "like a lady." Writers such as Caro and Low derive a great deal of inner strength from concepts that are entirely compatible with Nazi ideology: they take pride in being superior in terms of personal strength, class, and race.

Elisabeth Freund, a well-read lawyer's wife, wrote a memoir that applies narrative strategies traditionally taught in German composition classes, including direct speech, the present tense, and inner monologue to create suspense and immediacy. "Zwangsarbeit für Hitler. Berlin 1941" (n.d.) (Forced Labor for Hitler. Berlin 1941) discusses the intellectual and cultural oppression of the Jewish community. Freund expresses concern about the fact that the Jewish Cultural Association, the *Kulturbund*, is not allowed to perform works by non-Jewish composers. In view of her insights into political developments and social abuses and problems, her use of Nazi terminology comes as a surprise, even more so her appreciation for Germany and the Germans, including confirmed Nazis (Freund, 172). Freund, like Low, is an elitist, has a strong sense of rank and hierarchy. Like Caro, she also holds ethnocentric views, as her derogatory remarks about gypsies and the mentally disabled reveal.

The examples of Caro, Low, and Freund show that persons persecuted by the Nazis did not necessarily disagree with all aspects of Nazi ideology. Members of German society, they had assimilated, along with German culture, literature, and philosophy, discourses that National Socialism endorsed as well. Daniel Goldhagen writes: "Germany during the Nazi period was a country in which government policies, public acts of other sorts, and the public conversation were thoroughly, almost obsessively antisemitic" (Goldhagen, 29). Concerning the disabled and non-Germans such as Slavs and other groups, Goldhagen maintains that the Nazi view of humanity "informed the Germans' manner of treatment of conquered and subject peoples. This view divided human beings into a hierarchy of races, race being understood in biological terms" (Goldhagen, 410–411). Considering themselves Germans and Jews, Caro and Freund do not reject racial thinking per se, but only antisemitism, and Low in particular is influenced by Nazi rhetoric and ideas.

To explore the relationship between traditional literary models and spontaneous modes of expression in the works of Jewish women Holocaust writers, works by different authors will be examined, including texts by the social worker Gerty Spies, who became a poet after her deportation from her native Munich to Theresienstadt. In the ghetto, Spies, like other Holocaust poets such as Ilse Weber and Ilse Blumenthal Weiss, began to write for the sake of her psychological survival, although her autobiography suggests also a predisposition toward writing: Spies mentions several authors among her relatives whom she considered her role models. Writing did not come easy to Spies but required her complete concentration. However, engaging in such an intensive, even painful process, offset the effect of the Theresienstadt environment. Spies created poetry to keep alert during roll calls and while performing forced labor. By necessity, poetry became Spies's major genre. There was neither enough time nor paper to write prose. Prisoners were not allowed to write at all, so she composed her poems during the day and jotted them down secretly at night.

Spies was painfully aware of her shortcomings as a poet—she repeatedly expresses her desire to improve her writing skills. Yet developing her full creative potential is her most important objective during her imprisonment. Spies terms writing poetry "Digging for Coal" (Kohlen ausgraben), which places her into the Romantic tradition. Novalis, for example, had a predilection for the motif of the miner and mining. Indeed, like the Romantics, Spies considers writing an activity for the inspired, for the intellectual elite. She talks about writing as if it were a sacred mission.

Spies's style, her meter and rhyme patterns are simple. She favors four-footed iambic and trochaic verses—even pentameters are rare. In fact, her method and means of production do not allow for much variety—she had to memorize her rather lengthy poems before writing them down. Initially, writing was a solitary endeavor for her. Later some like-minded prisoners heard about her poetry, and her work became a means of connecting with a circle of intellectuals, artists, and poets, who engaged in poetological debates. Spies became the protegée of the most prominent member of the group, the poet Elsa Porges Bernstein, the illegitimate granddaughter of Franz Liszt and the mother-in-law of Gerhart Hauptmann's son Klaus. She was known primarily as an author of early feminist dramas (Starcke, 47–48). With Bernstein as her mentor, Spies achieved a measure of fame in the ghetto. She even received a literary award.

Except in the brief period preceding the inspection of Theresienstadt by a Red Cross Commission in 1944, anyone who participated in cultural events took a great risk. Spies mentions a group of painters who were deported to Auschwitz because their drawings documented everyday life in the ghetto (cf. Lorenz 1992, 98). However, Spies alludes to such hazards only in passing, stressing instead the significance of her poetry for herself and her friends: through their dedication they created a sphere of freedom that offered them a respite. Indeed, by maintaining their intellectual autonomy, they did resist the Nazis. The fallacies of this type of resistance have been discussed often: by ameliorating an intolerable situation, apolitical prisoners may have indirectly accommodated the Germans' work of destruction. On the other hand, for the young, the infirm, and the elderly, the benefits of the discipline and community spirit created by cultural activities must not be underestimated.

In her memoir, "Ein Stück Weges" (n.d) ("Part of the Way"), written soon after her return to Munich, and in her autobiography *Drei Jahre Theresienstadt* (1984) (*Three Years in Terezin*), Spies highlights her development as a poet. She published the first version of her accounts in 1948, concurrently with her first collection of ghetto poems, *Theresienstadt*. Despite their insights into the psyche of older women prisoners and the—at times—compelling images of ghetto life, Spies's poems pale compared to her prose. In her autobiographical accounts her rendering of subjective perceptions is more expressive and precise, while the conventional poetic forms impose greater limitations on her. When writing poetry Spies expects more of herself and is therefore more self-conscious. Her preoccupation with aesthetics detracts from her unconventional insights.

Likewise, Spies's narrative prose is encumbered by conventional literary devices. One of her major themes, the polarization of mind and body, art and reality, reveals her views on the role of literature, for example the opening sentence of her memoir: "As I was sitting there, my hands were working" ("Weges," 1) (Ich saß und meine Hände arbeiteten).* A slave laborer in an overcrowded workshop, Spies savors the exquisite alienation of the Romantic artist. Her idealism, the legacy of her Wilhelminian education, shelters her from her brutal environment, hence her trust in "the unique qualities of each human being" (die im Menschen ruhende Eigenart) despite her actual degradation. The camp routine is mentioned, to be sure, but it recedes behind her inner reality. To reflect her aspirations as a poet, Spies presents samples of her poetry within the prose text. To dismiss Spies's preoccupation with literary values as altogether escapist would be incorrect, rather, it constitutes a coping mechanism. Her obsession to become a great poet diverted her from the threat of death. In that sense, her work is a survivor's document. Also, her subject matter, life in Theresienstadt, shows that Spies did not actually avoid reality. Rather, she describes in minute detail the agony of the prisoners, including her own, and she focuses on the horrors experienced by older women. Moreover, irony, humor, and sarcasm are important devices in Spies's work. By concentrating on the grotesque aspects of her environment, by making light of her otherwise unbearable situation, Spies overcomes despair. Friendship, love, and tenderness play an important role as well. Through them Spies creates a semblance of privacy and eludes her loveless surroundings into a realm where she feels validated.

Although Spies claims that her topic is Theresienstadt "with its horrors, specters and darkness" (mit seinem Grauen, den Gespenstern, seiner Finsternis) ("Weges," 13), her narrative follows the linear structure of the educational novel: At the "time of terror" the protagonist/narrator reaches the apex of her career. Her delight at receiving the outstanding poetry award is second only to the joy at seeing the arrival of the Allied troops. In this rare instance she draws upon the tradition of Yiddish songs. "Sie sind da . . . " (They are Here) echoes the beat and style of the Yiddish partisan song by Hans Glik, "Sog nit kejnmal as du gejst dem letztn weg . . . " (Don't ever say that you are walking your last path . . .) (Weinreich 282)

---

*The translations are my own. DCGL.

The structure of the educational novel and Spies's story collide in a way similar to the content and form of her poetry. The author's experience after the liberation was anticlimactic: Spies remained in Theresienstadt for a period of time to work in the camp kitchen during a typhoid epidemic. Finally a shabby, long overdue bus arrived from Munich to pick up the survivors. Upon her return Spies learns about the extent of Germany's devastation and the demise of her friends. She also realizes through her encounters with other Germans that antisemitism has not ended with the Nazi regime (*Theresienstadt*, 179). Spies had to face the fact that her accounts were unwelcome to many, but she continued to write and speak publicly to admonish her contemporaries not to forget the past and to hold the perpetrators accountable, as in her poem "Auftrag" (Task). Clearly, the model of the educational novel is unable to sustain this kind of experience. Spies's accounts deteriorate toward the end. After the destruction of the Jewish community there is no society into which the narrator can be integrated: her story does not fulfill the expectations raised by the literary framework.

Similar problems arise in the works of other authors, one example being the accounts of Rahel Behrend, who escaped to Switzerland after surviving under exceedingly difficult conditions in Nazi Germany. The same is true for Inge Deutschkron, who survived the Nazi era as a young girl together with her mother under assumed identities. Neither Behrend nor Deutschkron took up residence in Germany after the liberation. The autobiographies of Lotte Paepcke and Ingeborg Hecht, authors of mixed German Jewish and non-Jewish background, who experienced discrimination and faced deportation, do not end in reconciliation and harmony either. Like Spies the latter two writers cannot imagine a home country other than Germany, but they never get over the experience of persecution and the destruction of their families. Spies, Behrend, and others wrote and rewrote their stories, some did so more than once. Dissatisfaction with their texts may have caused them to do so. Other women waited for decades until they found their own voice and genre. Many published under pseudonyms.

Established literary conventions affected younger and less educated authors to a lesser extent. Their lack of inhibition did not necessarily result in great literature, but it allowed more spontaneous and direct writing, as the Auschwitz memoir of Nina Weilovà shows. Weilovà survived in a mother-daughter team and wrote her brief memoir "Jude 71978" (n.d.) (Jew 71978) in correct and fluent German, as if holding her emotions in check. She obviously has no literary ambition, but she handles rhetorical devices effectively: contrasts and comparisons to denote surprise, misapprehension, and shock. Describing the arrival of the German troops in Prague, the narrator recollects naive childhood impressions as she enjoys the pageantry while her mother cries: she already knows about the persecution of the Jews in Berlin.

Weilovà's account contains no poetological and aesthetic passages. No attempt is made to portray the author or anyone else as a hero—if there were such a character, it would be the circumspect, gentle mother who dies before the liberation. Nowhere does the nonlinear account suggest a goal or showcase the narrator's development. The notion that pain and suffering serve a purpose does not arise—no moral victories or personal achievements crown Weilovà's transition from the camps into civilian life. As is the case in Inge Deutschkron's memoir, *Ich trug den gelben Stern* (*I Wore the Yellow Star*), Weilovà's elation over the Germans' desertion and the arrival of the Russian soldiers is short-lived. The narrator ends by describing herself as a twelve-and-a-half-year-old, underweight orphan girl who barely survived. Faced with an uncertain future, weakened by starvation and illness, traumatized by the death of her loved ones, she expresses neither hope nor self-confidence.

Weilovà's perceptions correspond with views expressed in Ilse Aichinger's novel *Die größere Hoffnung* (1948) (*Herod's Children*), which was based on personal notes the author had taken in Vienna during World War II. Clearly a work of literary aspiration and accomplishment, *Die größere Hoffnung* contains also autobiographical elements. Like Ellen, the protagonist, Aichinger had been classified as a *Mischling* and her life was deeply affected by the Nuremberg Laws. As in Weilovà, the daughter's loving relationship with the absent mother represents a life-sustaining force. Both narratives discuss the traumatic effects of the Nazi takeover on the child's psyche. From one day to the next the girls are barred from public places, parks, forests, movies, concerts, swimming pools, and restaurants, and are at school tormented by their non-Jewish classmates. Finally they are excluded from public schools and later from all educational programs. An important theme in Aichinger and Weilovà is the Yellow Star. Rather than accepting its intended derogatory meaning, both authors describe a process through which the girls come to regard it as an affirmation of their Jewish identity.

While the memoirs of authors who were adults during the Nazi era tend to describe cultural activities as a counterbalance to oppression, younger authors ascribe a similarly liberating function to games, play, and learning, especially the study of languages. Weilovà and Aichinger report that Jewish children risked their lives to study secretly with a private tutor. Game playing appears to have been equally important. Weilovà relishes her memories of the only playground accessible to Jewish children in Prague. Here she met her friends and role models, including the almost legendary educator Fredi Hirsch. The children in Aichinger's novel play wherever possible: at home, in the streets, at the forbidden amusement park, even at the cemetery.

Aichinger filters her experience in Vienna through her semiautobiographical protagonist Ellen—she stayed in Vienna until the end of the war. Weilovà and her mother were deported in 1942, first to Theresienstadt, then to Auschwitz. Weilovà's account evokes the chaos of the concentrations camps, the lack of hygiene, the substandard food, and the brutality. Aichinger examines the social disintegration under Nazi rule. In addition, both texts are also documents of remembering and mourning. In Aichinger it is the death of Ellen's grandmother that reflects the fate of the author's own grandmother, who died in the Holocaust. Weilovà commemorates the death of her own mother.

Both Aichinger and Weilovà reveal an insurmountable generation gap caused by the Holocaust. Although she loves her mother, Weilovà is glad when in Theresienstadt she is separated from the adults, because she cannot bear to listen to their depressing conversations. According to her, adults were even less resilient and able to cope than children (Weilovà, 15). Aichinger conveys an impression of adults unable to help and counsel the children. Ellen's grandmother surrenders by killing herself to elude a supposed arrest. By contrast, children are portrayed as creative and competent.

Compared to most literary and nonliterary texts about the Holocaust, *Die größere Hoffnung* stands out because it resists traditional patterns. The unusual poetic language expresses views and feelings that emanated from the way in which the author processed her experience. Aichinger does not need to insert poems into her prose, her prose is poetic. She mixes dramatic and descriptive passages and overlays them with poetic and reflective passages that evoke the Psalms, German Romantic and Nietzsche's ecstatic poetry. Structurally the novel is fluid and open. It defies the boundaries of established literary genres as well as the categories of character and identity. Rather than constructing a protagonist, Aichinger constructs narrative positions and ciphers in an ever-changing literary cosmos. Reintegration into society is not even an issue in Aichinger—the protagonist is killed by a bombshell. Aichinger's later, more directly autobiographic works suggest that Ellen's death signifies more than a device to conclude the novel. The essay "Vor der langen Zeit" (1964) (Before the Long Time) looks back at the narrator's childhood and the trust with which she embraced the world. Only during the war, and in the harsh postwar reality did the alienation and the mistrust set in that Aichinger has repeatedly thematized in her works.

A *Gymnasium* graduate, Aichinger was familiar with literary conventions. Contrary to Spies and Freund, however, she did not identify with the majority culture and its discourses. Her detachment is found in all stages of her career: as early as *Die größere Hoffnung* her language does not show the slightest trace of Nazi jargon. Neither does Nina Weilovà's memoir. In the works of many other authors Aichinger's age and older, even avowed antifascists, Nazi vocabulary occurs. It is present, for example, in the writings of survivors such as Freund, Hecht, and Paepcke.

Jewish women born after 1945, who write in German, continued the work begun by writers such as Aichinger. They had no personal recollections of the Holocaust but shared the previous generation's memories of the destroyed Jewish culture, Jewish communities and families. A sense of danger and insecurity, a feeling of not belonging, and images of persecution and genocide permeate their literature and films. The poetic abstract prose of the Swiss author Rahel Hutmacher, for example, conveys an awareness of difference and vulnerability, connected to gender and race, in her novel *Wildleute* (1986) (*Wild People*). Although Hutmacher's narrative avoids explicit historical references, its imagery and themes point to the Shoah. Another author, Lea Fleischmann, the daughter of Polish Holocaust survivors, who grew up in West Germany, expressed her frustration with West Germany in *Dies ist nicht mein Land* (1980) (*This is not My Country*). Her autobiographical account of growing up Jewish in an antisemitic society juxtaposes Germany, where she felt marginalized, with imagined memories of Jewish Eastern Europe, her illusory homeland. Fleischmann took residence in Israel. The essay *Unzugehörig* (1989) (*Not Belonging*) by Ruth Beckermann, the daughter of survivors, describes the alienation of a Jewish woman growing up in Vienna and raises the question where to position herself in terms of geography and ideology—Beckermann ultimately chooses Vienna. In her films of the 1980s and in her photo documentary *Die Mazzesinsel* (1984) (*The Matzo Island*), Beckermann captures images of Jewish Vienna and Eastern Europe prior to the Holocaust. Exploring the roots of her father's family in Romania, Beckermann finds herself confronted with ruins. So does the narrator of Barbara Honigmann's novel *Roman von einem Kinde* (1986) (*Novel of a Child*), a highly literary account of a journey into the past and the self that initiates the construction of a Jewish woman's identity.

These works of remembrance and mourning by authors who grew up after the Shoah reveal that the memories of Holocaust survivors have shaped the imagination of several generations of women. Familiar with the accounts of family members, the writings of survivors as well as historical and documentary works, they identify with the Holocaust testimonies as if they had become a part of their own personal memory. Most of the younger writers ignore traditional patterns of German literature. Their works possess a flowing, boundless quality. They stand between the genres, languages, and, as their biographies show, between cultures and countries.

The success of the autobiography of the Holocaust survivor Ruth Klüger, *weiter leben* (1992) (*Living On*), proves that the Holocaust has remained a pivotal topic. Klüger's account describes and reflects upon the Auschwitz experience and comments on literary and culture-critical Shoah-discourses. It is a literary landmark: Begun in the late 1980s, it signals the end of conventional Holocaust literature: survivors' correspondences, memoirs, and traditional literary and scholarly works about the Nazi concentration camps. While *weiter leben* possesses some elements reminiscent of older autobiographies such as Spies's—it intersperses poems into the prose text, for example, but it also shows some of the characteristics of the more recent literature. Like Nina Weilovà, Ilse Aichinger, and Behrend, Klüger entwines perceptions with biographical and historical facts. Childhood memories are recounted with great intensity, but they are told from a distance and integrated into the horizon of a woman of the 1990s.

It took Klüger decades to develop a literary voice to tell about her family and community as well as her survival of Theresienstadt and Auschwitz. When *weiter leben* was written, an extensive body of literature about the concentration camps existed already. Klüger's autobiography challenges universalizing notions, but also takes into consideration and validates earlier publications. Thus, the text is integrated into twentieth-century criticism and historiography. Against the background of authors such as Borowski, Wiesel, Adorno, and Fried, Klüger tells her story from a feminist point of view. She disagrees frequently with assessments made by male authors and critics, for example when she terms the discrimination of women a general social phenomenon and contends that authors such as Eli Wiesel have omitted or distorted women's experiences. According to Klüger they have diminished the suffering of women, and Holocaust fiction has represented the experience of women with prurient overtones or as pornography: "Concentration Camp pornography does exist since the notion of absolute power over others is titillating" (Es gibt ja eine Pornographie der KZs, die Vorstellung der absoluten Macht über andere erweckt Lustgefühle; Klüger, 236).

Klüger's autobiography stands in a class by itself because of its critical and literary merits. Indeed, Jennifer Taylor terms *weiter leben* as a "Jewish Woman's 'Letter to her Mother'" (77), in analogy to Kafka's *Brief an den Vater* (*Letter to his Father*). Such a comparison shows how fitting the German language is as a medium for this work, how appropriate the dedication: *Den Göttinger Freunden—ein deutsches Buch* (To the Friends in Göttingen—a German Book). With an amazing sensitivity for nuances, Klüger evokes ideological and historical contexts, moods, atmospheres in which she places her boldly drawn characters. Viennese intonation and Austrian expressions, along with occasional Yiddish terms, blend into a portrait of the conservative Viennese Jewish middle class of the 1930s. Klüger casts herself as a rebellious young girl, attracted to Zionism and insisting on changing her name to better express her personality (40). Similar to Aichinger's protagonist Ellen, Klüger's childhood character successfully resists the pressure to conform to the language of her racist environment. The Viennese timbre and vocabulary continues to set Klüger's adult narrator apart from the Northern German intelligentsia of the 1980s whom she encounters in Göttingen. Armed with their sporadic knowledge about Nazi and Holocaust history and their specialized vocabulary and body language reserved for such topics, these Germans try, but fail to achieve the much-discussed *Vergangenheitsbewältigung,* the task of coping with the past.

Germany torn by ethnic strife and xenophobia needs to listen to the mothers and daughters of the Holocaust. Klüger's autobiography bridges the gap between the different generations and genres of Holocaust literature in a unique way and asks questions about the past and the future that in the light of recent events are now more relevant than ever. The works discussed in this chapter show that coming to terms with the Shoah was and continues to be an intense personal process—no two experiences were alike, no two accounts are identical. Class, personal philosophy, education, age, and individuality were not suspended in the camps. They are significant factors in the works of women survivors who faced attacks on their identity and lives on a daily basis.

It is important to take into consideration the time of remembering and recording, as the comparison between earlier and later memoirs reveals. Since 1945 a tradition of Holocaust prose has arisen, building on an earlier body of texts. It continues to shape the language, images as well as the concepts and artistic expression of later works. Holocaust literature is made up of works by men and women. Each individual work is gender-specific—a generic Holocaust experience does not exist. The specificity of women's writing pertains, among other things, to issues regarding women's bodies, their socialization, and gender roles in pre-Nazi and Nazi Germany, in the concentration camps, and in postwar society. Gender-specific factors determine the ways in which women regarded themselves, how they conceive of their roles and their options, how they relate to others and, ultimately, how they write. There are distinct affinities between Jewish women writers based on similarities of perception and deliberate intertextualities, such as references to the works of other authors, or the citing of another's work. All of these are part of a distinct literary tradition that began in the camps and continues into the present and beyond.

Bibliography

Adorno, Theodor W. "Kulturkritik und Gesellschaft." In *Soziologische Schriften* X. Ed. Rolf Tiedemann. Frankfurt am Main; Suhrkamp, 1972, 11–30.

Aichinger, Ilse. "Vor der langen Zeit." In *Kleist, Moos, Fasane*. Frankfurt am Main: Fischer, 1987, 15–18.

———. *Die größere Hoffnung*. Wien: Bermann-Fischer, 1948.

Angress, Ruth K. "Lanzmann's *Shoah* and Its Audience." *SWC Annual* 3 (1986): 249–260. (During her career as a scholar of German literature in the United States, Klüger went by the name Angress.)

Beckermann, Ruth. *Unzugehörig*. Wien: Löcker, 1989.

———. *Die Mazzesinsel. Juden in der Wiener Leopoldstadt*. Wien, München: Löcker, 1984.

Behrend, Rahel. *Verfemt und Verfolgt*. Zürich: Büchergilde Gutenberg, 1945.

———. *Ich stand nicht allein. Erlebnisse einer Jüdin in Deutschland 1933–45.* Frankfurt am Main: Europäische Verlagsanstalt, 1964.

Bettelheim, Bruno. *Surviving*. New York: Knopf, 1979, 246–257.

Caro, Klara. "Stärker als das Schwert. Den Märtyrern von Theresienstadt zum Gedächtnis." Ts. Leo Baeck Institut Archive, New York, 1946, 1956.

Deleuze, Gilles, and Félix Guattari. *Kafka. Toward a Minor Literature*. Trans. Dana Polan. Minneapolis: University of Minnesota Press, 1986.

Deutschkron, Inge. *Ich trug den gelben Stern*. Köln: Verlag Wissenschaft und Politik, 1978.

Fleischmann, Lea. *Dies ist nicht mein Land*. Hamburg: Hoffmann & Campe, 1980.

———. "Identity Problems of Postwar Generation Jews in Germany. A Historical Perspective." In *Insiders and Outsiders. Jewish and Gentile Culture in Germany and Austria*. Ed. Dagmar C. G. Lorenz and Gabriele Weinberger. Detroit: Wayne State University Press, 1994, 301–307.

Freund, Elisabeth. "Zwangsarbeit für Hitler. Berlin 1941." Ts. Leo Baeck Institut Archive, New York, n.d.

Gilman, Sander L. *Jews in Today's German Culture*. Bloomington and Indianapolis: Indiana University Press, 1995.

———, and Karen Remmler, eds. *Reemerging Jewish Culture in Germany: Life and Literature since 1989*. New York and London: New York University Press, 1995.

———. "Jewish Writing in a Reunified Germany: Questions of Gender and Identification." In *The Jewish Experience of European anti-Semitism*. Ed. Hazel Kahn Keimowitz and Wolfgang Mieder. Burlington, Vt.: The Center for Holocaust Studies, 1995, 45–113.

Goldhagen, Daniel Jonah. *Hitler's Willing Executioners. Ordinary Germans and the Holocaust*. New York: Alfred Knopf, 1996.

Hecht, Ingeborg. *Als unsichtbare Mauern wuchsen. Eine deutsche Familie unter den Nürnberger Rassengesetzen*. Hamburg: Hoffmann und Campe, 1984.

Heinemann, Marlene E. *Gender and Destiny. Women Writers and the Holocaust*. New York: Greenwood, 1986.

Honigmann, Barbara. *Roman von einem Kinde*. Darmstadt und Neuwied: Luchterhand, 1986.

Hutmacher, Rahel. *Wildleute*. Darmstadt, Neuwied: Luchterhand, 1986.

Klüger, Ruth. *weiter leben. Eine Jugend*. Göttingen: Wallstein Verlag, 1992. (In the U.S. Klüger spells her name Kluger)

Lorenz, Dagmar C. G. *Verfolgung bis zum Massenmord. Holocaust-Diskurse in deutscher Sprache aus der Sicht der Verfolgten*. New York, Frankfurt, Bern: Peter Lang, 1992.

———. "Memory and Criticism: Ruth Klüger's *weiter leben.*" *Women in German Yearbook* 9 (1993): 207–224.

———. *Keepers of the Motherland. German Texts by Jewish Women Writers.* Lincoln: University of Nebraska Press, 1997.

Low, Erna. "I was in Oswiecim." Ts .Leo Baeck Institute, New York, n.d.

Lustig, Arnost. *The Unloved. From the Diaries of Perla S.* New York: Arbor House, 1985.

Paepcke, Lotte. *Unter einem fremden Stern.* Frankfurt am Main: Verlag der Frankfurter Hefte, 1952.

———. *Ein kleiner Händler, der mein Vater war.* Heilbronn: Eugen-Salzer-Verlag, 1972.

———. *Ich wurde vergessen. Berichte einer Jüdin, die das Dritte Reich überlebte.* Freiburg: Herder, 1979.

Reiter, Andrea. *"Auf daß sie entsteigen der Dunkelheit." Die literarische Bewältigung von KZ-Erfahrung.* Wien: Löcker, 1995.

Spies, Gerty. *Drei Jahre Theresienstadt.* München: Kaiser, 1984.

———. *Theresienstadt. Gedichte.* München: Freitag, 1948.

———. "Ein Stück Weges (ein Gedanke an Jahre schmerzvoller Reifung)." Ts. Leo Baeck Institute Archive, New York, n.d.

Starke, Käthe. *Der Führer schenkt den Juden eine Stadt.* Berlin: Haude und Spener, 1975.

Taylor, Jennifer. "Ruth Klüger's *weiter leben: eine Jugend:* A Jewish Woman's 'Letter to her Mother.'" In *Out from the Shadows: Essays on Contemporary Austrian Women Writers and Filmmakers.* Ed. Margarete Lamb-Faffelberger. Riverside, Cal: Ariadne Press, 1997, 77–78.

Weilovà, Nina."71978 Jude. Erinnerungen."Ts . Österreichisches Dokumentationsarchiv der Widerstandsbewegung, Wien, n.d.

Weinreich, Uriel. *College Yiddish. An Introduction to the Yiddish Language and to Jewish Life and Culture.* New York: YIVO, 1949

Part V

Women's Voices after 1945

11

Luise Rinser: Dialogues with the Past? The Problem of *Vergangenheitsbewältigung* (Coming to Terms with the Past)

Elke P. Frederiksen

The name Luise Rinser usually evokes strong emotions that are either a sign of great admiration or of total rejection. The admiration comes mainly from a large readership, which has made Luise Rinser one of the most successful German writers today. The rejection, even condemnation, stems from a persistently critical press and from literary scholars who do not hold her in high regard. The reasons for this rejection, however, have to be viewed from several perspectives. While she was looked down upon as a "woman writer" in the 1960s, and the literary merit of her texts was called into question (Frederiksen 1980, 43), nowadays her texts are tainted with the memory that she was an early participant in the Nazi movement. Nevertheless, the literary critic Ulrich Greiner does not even grant Luise Rinser the stature of being worth discussing, quite in contrast to personalities such as the philosopher Heidegger, the historian and media critic Werner Höfer, or the literary critic Paul de Man (*Die Zeit*, August 1988).

My own introduction to Luise Rinser goes back to the year 1978—initially through reading some of her diary texts. As a literary scholar, I was on an exploratory journey through German literature with the intention of discovering and uncovering the works of German women writers when I came across Luise Rinser's *Kriegsspielzeug* (*War Toy*). The text fascinated me because of its construction of opposites in the title, which links violence, and peace together in one word. In this text, Rinser takes fascism to task, as well as extremism, violence and terrorism, by referring to concrete historical and political events, for example the "Deutsche Herbst" ("German Autumn")—a journalistic hate campaign against left-wing intellectuals such as Günter Grass, Heinrich Böll, and Luise Rinser in September 1977, which was sparked by the terrorist murder of Hans-Martin Schleyer, then president of the employers' union. It was incomprehensible and upsetting to me that I had never before read anything by Luise Rinser. I began reading other works by her—*Mitte des Lebens* (*Nina*), *Septembertag* (*A Day in September*), and *Baustelle* (*Construction Site*)—and I decided then and there to deal more intensively with her writings. This first encounter with Luise Rinser and her texts would eventually force me to ask serious and essential questions concerning the meaning of literary texts and the meaning of my own work as a literary scholar.

The goal of this chapter is, first of all, to describe in more detail my initial encounter with the author and her texts. The specific focus will be on the changes, the ambivalence, and the doubts in my own position and perspective—partly caused by the disclosure of her publications in the years 1934–1937 in the Nazi-influenced magazine *Herdfeuer* (*Hearth Fire*), which entangled the author in a series of denials. My view of her has become much more critical, influenced in part by new scholarly approaches to the investigation of the 1930s and 40s in Germany. At the end of the 1980s a plethora of mainly historical research was published, dealing with the role of women under National Socialism, and more importantly, feminist scholars began to address the theoretical implications of National Socialism for women; for example, the historical studies by Angelika Ebbinghaus, *Opfer und Täterinnen* (1987) (*Victims and Collaborators*), and Claudia Koonz, *Mothers in the Fatherland* (1987).

If the main issue for historians, until the early 1980s, had been "to seek out clearly identifiable perpetrators, or heroic resisters and noble martyrs—male or female" (auf der Suche nach eindeutig identifizierbaren Täter/inne/n, heroischen Widerstandskämpfer/inne/n und edlen Märtyrer/inne/n; Koonz, 21)—the intention now (in the 1990s) is "to reconstruct the social networks in which individuals could weigh the advantages of collaboration against the price of resistance and search for ways to avoid becoming victims of the system" (die sozialen Netzwerke zu rekonstruieren, in denen die Individuen die Vorteile der Kollaboration und den Preis des Widerspruchs gegeneinander abwogen, und Wege suchten, nicht Opfer des Systems zu werden; Koonz, 21). Thus, it is no longer an either-or situation, but rather a victim-perpetrator dialectic, a much more differentiated view of history, which not only considers the extremes—victim and perpetrator—but includes also the category of "collaborators."

Secondly, it is the intention of this chapter to show—using a specific text example from Luise Rinser's prolific work—how and in what manner this controversial writer has tried to confront the Nazi past—and her own past in particular—in order to come to terms with it. This critical inquiry into Rinser's literary texts is an attempt at looking anew at her work while taking into consideration her Nazi past. Until recently, Rinser has almost always been regarded as an antifascist (Gill, Schnell, Weigel, Schwab, Frederiksen). The one exception is the recently published essay "The Case of Luise Rinser: A Past That Will Not Die," by Diana Orendi Hinze. However, in spite of her justifiable criticism and her important insights into the phenomenon Rinser, Hinze goes to the opposite extreme, accusing Rinser of having been a fascist, whose change of heart at the end of the 1930s was dictated by megalomania and opportunism.

The main focus of this discussion will be Rinser's lesser known novel *Der Schwarze Esel* (*The Black Donkey*), a fictional text published in 1974. Although I was inspired by historical research, my analysis here constitutes an approach to a literary text, which—of course—can never be direct representation. As is well known, in the process of literary writing, certain shifts or displacements occur when historical events are changed into specific perceptions of history, which are then translated into literary form (Ryan, 16). Judith Ryan, for example, makes the following comment:

> Where historiography tries to minimize the subjective element implied by written perspective, canceling it out as much as possible by its own self-criticism, literature points up the subjective nature of our view of reality by deliberately clothing it in fictional disguise. *What retrospective novels reveal are thus not the facts of a particular historical period, but specific views of it.* (Ryan, 17; my emphasis)

These diverse opinions and views refer to the relationship between the text and the reader who re-reads every text, at various moments in history, in a new and different context (Eagleton). Important categories of literary interpretation are therefore class, race, ethnicity, sexuality, religion, and nationality. Feminist literary and cultural scholarship—while taking the above categories into account—has placed its emphasis on the gender component. In her recently published *Gender, Patriarchy and Fascism in the Third Reich* (1993), Elaine Martin states: "In writings by women, the perceptions of history in literary form undergo a third gender-informed displacement: literature by women about the Nazi era integrates story and history from the unique perspective of her story" (12), which I would change to *her stories* or *their stories*, because women tell many different stories.

With regard to Luise Rinser, it is my intention, as indicated above, to look at this author as a reader and interpreter of the Nazi past. In her literary texts, Rinser constructs a dialogue-oriented discourse in which we as readers are asked to participate. But these dialogues are also conversations with herself about the German past, including her own. Rinser once characterized her novel *Der schwarze Esel* (*The*

Black Donkey) "as an attempt to deal with the German fascist past" (Als Versuch der Bewältigung der deutschen faschistischen Vergangenheit; Konzag/Schwab, 33). In her *A Woman's Prison Journal* (*Gefängnistagebuch*) (1946), she wrote years earlier:

> Only when we have fully "seen" our past, whether we committed the crimes or were victims of them, will we have a future. (6)
>
> (Wir werden keine Zukunft haben, ehe wir unsere Vergangenheit—ob wir sie als Täter oder als Opfer erlebten—ganz und gar "gesehen" haben.) (9)

The difficulty, or rather the impossibility, of coping with the horrors of this past was put into words by Alexander and Margarete Mitscherlich in their book *Die Unfähigkeit zu trauern* (*The Inability To Mourn*), where they point out that it is not possible to deal with the murder of millions (24). Nevertheless, they note the original meaning of the expression "unsurmounted past" (unbewältigte Vergangenheit) and refer to Freud, who understood this "dealing with an experience" to be a succession of steps to achieve insight, which he termed "remembering, repeating and working through them" (erinnern, wiederholen, durcharbeiten; 24). With regard to Rinser's text, the question arises as to how her text illustrates this "coming to terms with the past" and how this literary attempt can be reconciled with her repeated denials of her own past. In the context of our discussion it will be appropriate that the text be read as an intersection of gender, fascism, and patriarchy (Fascism and National Socialism as the most evil form of patriarchy).

My personal encounter with Rinser and her work (and I am writing here as a feminist, a German living permanently in the United States and specializing in German literature and culture) is marked by ups and downs, by an intense interest on the one hand, doubts, questions, and confusion on the other, all caused by the tensions and the contradictions in the life and work of this author. My interest was sparked at first by the fact that here was a well-known author of fictional and documentary prose who had not found entry into the scholarly discussions, who had after all published her first longer prose text *Die gläsernen Ringe* (*Glass Rings*) in 1941, and who now seemed to be politically, socially, and religiously extremely involved. This German, non-Jewish author who had written a letter in 1937 defending the painter Emil Nolde and who, from October 1944 until April 1945, was held in captivity at the Traunstein prison for committing high treason and undermining the war effort, also appeared consistently as an antifascist after the war. In the 1950s and 60s, she took a critical position toward the affluent West German society, severely criticized the Catholic Church, showed sympathy with the extra-parliamentary opposition, declared herself a socialist, and immersed herself deeply in East Asian politics and philosophy. In the 1980s she became involved with the pacifist movement.

The other side of the coin, however, is a writer who published between 1934 and 1937 in the journal *Herdfeuer*, a German magazine leaning toward National Socialism: her publications consist of a report describing her stay in a BDM camp (Camp for German Girls), three poems, and four stories. Already in 1981, an acquaintance drew my attention to the poem "Junge Generation" (New Generation), which was published in *Herdfeuer* in 1935 and which glorifies an unnamed leader with exaggerated pathos. However, my mind was put at ease by Rinser's own explanation in an interview in 1982, when she stated that she did not know how the poem was attributed to her and that all this was the result of a hate campaign waged by radical rightists who had published the poem in their newspaper, the *Deutsche Nationalzeitung*. I was unaware then of the fact that Luise Rinser had already lost a lawsuit against the publisher of this journal. But renewed doubts surfaced in my mind in January 1988, after seeing the television broadcast "Schreiben unterm Hakenkreuz" (Writing under the Swastika), when the historian Bernd Sösemann (Free University, West Berlin) tried to demonstrate Luise Rinser's Nazi past, using as evidence the *Herdfeuer* publications that the author had denied. In my own research I finally found the original publications, which unambiguously bear the name Luise Rinser.

My disappointment and confusion with regard to Luise Rinser came specifically from the fact that her autobiographical texts—which I had valued for their antifascist stance—were now cause for serious doubt: for instance, the diary *A Woman's Prison Journal* (*Gefängnistagebuch*) (1946), which describes the experiences of women in a National Socialist women's prison from the author's own perspective, based on her experience and re-experience, a text that protests against forgetting a dark past, because "the past is locked into the present and is inseparably one with it" (3) (Die Vergangenheit ist in die Gegenwart eingeschlossen, ist untrennbar eins mit ihr; 6) Rinser goes on to say:

> We must not allow what has been awakened to slip back into sleep. Only when we have fully "seen" our past, whether we committed the crimes or were victims of them, will we have a future. (6)
>
> (Wir dürfen nicht mehr einschlafen lassen, was wachgeworden ist. Wir werden keine Zukunft haben, ehe wir unsere Vergangenheit—ob wir sie als Täter oder als Opfer erlebten—ganz und gar "gesehen" haben.) (9)

A most problematic text relevant to this debate is her autobiography *Den Wolf umarmen* (1981)(*Embracing the Wolf*), in which she attempts to document the events as she experienced them herself since her birth in 1911. But she omits her Nazi past entirely and emphasizes instead her antifascist activities.

My reading of Rinser's *fiction* has also changed; particularly my reading of those texts that thematize events of the Third Reich, such as *Jan Lobel aus Warschau*,

Mitte des Lebens, or *Der schwarze Esel*, the novel under discussion here. For the benefit of those who are not familiar with *Der schwarze Esel*, let me briefly summarize the story. Through conversations and investigations, the first-person female narrator constructs a multifaceted family and city chronicle, quite condensed, yet very lively. The story focuses on eight separate characters whose lives are nevertheless intimately connected. There are four girls and four boys who grow up together in a small town in central Germany during World War I. One of the girls is the narrator, who returns to the town in 1973, wanting to find out what happened to her childhood friends.

Central to the story are the events of the Third Reich, which claimed the four men (in the story) as its victims. At first reading, the book appears to be an accusation, an antifascist text told by women who had first-hand experience. The book describes the aftereffects of National Socialism and World War II on the lives of the men and women in this small town, which is symbolic and representative for many others and which "is only a very small dot on the map of Germany and does not appear at all on the larger map of the world and which nevertheless cannot be ignored, a tiny little mirror image of the history of our century and itself a small world with its own fate that also matters" (. . . die auf der Landkarte von Europa ein sehr kleiner Punkt und auf der Weltkarte gar nicht vorhanden ist, und die doch nicht weggeleugnet werden kann, ein winziger Spiegel der Geschichte unseres Jahrhunderts, und selber eine kleine Welt mit einem Schicksal, das zählt; (*SchwE*, 18).

Through conversations—Rinser attempts a dialogic discourse here—the narrator rediscovers her own childhood memories, but at the same time she experiences history in a much wider context: World War I, the demise of the Weimar Republic, and above all the Hitler regime, World War II, the Postwar Era. Women play a dominant role in this panorama of a society of men and women, of Germans and Jews, of rich and poor, of those politically to the left and to the right, of Nazis and collaborators, of victims and resisters—before, during and after World War II. The part played by women in this story is a representation of *herstory*.

Therefore, my first reading emphasized *gender* as primary literary category. From a feminist perspective, in the tradition of Sigrid Weigel's concept of the "double focus" or "cross-eyed gaze," which establishes connections between political and text-oriented questions, I was primarily interested in the representation of women in this text, and in the author's relation to the dominant image of women in her culture. I was interested in the writing process, the writing strategies used by the author to shatter the "mirror image," in order to show women's self-understanding, women's existence as the "second sex," the "other," within certain historical and patriarchal norms.

In Luise Rinser's novel *Der schwarze Esel*, the female narrator—at first only tentatively—tries to uncover what lies buried and blocked. She does so with the help of the sisters Klara and Stefanie, and their cousin Berthie, all three belonging to the middle class, but also through Anna, a working-class woman. It is striking how well differentiated the figures of the women and their experiences are, while the men—most of them war victims—appear only indirectly and sketchily in the memories of the women. This multiperspective seems to open up the text; it certainly serves as a means to examine and question historical developments and events. As in earlier texts by Rinser, the text structure creates a constellation of tension, subtly developed here through the contrasts between the sisters Klara and Stefanie. These two elderly women are the central characters of the story (a sharp contrast to most male-authored prose texts from the mid-1970s). Klara and Stefanie are not only opposites in appearance, they also differ substantially in their philosophy of life. For one of them (Klara), her down-to-earth view makes it at least easier to deal with the Nazi past—which she experienced in the limited world of her small home town—while the other (Stefanie) represses the horrors of that time (she lost her fiancé Peter Niels, who fought against the Nazis). She retreats into a world of fantasy. All these women figures (including Mina, the mother, and Berthie, the cousin) live as outsiders in this bourgeois middle-class society whose norms they either do not fulfill or try to subvert.

The narrator leaves no doubt that she admires Klara, the hunchback, who conforms the least to the expectations society holds for a woman in this text, and who even shocks neighbors and friends because she has an "illegitimate" child. But a sober matter-of-factness, a certain distance, directness, and courage, make it possible for her to deal with her petit bourgeois life. After the crimes of the Nazi era, her relation to God has become that of a person, according to the text, "who has been severely and unjustly insulted and deprived" (. . . der tief und zu Unrecht Beleidigten und Beraubten . . . ; 95). But she takes her direction from a nonreligious principle of love, a "compassion for humanity" (Mitmenschlichkeit; Gill), which she follows unobtrusively without sacrificing her entire existence. All the incomprehensible and inexplicable events in her life, such as the Nazi terror, she subsumes under the formula of the "Black Donkey." This metaphor expresses her strategy for survival because she assigns to it all the answers to the problems concerning her own and other people's destinies (*SchwE*, 200–201).

With her "deformed" body Klara resembles an Oskar Matzerath, although, unlike him, she does not retreat to an insane asylum in order to look at the world, but rather continues to take an active part within it. The figure of Klara is as a very successful representation of a woman who has learned to use the cross-eyed gaze or the double focus, as she sees contradictions, confronts them realistically, and lives with them.

Inspired by the revelations concerning Rinser's past, my new and different reading of the novel focused more critically and intensively on the difficult problems of dealing with Germany's fascist past, which pursues us into the present and which we must remember, in Mitscherlich's sense, by not forgetting it and working through it. My interest now focused also on the male characters, Fleckmann in particular, who had seemed a minor figure before. In addition, I began to question the role of the narrator with respect to a dialogic structure of the text.

Luise Rinser has stated repeatedly that her main purpose in writing is to communicate with her readers. And it does seem at first glance that a dialogic multiperspectivity—a presentation of several perspectives through conversations between narrator and characters—achieves this purpose. But does it really succeed in opening the text, which could create an interplay of many possibilities for the reader?

In a feminist reading process, a dialectic communication ideally takes place, as demonstrated, for example, in Patrocinio Schweickart's analysis of a Dickinson essay written by Adrienne Rich. "In the paradigm of reading implicit in her [Adrienne Rich's] essay, the dialectic of *control* . . . gives way to the dialectic of *communication*. For Rich, reading is a matter of "trying to connect" with the existence behind the text" (Schweickart, 53). This paradigm of reading, of a "dialectic of communication" as opposed to a "dialectic of control" can be applied to the writing process also. The question is then: to what extent does the author/the text succeed in juxtaposing the different text characters without letting one voice drown out the other.

In *Der schwarze Esel*, several forms of dialogue are in competition with each other: we hear Mina's conversation with invisible forces, Stefanie's long monologues, the conversations among several women, and the question and answer game of the first-person narrator. The latter is of particular significance. Although at first she seems to be tolerant and full of interest toward her partners in the conversation, approaching them very cautiously, she assumes the dominant role very quickly. The narrator uses clever manipulation strategies to compel the women to open up, and she adds her own comments freely. Some parts read as if one or the other of the women were being put on trial, with the narrator taking on the role of cross-examiner. They actually become a sounding board for the narrator in confronting her own past and trying to gain a better understanding of it. Thus, the interplay of many possibilities is essentially reduced to one—the one of the first-person narrator. And she, the narrator, seems to leave the past behind at the end. The last sentence of the novel reads: "Such a journey one undertakes only once in a lifetime" (. . . So eine Fahrt macht man nur einmal im Leben; 202).

The text nevertheless presents a wide spectrum of different lives during the Nazi era, from dedicated National Socialists to Jewish victims to resisters. The text attempts to differentiate further between the different types of collaborators (e.g., Berthie, the communist who became a National Socialist), thereby breaking open the dualism of victim and perpetrator. The text focuses repeatedly on ambivalent characters such as Dr. Fleckmann, whose very name is revealing. A so-called "good Nazi" he is, but this figure makes the reader wonder; this chemist, councilmember, mayor, is described as "absurd and spooky" because "he belonged to the Nazis, but he did not really do anything evil" (der ganze Mann war absurd und unheimlich . . . weil er ein Nazi war und doch nichts Böses tat; 26). A National Socialist "because of his lack of understanding, or even conscious misunderstanding," who thought that "fascism was a great idea, and who needed great means . . . in order to achieve great things"; this is Klara's interpretation. (Er war ein Nazi, ja, aber aus vollem Mißverständnis, vielleicht aus bewußtem Mißverständnis . . . der Faschismus sei so eine große Idee, er brauchte etwas Großes . . . um große Dinge tun zu können . . . ; 28.) She admires him because he was "consistent" and killed himself on the white flag of surrender.

The character of Berthie illustrates perfectly how closely the status of perpetrator/collaborator and victim is connected. The gluttonous Berthie, who still mourns the Hitler era, becomes a frightening and upsetting example for her modern readers in her state of mental immobility and stagnation. But she also gives reason for reflection: "a woman whose fate was only partly her fault, to a very minor extent even, maybe a quarter, maybe a hundredth . . ." (eine Frau mit einem Geschick, das sie nur halb, nur viertels, nur zum hundertsten Teil selbst verschuldet hat; 141). Her pathetic state, her bigotry, her dismal life are best shown by the text itself:

> Stupid old Berthie, raised in the half-lit café between gossip and a craving for food, crushed between her fat, money-hungry and adulterous mother and the mean, calculating pastry cook Karl and the father for whom they had no respect . . . , then later, at school, brainwashed with Hitler propaganda, not even looked at by the Jew Erich Bernheimer whom she adored, but immediately made to succumb by the first seducer who happened to look like the ideal of the "nordic masterrace," . . . . . then pregnant and almost killed by fear of shame and disgrace in this small-town society, without hope of abortion (it carried a death penalty at this time), giving birth in secret to a baby hated by all and hidden at the mother's command, the slow murder also prompted by her mother and by her own helplessness, being caught in a libel action, pronounced guilty, paying the fine out of her mother's purse, abandoned to ridicule and condemnation, surviving bomb attacks—simply forgotten by fate, so that the long rest of her life is nothing but a walk through a blind alley of total incomprehension, a petrification that cannot be stopped, a lingering death. Did it have to be like this, was there no freedom, dignity or grace?
>
> (Dumme alte arme Berthie, aufgewachsen in dem dämmerigen Café zwischen Klatsch und Naschsucht, erdrückt zwischen der fetten geldscheffelnden ehebrecherischen Mutter, dem schnöden berechnenden Konditor Karl und dem sie alle verachtenden Vater. . . . dann in der Schule . . . mit Thesen in Hitlerdeutsch

> programmiert, vom heimlich Angebeteten, dem Juden Erich Bernheimer, nicht einmal angesehen, dem erstbesten Verführer verfallen, der zufällig dem Ideal der 'nordischen Herrenrasse' entsprach, . . . schwanger dann mit allen mörderischen Ängsten vor Schande und Verfemung in der scheinheiligen Gesellschaft der kleinen Stadt, keine Möglichkeit zur Abtreibung in jener Zeit (sie stand unter Todesstrafe) das heimlich geborene, auf Befehl der Mutter versteckte und von allen gehaßte Kind, der langsame Mord, angestiftet von der Mutter und der eigenen Hilflosigkeit, in einen Verleumdungsprozeß verwickelt, schuldig gesprochen, Strafe zahlend aus der Kasse der Mutter, der Lächerlichkeit und Verachtung preisgegeben, die Bomben überlebend, vom Schicksal einfach vergessen, so daß der lange Rest des Lebens nichts mehr ist als der blinde Gang durch Unverstandenes, die gnadenlose unaufhaltsame Versteinerung, der hinausgezögerte Tod. Mußte das so sein, wo war da Freiheit, Würde, Gnade.) (141)

The novel *Der schwarze Esel* also directs attention toward the Postwar Era—the years from 1945 on into the early seventies, and even extended into our time. That period is marked by the gradual *repression of guilt*. The reconstruction of the town and its industrialization after 1945 are sharply criticized in the narrator's reflections, vividly illustrated in the contrast of the garden idyll and the town now polluted by toxic fumes (44–45).

The characters in the text and particularly its women seem to exist in life's shadow, entangled in a net of perpetrators, collaborators, and victims. Some of them became collaborators, although National Socialism, this pinnacle of patriarchical thought and action, simultaneously used and oppressed them. Yet they also share in the guilt of repressing the past. The message of the text remains ambiguous. Klara asks herself at one point: "Why then, why should one not just forget. But I tell myself also one cannot know enough. The more one learns, the clearer the connections, and those do matter" (. . . Ich frage mich zwar, warum eigentlich, warum sollte man nicht vergessen, aber ich sage mir auch, man könne nicht genug wissen vom Leben, je mehr Material, desto mehr Zusammenhänge, und auf die kommt es an; 24–25). It is significant that it is the first-person narrator, however, who responds to Klara at some point: "Recovering through forgetting, that is the worst" (Gesundwerden durch Vergessen, das ist schlimmer als alles; 32).

Luise Rinser's novel *The Black Donkey* presents us with an attempt to confront fascism in Germany's past and present. Whether it really offers "Dialogues with the Past" is the question. I read the text instead as a monologue by a first-person female narrator—full of nuances, variations, and lively illustrations—who cannot forget although she would like to. It is precisely this conflict that mirrors the difficulty of coping with the past and the impossibility of forgetting.

Concerning the author, Luise Rinser herself, one can only wish that she would observe what Christa Wolf once formulated in an essay on Max Frisch: "The aversion to using one's creative work for the purpose of self-protection can grow to the point where it is self-defeating and one's self-esteem depends on the degree to which one opens oneself to one's readers" (Die Abneigung gegen das Erfinden zum Zwecke der Selbst-Schonung kann wachsen bis auf den Punkt, da sie unüberwindlich wird und die Selbstachtung davon abhängt, daß man mit offenem Visier vor die Leser tritt; *Spiegel*, 6/93, 198).

(Translation by Dorothy Krahn and Elke P. Frederiksen)

Bibliography

Ebbinghaus, Angelika. *Opfer und Täterinnen. Frauenbiographien des Nationalsozialismus*. Nördlingen: F. Greno, 1987.

Falkenstein, Henning. *Luise Rinser*. Berlin: Colloquium, 1988.

Frederiksen, Elke. *Luise Rinser: Leben—Literatur—Engagement*. Stuttgart: Akademischer Verlag Heinz, Forthcoming.

————. "Luise Rinser." In *Women Writers in German-Speaking Countries. A Bio-Bibliographical, Critical Source Book*. Westport, New York and London: Greenwood, 1998. 398–406.

————. "Luise Rinser." In *Neue Literatur der Frauen. Deutschsprachige Autorinnen der Gegenwart*. Ed. Heinz Puknus. Munich: C.H. Beck, 1980, 55–61, 316–318.

Gill, Gudrun. *Die Utopie Hoffnung bei Luise Rinser. Eine sozio-psychologische Studie*. New York/Bern/Frankfurt am Main/Paris: Peter Lang, 1991.

Greiner, Ulrich. "Gespenster: Heidegger, Höfer, Rinser, Waldheim, de Man und der Antifaschismus im Sonderangebot." *Die Zeit* (8 August 1988).

Hage, Volker. "Wir müssen uns dem Schicksal stellen." *Der Spiegel* 47.6 (8 February 1993): 197–199.

Hinze, Diana Orendi. "The Case of Luise Rinser: A Past That Will Not Die." In *Gender, Patriarchy, and Fascism in the Third Reich: The Response of Women Writers*. Ed. Elaine Martin. Detroit: Wayne State University Press, 1993, 143–168.

Konzag, Marianne. "Gespräch mit Luise Rinser." In *Luise Rinser: Materialien zu Leben und Werk*. Ed. Hans-Rüdiger Schwab. Frankfurt am Main: Fischer, 1986, 25–38.

Koonz, Claudia. *Mütter im Vaterland*. Trans. Cornelia Holfelder von der Tann. Freiburg (Breisgau): Kore, 1991.

Lennox, Sara. "Feminist Scholarship and Germanistik." *The German Quarterly* 62.2 (1989): 158–170.

Martin, Biddy. "Zwischenbilanz der feministischen Debatten." In *Germanistik in den USA: Neue Entwicklungen und Methoden*. Ed. Frank Trommler. Opladen: Westdeutscher Verlag, 1989, 165–195.

Martin, Elaine. "Women right/(Re)Write the Nazi Past: An Introduction." In *Gender, Patriarchy, and Fascism in the Third Reich*. Ed. Elaine Martin. Detroit: Wayne State University Press, 1993. 11–31.

Mitscherlich, Alexander and Margarete. *Die Unfähigkeit zu trauern*. Munich: Piper, 1967.

Raddatz, Fritz J. "Von der Beschädigung der Literatur durch ihre Urheber: Bemerkungen zu Heiner Müller und Christa Wolf." *Die Zeit* (5 February 1993): 17.

Rinser, Luise. *Gefängnistagebuch*. (1946). Frankfurt am Main: Fischer, 1973.

———. *A Woman's Prison Journal*. Trans. Michael Hulse. New York: Schocken, 1987.

———. *Der schwarze Esel*. Frankfurt am Main: Fischer, 1974.

Ryan, Judith. *The Uncompleted Past: Postwar German Novels and the Third Reich*. Detroit: Wayne State University Press, 1983.

Schnell, Ralf. *Die Literatur der Bundesrepublik. Autorem, Geschichte, Literaturbetrieb.* Stuttgart: Metzler, 1986.

Schwab, Hans-Rüdgier. "≫Soviel Sicherheit reizt mich zur Provokation . . .≪. Eine Skizze zu Werk und Wirkung Luise Rinsers." In *Luise Rinser. Materialien zu Leben und Werk*. Ed. Hans-Rüdgier Schwab. Frankfurt am Main: Fischer, 1986, 11–21.

Schweickart, Patrocinio P. "Reading Ourselves: Toward a Feminist Theory of Reading." In *Gender and Reading: Essays on Readers, Texts, and Contexts*. Ed. Elizabeth A. Flynn and Patrocinio P. Schweickart. Baltimore/London: Johns Hopkins University Press, 1986, 31–62.

Weedon, Chris. *Feminist Practice and Poststructuralist Theory*. Oxford/New York: Blackwell, 1987.

Weigel, Sigrid. "Der schielende Blick. Thesen zur Geschichte weiblicher Schreibpraxis." In *Die verborgene Frau: Sechs Beiträge zu einer feministischen Literaturwissenschaft*. Ed. Inge Stephan and Sigrid Weigel. Berlin: Argument Verlag, 1983, 83–137.

Wolf, Christa. "Eine Auskunft." *Berliner Zeitung* (21 January 1993).

Wolf, Christa. "Ich war nicht die Dichterin dieses Staates." *Frankfurter Allgemeine Zeitung* (2 February 1993).

12

Ingeborg Drewitz: Three Generations of Women Respond to Fascism

Margaret E. Ward

On January 18, 1952, Ingeborg Drewitz scrawled in the plain copybook that served as her personal diary:

> Strange feeling that one can only reach the next generation completely, which in reality is already foreign to us, has its own problems to deal with. But this desire to reach out is the bridge between the generations, which have been separated by deep chasms of suffering for at least the last 2000 years.
>
> (Seltsames Gefühl, daß man immer erst die nächste Generation ganz erreicht, die dann eigentlich schon wieder fremd ist, ihre eigenen Probleme hat und durchstehen muß. Aber dieses Erreichenwollen ist die Brücke zwischen den Generationen, die seit nunmehr fast 2 Jahrtausenden durch Schluchten von Leid getrennt sind.) (*Nachlaß* [unpublished papers], n.p.)[1]

Drewitz's keen awareness of the inevitable distance between herself and the next generation may be linked to her childhood memories of daily life in a crowded, working-class flat in Berlin (Moabit), which had been home to four generations of her family during the 1920s, but at this moment it was no doubt magnified by the fact that she had two young daughters, Dorit and Jutta, four and two years old. This diary entry seems to presage the estrangement she would experience in the late

1960s and 1970s, especially from the eldest of her three daughters. Nevertheless, a fierce determination to build bridges, to the previous as well as to the next generation of which she speaks here, characterized Drewitz's personal and public life, and much of her oeuvre.

As a member of that generation of postwar Germans, who were born in the mid to late 1920s and who had experienced the rise of National Socialism as schoolchildren, and the war years as young adults, Drewitz had a profound sense of the moral necessity to link the past to the present, especially that fascist past that many Germans were eager to forget. By the time of her untimely death in the mid 1980s, Drewitz felt that only a desperately fragile hope remained that any kind of communication with her daughters' generation *could* take place, but she never abandoned the conviction that she must try to build that bridge. Drewitz's motivation to write dramas, radio plays, essays, reviews, novels, and stories, as well as her tireless work for a variety of organizations and causes—against injustice and on behalf of minorities—have their source in this basic desire to close that gap to the next generation.

Literature has a special, twofold role to play in Drewitz's bridge building. She saw herself not only as a writer, but also as a reader and critic. It is noteworthy that she was one of the first to draw attention to the little-known oeuvre of those German writers who had resisted Hitler. As she stated in the introduction to her collection of essays on exile literature and the literature of resistance, *Die zerstörte Kontinuität* (1981) (*The Destroyed Continuity*):

> It was and is important to me to demonstrate that by reading, a part of reality can be recovered, which is in fact history, that through books, fates can be revealed which concern us.
>
> (Wichtig war und ist es mir, zu zeigen, daß sich lesend ein Stück Wirklichkeit, die ja immer auch Geschichte ist, einholen läßt. Daß hinter den Büchern Schicksale verborgen sind, die uns angehen.) ("Zu diesem Buch" ["About this Book"], 9)

More importantly, in her own works—from those first difficult years as she struggled to establish herself as a writer in the early postwar period, to her last literary sketches and diary entries—Drewitz repeatedly evoked her personal experiences of growing up in Nazi Germany. She constantly probed that private ground within the context of the times and asked the most difficult personal questions concerning guilt and responsibility. What possible meaning could the life of one individual have? She certainly found no easy answer. On the contrary, she often responded to both the German fascist past and its hallmarks in the present with a sense of utter helplessness, even bouts of depression. In fact, she always reacted quite emotionally and personally to the vast array of humanity's inhumanity—which reaches us daily through the media—recognizing her/our complicity in its various manifestations.

She lived vulnerably, the way she described a recurring nightmare in her diaries—"without skin"—painfully aware of the open wound left by Germany's recent past, and cognizant of "how small a step it is from simply not knowing what to do—something we face daily anew in this situation—to the total negation of our responsibility" (wie klein ist der Schritt von der Ratlosigkeit, in die uns diese Situation täglich von neuem bringt, zur Negation von Verantwortung; "Und ich weiß, daß ich damit nicht allein stehe . . ." [And I Know, That I Don't Stand Alone], 201).

Despite self-doubt, setbacks in private and public life, Drewitz resisted the seduction of repressing the past, for she firmly believed in the personal responsibility of every individual. She always seemed to discover within herself some small reserve of that hope she needed to continue the precarious balancing act between past and future which her bridge-building entailed. She argued, for example, in the December 14, 1980 speech, on receipt of the Carl von Ossietzky medallion from the German Section of the International League for Human Rights, that it is necessary for all of us to act in the here and now, to use "the small possibilities [we have] to prevent that which actually happens but which is unimaginable, and not to lose sight of the imaginable unreal that is utopia" (die kleinen Möglichkeiten, das unvorstellbar Wirkliche zu verhindern, das vorstellbar Unwirkliche, die Utopie, nicht aus den Augen zu verlieren; 202).

In an essay on the meaning of Ernst Bloch for her generation and for herself, written in 1985—only a year before her death—Drewitz admits how precarious the shifting terrain had become, on which she was still trying to build that bridge to the next generation.[2] She fully recognized that Bloch's hope was "yesterday's consolation," but she nevertheless admits:

> Without this consolation; without this expectation—however questionable—of an enlightened humanity . . . I couldn't live or write anymore. I know I just act as if this "Principle Hope" can be stretched out over the abyss in our reality; I act as if I weren't affected by my existential *angst*. The last philosopher of humanism Ernst Bloch, gives me once again the signs and the language to hang on. But—hope? [I] hardly [have] that anymore.
>
> (Ohne diesen Trost, ohne diese, wenn auch fragwürdige Erwartung der mündigen Menschheit . . . könnte ich nicht mehr leben, nicht mehr schreiben. Und ich weiß, ich tue nur so, als sei das "Prinzip Hoffnung" über den Riß in der Wirklichkeit zu wölben; ich tue nur so, als sei ich in meiner Existenzangst ungerührt. Der letzte Philosoph des Humanismus Ernst Bloch, gibt mir noch einmal die Zeichen und die Sprache, um standzuhalten. Aber—die Hoffnung?—kaum noch.) ("Ernst Bloch und meine Wirklichkeit" ["Ernst Bloch and My Reality"], 248)

In a brief autobiographical sketch, entitled *Lebenslehrzeit* (*Life's Apprenticeship*), published the same year she wrote the Bloch essay, Drewitz reveals another source for her slim, but persistent hope in the future, and her confidence in the importance of everyday resistance, in change measured only by millimeters—the example of her mother. She describes here her personal experience of those critical, formative years between 1932 and 1946. She truly believed, "Whoever wants to understand fascism must understand the everyday" (Wer Faschismus begreifen will, muß den Alltag begreifen; 29). By 1933 Drewitz had moved with her parents and younger sister to a small, third-floor flat in the petit-bourgeois neighborhood of Berlin (Friedenau). Her father, once again unemployed, unleashed his frustration in verbal and physical abuse of his wife and children. In *Lebenslehrzeit*, Drewitz describes the house in which they lived, and the spectrum of reactions to Hitler's assumption of power among her neighbors and schoolmates, some of them Jewish. She indicates that she learned during these years how easily categories blurred. What did it mean to be a perpetrator, a bystander, a victim, she asked herself. She realized that "the dividing line between guilt and complicity; between merely being affected by and being victimized is not so easily distinguishable . . ." (die Grenze zwischen Schuld und Mitschuld, zwischen Betroffensein und Opfersein nicht genau auszumachen ist . . . ; 25).

Gabriele, the main character of Drewitz's novel, *Gestern war Heute: Hundert Jahre Gegenwart* (1978) (*Yesterday Was Today: A Century in the Present*), asks herself some of the difficult, personal questions that arise out of this blurring of the categories:

> To understand being caught up in it all. The no-mans-land between guilt and guilt. That we didn't overthrow the Nazis? That we didn't see the camps, or didn't look at them carefully or didn't want to see them?
>
> (Verstrickungen begreifen. Das Niemandsland zwischen Schuld und Schuld. Daß wir die Nazis nicht gestürzt haben? Daß wir die Lager nicht gesehen, nicht genau gesehen haben oder nicht haben sehen wollen?) (232)

As Drewitz began to ask herself these same kinds of questions in the early postwar years, she realized that it was her mother, Hildegard Vogel Neubert, who had shown her that resisting might at least begin with everyday acts. Her formative years, then, provided the key source of that albeit fragile belief to which she afterward clung, and which made writing a necessity for her: that the individual must count, that the subject is the locus where ideology can take hold, but also where resistance must originate, even if it only begins as a kind of instinctive repulsion in the face of injustice. Gabriele, her alter ego in *Gestern war Heute,* reaches that same conclusion in the chapter depicting the period 1954 to 1957: "Then I realize, that I AM! That I can intervene in reality!" (Dann fällt mir ein, daß ICH BIN! Daß ich eingreifen kann in die Wirklichkeit! 241). Drewitz's oeuvre explores the subject as the locus of possible resistance to both political and personal forms of oppression, as well as the need to confront the manifestations of fascism in the everyday, and always in the present.

Drewitz's many autobiographical essays and vignettes, and some of her best fiction testify to the way this preoccupation can be traced to her relationship with her mother, which became closer because of the political events of the 1930s and the wartime experiences of the 1940s. As a ten-year-old, Drewitz claims to have been only dimly aware of her mother's "helpless anger" (der hilflose Zorn) as they stood together on the cold balcony in January 1933 and listened to the emboldened brown-shirts marching down the nearby avenue shouting: "'Jew, die!'" (Juda, verrecke!; *Lebenslehrzeit,* 9–10). Despite his anti-Nazi tirades at home, her father had joined the NSDAP in March 1933 in hopes of bettering his chances for employment, a decision that had created a further rift between husband and wife and left the daughter with a mixed message. Neither religious beliefs nor political ideology seem to have played any role in the strongly anti-Nazi sentiments of Drewitz's mother, but she clearly set an example.

Five years later, the so-called *Kristallnacht* (Night of Broken Glass) of November 9–10, 1938 proved a turning point, for only then did the daughter realize how the Nazi racial policies—to which she had been given a theoretical introduction in school—might be brutally applied. Drewitz had at first rebelled against the express wishes of her mother, by joining the BDM (Nazi youth organization for older girls) in 1936. While she herself could only barely disguise her antipathy for many of its goals, she admits she was flattered to have been assigned a minor leadership role. Since her membership had not actually been finalized, however, she was evidently able to withdraw from the organization after the burning synagogues and shattered storefronts brought her to her senses. When questioned about this, Drewitz emphasizes that she had been able to withdraw easily. No heroism had been required of her, and she did not want to suggest that, if it had been, she would have been capable of it.[3]

Drewitz notes that during the 1930s her mother—who had abandoned a promising musical career—had less and less time to play the piano. The daughter had become aware that her mother was trying to help some of their Jewish friends who had gone into hiding:

> She was taking care of people who at that time were not allowed to be people any more. A few oblique references to this, no more. Still, she was a model for me and has remained one.
>
> (Sie sorgte sich um Menschen, die damals keine Menschen mehr sein durften. Ein paar Andeutungen, mehr nicht. Doch, sie war mir Vorbild und ist es geblieben). ("Ich wünschte sie mir immer am Klavier" ["I Would Wish to Have Her Always at the Piano"], 81)

Drewitz interprets her mother's actions as mundane. She nevertheless considers them a modelling behavior that had been absolutely essential to her own formation.

It should be noted in this connection that social psychologists who have explored the personality traits of those few individuals who exhibited helping behavior toward Jews during the Nazi period, have found their altruism was often dependent on an intense identification with a parental model. The identification tends to be with only one parent, who is "not necessarily religious" but who holds "very firm opinions on moral issues" and serves "as a model of moral conduct" (London, 247). In a series of family vignettes included in the collection, *Hinterm Fenster die Stadt* (*The City behind the Window*), Drewitz highlights similar helping behavior on the part of her maternal grandfather, Gustav, who did volunteer social work in Berlin-Moabit right up until his death in 1939.[4]

In the sketch entitled "Hildegard (1896–1953)," Drewitz clearly sees the mother/daughter relationship as crucial, however. Like the figures of Susanne and Gabriele in her novel *Gestern war Heute*, Drewitz's relationship with her mother was problematic in many ways. The daughter resented what she viewed as her mother's subservience in marriage, for she carried from earliest childhood an image of her mother as a victim of mental and physical cruelty. In retrospect, the daughter now asks herself why this beautiful and talented young woman had given up her prospects as a concert pianist to marry such a weak man, and how she had been able to assume the role of caregiver to a multigenerational, extended family with such equanimity. More importantly, the daughter also wonders what her mother may have actually suspected or even known of the Nazi genocide before 1945.[5] Drewitz thus seeks to bridge the gap backward to the past generation, as well as forward to the next, as she probes Hildegard Neubert's complex motivations—as a woman and a German citizen—many years after the mother's death.

Having slowly peeled away the layers first of anger, then pity, Drewitz is left with some vividly remembered conversations, and even more importantly, moments of silence in which solidarity and understanding had brought mother and daughter momentarily close. She now can acknowledge her mother's decisive role in supporting her wish to pursue university studies against her father's will. By the 1980s, Drewitz appreciates that there was some solid core of courage in her mother's seemingly mundane actions:

> What does that mean, to be a model? Is there only one? Certainly I am equally indebted to Rosa Luxemburg and Ricarda Huch and Käthe Kollwitz, examples of political intelligence and courage, historical insight and courage, artistic individuality and courage. . . . However, the power of an example is, after all, the power to make an impression which forms one during ones childhood and youth.
>
> (Was ist das, ein Vorbild? Gibt es nur eines? Sicher bin ich Rosa Lusemburg [*sic*] und Ricarda Huch und Käthe Kollwitz gleichermaßen verbunden, der politischen Intelligenz und dem Mut, der historischen Klugheit und dem Mut, der künst-

> lerischen Eigenheit und dem Mut. . . . Aber, die Kraft des Vorbilds ist doch die Prägekraft, die einen in der Kindheit und Jugend formt.) (83)

Drewitz especially remembers her mother's subtle, pedagogical style:

> Come, my mother said, and showed me a rose blooming in the Berlin Tiergarten. Come, she said, and showed me the blood stains on the pavement in Moabit after the political street fighting before 1933. Come, she said, and showed me the cabbage beds in the kitchen-gardens; we can live on this. Come, she said, and went with me into the apartments and the cellars in which Jewish families were trying to survive during the early 1930s. . . . And still that was never an order, never a pedagogical measure taken, she never had ready explanations. For she trusted us as children and as we were growing up. She was sure that we had eyes to see and ears to hear.
>
> (Komm, sagte meine Mutter, und zeigte mir im Berliner Tiergarten im Rosengarten eine Blüte. Komm, sagte sie und zeigte mir in Moabit die Blutflecken auf den Straßen nach den Straßenschlachten vor 1933. Komm, sagte sie und zeigte mir die Kohlbeete in den Laubengärten, davon kann man leben. Komm, sagte sie und ging mit mir in Wohnungen und Kellerwohnungen, in denen jüdische Familien in den frühen dreißiger Jahren noch zu überleben versuchten. . . . Und doch war das nie ein Befehl, nie eine "pädagogische Maßnahme", hatte sie nie Erklärungen bereit. Denn sie vertraute uns Kindern, uns Heranwachsenden. Sie war sicher, daß wir Augen hatten zu sehen, Ohren zu hören.) (83)

In the speech with which Drewitz accepted the Carl von Ossietzky medal, she also began with a remembered conversation she had had with her mother in the summer of 1945. This clearly marked another important turning point, in which the historical moment precipitates a personal crisis, as the full extent of the Nazi wartime atrocities and the Shoah was being revealed to the German public. In another autobiographical sketch in *Hinterm Fenster die Stadt*, Drewitz names these revelations, with their "horrible truth about the murder of the Jews and the brutality of the Nazi conduct of war" (entsetzliche Wahrheit der Ermordung der Juden und der Brutalität der nazistischen Kriegführung; "Deine Stadt, meine Stadt" ["Your City, My City"], 11), as the reason she became a writer. It was not so much a wish, but rather a compulsion to write, "to unmask that which was against all reason, to find a beginning behind the pain" (diesen Widersinn zu entlarven und hinter dem Schmerz den Anfang zu finden; 11). Significantly, in this same sketch, Drewitz tells that she wrote one of her first works, a drama entitled *Alle Tore waren bewacht* (*All the Gates Were Guarded*) for her mother (16).[6]

It took a considerable amount of daring in 1951 for this virtually unknown young woman to write a play that is set in a concentration camp. Drewitz received the Carl

Zuckmayer prize for it, and eventually the play was performed, but not until 1955, two years after her mother had passed away. By the 1960s Drewitz's attempt to deal with the unspeakable had certainly been conveniently forgotten, and writers such as Rolf Hochhuth and Peter Weiss were hailed as the first to attempt to bring this difficult subject matter to the German stage. One reason for the negligible impact of Drewitz's play may have been the attention she pays in it to the lives of women. Some of the most effective scenes take place in the women's barracks of the unnamed camp. Drewitz actually tries to imagine the everyday life of a small group of Jewish women, their petty jealousies, but also their solidarity with each other in the face of death. The action concerning the possibility of resistance is carried by a male protagonist, however. Although his attempt to save one woman fails, the message of the drama is clear: "We must resist. Perhaps somewhere the net will tear. . . . The state is created by human beings. . . . Human beings pull the strings" (Wir müssen uns wehren. Vielleicht reißt irgendwo das Netz. . . . Der Staat ist Menschenwerk. . . . Da ziehen Menschen die Fäden; unpublished ms. in *Nachlaß*, 16–17).[7]

Drewitz's choice to write mostly dramas and radio plays in the 1950s may well have been due to her belief that the dramatic genre was the best one with which to confront the German public with the Nazi past.[8] It was probably for this reason that she started to write dramas again near the end of her life, at a time when she felt a renewed urgency for that confrontation with the repressed past to take place as a fourth generation—that of her own grandchildren—reached school age. By the early 1960s Drewitz had turned increasingly to narrative forms. In her early fiction she continued to play out moments of possible resistance in everyday settings. Some of these variations on the theme are based on her own experiences, as comparison with the autobiographical sketches and vignettes published in the 1980s clearly reveals. In almost every case the central characters are figures of the middle generation to which Drewitz belonged.

In a story written in the 1950s and entitled "Brenna," for example, it is a young woman who thinks back to the 1930s and early 1940s. The first-person narrator admits her ambivalent feelings about a close friend from her school days, a Jewish girl named Brenna, who had moved to another part of the city. She had been excited to meet Brenna again by chance in the elevated train one day. Against her parents antisemitic objections, she had even invited Brenna to her wedding. But when the Jewish girl sought her out several years later, hoping the narrator might offer her a place to hide, she had turned Brenna away. The narrator had been unwilling to do anything that might jeopardize her own safety or that of her two young children. The moment of decision is not portrayed as dramatic, however, for there are no dialogues in which the conflict can be joined. Both the request and the refusal are not even articulated; everything hinges on what the two women understand without saying anything to each other. By the following day the narrator has had second thoughts about her silent rejection of Brenna's unspoken pleas. She returns to Brenna's flat, but finds her gone. Perhaps she has already been deported. After that the narrator can not overcome her deep sense of complicity in the Nazi crimes, as the blurring of the borders between the role of bystander and perpetrator is enacted ("Brenna," 7–20).

In her early fiction Drewitz often projected her own experiences onto a male figure. In the novel *Das Karussell* (1962) (*The Carousel*), for instance, Andreas, a sixteen-year-old schoolboy, in love with a Jewish girl, is profoundly affected by the events of November 9–10, 1938, as he and Golde meet on the street and together watch the burning synagogue in the Fasanenstraße, Berlin. Shortly thereafter he withdraws from the Hitler Youth. One recognizes this as a fictionalized version of Drewitz's own story. The action of the novel is divided into three parts: 1938, 1945, and 1953. After the war Andreas tries to make a new start, but he hasn't forgotten what happened during the Nazi era. A professor who had been imprisoned because he was a communist, now helps Andreas launch a small theater group. When the young man is called upon to make what he considers a foul political compromise, he tells the professor what he learned about the need for civil courage at the time he witnessed the 1938 pogrom (185). Fortified by that memory, he is now able to act in accordance with his ideals.

While not as fully drawn as the figures of the parental generation in *Gestern war Heute*, Andreas's mother and father share some of the same character traits as Gabriele's mother and father in that novel. In *Das Karussell,* it is also the mother who is willing to remember the past in the present, and who points to one reason for hope in the future—the birth of a grandchild. However, Drewitz's choice of language makes it clear, that the key relationship that builds a bridge of understanding might be with either parent: "To walk next to a child, to be able to withstand his/her questions" (Neben einem Kind hergehen, seinen Fragen standhalten; *Das Karussell*, 160).[9] Andreas, who is about to become a father, worries about his ability to forge that link. He remains pessimistic about Germany's future and his ability to answer those questions he imagines his son will inevitably pose about its past. He tells his wife, for example, "We're not going to make it; we'll never clear away the guilt which has come upon us, Barbara—" (Wir schaffen's nicht, wir tragen die Schuld nicht ab, die auf uns gekommen ist, Barbara—; 188).

By the time Drewitz published *Gestern war Heute* in 1978, the generation spoken of in the 1952 diary entry—the generation of Andreas's son and of her own daughters—had come of age. In many of her novels of the 1970s and 1980s it is the mother/daughter bond that serves as the central vehicle for exploring the possibility of actually reaching that next generation. As Monika Shafi has shown in her article, "Die überforderte Generation: Mutterfiguren in Romanen von Ingeborg Drewitz" (1991) ("The Overburdened Generation: Mother Figures in the Novels of Ingeborg Drewitz"), it is the middle-generation mother's perspective that dominates the plots, as she must stand up to the questions of her daughters. Drewitz no longer shied away from her autobiographical impulse, nor did she feel the need to hide her female subjectivity behind an imagined male protagonist.

By the 1980s gender has become a more important category for the writer in this constellation, for Drewitz now clearly shows women as the ones most willing to confront the Nazi past, and as the ones most eager to build a bridge of communication to the next generation and beyond. This can best be illustrated by two plays, *Gestern war heute* (*Yesterday Was Today*), using motifs from the novel of the same name, and *Das Gartenfest oder Eine deutsche Idylle* (*The Garden Party or A German Idyll*).[10] In both, Drewitz simultaneously explores the way both generational and gender differences may color all three generations' responses to National Socialism. In *Das Gartenfest*, an English journalist, Charlotte Weiss, returns repeatedly to West Germany to find out about the motivations of the people in her home town. We learn that her mother, who had stayed behind in 1933, had perished in one of the death camps. Among the people the daughter confronts in their German idyll of the '50s, '60s, '70s, and '80s, it is the women of that middle generation who are gradually able to admit complicity. During the Vietnam war, several of them have allied themselves with rebellious children who are active in the radical student movement.

The dramatic version of *Gestern war heute* makes this generational shift most clearly, as the daughter's position is finally given prominence, and she confronts the mother on the very issue of repressing the fascist past. In the novel, by contrast, the rift between mother and daughter is more subtle. Much is left unspoken. The daughter's accusations have primarily to do with compromises she has seen her mother make in the tradeoff between family and career. The narrative also ends with a passage told from the mother's perspective, in which her sense of identification and solidarity with the daughter softens the conflict between the generations (382).

Drama was intended to produce a public shock effect, in Drewitz's view. Thus, in the play adapted from the novel, a much deeper divide separates the first and second generation. Unlike the narrative, in which metaphors and other textual features emphasize the maternal viewpoint (Shafi), here the daughter takes center stage. And the Nazi past becomes the point of departure for her critique, as she rejects her mother's example, both in the private and public spheres. The problems of this next generation and of the recycling of fascist tendencies in the present can now come to the fore. The action is set in a frame that brings mother and daughter together at a moment when the daughter's boyfriend, Knut, a member of the radical left, is facing bank robbery charges. But the daughter, Cornelia, goes on the offensive immediately:

> CORNELIA: You were a part of it back then when the world was out of kilter. How did you live when those with the stars on their lapels were driven into the street? Did you look the other way? Why didn't you . . . why didn't you all tell [the next generation]: be different. Scream, when you see injustice! Cry out! Destroy!
>
> (Du warst doch dabei, als die Welt nicht in Ordnung war. Wie hast du denn gelebt, als die mit dem Stern auf dem Mantelaufschlag auf die Straßen mußten? Hast du da weggesehen? . . . Warum hast du . . .warum habt ihr nicht alle gesagt: werdet anders! Brüllt, wenn ihr Unrecht seht! Schreit! Zerstört!) (167)

This accusation forces the mother to retrieve her past in a series of flashbacks. Ursula appears as a young BDM member in the late 1930s, but we learn of her affection for a Jewish boy. In the next scene (I, 2) she returns home with the packages intended for his family in hiding; they have been transported to some unknown destination in the East. Ursula, like Andreas in *Das Karussell*, had clearly thought that her small acts of faithfulness to an individual she cared for could make a difference. This belief is now exposed by the next generation as naive. Such mundane caring is insufficient. Much more explicit political action is required. In this instance, we learn, as soon as the war was over, Ursula and her husband had done everything they could to repress the Nazi past, to put it behind them as quickly as possible. They wanted to start a new life, to have a child whose name would remind them of nothing. They wanted to protect their child from that recent German past and from any future experience of pain.

In a key scene (II,2) there is a glimmer of hope as the pregnant Ursula recognizes the way in which each of them nevertheless unwittingly continues to pass on the past in the present, if only by means of the familial stories they tell, or refrain from telling (173). There is no cosmic vision here of a new birth that will redeem, but rather fear of a wound that may never heal because the means to do so can be thoroughly repressed. Once Cornelia is born, the parents' repression is in fact so complete that it is left to the next generation to ask the difficult questions. In a first confrontation with her mother, which occurs in one of these flashbacks, (II, 4) the daughter accuses:

> CORNELIA: (almost screaming) You haven't learned anything. Nothing! Nothing! And I'm supposed to learn from you two. You lie for every bit of money like Judas. You lie along with the others. You forget along with the others. You fail to listen along with the others. You don't want to admit that all of you—even you and father—all of you are guilty And that's why you hit me.
>
> ([fast schreiend] Nichts habt ihr dazugelernt. Nichts. Nichts! Und ich soll von euch lernen. Ihr lügt doch für jeden Judaslohn. Lügt mit. Vergeßt mit. Überhört mit. Wollt nicht wahrhaben, daß ihr alle—du und Vater—alle Mitschuldige seid. Und darum schlägst du mich.) (175)

Soon thereafter, Cornelia leaves home after having joined the radical student movement. In the next scene (II, 5) Ursula overhears her giving a political speech one day on the street in opposition to the Vietnam War:

> CORNELIA: We have already been guilty once. We kept silent once, when the gas chambers and the crematoriums were built. . . . Friends, comrades, let us unmask our industries and our banks, that financed the building of the gas chambers and crematoriums back then. ... Let us gather in front of the directors' villas. Let us disturb their idyll. . . . Let us no longer remain silent! Don't remain silent any longer.
>
> (Wir sind schon einmal schuldig geworden. Wir haben schon einmal geschwiegen, als die Gaskammern und die Verbrennungsöfen gebaut wurden. . . . Freunde, Genossen, stellen wir unsere Konzerne und unsere Banken bloß, die schon einmal den Bau der Gaskammern und der Verbrennungsöfen finanziert haben. . . . Treffen wir uns vor den Villen der Direktoren! Stören wir sie in ihrer Idylle. . . . Schweigen wir nicht länger! Schweigt ihr nicht länger!) (176)

Then, in the scene that closes the frame, as the play returns to the present, Cornelia again refers specifically to her mother's personal past, rather than more generally to German guilt. "Did you run into the street when they came for your friend back then? Did you call out, be good?!" (Bist du denn auf die Straße gelaufen, als sie deinen Freund holten? Damals? Hast du denn gerufen, seid gut?! 181). Ursula cannot respond; she has no answers. She doesn't condone her daughter's current resort to violence, but she begins to be able to acknowledge the validity of the daughter's anger and her own complicity in Nazi crimes against humanity. The father, on the other hand, simply worries that Cornelia's whole generation is putting his postwar German idyll into question (177).

In the last years of her life Drewitz seemed to be driven by the compelling need to find some suitable response to the kinds of accusations the daughter makes in this play. If communication with the next generation had become too difficult, then at least links could still be forged to her grandchildren, to whom she wrote "Flaschenpost" (messages in a bottle). One is reminded of the way in which a single familial story about the uncle who had witnessed the storming of the Winter Palace in St. Petersburg in January 1905 is handed down from grandmother to granddaughter in the novel, *Gestern war Heute*. It plays a key role in Gabriele's emerging self-concept (157) and she in turn, passes this story on to her daughter, Renate, at a moment of family crisis, when the latter is only eight years old (273).[11] It is noteworthy that this vital familial story-telling role is assigned to women from one generation to the next. It may also be significant that Drewitz wrote quite differently to her only granddaughter, suggesting a special bond between women. This message in a bottle is written in a poetic language quite distinct from the speech used for the two boys, and it clearly echoes her remembrances of her mother's pedagogical style:[12]

> Come, come, I want to write, say, call out, come, I'll show you the ways through the streets and back alleys of the city, where the children play with the garbage can lids and with hate and they mock you because your friendliness seems strange to them.
>
> (Komm, komm, will ich schreiben, sagen, rufen, komm, ich zeig' dir die Wege durch die Straßen und Höfe der Stadt, wo die Kinder mit den Mülltonnendeckeln spielen und mit dem Haß und dich ihr Hohn trifft, weil deine Freundlichkeit ihnen fremd ist.) ("Flaschenpost: An meine drei Enkel" [Messages in a bottle: To my three grandchildren], 81-82)

Among Drewitz's final literary sketches in the back of the copybook that served as her last diary, one finds plans for a series of short plays for children, a cycle with scenes from the years 1929, 1932, 1934, 1938, 1945, and into the present. In the one for 1938 children are pictured as standing by while the synagogues burn and the stores are looted. Drewitz engages her potential, young audience directly, asking them to imagine themselves the next morning in school. She conjures up the scene from her own childhood which she had also used in *Gestern war Heute*. The history teacher, still in uniform, says "that it was the Jews' own fault" (daß sich die Juden das selber zuzuschreiben hätten; 97). In the planned play, Drewitz can go beyond that narration of the past, unleashing a series of rhetorical questions that are posed quite directly:

> Just imagine: A November morning, school begins. . . . What would you have done? Swear? Scream? Write letters to the editor? Pass out leaflets? Swear at home, of course (quietly please)! Would you have wanted to discuss it in school (stoney silence).
>
> (Stellen Sie sich vor: ein Novembermorgen, Schulbeginn. . . . Was hätten Sie getan? Schimpfen? Schreien? Leserbriefe schreiben? Flugblätter verteilen? ZuHause schimpfen, ja (leise bitte)! In der Schule diskutieren wollen? (eisiges Schweigen). (unpublished diary from April-November 1986, *Nachlaß*, n.d., n.p.)

In one of the last diary entries made before her death in November 1986 Drewitz noted: "Hate against minorities is lurking in all of us" (Der Haß gegen Minderheiten lauert in uns allen; n.d., n.p.). She knew one need not look very far to see how quickly hate could be mobilized among disaffected youth, and the attacks against foreigners in Hoyerswerda, Rostock, Mölln, or Solingen would probably not have surprised her had she lived to witness them. Yet she did not look to lay blame on others. Her last entry reads: "To be afraid of one's neighbor" (Angst vor dem Nächsten; n.d., n.p.); this too can be read as a final admission of complicity.

In an essay appropriately entitled "Gegenwart und Zukunft" (1971) ("The Present and the Future"), Christa Wolf has written of the difficulty of belonging to this particular "Zwischengeneration" (generation between): "Perhaps our contribution to literature will have to consist in finding the courage to tell the material of our own life relentlessly and truthfully" (Vielleicht wird unser Beitrag zur Literatur darin bestehen müssen, daß wir den Mut finden, unseren eigenen Lebensstoff schonungslos und wahrheitsgetreu zu erzählen; 37). It was this sort of courage that Drewitz admired in others and that she exhibited herself to such a remarkable degree. In addition, she gave speeches, participated in political demonstrations, wrote letters, and organized countless exhibits and conferences, drawing attention to previously ignored groups: exiled and women writers, Turkish authors, and prisoners, among others. Her outspoken support for causes viewed by some as left-wing resulted in name calling from the right, even anonymous threats. She countered these with civil courage and good humor, but she never lost her capacity to be frightened, to be ashamed, to grieve, to desire change. By using the material of her own life in both her fiction and nonfiction, she tried relentlessly ("schonungslos") to build bridges across the generational divides in both directions.

Drewitz also seems to have at least considered, that this compelling sense of wanting to reach out, especially in its literary manifestations, might be gender specific. In a 1955 essay she had already written of women's problematic relationship to the dramatic genre as follows: "She [woman] doesn't open up the abysses between gods and humans, between the sexes, between the generations and between world orders without simultaneously believing in their reconciliation" (Sie reißt die Abgründe zwischen Göttern und Menschen, zwischen den Geschlechtern, zwischen den Generationen und zwischen den Weltordnungen nicht auf, ohne nicht zugleich an die Überbrückung zu glauben; "Wege zur Frauendramatik" ["Ways to a Women's Drama"], 153). A literal translation of the German word "Überbrückung" would be "to bridge over."

Notes

1. The entire *Nachlaß* (unpublished papers), 1.59, is now located at the Akademie der Künste (Academy of Arts), Berlin. I would like to express my deepest appreciation to Mr. Bernhard Drewitz, who let me have access to Ingeborg Drewitz's diaries—which were then in his posession—while I was on sabbatical in Spring 1991, supported by a Fulbright research grant. Mr. Drewitz also greatly facilitated my access to the material already in the archive, which was not open to the general public until 1993. Without his generous personal commitment, my research projects in the *Nachlaß* could not have been accomplished at that time.

2. The philosopher Ernst Bloch (1885–1987) started writing his major treatise, *Das Prinzip Hoffnung*, while in exile in 1938. The first two volumes were published in 1954–55 and

the third in 1959. Drewitz claims to have received a copy from an acquaintance in East Berlin in the late 1950s. See Ernst Bloch, *The Principle Hope*, trans. Nevil Plaice, Stephen Plaice, and Paul Knight, 3 vols. (Cambridge Mass: MIT Press, 1986).

3. See, e.g., the interview with Günter Demin for Radio Bremen, 15 Feb. 1982.

4. See the vignette, "Gustav (1868–1939)," in *Hinterm Fenster die Stadt,* 28–29, as well as the figure of the maternal grandfather, Gustav, in the novel, *Gestern war Heute*, 75–79.

5. See the vignette, "Hildegard (1896–1953)," in *Hinterm Fenster die Stadt*, 25–27.

6. For more on this and other early dramas see Häussermann, 32–34, 125–126.

7. There are at least five different undated versions of this drama in multiple mss. in the *Nachlaß*. I quote here from scene 6 of the twenty-two-page version, probably prepared for the 1955 performance by the Vagantenbühne, Berlin (Steglitz).

8. See Margaret E. Ward, "Ingeborg Drewitz's Forgotten Dramas of the 1950s," in *Thalia's Daughters: German Women Dramatists from the Eighteenth Century to the Present*, ed. Susan L. Cocalis and Ferrel Rose (Tübingen: Francke, 1996), 173–190.

9. The German pronoun here [sein] agrees with the gender of the noun [das Kind], which is neuter. Therefore the child might be thought of—like the parent—as male or female.

10. The dramatic version, "Gestern war heute," premiered January 26, 1985, at the Goethe Theater in Frankfurt am Main. These two plays were only published after Drewitz's death in 1986 under the combined title, "Gestern, heute, morgen . . . Zwei Stücke" *die horen: Zeitschrift für Literatur, Kunst und Kritik*, 165–205.

11. Cf. the vignette, "Paul (1869–1909)," in *Hinterm Fenster die Stadt*, 32–34, which shows that this too was a story from Drewitz's own family.

12. See "Flaschenpost: An meine drei Enkel," in *Hinterm Fenster die Stadt*, 75–82.

Bibliography

Bloch, Ernst. *The Principle Hope*, trans. Nevil Plaice, Stephen Plaice, and Paul Knight. 3 vols. Cambridge Mass.: MIT Press, 1986.

Drewitz, Ingeborg. *Alle Tore waren bewacht*. Unpublished drama ms. in Nachlaß 1.59. Akademie der Künste, Berlin.

———. "Brenna." In *Auch so ein Leben: Die Fünfziger Jahre in Erzählungen*. Göttingen: Herodot, 1985, 7–20.

———. "Ernst Bloch und meine Wirklichkeit." In *"Die ganze Welt umwenden": Ein engagiertes Leben*. Ed. Uwe Schweikert. Munich: Goldmann, 1989, 243–248.

———. "Gestern war heute." *die horen* 32.1 (1987): 165–181.

———. *Gestern war Heute: Hundert Jahre Gegenwart*. 1978. Munich: Goldmann, 1985. 2nd ed. Hildesheim: Claassen, 1992.

———. *Hinterm Fenster die Stadt: Aus einem Familienalbum*. Munich: Goldmann, 1988.

———. "Ich wünschte sie mir immer am Klavier." In *"Die ganze Welt umwenden": Ein engagiertes Leben*. Ed. Uwe Schweikert. Munich: Goldmann, 1989, 81–84.

———. Interview with Günter Demin, "Mensch und Werk: Ingeborg Drewitz." Radio Bremen. 15 Feb. 1982.

———. *Das Karussell*. Göttingen: Sachse & Pohl, 1962.

———. *Lebenslehrzeit*. Stuttgart: Radius, 1985.

———. "Und ich weiß, daß ich damit nicht allein stehe. . . ." *1984—am Ende der Utopien: Literatur und Politik, Essays*. Munich: Goldmann, 1984, 200–205.

———. Unpublished diaries. Notebooks in Nachlaß 1.59. Akademie der Künste, Berlin.

———. "Wege zur Frauendramatik." *Neue deutsche Hefte* 2 (1955–56): 152–155.

———."Zu diesem Buch" (Introduction). In *Die zerstörte Kontinuität: Exilliteratur und Literatur des Widerstandes*. Vienna/Munich/Zurich: Europaverlag, 1981, 9.

Häussermann, Titus, ed. *Ingeborg Drewitz: Materialien zu Werk und Wirken*. 2nd. ed. Stuttgart: Radius, 1988.

London, Perry. "The Rescuers: Motivational Hypotheses about Christians Who Saved Jews from the Nazis." In *Altruism and Helping Behavior*. Ed. Macaulay & Berkowitz. New York: Academic Press, 1970, 241–250.

Shafi, Monika. "Die überforderte Generation: Mutterfiguren in Romanen von Ingeborg Drewitz." In *Women in German Yearbook* 7. Lincoln: University of Nebraska Press, 1991, 23–41.

Ward, Margaret E. "Ingeborg Drewitz's Forgotten Dramas of the 1950s." In *Thalia's Daughters: German Women Dramatists from the Eighteenth Century to the Present*. Ed. Susan L. Cocalis and Ferrel Rose. Tübingen: Francke, 1996, 173–190.

Wolf, Christa. "Gegenwart und Zukunft." In *Die Dimension des Autors: Essays und Aufsätze, Reden und Gespräche 1959–1985*. Darmstadt: Luchterhand, 1987, 36–40.

13

Fact, Fantasy, and Female Subjectivity: *Vergangenheitsbewältigung* in Christa Wolf's *Patterns of Childhood*

Robert C. Holub

The controversies about Christa Wolf in the German press in January 1993 compel me to preface my chapter with a few remarks relating to her political activities and the controversies that have surrounded her since German unification. When I originally conceived of this essay in 1992, Wolf had already been the subject of one campaign to discredit her works in the summer of 1990. At that point, following the publication of *Was bleibt* (1990) (*What Remains*), she was attacked by Ulrich Greiner and Frank Schirrmacher, who portrayed her as a "state poet" trying to cover her loyalty to the repressive regime in the GDR by claiming the status of victim.[1] Since the criticism contained in these attacks was transparently an attempt to disqualify intellectual opposition to the orchestration of unification by the CDU (Christian Democratic Union) and the concomitant attempt to repudiate the entire tradition of leftist intellectual activity, particularly as it related to literary engagement, I did not feel that I had to deal with this initial controversy in my essay. By the time I revised this chapter in February 1993, however, a new controversy had erupted that I could no longer ignore. Since this volume focuses on how women writers came to terms with fascism, and since I had planned to present Wolf's novel *Kindheitsmuster* (1976) (*Patterns of Childhood*) as an exemplary work in this genre, the revelations about her own "unmastered" past seemed relevant to my discussion.

Wolf's activities from 1959 to 1962 as an IM or "Inoffizieller Mitarbeiter" (Unofficial Co-Worker) for the German secret police (Stasi)[2] appear to have direct bearing on the themes of *Patterns of Childhood*, since this novel deals centrally with memory, cooperation, victimization, cooptation, propaganda, subjectivity, and silence under a politically repressive regime. That Wolf herself had made such a seminal contribution to coming to terms with the National Socialist past, but had evidently failed so miserably in coming to terms with her own "Stalinist" past presented me with a new and unwanted problem.

To defend Wolf, as many others have done, I could simply state the obvious: that her involvement with the STASI was of short duration, that she had more than forty "victim" files compared to one brief IM file, that she had been removed from the list of candidates for the Central Committee because of her political positions, that *Nachdenken über Christa T.* (1968) (*The Quest for Christa T.)* as well as other works were severely criticized in the GDR (German Democratic Republic), that she signed the petition protesting the expatriation of Wolf Biermann in 1976, or that she was known in the GDR and in the West for her support of the nonofficial peace movement. Since the most brutal attacks on Wolf have involved her status as a "party poet," however, my comment should more appropriately take the form of a brief look at selected parts of *Patterns of Childhood* in which Wolf herself criticizes the GDR and its policies. Although the euphoria of a conservatively driven unification has apparently caused widespread amnesia in some observers of the literary scene, especially those who write for the popular press, almost all commentators on Wolf's work had noted prior to 1989 that Wolf was consistent in her criticism of the GDR for its lack of personal freedom. There is no doubt that she supported socialism as a general principle for organizing society politically and economically—and this view evidently tempered to a degree her remarks on the GDR. But there is also no question that she did not believe that the GDR was living up to its responsibilities or potential as a socialist state. In her early works, the very fact that, in *Der geteilte Himmel* (1963) (*Divided Heaven*), the erection of the wall compels Rita and Manfred to break off their relationship, and that Rita almost dies as a result of the personal impact of this political act; or that Christa T., in no way an antisocialist figure, is unable to find a comfortable place in the GDR, demonstrate that Wolf was hardly unaware of the conflict between individual liberties and personal fulfillment, and the governing practices of the East German regime. That this conflict was not depicted as drastically or as absolutely as in some other authors is partly due to Wolf's optimism with regard to the GDR—which diminished over the years—and partly to her stylistic and thematic concerns.

Wolf's criticism of the GDR in *Patterns of Childhood* takes many forms, the severest of which occurs when she compares the practices of the GDR with those of National Socialism.[3] In chapter 7, for example, the narrator informs us that she has been reading old editions of the *Landsberger General-Anzeiger* (the newspaper in Landsberg, where Wolf grew up) in the library to see what was reported officially to the population about foreign affairs. On 14 May 1937 the newspaper evidently contained an article dealing with the purges of Stalin. These reports seem very pertinent to the narrator, even in, or perhaps especially in, a book written about growing up under fascism. One of the recurring themes of the novel is how little the child Nelly knew, how information was not consciously absorbed even when it was published and available. The parallel with the GDR is evident, and it becomes more explicit when Lenka, the narrator's fourteen-year-old daughter, asks who Khrushchev is. The education of the youth in the GDR is evidently in some respects just as deficient as the education during the Third Reich, and the narrator comments that she felt she could no longer put off the duty "to describe what has happened to us" (anzudeuten, was mit uns geschehen ist; 147). She then continues by speaking of the taboo that the Stalinist trials were (and are) for socialist countries. We are then allowed to read the report from 14 June 1937, which announced the execution of eight soviet generals. The suggestion from all this—and it is rather apparent for most readers—is that socialism, as well as National Socialism, has a past with which it must come to terms, and that this process of "mastering the past" is not occurring. Indeed, part of the reason for the absence of a socialist "mastering of the past," one might conclude from this novel, is that the fascist past still haunts the social body. The point is that Nelly lives on inside the narrator: the repressive mechanisms that have obscured the past are generalizable across regimes.

Perhaps one further incident will demonstrate how Wolf, even in a novel that is ostensibly not about the GDR or the socialist past, is alert to the failings of the communist regime. In chapter 5 she alludes to the suicide of the German teacher M. Although we do not find out very much about him, he was obviously someone sensitive to contradictions in GDR ideology and somewhat cynical with regard to his role as teacher. We are told, for example, that "he was able to prove any theory and then prove the contrary in the next class. And he'd smile irritatingly when she [Ruth, the narrator's other daughter] wanted to know what he really thought" (Er konnte der Klasse jede These beweisen, und in der nächsten Stunde ihr Gegenteil. Und er lächelte auf eine irritierende Art, wenn sie erfahren wollte, was er wirklich dachte; 101). His gesture of opposition—and it is a faint one by any standard—comes when he rearranges the seating in the seminar room so that the teacher no longer sits at the head of the class in a position of absolute authority; we are told that the old arrangement reappeared after his suicide. It is not insignificant that the discussion of M. is interrupted by the narrator's reflections on Nelly's school experiences; again, the continuity, and not just the contrast, is suggested by this narrative juxtaposition. Returning to M., the narrator tells us that he had returned to her Robert Musil's novel, *Der Mann ohne Eigenschaften* (*The Man without Qualities*), the evening that he and his young girlfriend committed suicide. As readers of Wolf's work we are left with the question of why they committed suicide. The reason for their action is never given in an explicit fashion, but it is obvious that it has something to do with the oppressive and unjust climate in East Germany. M.'s girlfriend, obviously a talented student, had been recently turned down for admission to medical school for the second time. What could be the reason for this? Again, it is never stated, but if she is like M., then it may be that she, too, was too much of a free thinker for a system that enforces conformity. The report of M.'s suicide is, of course, complex. It is introduced by a reflection on the word *pretending* (*Verstellung*), and M. is shown to be dishonest in some respect for not showing his true feelings and thoughts. His suicide is also attributed to an "uninterrupted incapacity to put up with life" (seiner andauernden Unfähigkeit, das Leben zu ertragen; 108). To some degree he is seen as a coward, or at least as someone who takes the easy way out of a difficult situation. But just the fact that it takes unusual courage to live in the GDR says something rather unflattering about the systematic oppression in that country. Here again, Wolf hardly idealizes the virtues of her country; rather, she subjects it to a critical appraisal that few of her fellow writers or citizens dared to voice in public in the 1970s, or at any time until after the fall of the wall in 1989.[4]

These reflections on the nature of Wolf's political criticisms of the GDR are not irrelevant to my main purpose in this chapter since the tenet I would like to suggest for the evaluation of *Patterns of Childhood* as a book of *Vergangenheitsbewältigung* or "mastering the past" (in its now-established double reference) has to do with how we measure its importance against a background of discourses. In the most general sense, the significance of a work of literature—or any cultural document for that matter—is determined by its relationship to the discourses in which it is situated. Those works that conform to expected norms of a given discourse, will be evaluated accordingly as derivative and epigonal; works that establish a discourse, or that significantly alter the parameters of a discourse will be judged to be important events.[5] Literary quality is thus not always the determining factor for the significance of a literary work—unless one chooses, as the Russian Formalists did, aesthetic or formal criteria as the sole measure of significance—since novels, plays, and poems are always participants in a more encompassing cultural environment. Every work, of course, is potentially located in an infinity of discourses. What is deemed important about a work at the time of its appearance may not be the same thing that appeals to later audiences, or the work may lose its appeal entirely based on a decrease in importance of the original discourse. Similarly, a literary work may have no appeal to an original audience, yet speak to later readers based on changed sensibilities and perceptions. Works by women authors from previous centuries, for example, which may formerly have been considered part of travel literature or romances, may now be viewed in the context of centuries of women's struggles as significant inaugurators or anticipators of feminist discourse. Conversely, works by male authors, hailed by male critics and scholars, may not fare well at all when placed in a discursive context of gender equality.

If we consider the contribution to an ongoing discourse to be the most important feature for evaluating the significance of a text, then Wolf's *Patterns of Childhood* was undoubtedly one of the most significant works to appear in the postwar era. Wolf's novel impacted two seminal cultural discourses in Germany, and in both cases altered the way in which we think about these discourses. The first of these discourses may be identified for purposes of simplicity with the popular, but somewhat misleading term *Vergangenheitsbewältigung*, which I render as "mastering the past," rather than "coming to terms with the past" or "overcoming the past" because the term *mastering* captures the notion of force or even suppression implicit in *Vergangenheitsbewältigung*. In essence, what I mean by this term is the large complex of discussions, policies, and cultural responses that dealt with World War II, but in particular those reflections that tried to come to terms with the atrocities against foreigners and minorities committed by the National Socialist regime. This topic has been a preoccupation of all the foremost writers and thinkers in Germany since the end of the war and has had a profound effect on every aspect of German society, from linguistic usage to foreign relations. In the West the terms that were set for "mastering the past" were primarily moral, and the central guidelines were established at a rather early date in Karl Jaspers's essay on *Die Schuldfrage* (1946) (*The Question of German Guilt)*. There have been some challenges to the universal and moral opprobrium connected with the Third Reich in Jaspers's text: during the 1980s there was an attempt to lay the past to rest that was manifested politically in Chancellor Helmut Kohl's invitation to have President Ronald Reagen attend a ceremony for the dead at Bitburg, where members of the SS were buried; and intellectually in the historians' debate, in which conservative historians endeavored to relativize the Holocaust and to propagate a German history unincumbered by the Nazi legacy. Both of these "revisionary" attempts failed, however, and the uniqueness of the Holocaust and the absolute evil of the Nazi regime have remained the unstated parameters of most official discourses even to the present day.

The situation was somewhat different in the GDR. Until the outbreak of the Cold War, that is, at a time when the GDR had not yet emerged from the Soviet Occupation Zone (SBZ), the response in the East, particularly with regard to cultural politics, was not very much different from the response in the West.[6] This parallel development in East and West was short lived and encompasses at most the first few years after the war, but during this time the cultural politics in Germany could be characterized by a common, general humanitarianism. With the beginnings of the Cold War, and especially since the early fifties, the GDR assigned all vestiges of the Nazi past to the Western world. Fascism and National Socialism were viewed solely as the heritage of the FRG (Federal Republic of Germany); the GDR simply declared itself to be antifascist on the basis of its communist heritage. There is a certain logic to this declaration, of course, since the communists were the first internal victims of the National Socialists, and since National Socialism was always virulently anti-Bolshevik. But the net result of such a myopic, Cold War position with its concomitant cultural politics was that the past was neither confronted nor mastered nor understood, but instead swept under the carpet. Typical of the glorification of communist deeds in the face of fascism was a film such as Slatan Dudow's *Stärker als die Nacht* (1954) (*Stronger Than the Night*), which depicted communist resistance in Hamburg. The hero becomes a veritable martyr to the cause, a man who in a Christlike conclusion is admired by friend and foe alike for his bravery and convictions. Another consequence of the Cold War and its effects on the GDR was a certain brushing aside of the Jewish question and of antisemitism. This is even reflected in *Patterns of Childhood*, where the narrator remarks that Eichmann is hardly mentioned in her daughter's history book when it deals with World War II. The Jewish question and racism in general were always seen as secondary to sociopolitical issues and the class struggle. Fascism was explained as the most extreme phase of imperialist capitalism; antisemitism was thus at most a smokescreen for capitalist exploitation or an unimportant side issue to the proletarian struggle. In the social science literature of the GDR the Holocaust is virtually ignored. Only in the early 1980s, when Kurt Paetzold edited a volume of documents on Jews in the Third Reich, and then later a collection of materials on the so-called *Kristallnacht* (the night of anti-Jewish pogroms unleashed by the SS in November 1938), do we find the much-belated beginnings of a reflection on the racist dimension of National Socialist hegemony. The topic surfaces somewhat more frequently in literary works and films, where many important issues seem to have had their only extensive public discussion. Jurek Becker's *Jakob der Lügner* (1976) (*Jacob the Liar*), a popular novel that was also made into a film, described life in a Polish ghetto, but it is certainly not coincidental that Bruno Apitz's *Nackt unter Wölfen* (1958) (*Naked among Wolves*), perhaps the most noted GDR work dealing with a concentration camp, emphasizes the political prisoners and not Jews, Gypsies, or homosexuals. Thus, the topics Wolf deals with in *Patterns of Childhood* and in particular the way in which she deals with them, although not foreign to the GDR, were relatively new at the time of its appearance in 1976, and in the West, where "mastering the past" had been more insistently pursued, they were most often framed by abstract moral formulae.[7]

The second discourse into which *Patterns of Childhood* inserts itself revolves around the topic of women and fascism. Although during the past decade and a half both historical accounts—for example, Claudia Koonz's *Mothers in the Fatherland* in 1987[8]—and a variety of cultural products—for example, Helma Sanders-Brahms's film *Deutschland, bleiche Mutter* (1980) (*Germany, Pale Mother*)—have contributed to a more differentiated view of women's activities during the Third Reich, we should recall that in the mid-seventies women's involvement in National Socialism had been a marginal and somewhat trivialized issue. In most of the prominent cultural products throughout the sixties women were viewed either as adjuncts and aids to male protagonists or as flighty, impressionable fellow travellers of the Third Reich. Representative for the former attitude is Susanne Wallner in Wolfgang Staudte's *Die Mörder sind unter uns* (1946) (*The Murderers Are among Us*). Although, as an inmate of a concentration camp, she was the most obvious victim of National Socialism—we are also led to believe that she lost her father to Nazi terror—her function in the film is to help Hans Mertens overcome his psychic disturbance and assist his reintegration into the new postwar social order. The type of woman who simply goes along with National Socialism out of stupidity, naivete, or habit, finds early representation as Ruth Mamlock in Friedrich Wolf's *Professor Mamlock* (1934), but reaches a misogynist climax in the figure of Helga in Rolf Hochhuth's *Der Stellvertreter* (1963) (*The Representative*). Helga is the young woman who is inexplicably attracted to the Doctor, a thin disguise for Josef Mengele, while she tries to remain faithful to her more mundane German fiancé, an SS officer serving in Auschwitz. Let me cite a bit of Hochhuth's description of her in his stage directions to give you a flavor of how women under fascism were portrayed publicly even in the sixties in one of Germany's most important dramas:

> A little more about Helga. The specifically feminine abilities, first to be completely in agreement with the opinions of those who make an impression on her and, secondly, the ability to ignore anything that might disturb the view, are powers which she has not even needed to develop particularly. Like any markedly feminine characteristics, they are inborn in her to such an extent that if she were ever actually to reflect on the subject she would find even Auschwitz to be "quite in order." Of course, she never does reflect on the subject. For this reason, she is a particularly attractive kind of sleeping pill for the men here, who are from time to time troubled at night by ghosts. . . . Like all young girls, she is completely manageable, not simply pliable material in the hands of a lover, but in the way that many secretaries, even in their deepest likes and dislikes, are nothing more than parrot-like repetitions of their bosses.
>
> (Noch einiges über Helga. Die spezifisch weiblichen Fähigkeiten, völlig der Meinung derer zu sein, die auf sie Eindruck machen, und nichts zu sehen, was den Blick trüben könnte, hat sie nicht einmal besonders entwickeln müssen, da sie ihr, wie alles betont Weibliche, in solchem Maße angeboren sind, daß sie selbst Auschwitz "in Ordnung" fände, wenn sie je darüber reflektiert hätte. Natürlich reflektiert sie niemals. Deshalb ist sie für die Herren hier, die nachts doch hin und

> wieder Gespenster sehen, ein besonders verlockendes Schlafmittel. . . . Doch ist sie, wie fast alle jungen Mädchen, vollkommen dressierbar, nicht nur schmelzendes Material unter der Hand des Liebhabers, sondern wie auch viele Sekretärinnen bis in ihre intimsten Sympathie- oder Antipathiekundgebungen nichts als der Papagei ihres Chefs.) (212–213)

Thus, until the seventies women under fascism were viewed through two stereotypical categories: they were seen, on the one hand, as naive, pliable beings who swoon under the influence of Hitler's propaganda and who are attracted to the shiny buttons on the Nazi uniforms. Or they are considered, on the other hand, as equally apolitical, but as people who were not emotionally involved with National Socialism at all.[9] During the immediate postwar period women could therefore function more readily, at least in literature, as a source of humanism, Iphigenie-like in their purity, undefiled by ideology and war. Matters were, of course, a bit different in the GDR. Especially in several early plays—Erwin Strittmatter's *Katzgraben* (1953) or Friedrich Wolf's *Bürgermeister Anna* (1950) (*Mayor Anna*)—women were more often portrayed as agents of change as the Socialist Unity Party (the Sozialistische Einheitspartei Deutschlands [SED], the equivalent party to the Communist Parties in other East Bloc countries) recruited them for the new socialist society. But behind this more positive portrayal is the same stereotype that was operative in the West. Women, because they were not active politically, because they were involved solely with the home and the family, are somehow instinctively antifascist. The transformation in the depiction of women in the cultural products of the GDR proceeds quickly from the Susanne Wallner figure, the nurturing, self-sacrificing, patiently suffering woman dedicated to one man, to a more brazen, prosocialist, quasi-feminist activist who confronts males with their undemocratic and misogynist legacy.[10] Although this representation may be more flattering to women, it is surely no less stereotypical and distorted than the less complimentary images in the West.

The two related discourses I have outlined—the almost ubiquitous discussion of "mastering the past" and the concern with how women related to National Socialism—are marked by an adherence to dichotomous thinking. *Vergangenheitsbewältigung* in the discourse of East and West Germany either assumed an ahistorical moral posturing that moved it into the proximity of penance, sin, purification, or other quasi-religious vocabulary; or it relied on a one-dimensional historical explanation that attributed individual decisions and actions to reflexes of economic or political interests. The discourse on women and fascism tended to reduce the role of women to enthusiastic, but naive spectators, or else to apolitical keepers of the Holy Grail of family and humanism. I would like to suggest that Wolf's contribution to both of these discourses can be conceived more as a deepening and expanding of the conventional views about the past than a cancellation of them. She continues to employ many of the traditional discursive parameters, and to a degree she urges acceptance of them. But she provides a level of understanding concerning these discourses that sets new stakes for future contributions. I would like to demonstrate how Wolf does this by looking at two exemplary episodes from *Patterns of Childhood*: in the first the narrator discusses the anticommunist demonstrations in L., while in the second Wolf demonstrates how antisemitism is unconsciously inculcated into Nelly by associations and innuendo. In both of these episodes Wolf exhibits a threefold structuring that is typical for her procedure throughout the novel: the questioning of fact, the effect of fantasy (in the sense of imaginative and associative powers), and the production of female subjectivity.

The tripartite structure of Wolf's novel allows her often to thematize "facts." Since she is writing about memories from the thirties and forties, but reflecting upon them in both the narrative of the trip to L. in July 1971 and the process of writing from 1972 until 1975,[11] she has occasion to question the materials associated with most earlier historical and literary accounts: not only facts, but also memories and experiences.[12] Chapter 3 contains the most sustained reflection on the inadequacy of facts for representing the past. The reader has just been told the story of Elvira, who was a maid at the Jordans, but who came from a family of communists. Elvira reported to the young Nelly that she and her family cried when the communist flags were burned. The fact that Elvira was a communist, of course, sits rather uneasily in the young child's mind. Communists and communism had obviously been a topic in the Jordan household, and Nelly has already developed an image of what communists are. Elvira, a kind and sympathetic person whom she has known rather well, does not fit the stereotype she has formed; from her limited experience, and most likely from conversations in her home, she has been led to believe that "Communists raise their fists, shouting 'Red Front'!" (52). The confrontation between the real communist Elvira and the distorted stereotype of a communist is only one of many occasions throughout the novel where experiences clash with propaganda, or where experiences clash with each other. In an attempt to clarify her own feelings at the time, the narrator first turns to what she facetiously calls "the facts." That this can only be meant facetiously is obvious from the source of her "facts": to prepare for her trip back to L., the narrator has been reading old editions of the local newspaper, the *General-Anzeiger*.[13] Under Nazi control, this newspaper does not just print facts; it also supplies propagandistic interpretations of these facts in support of the new regime. Despite its partisan politics the newspaper does supply her with a reliable, albeit slanted, account of the anticommunist demonstration that took place in March 1933.

What is more interesting for Wolf and Wolf's narrator, however, is what is occurring in the fantasies of the various spectators and participants in this demonstration. Beyond the mere factual details of when and where and why, she is concerned with the mental processes, the psychic reactions, the secret, subjective, subconscious, internal responses to the march, to the burning of the communist flags, and to the attendant glorification of National Socialism. What is important for the narrator in coming to terms with history is thus in most cases precisely what escapes official histories:

> Nobody will ever know if the night of March 17 was the night when Charlotte thought—or dreamed—for the first time, with a shock: It's all wrong. It is precisely this kind of unreported, statistically unrecorded fact which would interest you today. More than the fact that every town experienced the National Socialist takeover. Or that—according to the *General-Anzeiger*—the population of L. stood shoulder to shoulder along the main streets, waiting for the SS and SA torchlight parade to approach during the eighth hour of evening. . . . What were the thoughts that went through people's heads, that they preferred not to know about: that's what you'd like to know.
>
> (Ob die Nacht des 17. März auch die Nacht war, in der Chrlotte zum erstenmal mit Schrecken dachte—oder träumte—: Alles ist verkehrt!, das wird niemand je erfahren. Aber gerade diese Art Tatsachen, die keine Zeitung berichtet und keine Statistik erfaßt hat, sind es, die dich heute interessirren könnten. Nicht, daß es in jeder Stadt die nationale Erhebung gegeben haben muß. Nicht einmal nur, daß—laut 'General-Anzeiger'—die Bevölkerung von L. dicht bei dicht die Hauptstraße gesäumt hat, auf denen in der achten Abendstunde, [vom Adlergarten herkommend,] der Fackelzug von SS und SA sich näherte. . . . Was man da gedacht und gefühlt haben mag, ohne selbst davon wissen zu wollen: Dies wäre es, was du gerne wüßtest.) (53)

Wolf is interested less in what happened than in how subjectivity is constituted, and in particular, with regard to her mother, Nelly, and the women of the novel, how female subjectivity is formed and transformed in the passive role of spectator. If we could delve into the consciousness of each individual, we would surely find compliance with the new regime, but simultaneously, Wolf suggests, we would encounter sites of ambivalence and furtive resistance even in apparently docile acquiescence. Facts are thus inadequate, but not because they reveal too little, but because there are too few of them to tell us about what is really important. Later in the same passage she questions the "factual" newspaper report that people were standing "shoulder to shoulder." At the very least we would have to know how many rows deep as well.

> In any case, statistics [she continues] are too coarse for your purpose. Even in the face of exact figures, you'd still want more information, and it's unobtainable in this world. After the tears you'd want to count the beads of sweat—of fear—on the brows of some in the cheering crowd. The palms that turned moist with disgust. The hearts that skipped as they beat faster.

> (Statistiken wären in jedem Fall für deine Zwecke zu grob. Selbst angesichts genauer Zahlen kämest du mit neuen Wünschen nach Angaben, die nun mal auf dieser Welt nicht zu erbringen sind. Und nach den Tränen würdest du die Schweißtropfen zählen wollen, die unter den jubelnden Massen an diesem Abend einzelnen als Angst auf die Stirnen traten. Die Hände, die vor Ekel feucht wurden. Die Herzschläge, die stockten, mitten im Höherschlagen.) (55)

Not that these details would exonerate the people who stood shoulder to shoulder to rail against the communists and support the fascist regime. Ethical categories are not cancelled in Wolf's novel; she does not seek moral exculpation for the citizens of Landsberg based on beads of sweat. Nor does she want to derive morality deterministically from political and economic structures. The key to understanding National Socialism lies in neither the autonomous moral individual nor the social nexus, but rather in the complex interactions that explain and escape these extremes. Documents, statistics, facts, and reports do not and cannot tell the whole story, because they are partial in their apparent impartiality. The same holds true for reports based on "experience":

> But memory's recall—which incidentally varies markedly in people who seem to have had the exact same experience—may not be a matter of biochemistry, and may not universally be a matter of choice.
>
> If this were not so, some people's assertions would be accurate: documents could not be surpassed: the narrator would therefore be superfluous.
>
> (Doch ist das Abrufen der Gedächtnisinhalte—die sich übrigens bei verschiedenen Leuten, die akkurat das gleiche erlebt zu haben scheinen, bemerkenswert unterscheiden—wohl keine Sache der Biochemie und scheint uns nicht immer und überall freizustehen.
>
> Wäre es anders, träfe zu, was manche behaupten: daß die Dokumente nicht zu übertreffen sind und den Erzähler überflüssig machen.) (69)

This chapter, which amounts to a justification for the very novel in which it is included, presents us with a trenchant critique of the history of *Vergangenheitsbewältigung* conceived in terms of factual records and private recollection. Avoiding the facile reliance on both individualistic ethics and supra-individualistic structures without rejecting the validity of either, Wolf presents us with a mode of comprehending the past in terms of process, fantasy, and the formation of subjectivity.[14] My second illustration clearly shows how facts turn into fantasy and lead to subjective formations that are constitutive for fascism. Chapter 6, which is devoted centrally to antisemitism, demonstrates one of the many mechanisms by which prejudices are passed from one generation to the next via hints, associations, and even silences. In the first half of this chapter the narrator relates Nelly's experience with Lori Tietz, the daughter of a rich factory owner. Significant in this relationship is that for the first time Nelly perceives herself as a split consciousness; she is able to witness herself acting. The "I" that had initiated the novel (5) has here become bifurcated; under social conditions infused with hierarchy and power subjectivity is damaged. In countering the falseness of the Tietz family, who only want Nelly to visit Lori so that the brighter girl can help her slower classmate with homework, Nelly finds herself acting instrumentally. She opposes the hypocrisy that emanates from the Tietz family, but her only weapon is imitation of their mendacity. Thus, in a gesture that is typical for Wolf's works, a potential opposition amounts to a similarity. Nelly does not counter falsehood, she participates in it.

The resulting damaged subjectivity reveals itself as a necessary prelude to her introduction to antisemitism, which is not a sudden revelation, but a series of occurrences with various dimensions and implications. The most direct indoctrination into anti-Jewish attitudes results from a visit by the bookseller, Leo Siegmann, an ardent Nazi who is known as the vendor of the quasi-mandatory photos of Hitler. Siegmann relates his experience with an unnamed Jewish child in secondary school. While the Jewish child would sit innocently at his place, his classmates would file by him and "sock him one." Siegmann explicates as follows: "It was instinct, say what you will. He just gave off an offensive odor, or whatever it was" (Das war Instinkt, da kann einer sagen, was er will. Er roch einfach widerlich, oder was es war; 133). Despite the incoherence of his explanation, Siegmann's tale obviously leaves an impression on Nelly. Her fantasy involves her in a similar incident, which she embellishes with suitable details gleaned from her racist environment. "Nelly can see him clearly. He is pale, with a pointed face, dark, wavy hair, and a few pimples. For some reason he always wears knickers. He sits at his desk like a sack of wet flour, and everyone who walks by him . . . She, too, has to walk by him. She, too, will 'sock him one'" (Nelly sah ihn deutlich. Er ist blaß, hat ein spitzes Gesicht, welliges dunkles Haar, ein paar Pickel. Aus irgendeinem Grund trägt er immer Knickerbocker. Hockt da wie ein nasser Sack, und jeder, der vorbeikommt . . . Auch sie muß vorbeigehen. Auch sie wird ihm also 'eine reinhaun'; 133). Her associations go on, using the clichés she has heard about Jews. She will have to sock him, we read, because he speculates that she may not. All Jews are speculators. She convinces herself that the Jewish child is making her hit him. It's really his fault; she is doing her duty.

The story told by Leo Siegmann leads to another memory, obviously one also associated with the word *Jew*. The remembered event occurred at the local railroad tracks where a man exposed himself to Nelly. Nelly's disgust with this incident results in her avoidance of reptiles and insects. The connection among all these associated memories is far from clear, even to the narrator reflecting back upon them: "It's a touchy matter to this day to inquire into the connection—it must have established itself at that time—between the nameless Jew boy, whom Nelly has come to know through Leo Siegmann, and the white snake [the penis of the man who exposed himself to her]. What does the pale, pimply boy have to do with toads, spiders, and lizards?" (Heikel bis heute, der Verbindung nachzugehen, die sich damals zwischen dem namenlosen Judenjungen, den Nelly durch Leo Siegmann kannte, und der weißen Schlange hergestellt haben muß. Was hat der blasse, picklige Junge mit Kröten, Spinnen und Eidechsen zu tun?; 135). All these items are then subsequently identified with the ideologemes of National Socialism.

> One doesn't know how, then. But it came about that by the blending and fusing of seemingly unrelated components, she, Nelly, could no longer hear the word *unchaste* without having a simultaneous vision of vermin, the white snake, and the face of the Jew boy. We know very little as long as we don't know how these things come about; as long as one can only wonder at the fact that these images didn't evoke hate or disgust in Nelly, only awe—a feeling very close to the first stages of fear.
>
> (Wie, weiß man also nicht. Doch es geschah, daß sie, Nelly, durch eine Vermischung und Verquickung scheinbar entlegener Bestandteile das Wort 'unrein' nicht mehr hören konnte, ohne gleichzeitig Ungeziefer, die weiße Schlange und das Gesicht jenes Judenjungen zu sehen. Wir wissen wenig, solange wir nicht wissen, wie dergleichen geschieht; solange man sich nur wundern kann, daß in Nelly mit jenen Bildern nicht Haß oder Abscheu aufkam, sondern Scheu—ein Gefühl, sehr nahe den Vorstufen der Angst.) (136)

The chapter closes with an incident in which the Aryan heritage of Bruno Jordan is questioned. When Nelly, only about eight years old, hears of the inquiry, she "utters the remarkable words: I don't want to be Jewish! and Charlotte addresses the no less remarkable question to an unnamed court: How on earth does this child know what Jewish is?" (Da äußert Nelly den bemerkenswerten Satz: Ich will keine Jüdin sein!, und Charlotte richtet an eine nicht zu benennende Instanz die Frage: Woher um alles in der Welt weiß dieses Kind, was eine Jüdin ist?) The chapter then closes with the laconic remark: "The answer to this question cannot be determined" (Auf diese Frage ist eine Antwort nicht zu ermittlen; 140). But the point is that this chapter has shown, perhaps as precisely as possible, the mechanisms by which Nelly comes to "know" what Jewish means.[15] The paths of prejudice, of irrational hatred and racism, are certainly not elucidated with the descriptive logic that we find in historical accounts (see Pickerodt). But Wolf's chapter is nonetheless probably closer to the reality of National Socialism as it was experienced than the scores of books and essays that relate the "facts" of antisemitism. National Socialist ideologemes function by processing dubious facts through fantasy to alter damaged subjectivity.[16]

And in this case the subjectivity that is constituted is distinctly female. Antisemitism in the mind of the young girl is intimately connected with, and effectively reinforced by, sexual apprehensions. What we witness in this chapter and throughout the novel, therefore, is the formation of female subjectivity under fascism; here the important stages are the division of the subject as agent and onlooker and the introduction into this damaged subjectivity of antisemitism by association, fear, and the redirection of sexual energies. But what is more important for the discourse of women and fascism is that Nelly, her mother, her aunts, and her classmates are depicted not as naive enthusiasts or as innocent victims, but as conflicted participants in a complex social process. There is certainly good reason to characterize National Socialism as a form of patriarchy, since it is clear in everything from its propaganda to its legislation that it propagated a male-dominated social hierarchy. But for patriarchy and male domination to continue in German society—or in any society—the cooperation and cooptation of women is essential. That women too were involved in myriad ways in the complex process of passing on and complying with fascist attitudes and values may seem a trivial assertion today, but it certainly was not a prominent theme in discussions during the three decades after the war. Wolf's *Patterns of Childhood* thus contributes significantly to a transformation in the way we conceive of both fascism, our ability to come to terms with the fascist legacy, and our complicity with it. Because of this, it is also an initial and necessary step in the most important task of locating the sites and mechanisms of resistance.[17]

Notes

1. Even this attack had a prehistory. As Thomas Anz documents, Marcel Reich-Ranicki had anticipated the debate in 1990 when he took issue with Wolf's remarks about Thomas Brasch when the latter was awarded the Kleist Prize in 1987. Reich-Ranicki's diatribe against Wolf, "Macht Verfolgung kreativ?" ("Does Persecution Make One Creative?"), which appeared in the *Frankfurter Allgemeine Zeitung*, Germany's leading newspaper, on 12 November 1987 (rpt. on pp. 35–40 of Anz), accused Wolf of cowardice and self-serving behavior, as well as of being an overrated writer. These criticisms from the pen of Reich-Ranicki, which have been repeated in other contexts in subsequent years, have an added dimension now that it has been revealed that he himself spied on the Polish exile government in England for the Polish Communist Party in the immediate postwar period.

2. The full record of this involvement is documented in Vinke.

3. I will be citing parenthetically from the English edition of *Patterns of Childhood*. The first translation of *Kindheitsmuster* appeared under the title "A Model Childhood." The choice of a title, like the entire writing of the book, is thematized and specifically mentioned in the novel itself: "Tentative titles, while shopping with H." (Titelproben, beim Einkaufsweg mit H.). The narrator goes on to mention her thoughts: "Basic Patterns, Behavior Patterns, Childhood Patterns. A Model Childhood" (Grund-Muster. Verhaltens-Muster. Kindheitsmuster; 36). We can see from these reflections the kind of associations that Wolf wants. Actually the German title is ambiguous, and this is probably the reason for the indecision

with regard to the English version. The German word *Muster* means model and pattern; as a neuter noun the singular and the plural forms are identical. Thus we can have the title associated with Nelly's childhood being a model, and exemplary childhood: the word *Musterkind* is an exemplary child; analogously a *Musterkindheit* or a *Kindheitsmuster* could be an exemplary childhood. If we used this translation, however, I think we would have to regard it with some irony. What was exemplary for a child under fascism is not viewed by the narrator as exemplary at all. There is thus a tension between what is the model for childhood then and now, concretized to a degree by Nelly and her present-day counterpart Lenka. If we take the second possibility expressed in the more recent English version: Patterns of Childhood, then we have another field of meaning. What Wolf is exploring are the various patterns that get ingrained in a child undergoing socialization. As she says in her reflections: "Behavior Patterns" or, we might add, "Socialization Patterns." Patterns are ways of action that preclude reflection, something like habits, something one does without subjectivity. Like Adorno, whose claim was that fascism (and modern societies in general) evidence a damaged subjectivity, Wolf seems to thematize the lack of authentic subjectivity in Nelly's youth.

4. Wiesehan emphasizes an opposing point of view, when she points to the harsh criticism of the West that exists throughtout the novel and finds that the criticism of the GDR is lacking in comparison (80).

5. I have obviously modified the views of Hans Robert Jauss on evaluation, since they prove to be too narrowly literary. My concern is with cultural discourses, not with literary history.

6. The first postwar German feature film, Wolfgang Staudte's *The Murderers Are Among Us* (1946), was produced in the studios of DEFA (Deutsche Film-AG) in the eastern part of Berlin, but it contains a moral message that was similar to the one we find in the early writings of Wolfgang Borchert or Heinrich Böll. We could also note that in the East, as in the West, most theaters, for rather transparent reasons, opened or scheduled two plays in the late forties: Gotthold Ephraim Lessing's *Nathan der Weise* (1779) (*Nathan the Wise*) and Johann Wolfgang Goethe's (1787) *Iphigenie auf Tauris*, both of which have tolerance and humane treatment of other people as their themes.

7. Wolf, of course, was fully conscious of the incomplete "mastering of the past" (*Vergangenheitsbewältigung*) in the GDR and thus of the context within which her novel appeared. At the Writers Congress of the GDR in 1973, she made the following statement: "But we have considered this problematic [of working out intellectually the influences of the fascist period] to be taken care of too early. That coincided with a phase of mastering the past in our society during which we were tempted to relegate fascism to 'the others' as their tradition and as their past. I believe that this time is past. We don't do that any more. But it is no coincidence that we did this, and it seems to me that our discussion of the 'fathers' still shows traces of this attitude. Naturally one can also adopt spiritual fathers; one can even do that more than once in one's life. But one cannot adopt a biological father, never, although perhaps an entire generation would not have been disinclined to do so. One cannot, however, simply choose to be rid of him, and one cannot ever get rid of a childhood, which was experienced not only as an object, passively, and which was also had a formative effect"

(doch haben wir die Problematik zu früh für "erledigt" gehalten: Das fiel zusammen mit einer Phase der Vergangenheitsbewältigung in unserer Gesellschaft, in der wir versucht waren, den Faschismus an "die anderen" zu delegieren als Tradition und als Vergangenheit. Diese Zeit scheint mir vorbei. Wir machen das nicht mehr. Aber es war kein Zufall, daß wir es gemacht haben, und mir kommt es so vor, als ob unsere Diskussion über die "Väter" noch Spuren dieser Haltung zeigte. Natürlich kann man sich geistige Väter adoptieren; man kann das sogar mehrmals in seinem Leben tun—aber man kann sich keinen biologischen Vater adoptieren, niemals, obwohl eine ganze Generation gar nicht so abgeneigt gewesen wäre, das zu tun. Man kann ihn aber auch nicht wegdelegieren, und man kann eine Kindheit, die man nicht nur als Objekt, also passiv, erlebt hat und die einen geformt hat, nicht wie niemals gewesen von sich abtun; *Die Dimension des Autors* 433–434).

8. In the "Acknowledgements" Koonz speaks of the "scarcity of published documents and secondary works in the mid-1970s" about women in Nazi Germany. It is a tribute to Wolf and an obvious recognition of her pioneering spirit that Koonz takes as the motto to her book the initial paragraph from *Patterns of Childhood*.

9. Because of these stereotypes Sigrid Weigel has remarked that there was a thirty-year delay in dealing with the topic of women and fascism (152).

10. I am thinking here of women characters from Suse Rieck in Eduard Claudius's *Menschen an unserer Seite* (1951) (People on Our Side) to Tinka in Volker Braun's drama of the same name (1976).

11. Technically we should recognize that there is a fourth structural level, one on which general statements are made. An example occurs in the opening sentences of the novel: "What is past is not dead; it is not even past. We cut ourselves off from it; we pretend to be strangers" (Das Vergangene ist nicht tot; es ist nicht einmal vergangen. Wir trennen es von uns ab und stellen uns fremd; 3). Such a statement may belong to the period of the writing of the novel, but it seems distinct enough from that process to be accorded a level of its own. It goes almost without saying that Wolf moves quickly and often seamlessly among these levels.

12. In contrast to history of daily life (*Alltagsgeschichte*)—especially histories that are written naively, as if recollections from daily life reflect unmediated, actual experience—and the cultural modes based on it—for example, in Edgar Reitz's television film *Heimat*—Wolf shows a healthy distrust of memory. The narrator repeatedly calls memory into question: "People with memories linked to people, memories whose unreliability could be easily tested; take for instance the word 'prewar'" (Personen mit personengebundenem Gedächtnis, dessen Unzuverlässigkeit leicht zu testen wäre; beispielsweise an dem Stichwort 'Vorkrieg'; 142). The instability and potential inaccuracy of memory is captured in the following passage relating a hypothetical response of Nelly's mother to the notion of "prewar times": "Prewar times? What happy years! she would have said at first. Later perhaps: A lot of work. And finally: One big fraud. This only to make it clear that memory is not a solid block fitted into our brain once and for all; rather, perhaps—if big words are permitted—a repeated moral act" (Vorkrieg? Ach, glückliche Zeiten! hätte sie zuerst gesagt. Später vielleicht: Viel Arbeit. Und zum Schluß: Ein einziger großer Beschiß. —Nur um klarzustellen, daß das Gedächtnis kein festgefügter Block ist, der in unserem Gehirn un-

veränderlich festsitzt; eher schon, falls große Worte erlaubt sind, ein widerholter moralischer Akt; 143). Memory must obviously be checked with facts—what really happened in German prewar society—and, above all, reflection.

13. The narrator is obviously referring to the *Landsberger General-Anzeiger*, although Wolf refrains from identifying her former home town with anything more than the initial "L."

14. Among the more interesting interpretations of *Patterns of Childhood* in the context of *Vergangenheitsbewältigung* are the essays by Sabine Wilke.

15. It is significant that the strongest attack on *Patterns of Childhood*, penned by Annemarie Auer, pointed to the lack of clarity and specificity about mechanisms of National Socialist hegemony. Auer misses the point entirely: it is exactly the invisible and therefore more pernicious paths of fascist ideology that present the greatest danger, because they are the most persistent. When Auer writes: "The investigation remains too tentative; it does not penetrate through to the real historical and moral core of the people" (Aber die Untersuchung bleibt zu zaghaft, sie greift nicht durch bis auf den wirklichen historisch-moralishen Fundus in den Leuten; 874), we can see that she is simply demanding adherence to the worn maxims of the first thirty years. By calling Wolf's novel an investigation (Untersuchung) and subjecting it to criteria appropriate to social science, she shows that she does not understand the significance of Wolf's contribution. It is not surprising that she later insists that the GDR has already come to terms with National Socialism, a statement belied, at the very latest, by the most recent right-wing activities in East Germany.

16. For a more psychoanalytically oriented interpretation of this episode, see Zahlmann (173).

17. For an interpretation of this novel as a practice of resistance, see Gättens.

Bibliography

Anz, Thomas, ed. *"Es geht nicht um Christa Wolf": Der Literaturstreit im vereinten Deutschland*. Munich: Spangenberg, 1991.

Auer, Annemarie. "Gegenerinnerung." *Sinn und Form* 30 (1976): 847–878.

Gättens, Marie-Luise. *Women Writers and Fascism*. Gainesville: University of Florida Press, 1995.

Hochhuth, Rolf. *The Representative*. Trans. Robert David MacDonald. London: Methuen, 1963.

Jaspers, Karl. *The Question of German Guilt*. Trans. E. B. Ashton. New York: Capricorn Books, 1947.

Jauss, Hans Robert. *Toward an Aesthetic of Reception*. Trans. Timothy Bahti. Minneapolis: University of Minnesota Press, 1982.

Koonz, Claudia. *Mothers in the Fatherland*. New York: St. Martin's Press, 1987.

Pickerodt, Gerhart. "Christa Wolfs Roman Kindheitsmuster. Ein Beitrag zur 'Vergangenheitsbewältigung'?" In *Exit: Wirkung und Wertung: Ausgewählte Beiträge zum fünften Symposium über deutsche und österreichische Exilliteratur*. Ed. Donald G. Daviau and Ludwig M. Fischer. Columbia, S.C.: Camden House, 1985, 293–307.

Vinke, Hermann, ed. *Akteneinsicht Christa Wolf: Zerrspiegel und Dialog*. Hamburg: Luchterhand, 1993.

Weigel, Sigrid. *Die Stimme der Medusa: Schreibweisen in der Gegenwartsliteratur von Frauen*. Dülmen-Hiddingsel: Tende, 1987.

Wiesehan, Gretchen. "Christa Wolf Reconsidered: National Stereotypes in *Kindheitsmuster*." *Germanic Review* 68.2 (1993): 79–87.

Wilke, Sabine. "'Dieser fatale Hang der Geschichte zu Wiederholungen': Geschichtskonstruktionen in Christa Wolf's Kindheitsmuster." *German Studies Review* 13 (1990): 499–512.

———. "'Worüber man nicht sprechen kann, darüber muß man allmählich zu schweigen aufhören': Vergangenheitsbeziehungen in Christa Wolfs Kindheitsmuster." *Germanic Review* 66.4 (1991): 169–176.

Wolf, Christa. *Die Dimension des Autors: Essays und Aufsätze, Reden und Gespräche 1959–1985*. Darmstadt: Luchterhand, 1987.

———. *Patterns of Childhood*. Trans. Ursule Molinaro and Hedwig Rappolt. New York: Noonday Press, 1980.

Zahlmann, Christel. *Christa Wolfs Reise "ins Tertiär": Eine literaturpsychologische Studie zu "Kindheitsmuster."* Würzburg: Königshausen + Neumann, 1986.

14

Grete Weil: A Jewish Antigone

Elke Liebs

A "Jewish" Antigone? The formulation is of course provocative, at least in Grete Weil's view. Once, in a contribution to a volume on attituds toward Germany, she wrote that *her* Antigone was always a *German* Antigone, that is, she knew her only in German translations of the Greek texts. And she added: "just as I am a German" (wie ich eine Deutsche bin; "Vielleicht irgendwie," 58) A bit later: "I am a European." (Ich bin eine Europäerin; 60). And then the title: *Meine Schwester Antigone* (1983) (*My Sister Antigone*).[1] Sisterliness as a metaphor of closeness as well as estrangement. "Elective affinity." Tender affection for this creature of infamy, daughter and sister alike to her father, daughter and granddaughter of her own mother. There is a fascination transcending ethnic and geographic boundaries with a woman whose very existence denies the laws of social order and decency. Faithful unto death to her father/brother, she whose existence is conditioned on the abnormal cannot live in the world of "normality," she must repudiate it. Therefore: one must put oneself outside the accepted social order to see its disorder, to be able to say *no*. The fellow traveller cannot see the whole. Those who go along are accomplices. Those who obey betray themselves.

Grete Weil's book is a text about living and dying, and continuing to live after death. Antigone's refusal is aimed at the "normality" of war, murder, and contempt for humanity. But her refusal is also aimed at the forcible deformation of her most private feelings. It is not religion that drives her to rebellion, but an incestuous love for her incestuously conceived brother. In such myths the most private intimacy finds expression. A hypertrophic relationship corresponding to an elective affinity. Two totalities are in collision here: a totalitarian regime (Kreon) and the totality of an individual's claim to autonomy, that is, of her feelings, dignity, and identity (Antigone). Because Antigone dies for this, she is able to live on into the present day, and Grete Weil's book lives from her, with her. But it is life lived *as resistance*, in several meanings of the term. First: resistance to the alien violence of myth, to the severe appeal of an artistic figure who does not awaken to life until the life of its author is threatened by death. Resistance, then, to the law of survival—as against the much more "natural" death wish at a time of extreme barbarity; and finally, resistance to the absolute loneliness that comes out of such a "relation," resistance to the vain arrogance of martyrdom, and the intransigence of the martyr's capacity for self-annihilation.

What makes Grete Weil's text so disturbing is precisely this inescapable linking of myth, history, and private experience. She unmasks the false heroism or arrogance that often accompanies martyrdom; just as consistently, she exposes the sentimentality of the victims, and the absurdity of (Jewish) survivor's syndrome, from which she herself suffers so much. Envy and admiration are intensified to defensiveness toward the one able to follow the path to its end, following only her own laws.[2]

The Danish philosopher Kierkegaard rightly pointed out a significant difference in his conception of Antigone: in calling her the "bride of grief," he consciously distinguishes the idea of grief from that of pain (I, 158). Sophocles' Antigone goes to her doom as if petrified by pain, while Kierkegaard puts the "fruit of grief into the bowl of pain" (I, 156). That which is manifest externally in Sophocles is unfolded inward, so to speak, by Kierkegaard, and is continued by Weil into that most inward and private variant of pain: remorse. The dynamic of the steps from pain via grief to remorse could be seen as analogous to the three stages of psychoanalytic "grief work" according to Freud: remember, repeat, work it through. It is not without reason that Alexander Mitscherlich's work on psychic reappraisal of the events and consequences of World War II is known as: "The inability to grieve." One of Mitscherlich's central concepts is that of "overcoming the past" *(Vergangenheitsbewältigung)* against which he argues as vehemently as does Grete Weil. *Bewältigung* (confronting) is still associated with *Gewalt* (force), and a sense of this *Gewalttätigkeit* (violence or powerful exertion) in the process of working it through, attaches to the concept of *collective guilt*, which in this context is similarly controversial and dangerous. Collective guilt tends to exonerate the individual more than it involves him or her in co-guilt. But the focus of attention in the texts we are concerned with here is the action of a single individual, the apparent senselessness of which cannot deny the fact that it has unforeseeable consequences and that it, inevitably, has meaning for us directly.

Grete Weil's book is living proof of this; it continues a dialogue between the individual and the "other" that began more than two thousand years ago and that in view of recent historical events in the whole world, but especially in Germany, has taken on a new and disturbing relevance. Alongside "overcoming the past" and "collective guilt," a new concept has emerged, which appears to sabotage both of these: the idea of the *Feindbild* (image of the enemy). This concept contains a potential for manipulation which could not be structured more explosively than it was by Sophocles: Not I, but the State, decides who my brother is; not those "natural" relationships, but the current regime or political climate. My brother today can be declared an alien tomorrow, an enemy of the state, and the day after tomorrow be declared again my brother: regardless of proximity. Whether we consider the Nazi regime or the Soviet empire, the German Democratic Republic or Yugoslavia, Los Angeles or Mölln, the Jewish pogroms all over the world that have occurred since the beginning of Christianity or modern manifestations of xenophobia in all parts of the world: it is always someone else telling us who our brother, who our sister is, and always the radical task of decision is directed *against* dictates, against dictatorship, and ultimately against oneself.

Grete Weil's astonishing achievement in this book is that she thematizes and presents the ambivalence and the pain that alone proceed from the necessity of such a decision; she does this openly and unreservedly, even when turning against herself. There literally is no other theme for her—from her 1949 tale *Ans Ende der Welt* (*To the End of the World*) up to her 1992 volume *Spätfolgen* (*Late Consequences*).

It is not by chance that her most important book is called *Meine Schwester Antigone* (*My Sister Antigone*). Artfully, this title leaves open the question of whether the author identifies herself first and foremost with the radical Antigone or the timid, obedient Ismene, who cannot bring herself to participate in the revolutionary act of humanity. Sisters they are, and sisters they remain, even in fear, failure, and remorse.

A totally unexpected and surprising new variant of this problematic arises from the opening of the STASI[3] and KGB archives. Since we are insufficiently informed by the media, in particular emotionally "underinformed," we tend all too easily to demand a radicality and unambiguity (which we have never demanded of ourselves) from those who in fact had to live under the dictate of an always potentially murderous partisanship. In the context of a system in which any public announcement can jeopardize one's very existence, only one argument has real validity: did someone, without immediate risk to life or limb, that is, for personal gain, knowingly and willfully denounce someone else, or not?

Germans have a well-known tendency to make moral judgments about others, and to a certain arrogance with regard to "detours" or "shortcuts" to whatever "ideal" is currently subscribed to. For example, in the recent *Literaturstreit* (literary controversy) about Christa Wolf, it seems the public wanted to punish her because they had stylized her, without consulting her, as the "conscience of the nation." This psychic mechanism would make it seem prudent to fear *any form* of admiration, because the power (*Gewalt*) implicit in this form of "confrontation," especially collective confrontation, will always eventually, inevitably, erupt.

One suddenly discovers that every Antigone (and every Cassandra) has an Ismene for a sister, and has something of this sister in herself, equal and not equal at the same time, filled with grudging love, with fear for one another, fear of one another; in Jung's views, only two of the multiple aspects of one and the same person.

It is precisely this fear, which Grete Weil also describes, and about which she understands that it forces one constantly to make decisions, if one is to remain a human being, that is, if one is not to become petrified in Sophoclean pain. Because she does not believe in collective guilt, she returned to Germany shortly after the war, and admitted her linguistic roots, namely, a feeling of rootedness, a *Heimatgefühl*, whose spiritual and cultural legacy survived political and ideological defacement. Like Jean Améry, who was himself in Auschwitz, she feels "Jewish" only when Jews (and other members of humanity) are spoken of in categories.

But the "wound" remains open: the wound, that is, of her having been irreversibly injured in her understanding of herself; of having done nothing to save her husband from the Nazi henchmen at Mauthausen, or to avenge his murder. The "wound," of having survived in a time in which it was "indecent," or, as Brecht says, "a crime" to survive (172–173); the "wound": having been both victim and perpetrator—as a member of the Jewish Council *(Judenrat),* as an emigrant or fugitive, as a re-immigrant, as a writer and as one who maintained silence. From the "wonder" of having survived, especially of having saved her mother, came this "wound" that can only be made bearable by writing, by bearing witness, for herself and others. But until her last moment Grete Weil will always refuse to see anything "bearable" or "understandable" in the events of the Holocaust. The incomprehensibility and inconceivability of that which happened finds its most immediate expression in that novel in which she included an authentic report of an eyewitness who as a soldier had been present at the massacre in the Polish town of Piotrkow in 1943 (officially called "ghetto liquidation"; Chapter 15, pp. 151–178 in English translation). It speaks for itself that almost all reviews of the novel made no mention of this horrifying document, which was left unchanged and uncommented. This is a text no German youngster should be allowed to leave school without reading; written for the sole purpose of bearing witness to the monstrous acts of which human beings are capable. I remember clearly and yet with a certain dreadful irony, a point in my Greek studies in a "humanist" *Gymnasium* (high school) in postwar, "Economic Miracle" Germany, where we were made to memorize, completely straightforwardly and with no sense of irony, the Song of Fate (*Schicksalslied*) from Sophocles' *Antigone*:

"Polla ta deina . . . " "Many the marvelous [also in the sense of awesome, overwhelming, dreadful, powerful] things; but none that can be/More of a marvel than man!" (lines 308–309)

"Our task is remembrance" ("Erinnerung ist unsere Aufgabe"; *Vermächtnis*, 66), wrote Heinrich Böll. If Grete Weil seems to extend this specifically German assignment of rememberance over a period of two thousand years, she is doing this in the name of cultural memory, the task of which is to be not superhuman, but human, in an inhuman time. One could thus justifiably align the rather more "silent opposition" of an Antigone, or even that of resistance fighter Sophie Scholl with the desperately misguided activities of the Baader-Meinhof terrorist "sympathizers," one of whom in fact suddenly drops in on the narrator. Here the narrator sees herself confronted at close range with exactly what she is writing about: a deadly—and suicidal—radicality, whose claims literally take her breath away. When the vital needs of one individual mean denying life to another, where a society or political situation can bring about such perversion, then those affected, those willing to say "no" fall into that great, nameless loneliness, which Grete Weil, on every imaginable level, makes her theme. It is a loneliness that isolates even the various "sympathizers" from each other, freezes their actions into helpless gestures—this loneliness that could flow among them like a living stream. When the young girl Marlene, fleeing the power of the state, has a nervous breakdown in the narrator's home, it is not merely the crass disproportion of cause to effect, as in *Deutschland im Herbst* (1978)(*Germany in Autumn*); it is also a farewell to age and continuity, to reflection and responsibility, farewell to the rationalizations of resistance and restraint, of intellect and intransigence. The older woman shrinks in horror from the unconditional radicality of the younger, from the spiral of violence she represents, whose consequences she does not want to be responsible for. At the same time she is fascinated by the contrastive oscillation of fragility with toughness. Unthinkable that she, once persecuted herself, could ever betray another victim. But it dawns dimly on her that she could not have borne the totalitarianism of an Antigone. It too is strangely inhumane and opposed to life, if need be, even to her own. And, because she is completely isolated in the knowledge and acknowledgment of her own ambiguity, the young people leave her alone with the burden of history, *her* history.

It was the idea of an "other Germany" that caused Grete Weil, also Thomas Mann and many other fellow writers, to return to Germany after the war. And it is for this other Germany that Sophie Scholl and her friends stand; it is hard to imagine a more vivid memorial than that which Weil has set them in her Antigone novel. Critics have only recently and reluctantly come to grips with this analogy; indeed, not until she won the "Geschwister Scholl Prize," albeit for the much later novel *Der Brautpreis*, (1988)(*The Bride Price*). This, too, is a work of radical love, radical pain and radical refusal offered up against the mechanisms of force. It is perhaps not coincidental that both works concern "brides"; Sophie Scholl, too, was a bride of grief, as Kierkegaard called his Antigone: Scholl, writing to her fiance of her despair at the knowledge that every sock knit by German women for their soldiers at the front would lengthen the war, said she would immediately stop knitting any. A German Antigone? Such statements are certainly corroborated by the most recently discovered documents: the members of the *Weiße Rose* were well aware of the mortal danger under which they worked, even the youngest, and the women, too.

Grete Weil speaks almost tenderly of the "dilettantism" of these rash, no, unhesitating, passionate people who were willing to say "no"; these sisters bound together over two thousand years, who so desperately needed that little bit of luck, which they were not to have. And yet: how much poorer would the world be without Antigone, without Sophie, even though they perhaps changed nothing. To avert Sophie's horrifying, degrading death, at least fictionally, Weil has her Antigone not passively await her end, but commit suicide: not to hasten her death, but actively to escape the "normality" of living on at odds with her own inner "law." Living on (*weiter leben*)[4] versus surviving (*überleben*) via death—the old dichotomy once again. Can the one ever balance out the other? In her confrontation with the third "bride," Marlene, the terrorist's bride, Grete Weil gives us an uncomfortable answer: she doesn't expressly *compare* the resistance to the tyranny of the Third Reich with the terrorist acts of the Red Army Faction; but she warns and reminds us that we cannot discuss the one without the other. These two extremes of radicality, where thought and action coincide, in outlining a historical horizon, illuminate mutually their differences and similarities.

> "I am a tired old woman. I don't care what happens to you [i.e., Marlene]. Even though you girls have not told me anything, I know you are a terrorist's moll. I reject violence and those who support violence. I reject your belief that there can be a paradise on earth, and I certainly reject your hellish ways of bringing about this paradise. You are playing war games, meaningless, sickening games. And I want peace." (149)
>
> (Ich bin eine müde alte Frau. Es ist mir egal, was mit dir [= Marlene] geschieht. Zwar habt ihr mir nichts gesagt, aber ich weiß, daß du eine Terroristenbraut bist. Ich bin gegen Gewalt und gegen Sympathisanten von Gewalt. Ich bin gegen euren Glauben, daß es ein Paradies auf Erden geben kann, und noch viel mehr gegen euren höllischen Weg zu diesem Paradies. Ihr spielt Krieg. Einen sinnlosen widerwärtigen Krieg. Und ich will Frieden.) (164)

The tired, old Antigone, then? Yes and no. An Antigone tired of being her own sister. Who would not understand that the burden of such forbidden "nearness" to one's own self is depressing beyond pain, and that to continue to live, like that, has less and less point. Grete Weil is tired. But only those who love life as strongly as she does, can distinguish between "living on" and "surviving," with such wisdom, that being this tired becomes expressible—without bitterness, coquetry, or heroism. Saying "no" is tiring, and even more so the stock taking of one's life: writing. But most tiring of all is the "pain of lost pain." The external changes wrought by aging are bad enough. But they cannot be compared with the humiliation of having no control over the inner changes. A pain that no longer hurts—is just rhetoric.

So Grete Weil's last battle is directed—as was the first—against the dulling of memory, against forgetting and against self-pity—three enemies we constantly succumb to, and not just in old age. She does this by repeatedly staying in touch with her pain, even her most personal. In the unremitting pain of remembering her husband, murdered in a concentration camp, she too is a "bride of grief"; the poetic outcome of the violence of "her" history is that she uses the power of myth to work against "mythologizing." In every life there comes the decision to be an Antigone. Only when one recognizes that the typical and the mythical are identical, does it become clear that resistance is never a unique decision in a particular historical moment, but that it becomes an existential process or an inner constitution: "to say 'NO'—the only indestructible freedom."

In writing the truth, in bearing witness like Wolf's Cassandra,[5] in writing against the fleeting quality of the remembered past (*Flüchtigkeit*), and against aiding a fugitive (*Fluchthilfe*), (which she clearly is also doing), Grete Weil remains in search of herself. This self-investigation in the light of her creation of Antigone contributes, surprisingly, both directly and indirectly to the *Historikerstreit* (historians' feud).[6] She does this by comparing realities in order to show that they are in fact noncomparable. At the same time she has created a novel of visionary and linguistic density, whose relevance is constantly being demonstrated, whose leitmotifs are timeless, and whose poetic images reveal both intellectual and emotional processes, familiar to us all. She was one of the first to point out the analogy between Antigone and Sophie Scholl, and only the timing of its appearance prevented her *Antigone* from receiving as much praise as Wolf's *Kassandra* novel, which Weil regarded highly. Weil's work is open and direct and appeared too early, at a time when the Germans were not yet ready to deal with their past. Wolf's message is encoded and her book appeared much later, when the past was being discussed in Germany.

It looks as if they are all a bit tired: Antigone and Christa Wolf, Cassandra and Grete Weil. But Antigone, according to Hölderlin, "der Jungfrau'n herrlichste Natur" (maidenhood's finest creation; stanza 4.1, verse 115) is not subject to such human foibles. She has survived, and will live on, ever more eloquently she will speak in such imposing, yet simple statements as the one Sophie Scholl wrote to her brother: "Just because all things are filled with contradictions, humans don't have to be the same" (Der Mensch soll ja nicht, weil alle Dinge zwiespältig sind, deshalb auch zwiespältig sein; 147). Antigone could have said this. Or Grete Weil. Or Cassandra or Christa Wolf. In any case one of the "sisters."[7]

Notes

1. An English translation by Krishna Winston was published under the title *My Sister, My Antigone* (New York: Avon Books, 1984). All quotations from the novel are from this edition, with the German original given in parantheses.

2. For a discussion of Weil's somewhat different linking of private experience, history, and old testament narrative, see Miriam Fuchs, "Recalling the Past and Rescuing the Self: Autobiographical Slippage in Grete Weil's *The Bride Price: A Novel*." The essay examines ways in which Weil's revisioning, feminizing, and intertextualizing of Michal, David's first wife, is used as a mechanism for autobiographical reflection. According to Fuchs, "Weil's portrayal of Michal's portrayal of King David dramatizes the deep ambivalences that have characterized Weil's life—her love for and resentment of her birth country, which is implicated in violence, but where she chooses to live; her disengagement from, but acknowledgment of, a religion that has torn apart her life; an avowed distance from, but obvious affection for Michal, King Saul's daughter as she has created her; and a profound bond with her husband and millions of others who died at the hands of the Nazis, which on all levels she wishes she did not have."

3. *Staatssicherheitspolizei*, the East German secret police.

4. See Ruth Klügers autobiography *weiter leben—Eine Jugend*.

5. The main character in the novel by Christa Wolf, *Kassandra*.

6. This film shows the radical position of the young German leftists in their struggle against capitalism and the power of the state. Their terrorist acts were motivated by the same radical idealism as the deed of Antigone or the phantasies of Grete Weil in her book about Antigone. But Weil's position toward violence is clear: she is against it, at least in her old age.

7. An earlier German version of this chapter was published as "Grete Weil: Eine jüdische Antigone," *Sinn und Form* 26 (1994): 291–298; and in *Ein Text für Christa Wolf* (Berlin: Janus Press, 1994). Translation of this essay from the original German by John A. Hargraves.

Bibliography

Aurenche, Emmanuelle. "Grete Weil et le myth d'Antigone." *Cahiers d'Études Germaniques* 26 (1994): 99–105.

Böll, Heinrich. *Das Vermächtnis. Erzählung*. Bornheim: Lamur Verlag, 1982.

Brecht, Bertold. *Selected Poems.* Trans. H. R. Hays. New York/London: Grove Press, 1954.

Fuchs, Miriam. "Recalling the Past and Rescuing the Self: Autobiographical Slippage in Grete Weil's *The Bride Price: A Novel.*" *Shofar: An Interdisciplinary Journal of Jewish Studies.* Special issue: *Women in Jewish Life and Culture* (Fall 1999).

Hölderlin, Friedrich. "Der Tod des Empedokles." In *Hölderlin Werke und Briefe.* Ed. Friedrich Beißner and Jochen Schmidt. Vol.2. Frankfurt am Main: Insel Verlag, 1826.

Inge Jens, Hans Scholl, Sophie Scholl. Briefe und Aufzeichnungen. Frankfurt am Main: S. Fischer, 1984.

Kierkegaard, Søren. *Either/Or.* Part I. Ed. and Trans. with Introduction by Howard V. Hong and Edna H. Hong. Princeton: Princeton University Press, 1987.

Klüger, Ruth, *weiter leben. Eine Jugend.* Göttingen: Wallstein Verlag, 1992.

Meyer, Uwe. "'O Antigone . . . stehe mir bei': Zur Antigonie -Rezeption im Werk von Grete Weil." *Lili: Zeitschrift für Literaturwissenschaft und Linguistik* 26 (1996): 147–157.

Mitscherlich, Alexander and Margarete. *Die Unfähigkeit zu trauern: Grundlagen kollektiven Verhaltens.* Munich: R. Piper, 1977.

Nussbaum, Laureen and Uwe Meyer. "Grete Weil: unbequem, zum Denken zwingend." *Exilforschung: Ein internationales Jahrbuch* 11 (1993): 156–170.

Weil, Grete. *Ans Ende der Welt.* Berlin: Volk und Welt, 1949.

———. *Der Brautpreis.* Zurich/Frauenfeld: Nagel and Kimche, 1988.

———. *The Bride Price.* Boston: D. R. Godine, 1991.

———. *Meine Schwester Antigone.* Zurich/Cologne: Benzinger, 1983.

———. *My Sister, My Antigone.* Trans. Krishna Winston. New York: Avon Books, 1984.

———. *Spätfolgen: Erzählungen.* Zurich/Frauenfeld: Nagel & Kimche, 1992.

———. "Vielleicht, irgendwie . . . ." In *Lieben Sie Deutschland? Gefühle zur Lage der Nation.* Ed. Marie Louise Janssen-Jurreit. Serie Piper 368. Munich: Piper, 1985.

Wolf, Christa. *Kassandra.* Darmstadt: Luchterhand, 1984.

———. *Cassandra.* Trans. Jan van Heurck. New York: Farrar, Strauss, Giroux, 1984.

Sophocles. "Antigone." In *Norton World Masterpieces.* Trans. Robert Fagles. 6th ed. Vol. 1. New York: W. W. Norton, 1992.

15

Gender, Film, and German History: Filmmaking by German Women Directors from Weimar to the Present

Richard W. McCormick

The historical period stretching from the Weimar Republic to the present contains almost all of the work done by women film directors in Germany, who represent another type of female "author." This is in obvious contrast to the situation of women writers, who have been writing literature in the German language for centuries. Filmmaking began in Germany in the same year as in France, 1895, but there is no record of a German film being made by a woman until 1913, when Olga Wohlbrück's *Ein Mädchen zu verschenken* (*A Girl for Giving Away*) appeared. A few other women are known to have directed films in the 1910s—Fern Andra made five films, and Hanna Henning had made more than forty before she died in 1925—but few of these films still exist. Only three female names get much mention in film histories, and those women worked in the Weimar Republic, most conspicuously in its later years. Lotte Reiniger is known for her short animated films, which she began making in 1925.[1] The other two women are much better known: Leontine Sagan's 1931 film *Mädchen in Uniform* (*Girls in Uniform*) can be found in video stores across the United States; Leni Riefenstahl's 1932 directorial debut film, *Das Blaue Licht* (*The Blue Light*), is not as well known, but her name is probably better known than any other pre–World War II German film director's, male or female. This fame is of course due to the state-sponsored films she made in the Third Reich (especially *Der Triumph des Willens*), not for *Das blaue Licht*.

Both Sagan and Riefenstahl were exceptions in a period of intense concentration in the German film industry; as fewer and larger corporations resulted, opportunities for women directors disappeared. Women would not again get the chance to direct films until the 1960s, and not in any significant numbers until the mid- and late 1970s, when after much struggle West German women were finally able to begin taking advantage of the state subsidies that had been going to independent male filmmakers associated with what we have come to call the "New German Cinema." In spite of this late start, by the late 1980s Thomas Elsaesser would write that the West German cinema had proportionally more women filmmakers than any other national cinema, a distinction that is probably still valid in now-unified Germany.[2]

The first two German films directed by women that are still widely known today, then, were made at the end of the Weimar Republic, just before Hitler came to power in 1933. Obviously, Riefenstahl's work cannot be discussed without reference to her complicity with German fascism. Sagan's *Mädchen in Uniform*, on the other hand, can be considered an antifascist film; indeed, until the 1970s that was more or less the only way it was discussed critically, at the expense of its exploration of female identity and relationships between women. As a matter of fact, however, both *Mädchen in Uniform* and *Das blaue Licht* thematize female identity, albeit in very different ways, and with very different politics; certainly it is no surprise to the viewer of *Mädchen in Uniform* to learn that its director left Germany in 1933. The two films can be used to mark two ends of a spectrum that defines the way in which the work of subsequent German women filmmakers has been viewed. At one end there is Riefenstahl's romantic depiction of feminity as exotic "otherness" in *Das blaue Licht* and her subsequent notorious complicity with the Third Reich; at the other end is Sagan's film about an antiauthoritarian female bonding at odds with German militarism and pronatalism.

While in the postwar period there has been no female director whose work places her in proximity to Riefenstahl, the critical reception of some films by West German women directors has not been so unambiguous. Some films have been criticized for manifesting a type of essentialism apparently characteristic of some West German feminists, who assert that German women as a group are innocent of any complicity with fascism. Arguments about women's general victimization within patriarchy are used to exempt German women from any responsibility for the events of German history—a special "feminist" variant of the art of finding ways to depict the Germans as victims, an old apologist strategy of the German right wing with regard to World War II, but variants of which have been noted as well on the West German left since the 1960s.[3] Such criticism may well be valid with regard to some West

German feminists; it certainly seems to explain the negative reaction by some feminist historians in West Germany to Claudia Koonz's book *Mothers in the Fatherland*, which investigates how it was that so many German women supported the Nazis.[4]

But with regard to the feminist cinema created by West German women directors in the last twenty years, the films that have most explicitly dealt with the experience and legacy of German fascism provide little evidence of this tendency. Indeed, I would argue that, on the whole, women directors in Germany have been more forthright about confronting fascism and the German past than male filmmakers.

In this chapter, I will provide a general survey of filmmaking by women in Germany, with a special emphasis on films that specifically address German fascism, antisemitism, or racism, and films that are otherwise relevant to discussions of those topics. As many of them are also feminist investigations of female identity, the complex intersections of identity politics and "otherness" in terms of class, race, gender, ethnicity, and sexual orientation will also be addressed—without ignoring the specific historical context of German experience in the twentieth century.

Sagan versus Riefenstahl: Resistance versus Exoticism in Late Weimar

Leontine Sagan directed *Mädchen in Uniform* in 1931. The film was produced by Carl Froelich and based on the play *Gestern und Heute* (Yesterday and Today) by Christa Winsloe; Sagan had already directed the very popular Berlin production of the play. Up until this point Sagan had made her career in the theater, as an actress and then as a director. *Mädchen in Uniform* was the first of only two films she directed, and it became an international success.[5] Given that we know the film today primarily because it was rediscovered by the women's movement in the early 1970s and then became a favorite especially among lesbian audiences, it is perhaps surprising to learn that the homoerotic aspect of the film was not much emphasized in its critical reception up until that point; it was discussed almost exclusively as an antiauthoritarian film. Siegfried Kracauer, one of its few detractors, considered it an antiauthoritarian film that did not go far enough, merely a "timid heresy."[6]

The film tells the story of Manuela, an adolescent pupil in an oppressive Potsdam boarding school for the daughters of somewhat impoverished Prussian aristocracy. Manuela creates a scandal by openly declaring her love for the only teacher in the school who treats the girls kindly, Fräulein von Bernburg. For those who have seen the film, the most memorable scene is probably the "kiss" scene, which is the closest thing to anything openly erotic in the film and thus is quite famous.[7] In context, however, it is only the first hint that something more than a mother-daughter relationship is developing between Manuela and her teacher, who gives every girl in her dormitory a very ritualized good-night kiss on the forehead.

Manuela breaks the rules of the ritual by an exuberant embrace of Bernburg, who responds with a brief kiss on the lips, which is shown in close-up.

Sagan's Berlin production of the play had apparently quite openly highlighted the homoerotic side of the relationship between the two women; Carl Froelich wanted to play this down in the film for commercial reasons and thus appears to have been working at cross purposes with Sagan (Thiele, 32, 34). In the early 1980s, the critic B. Ruby Rich wrote a very convincing article on the film reclaimimg it as a lesbian film, at the same time insisting that the film's lesbianism does not "undo" its antiauthoritarianism. This can be demonstrated by defining the basic conflicts in the film: according to the film's "villain," the school's authoritarian headmistress, the school's mission is to raise the daughters of Prussian soldiers to become suitable *Soldatenmütter*, the mothers of soldiers.

The ideology represented by the headmistress and the school she administers is a militaristic, nationalistic, and antidemocratic Prussianism, central to which was a pronatalist policy. With uncanny accuracy the headmistress predicts the role all ("Aryan") women will be expected to play under National Socialism: to be mothers of soldiers. A more democratic and humane treatment of her charges threatens such goals, for it is at odds with the training appropriate for women in an authoritarian, militaristic society. This "threat" is only increased by the possibility of emotional relations between women that in any way subvert the molding of women into obedient wives and mothers. Thus, any hint of lesbianism must be crushed, as must any generalized female solidarity of the type that mobilizes the schoolgirls to save Manuela from committing suicide.[8]

Whereas Sagan's film is clearly antiauthoritarian and should also be seen in relation to various progressive campaigns for sexual emancipation in the Weimar Republic, Riefenstahl's debut film *Das blaue Licht* has been viewed primarily as reactionary. Indeed, it has often been considered a proto-fascist film. This is understandable, given the filmmaker's subsequent career, but the situation is a bit more ambiguous. The film is not unequivocally fascist simply because it an example of the popular genre of "mountain films"; as Eric Rentschler has demonstrated, this was not a genre beloved only by the right wing in Weimar, in spite of Siegfried Kracauer's influential verdict (257–258).[9] And neither is the film itself unambiguously fascist in its specific aesthetic and textual structure, as Linda Schulte-Sasse has demonstrated.[10] I would suggest that it is probably in the film's gender politics that the problem lies: that is, in Riefenstahl's representation of an "elemental" femininity so socially isolated, so outside of history, so romantically "other." Such complete "otherness" can perhaps be compared to the concept of a "separate sphere" for women; according to Claudia Koonz, the belief in such a sphere explains the willingness of many conservative German women to collaborate with the obviously misogynistic Nazis.[11]

Riefenstahl herself did go on to collaborate, of course. She explains her collaboration now to be due to an apolitical naiveté, as for example she insists in the interviews in Ray Müller's film *Die Macht der Bilder* (U.S. release title: *The Wonderful/Horrible Life of Leni Riefenstahl*, 1993). But at the very least her "naiveté" was an extremely opportunistic one, I would insist.[12]

The gender politics of *Das blaue Licht* can be illustrated with reference to its very first scene: the mountain girl Junta (played by Riefenstahl herself) is shown retrieving magic crystals in a mountain stream, high above the valley below, in which a carriage is shown approaching. It bears a man from the city who will ultimately be responsible for Junta's death. In contrast to the shots of the carriage from the city on the road below, Junta is depicted against a mountain waterfall. She is identified romantically with an elemental nature in opposition to the more civilized world below. She is feared by the people of the nearby village and considered a "witch"; she is desired by the male protagonist from the city: and she is completely isolated from other women (and almost any social contact).

Women Filmmakers in the "New German Cinema": The Breakthrough in the 1970s

The career of Riefenstahl during the Third Reich is well known, but again, as a woman she was an isolated exception among the directors making films in Germany during the 1930s and 1940s. Women in postwar West Germany did not direct films until the 1960s. In that decade what we now call the "New German Cinema" emerged. Although it was a cinema very much in opposition to the style of filmmaking that had developed in the Third Reich and remained dominant in West Germany through the 1950s, it was still an overwhelmingly male-dominated phenomenon. Only at the end of the 1960s did two women make significant feature films on their own, and even then May Spils and Ula Stöckl were rare exceptions (Knight, 7).[13]

It was not until the mid-1970s that women directors in West Germany finally gained prominence. One of the first films by women to attract favorable critical attention was Helma Sanders-Brahms's film for television, *Shirins Hochzeit* (*Shirin's Wedding*), which won two film prizes in 1976. This film is of special interest today, given the xenophobia that has troubled unified Germany in the 1990s. Anti-"foreigner" sentiments have had a long history in West Germany, where they have been worsening since the recession of the early 1970s; in East Germany such feelings were better repressed, but they have certainly flourished since German unification. *Shirins Hochzeit* depicts the experience of a Turkish woman who flees her rural village in Turkey to find work in a German factory, only to be laid off in the recession, and then to experience downward mobility in spite of great determination, becoming first a cleaning woman and then a prostitute. The film attempts to thematize Shirin's oppression in West Germany both as a member of an ethnic minority and as a woman.[14]

It was in 1977, however, that a number of films by women appeared and attracted attention. In that year Margarethe von Trotta's *Das zweite Erwachen der Christa Klages* (*The Second Awakening of Christa Klages*), Helke Sander's *Die allseitig reduzierte Persönlichkeit/REDUPERS* (The All-Around Reduced Personality), and Ulrike Ottinger's *Madame X* were released—first feature films by three women who along with Sanders-Brahms would become leading figures in Germany's emerging feminist cinema. For Helke Sander especially this achievement had been long in coming. She had been making films since her days in film school ten years earlier, but because of her involvement in the student movement and even more so in the women's movement (Sander was one of the founders of the West German women's movement in the late 1960s), none of her film projects had been funded for much of the early and mid-1970s.

All three of these films are in their own ways important contributions to feminist politics and are not unrelated to the issues at stake in this chapter, but it was the next phase of filmmaking by West German women in which films were made that interrogate Germany's fascist past from feminist perspectives. Indeed, the films can be seen as part of a broader trend evident in the late 1970s and early 1980s in "New German Cinema," the advent of the "history film," or what Anton Kaes called the "return of history as film."[15] This trend has been explained in part as a response to the trauma of the "German Autumn" of 1977, when the hysteria and polarization around the activities of the terrorist "Red Army Faction" reached its peak, and memories of earlier periods of turbulence in twentieth-century German history were awakened. Certainly this was the reason that people such as Fassbinder, Schlöndorff, and Kluge worked on the collective film *Deutschland im Herbst* (1978) (*Germany in Autumn*); that project in turn led to Kluge's next film, *Die Patriotin* (1979) (*The Patriot*), and Fassbinder's history trilogy as well, especially its first part, *Die Ehe der Maria Braun* (1979) (*The Marriage of Maria Braun*). Clearly, Margarethe von Trotta's 1981 film *Die bleierne Zeit* (U.S. release title *Marianne and Juliane*) also had its origins in the events of 1977.[16]

But von Trotta's film, like the three films I will discuss in depth here, Helma Sanders-Brahms's *Deutschland, bleiche Mutter* (1979) (*Germany, Pale Mother*), Jutta Brückner's *Hungerjahre* (1980) (*Years of Hunger*), and Marianne Rosenbaum's *Peppermint Frieden* (1983) (*Peppermint Peace*)—among other films by West German women during this period—are different from the history films by Kluge and Fassbinder in some interesting ways. In my opinion this difference has to do with the feminist autobiographical project. Let me formulate this even more simply: it has to do with the feminist dictum that the personal must be seen as political. In these films German history, West German identity, female identity, and personal identity are all explored. Each filmmaker's personal investment in her project results in films that address the spectator much more directly than Fassbinder's gaudy but distanced allegorical melodramas and Kluge's clever but not readily accessible essayistic montage films. This direct address is not necessarily pleasant—often it is painful, and sometimes embarrassing—but it results in attempts to come to terms with the past that I would call especially honest.

Women, Fascism, and the War: Helma Sanders-Brahms's *Deutschland, bleiche Mutter* (1979–80)

The film in this group of feminist "history" films that has raised the most controversy is Sanders-Brahms's *Deutschland, bleiche Mutter*, attacked first of all by predominantly male critics in West Germany. Their vehement rejection of the film was analyzed—correctly, I believe—by Olav Münzberg as a defensive reaction against any such personal confrontation with the fascist past; to this day German critics have apparently not "forgiven" Sanders-Brahms for this film.[17] The film has also been criticized by some feminists, including Ellen Seiter, E. Ann Kaplan, and Angelika Bammer in the United States.[18] All of these three critics accused the film more or less of "essentialism," although this meant something different to Kaplan from what it meant to Seiter and Bammer.[19] The latter two criticize the film for its depiction of Lene, the filmmaker's mother, whose experiences during the Third Reich and the postwar era form the basis of this biographical/autobiographical film. They assert that Lene is portrayed too much as a passive victim of history, even as being outside of history. That sort of ahistorical depiction is problematic for feminism in general, but even more so with reference to German history, for as Seiter stresses, it is especially troubling that the story of the Third Reich and World War II is told in such a way that a non-Jewish German woman appears to be its primary victim (570–572).

Such concerns are clearly valid, but in my opinion they are based on inaccurate characterizations of the film.[20] The film does focus on the story of Lene, and she is in many ways a victim—but she is not really a victim of the war. Indeed, if anything she thrives during the war. Rather she is a victim of the postwar era and its restoration of traditional gender roles. She loses the autonomy she had developed while her husband was away, serving as a soldier in the war, and this loss makes her bitter, depressed, and suicidal. Whereas Lene is strong enough to survive rape by allied soldiers at the end of the war, in the postwar era she can barely survive being reunited with her husband. She abandons her suicide attempt at the last moment, but only for the sake of her daughter. During the war itself, if anything is problematic it is how happy and independent she becomes struggling to support her child alone. If this seems to idealize the war, however, it is precisely at this point in the film when Sanders-Brahms inserts documentary footage of the horrors of the war so that the child's idyllic memory of her mother is relativized. And Sanders-Brahms constantly makes clear with her voiceover that the whole film is her reconstruction of her mother's story, another way in which the limits of the daughter's perspective and the project of the film as a whole are—openly and very honestly—foregrounded.

For example, after their house has been destroyed in the bombing, Lene and her baby daughter Anna find refuge at the apartment of rich relatives in Berlin. In one scene they take a bath together, and here Seiter's critique of the film's "mystification" of the mother-child symbiosis seems most justified. Over a shot of the playful interaction of mother and toddler, Sanders-Brahms's narrative voiceover tells the viewers that she and Lene loved each other in the bathtub, and that they flew like witches together over the roofs. But as she mentions this fantasy of flying, the scene shifts, and documentary footage is inserted: aerial footage shot from a plane flying over the bombed-out buildings of Berlin. Here the documentary footage provides the corrective to the idealized fantasies of the child, showing what it would actually have meant to fly over the houses of Berlin, many of which by then had no roofs.

The film is not a glorification of the war. It is clearly an antiwar film based on a feminist critique of militarism in general, and of fascism in particular, as especially negative forms of patriarchal domination. Nor is the depiction of the filmmaker's father unfair: it shows how his socialization as a soldier and his experiences in the war transform him from a sensitive (if apolitical) young man to a bitter old man who tyrannizes wife and child in the postwar era.

The film (like so much discourse of the 1970s) could perhaps be said to be guilty of a certain narcissistic "politics of identity" in that its primary focus is on the story of a non-Jewish German woman.[21] But the film is not silent about the most obvious victims of German fascism, the Jews. Both parents, Lene even more than her husband, are criticized for their apolitical indifference; indeed it is through this attitude that they become complicit with the Third Reich. Their belief in their ability to escape history into the "private happiness" of their own romance is one illusion that the film destroys completely, and this is depicted for Lene precisely through her willingness to ignore the plight of the Jews. Early in the film, Lene and her sister Hanne hear glass breaking and screams outside their bedroom window (in what seems a direct allusion to the *Kristallnacht*). Looking out the window, they see their Jewish classmate Rahel Bernstein being carried away by some men. It is the "unpolitical" Lene who closes the shutters on the violence, not Hanne, the Nazi, who reproaches Lene for her coldness. Lene wants instead to talk about suitors; she believes politics (and "history") can be evaded by retreating into the private sphere, an illusion that not only facilitates her complicity with the status quo, but also one that will be eventually be her undoing.

At another point in the film, Lene is indicted even more clearly. It is early in the war, and Lene is embroidering a blouse to wear for her husband Hans, about to return on his first leave from the army. She is so eager to finish the blouse that she registers no reaction when told that the Ducksteins, the Jewish owners of the store where she buys thread, have been deported. Instead she goes to the boarded-up store and begs a neighbor to let her in. Here she participates in the expropriation of Jewish property without even thinking about it. The narrator, however, takes her parents to task for their thoughtless compliance in the Third Reich in voiceover narration: "You say you didn't want it, but you did nothing to stop it."[22]

While the filmmaker's voiceover tempers her critique of her parents by problematizing her own tendency to be self-righteous as a member of the privileged postwar generation, the film nonetheless depicts Lene's faith in "private," apolitical, domestic happiness as her downfall. For after the war the "private sphere" and its traditional gender roles are restored, along with the general restoration of a conservative status quo in West Germany, the rehabilitation there of many ex-Nazis, and Germany's remilitarization (the film alludes to all of these political developments). And the "private sphere" that is restored becomes Lene's personal prison.

Political and Sexual Repression in the 1950s: Jutta Brückner's *Hungerjahre* (1979–80)

Brückner's *Hungerjahre*, like *Deutschland, bleiche Mutter*, premiered at the 1980 Berlin film festival. Unlike the latter, Brückner's film was generally well received by critics, but the relative lack of controversy was also a disadvantage, for it would be years before the film received much scholarly attention in any depth.[23] This autobiographical film is also accompanied by the filmmaker's own voiceover, although the use of voiceover is more complex in this film. The film tells the story of Ursula, an adolescent girl who over the course of three years—1953 to 1956—develops a severe identity crisis, which results from difficulties in coping with her emerging sexuality in the repressive atmosphere within her own family in particular, and within the West German society of the 1950s in general. Off-camera voiceover is used to present internal monologues by three characters: primarily by Ursula, the character corresponding to the filmmaker as an adolescent (in the voice of the actress playing Ursula), but also by her mother and father. There is also voiceover commentary presented from the adult perspective of the autobiographical narrator (in the filmmaker's own voice).

As in *Deutschland, bleiche Mutter*, there is use of historical documentary footage to contextualize the fictionalized autobiographical reconstruction of the adolescent girl's experiences. The difference is that Brückner does not attempt to integrate them into the fiction so completely as Sanders-Brahms does at various points in her film; they remain more separate from Ursula's "personal" story. But their function is similar: to provide the larger political context within which Ursula's personal story unfolds. A striking example is the documentary footage shown of the suppression of the June 1953 uprising in East Berlin: over the shots of Soviet tanks and milling crowds we hear first an East German commentator, and then Konrad Adenauer himself discussing the events of June 17. For a while both voices are heard simultaneously, both providing opposed but equally distorted explanations of the visual reality being shown to us.

Here the complexity of the use of the soundtrack can be illustrated. As mentioned above, the three main characters in the "personal" story are granted voiceover; the overall effect is such that at moments in the film there seems to be a number of disembodied voices floating over the visual reality being depicted. In the June 17, 1953, footage this is shown to be true on the political level as well as the personal level of the story: conflicting voices and viewpoints attempt to explain reality—and no one voice is especially reliable.

After the documentary footage of the Soviet tanks in East Berlin, Ursula confronts her mother with questions about the political situation, especially about the concept of "freedom" stressed so much in Western accounts of the events. Ursula's mother defines freedom as "when things are going well for us and we don't need to be afraid" (wenn es uns gut geht und wir keine Angst haben müssen). The inadequacy of this definition is emblematic for West Germany in the period of postwar reconstruction: there is little about freedom or democracy in it. Instead it manifests a concern about economic prosperity and political stability.

This somewhat repressed notion of political freedom also accompanies a repressed attitude about physical affection; the viewer sees here one of the few examples of mother and daughter hugging in the film, and it is Ursula who initiates it. The daughter comforts her anxious mother, who upon composing herself pulls away. The mother's negative attitudes about affection and the body—especially the female body—become internalized by Ursula, and later they are crucial among the factors leading to her mental crisis. The film makes the social causes of the mother's repressed attitudes clear, especially her fear of pregnancy in an era in which birth control was much less available, socially condemned, and primarily the responsibility of women. Documentary footage of beauty pageants demonstrate another message that girls were given in the 1950s about their bodies. Sexual objectification as well as sexual repression of women's bodies was being propagated at the same time.

Later on, when Ursula's identity crisis has become severe, she seems to have internalized many of these self-destructive, often conflicting messages, which are represented on the sound track as internal voices (spoken by Brückner herself). The voices speak among other things of a coldness to be destroyed by fire. This somewhat schizoid chorus of voices that exteriorize conflicts within Ursula—voiced "over" the visual image of Ursula—recalls an equally schizoid conflict of voices over the disputed "body" of the nation itself earlier in the film (that is, conflicting commentaries heard over the footage of the Berlin uprising put down on June 17, 1953). In Brückner's film the "personal" is always contextualized in terms of the "political," and vice versa.

And here, too, political parallels are immediately made evident in a montage of documentary footage right after we hear the voices in Ursula's head: some famous footage of U.S. nuclear tests in the 1950s is shown, ending with human figures (test dummies) lying prone after an explosion. From the documentary footage we go right back to the "personal story": there is a cut from the prone dummies to Ursula lying in the grass in a park. Ursula then begins to play with matches, lighting her dress on fire in a somewhat dazed self-destructive act. She runs to a fountain in the park, where an Algerian man helps her put out the fire. The montage leads from the voices in Ursula's head speaking of fire, to the fireball in the sky (the atomic test footage), and then to the fire in Ursula's lap. In this manner the film introduces Ursula's ambiguous experience with the Algerian, a revolutionary temporarily in Germany who will provide her with her first sexual encounter.[24]

With regard to the German past, however, there is no ambiguity. The film is very explicit in its critique of the inadequacy of West Germany's attempts in the 1950s to come to terms with the fascist past, as an encounter of Ursula and other pupils with their teacher demonstrates. Having found some sheet music during gym class, they ask the teacher what it is; she looks at it and smiles, then tells them that it was a song she and others used to sing "in those days" (damals). She confesses that as a child in the Third Reich she too had thought great things were coming, but then suddenly one day there were millions dead, and nothing could make it right again. She says that she belongs to the Association for Christian-Jewish Cooperation. Ursula asks her if they will learn about these events in school, and the teacher says yes, just before they graduate, but they should discuss it first with their history teacher. Another girl says that there is never time for it, according to her older sister. The girls then disperse, and the teacher begins to play the song at the piano, singing (at first somewhat falteringly) the lyrics of the anthem of the Hitler Youth ("Unsere Fahne flattert uns voran"—"Our Banner Flies Before Us"). As she sings, a montage of documentary photos of the *Bund deutscher Mädel* (the "League of German Girls," the female counterpart to the Hitler Youth) is shown—photos of uniformed girls saluting the Nazi flag. The montage ends with a photo of a military hospital hall filled with beds.

This sequence underscores a number of points about German history. There is the appeal of fascism to young German girls, some of the tragic consequences of that ideology—the military casualties represented by the hospital beds—and of course the insufficiency of West German attempts to deal with that legacy. Added to this is its nonexistence in the curriculum and the somewhat hollow phrases about it from the teacher who then with such wistful nostalgia sings the old Hitler Youth song.

From a Child's Perspective: Fascism, Genocide, and the Cold War in Marianne Rosenbaum's *Peppermint Frieden* (1983)

Like *Hungerjahre*, Marianne Rosenbaum's *Peppermint Frieden* (1983) is autobiographical, and it concentrates on the relation between sexual repression, fascism, and the Cold War in West Germany of the postwar era. Unlike *Hungerjahre* this film is constructed from the perspective of a small girl, not an adolescent; its defamiliarization of conventional fiction comes not from the insertion of documentary footage or the use of voiceover but rather from distorted camera angles and lenses that attempt to provide the perspective of a small child on the adults looming over her, who attempt to socialize her into the bizarre world of war, genocide, repressive religion, and Cold War hysteria that characterize Germany between about 1943 and 1950. This film, made at the height of West Germany's peace movement, consists mostly of black and white footage that is often tinted, but it also contains surreal dream sequences in full color in which the child Marianne's confused understanding of the events around her is condensed into some obvious critiques of German reality.[25]

How does this film address the Holocaust? After Marianne's father has been sent with the German army to the Eastern Front, she becomes attached to Dr. Klug, a Jewish doctor; then all too soon he disappears suddenly from her life. In one shot, Marianne runs down the stairs to meet him at the door and is overjoyed that her special friend has come to visit. The next shot corresponds exactly to the first one in terms of camera placement and action: Marianne runs down the stairs to meet Dr. Klug, but this time it is her grandmother at the door. Marianne asks her where Dr. Klug is, and the grandmother says he is away ("verreist"), meanwhile whispering to Marianne's mother that "they" came and took him away. In the next scene, Marianne's mother diverts her daughter's eyes from an unpleasant sight, forcing her to look into a shop window, on which the viewer sees the reflection of the sight the mother does not want Marianne to see: gaunt prisoners with shaved heads being led down the street by armed soldiers. Soon thereafter the adults whisper about Theresienstadt, and there is a shot of smokestacks in the distance that will recur in Marianne's mind.[26]

In addition to making reference to the Holocaust, these scenes emphasize the attempt by the adults to hide its reality from the children—to keep them from seeing and hearing what is really going on. But not only are the children taught to avert their gaze from forbidden realities; they are taught further repression by learning to view themselves as under surveillance by an external power. In the postwar era it is no longer the fascist state that teaches this, but rather the Church, as the example of the village priest in a classroom scene demonstrates.

The priest attempts to squelch the playful orality of the children, who are fascinated with the ubiquitous American chewing gum. His real concern is not openly addressed, but it is obviously the sexual freedom manifested by an unmarried German woman in the town who is having an affair with an American soldier, "Mr. Frieden," the American who gives the children gum. Gum becomes the symbol of a sin against chastity; an illustration of Adam and Eve being expelled from the Garden of Eden at his back, the priest holds the gum up and quotes the Biblical serpent's temptation to "try it." He then declares that God sees everything, as the camera zooms in on another illustration, a famous mystical symbol depicting a large eye enclosed in a triangle (also to be found on the U.S. dollar). God is associated here with a gaze of surveillance, especially with regard to sexuality; the children are supposed to learn to internalize the feeling of being under surveillance so that they will police themselves and discontinue any playful sexual experimentation.

The priest tries to impress this idea of eternal surveillance upon the gum-chewing Marianne by having her look from various viewpoints at a likeness of Jesus whose eyes appear to move, seemingly staring at the child no matter where she turns. This kitschy, absurd prop (which nonetheless does intimidate Marianne) is typical of the humor in *Peppermint Frieden*, a quality that distinguishes this film somewhat from *Hungerjahre* and *Deutschland, bleiche Mutter*, two very powerful but not particularly playful films. *Peppermint Frieden* is by no means a "light" film, given its critique of sexual and political repression in postwar Germany, but it is characterized by a playfulness and humor that derive from the perspective that dominates the film, the perspective of a small child.

After "New German Cinema": Comedy, History, and Women's Cinema Since the Mid-1980s

The playful qualities in *Peppermint Frieden* create an affinity between it and subsequent West German films of the 1980s, in which humor came to be an ever more desirable quality, one that so much of the New German Cinema had lacked—in films made by both men and women. Part of this move toward humor had to do with a move away from the more explicitly political filmmaking that had been a part of the New German Cinema—especially its feminist wing. This shift was also in part generational: the comedies of Doris Dörrie and Monika Treut, to mention two directors whose styles are quite different, were made by women born in the 1950s, as opposed to the late 1930s and early 1940s. In part comedies represented an attempt to reach German audiences, with whom New German Cinema was never particularly successful; in part they were a response to the conservative politics of the 1980s in West Germany, which definitely had its effect on the film subsidy politics that had been developed during the 1970s while the SPD had been in power.

The New German Cinema may not have survived the 1980s, but women filmmakers have. And even if the "history film" may have waned, there is still political filmmaking. Even Doris Dörrie's entertainment films can have political resonance: she made *Happy Birthday Türke* (*Happy Birthday, Turk*), a film whose hero is a Turkish detective, in 1991, with xenophobic violence against so-called "foreigners" on the rise in unified Germany; her next comedy, *Keiner liebt mich* (1994) (*Nobody Loves Me*), thematizes multicultural diversity in unified Germany, featuring one main character who is an Afro-German gay man (if in a not entirely unproblematic fashion). And certainly Monika Treut's gender-bending lesbian comedies can be read as subversive. Ulrike Ottinger's *Countdown* (1990) is a long but beautiful—and critical—documentary about Berlin after the opening of the Wall. Films are still being made in Germany that deal with the fascist legacy and the Holocaust—although now such films are sometimes marketed (and not entirely without justification) as comedies, in spite of the dark history they explore. Two examples would be Michael Verhoeven's *Das schreckliche Mädchen* (1990) (*The Nasty Girl*) and Agnieszka Holland's *Hitlerjunge Salomon* (1991) (U.S. release title *Europa, Europa*).[27]

Helke Sander, from the founding generation of West German women filmmakers, can still be counted on to provoke; her filmmaking in the late 1980s and early 1990s has manifested a more directly political feminism. Her 1989 film *Die Deutschen und ihre Männer* (*The Germans and Their Men*)—which also employs humor—is a mixture of fiction and documentary: a fictional character interviews real people, namely West German men, mostly of the political class. These men, especially the leftists, turn out to be for the most part quite adept at problematizing their national identity—that is, they seem always ready to admit to feeling shame, or at least responsibility, for the crimes of the German nation during the Third Reich. But almost "to a man" they are unwilling to problematize their gender identity—to admit any collective responsibility for the many crimes of sexual violence committed every year by men against women, even when confronted by statistics showing how widespread such crimes actually are. This polemical strategy implies a comparison of the crimes of the Holocaust with the crimes of sexual violence against women. But its purpose, I would argue, is not to relativize or diminish the Holocaust, but rather to suggest a collective or structural explanation of sexual violence against women and to demonstrate the inadequacy of the common attitude to such crimes—that they are merely the result of individual aberration.

This emphasis on sexual violence—on rape—carries over into Sander's film, *BeFreier und Befreite* (1992), which has been translated somewhat unfortunately as *Liberators Take Liberties*. It focuses on the numerous rapes committed against German women at the end of World War II, especially by Soviet troops. Sander thus investigates a phenomenon that is striking both for the immense frequency with which it occurred and for the almost complete lack of historical discussion about it. The silence had much to do with taboos of the Cold War, taboos that did not relax during *perestroika*; Sander encountered immense resistance on the part of television networks approached for funding to make the film.[28]

There have been strong reactions against Sander's film, especially on the part of the German left (including feminists). These reactions have much to do with genuine remorse about the German crimes of World War II: what right did Germans have to talk about their victimization at the end of the War—especially at the hands of Soviets, given what the Germans had done in the Soviet Union? But it is also worthwhile to challenge the longstanding tendency of the international community not to treat rape seriously as a crime of war, an attitude that only recently has begun to change as the facts about the ethnic wars in the Balkans have become known.

Sander has been criticized for making a film depicting German women as victims of World War II, and indeed some have asserted that her film is close to apologist/revisionist recuperations of German nationalism (associated with right-wing arguments from the *Historikerstreit* [Historians' Debate] of the 1980s) and/or that the film is essentialist. These arguments have been made most persuasively by respected feminist critics such as the historian Atina Grossmann and the film scholar Gertrud Koch.[29] I too oppose any attempt to suggest some kind of universalized or essentialized victim status for any group of women, German or otherwise, that allows them to deny the social privilege that they enjoy due to class, ethnicity, or national identity—the privilege of an "Aryan" ethnic identity was a matter of life and death during the Third Reich. But Sander is hardly trying to validate the stories of victimized German women in some kind of right-wing, nationalist agenda to avenge the "honor" of German women. Nazi rapes and atrocities in the Soviet Union are clearly addressed in her film. It is clear she has no great respect for national myths but rather wants to focus on the neglected topic of rape and sexual violence as part and parcel of the militarist mindset of patriarchy. Indeed, she tends to deconstruct "national identity" precisely to focus on a number of issues concerning sexuality and gender in wartime. Gender is obviously a very significant category in an investigation that centers on wartime rape. If it is not foregrounded, the traditional focus on the national or ethnic identities in conflict during war tends to make rape invisible (or merely a function of those other conflicts). For in World War II—as in most wars—all parties to the conflict raped.

Gender, History, and German Feminist Cinema

Gender is no absolute or universal category outside of history, and it is by no means the only category necessary to understand the nature of social oppression. But there is an obvious value to foregrounding it where it has been too long ignored, and that is a project that is crucial to feminist politics. German women filmmakers have made a number of films that demonstrate a feminist politics that is differentiated and sensitive in its approach to the crimes of German history. In general I find in these films little evidence of an essentialism that would depict German women only as victims.

These films are not perfect, and I would not claim that certain blind spots typical of postwar West German thinking cannot ever be found in any of them.[30] But such blind spots are hardly exclusive to the women directors. Like a number of other critics, I find the "history films" by filmmakers such as Helma Sanders-Brahms, Margarethe von Trotta, and Jutta Brückner to be especially valuable.[31] Their cinematic confrontations with German history have been both more forthright and more political than what is generally to be found in films by the male auteurs of the New German Cinema. The women directors have been more insistent on a political interrogation of the personal and the everyday; without interrogation at that level, there is no way one can adequately determine the legacy of any historical experience.

Notes

1. Julia Knight, *Women in the New German Cinema*, (1992), 2–4.

2. Thomas Elsaesser, *The New German Cinema* (1989), 185. In this chapter, to the extent I am focusing on postwar German film, I discuss only women filmmakers from West Germany (and even of that group I am discussing only some of the most famous names). This is due both to the fact that there was no comparable feminist film culture in the German Democratic Republic (East Germany) and to the fact that I am not as knowledgeable about filmmaking in that German state. There were certainly women working in GDR cinema, especially in the area of documentary films; Helke Misselwitz would be one notable example. Sibylle Schönemann also was a filmmaker in the GDR before she was expelled to West Germany in the mid-1980s.

3. Andreas Huyssen, in his article "The Inevitability of Nation: German Intellectuals after Unification" (1992), cites Klaus Hartung's point in a column in *Die Zeit* (16 Aug. 1991), that members of the West German protest culture avoided historical guilt by blaming others (especially the U.S.) and by identifying themselves as victims (Huyssen, 71).

4. See Atina Grossmann, "Feminist Debates about Women and National Socialism," (1991).

5. On *Mädchen in Uniform* see Richard Dyer, "Lesbian and Gay Cinema in Weimar Germany" (1990): 31–60; B. Ruby Rich, "From Repressive Tolerance to Erotic Liberation" (1984/1993), and Hertha Thiele, "Ein Gespräch mit Hertha Thiele" (1981).

6. Siegfried Kracauer, *From Caligari to Hitler* (1947), 228–229. On the history of the film's reception, see Rich (1984/1993) and Dyer (1990). Although Kracauer's 1947 discussion of the film entirely neglects any mention of a homoerotic component to the film, Lotte Eisner's discussion (1969; orig. 1952) does hint at it, and in 1931, many critics did note it, even if they did not emphasize it much in their interpretations—see, e.g., Eggebrecht 1931. (Because we know now that Kracauer himself was gay—see, e.g., Hansen 1997, 173 and n. 36, 173–44—his complete silence on the topic in his 1947 discussion of the film seems interesting in a new way.)

7. The kiss scene is apparently quoted in the American film *Henry and June*.

8. Kathryn Reisdorfer asserts in her interpretation of the film that, beyond the lesbian relationship, what is celebrated in the film is female solidarity; she relates this vision of solidarity to the long tradition of German feminism. Reisdorfer, "Seeing through the Screen: Women in Soviet and German Films from 1919–1939" (1993), 192–203.

9. Eric Rentschler, "Mountains and Modernity" (1990); see, e.g., 142–145.

10. Linda Schulte-Sasse, "Leni Riefenstahl's Feature Films and the Question of a Fascist Aesthetic" (1992); see esp. 158–163. See also Eric Rentschler, "Fatal Attractions: *The Blue Light*" (1989), as well as the later version in his book *The Ministry of Illusion* (1996), 27–51.

11. Claudia Koonz, *Mothers in the Fatherland* (1987), e.g., 1–17.

12. Müller does a good job of exposing one of her baldest lies; when she asserts that she never used concentration camp inmates during the filming of *Tiefland*, he cuts to archival documents proving that she did. Cf. also Riefenstahl's autobiography, *Leni Riefenstahl: A Memoir* (New York: St. Martin's Press, 1993).

13. Danielle Huillet was making films with her husband Jean-Marie Straub.

14. Angelica Fenner has argued that there is something problematic about the power relations in the dialogue between the two voices that provide the voiceover in the film, that is, between the high-German-speaking narrator (the voice of Helma Sanders-Brahms) and the fictional Shirin, whose German is broken (the voice of the actress who plays Shirin). "Look Who's Talking: Pluravocity as Narrative Strategy in Helma Sanders-Brahms's *Shirins Hochzeit*" (1993).

15. This is the subtitle of Anton Kaes's *From Hitler to Heimat* (1989) as well as its original German version: *Deutschlandbilder: Die Wiederkehr der Geschichte als Film* (1987).

16. Von Trotta met Christiane Ensslin, the sister of Gudrun Ensslin and the model for the character Juliane, while accompanying Volker Schlöndorff as he filmed the documentary footage he contributed to *Deutschland im Herbst* (1978) (*Germany in Autumn*). For a discussion of *Die bleierne Zeit*, see Barton Byg, "German History and Cinematic History Harmonized" (1993); Byg cites much of the film's (largely negative) reception history and is very critical of the film himself. For positive evaluations of the film, see Paul Coates, *The Gorgon's Gaze* (1991), 193–228; and Susan E. Linville, "Retrieving History" (1991). See also Linville's book, *Feminism, Film, Fascism* (forthcoming).

17. On the German critics, see Renate Fischetti, *Das neue Kino* (1992), 121–124; Olav Münzberg, "'Schaudern vor der *bleichen Mutter*'" (1980).

18. Ellen Seiter, "Women's History, Women's Melodrama" (1986); E. Ann Kaplan, "The Search for the Mother/Land" (1986); and Angelika Bammer, "Through a Daughter's Eyes" (1985).

19. For Seiter and Bammer, whose concerns were more political, this seems to mean an idealization of woman as essentially maternal and separate from history. For Kaplan, writing from the perspective of the more Lacanian-oriented feminist film theory of the early 1980s, it was the film's autobiographical and realist tendencies that betray its "naive" attempt to represent "real" women—this is what is "essentialist" about it.

20. See my discussion of the film in my book *Politics of the Self* (1991), 186–207; it appears in abridged form as "Confronting German History" (1993) in Frieden et al. See also Susan E. Linville's "The Mother-Daughter Plot in History" (1992); Gabriele Weinberger, *Nazi Germany and its Aftermath* (1992), 37–104; and Roger F. Cook's "Melodrama or Cinematic Folk Tale?" (1991). See also Linville's forthcoming book, *Feminism, Film, Fascism*.

21. In my book *Politics of the Self* I concentrated on the progressive and postmodern aspects of the investigation of subjectivity on the part of feminists and others in West Germany's counterculture during the 1970s. But any too narrow insistence on speaking exclusively about the experiences of groups to which one has personal/autobiographical ties will of course marginalize the experiences of others, which is particularly problematic if the experiences of those others tend to be marginalized anyway because they are not part of a society's majority or of its dominant groups. Indeed, if because of the progressive idea that one ought not to speak on behalf of groups to which one does not belong, one ends up having an excuse to ignore those groups, this seems to me a not especially progressive consequence. What this has meant in Germany is that Germans have told stories that focus on "Germans" without the category of "Germanness" being interrogated critically for what it includes and excludes—and in the case of the Jews and some other minorities, this has a very problematic history.

22. And the blouse she is so concerned about will be ripped off of her by Hans, who barely notices it. His attitude toward sex is changing even as he attempts to resist the typical socialization of soldiers with regard to women and sex.

23. As Gabriele Weinberger points out (165), until 1988 no article had been published exclusively devoted to *Hungerjahre*. See Sandra Frieden, "'For Heaven's Sake, Anything But That!'" (1988); Weinberger, *Nazi Germany and its Aftermath* (1992), 165–220; Barbara Kosta, "Representing Female Sexuality" (1993), and the chapter on *Hungerjahre* in her *Recasting Autobiography* (1994), 153–181; and Susan E. Linville, "Self-Consuming Images" (1996). See also Linville's forthcoming book, *Feminism, Film, Fascism*.

24. This sexual encounter is more or less a rape. There is a disturbing ambiguity in the episode about the Algerian—up to the rape, he has been portrayed in primarily a positive light. In some ways this Third World revolutionary seems to parallel Ursula's father, whose leftist credentials had caused Ursula to expect a more equitable treatment of women.

25. See Gabriele Weinberger's article "Marianne Rosenbaum and the Aesthetics of Angst" (1993), and the even more exhaustive discussion in her book, *Nazi Germany and its Aftermath* (1992), 105–164.

26. The shot of smokestacks implies the cremation of gassed corpses, and one might object that this did not occur at Theresienstadt. In my opinion the filmmaker "condenses" here a number of allusions to the Holocaust into a few shots, and that this is a justifiable instance of poetic license. Dr. Klug's disappearance, Theresienstadt, and some smokestacks become associated with the Holocaust—and in a larger sense this is no distortion, in spite of Theresienstadt's specific status as a waystation to the "actual" death camps such as Auschwitz and Treblinka.

27. See Robert J. and Carol J. Reimer, *Nazi-Retro Film* (1992), 145–147, on the film and the controversy surrounding it.

28. See Helke Sander and Barbara Johr, *BeFreier und Befreite* (1992), 12.

29. See the pieces by Koch, Grossmann, and also by David Levin in the Fall 1995 special issue of *October* devoted to Sander's film. The film, which premiered at the 1992 Berlin Film Festival, at first got mostly positive reviews in Germany, but there were a few negative ones: Ingrid Strobl apparently attacked the film as "revanchistisch" in a review in *Konkret* (cited by Eva Hohenberger, *Stadtrevue Köln*, Oct. 1992, 128); Christiane Peitsch criticized it for an essentializing, biological depiction of gender differences in two articles in the *tageszeitung* (25 Feb. 1992 and 8 Oct. 1992). Gertrud Koch also published a negative review in the *Frankfurter Rundschau* (1992). In this country, the film has had a positive treatment in articles by Sheila Johnson ("The Crime: Rape. Helke Sander's 1992 Documentary, *BeFreier & Befreite: Krieg, Vergewaltigungen, Kinder* and Postmodernism") and by Irit Rogoff (she devotes four pages to it in her "From Ruins to Debris: The Feminization of Fascism in German History Museums"); it has also been discussed positively in two dissertations, Zinn (1995) and Smith (1996). But the film was also the subject of intense criticism at a showing at the Goethe Haus, New York, on October 30, 1993. The papers of two of the panelists at that showing—Grossmann and Levin—were published in later versions in the special issue of *October* (Spring 1995), along with Koch's piece, "Blood, Sperm. . . ." The latter, like Grossmann's piece ("A Question"), had first appeared in German in the journal *Frauen und Film* (1994). Kosta's article is also critical of the film.

30. Again, I would suggest that there is always a danger of narcissism in a too-narrow adherence to an identity politics of any kind, and this can result in some insensitivity to the positions of others.

31. See Linville's articles on *Die bleierne Zeit* (1991), *Deutschland, bleiche Mutter* (1992), and *Hungerjahre* (1996); see also her forthcoming book, *Feminism, Film, Fascism*. Coates devotes a whole chapter to *Die bleierne Zeit*, asserting that it is the only truly effective German film about German history (*The Gorgon's Gaze* (1991), 193–228). Robert C. and Carol J. Reimer suggest in their book *Nazi-retro Film* (1992) that *Deutschland, bleiche Mutter* is the best and most honest of the films examining the German past (204).

Bibliography

Die allseitig reduzierte Persönlichkeit / REDUPERS. (The All-Around Reduced Personality.) Dir. Helke Sander. 1977. 98 min.

Bammer, Angelika. "Through a Daughter's Eyes: Helma Sanders-Brahms's *Germany, Pale Mother*." *New German Critique* 36 (Fall 1985): 91–109.

BeFreier und Befreite: Krieg, Vergewaltigungen, Kinder. U.S. Title *Liberators Take Liberties*. Dir. Helke Sander. 212 min.

Das blaue Licht. (*The Blue Light*.) Dir. Leni Riefenstahl. 1932. 70 min.

Die bleierne Zeit. U.S. Title *Marianne and Juliane*. Dir. Margarethe von Trotta. 1981. 106 min.

Byg, Barton. "German History and Cinematic History Harmonized in Margarethe von Trotta's *Marianne & Juliane*." *Gender and German Cinema* 1 (1993): 259–271.

Coates, Paul. *The Gorgon's Gaze: German Cinema, Expressionism, and the Image of Horror*. Cambridge: Cambridge University Press, 1991.

Cook, Roger F. "Melodrama or Cinematic Folk Tale? Story and History in *Deutschland, bleiche Mutter*." *Germanic Review* 66.3 (Summer 1991): 113–129.

Die Deutschen und ihre Männer. (*The Germans and their Men*.) Dir. Helke Sander. 1989. 105 min.

Deutschland, bleiche Mutter. (*Germany, Pale Mother*.) Dir. Helma Sanders-Brahms. 1979–80. 130 min.

Deutschland im Herbst. (*Germany in Autumn*.) Dir. Rainer Werner Fassbinder, Alexander Kluge, Volker Schlöndorff et al. 1978. 116 min.

Dyer, Richard. "Less and More than Women and Men: Lesbian and Gay Cinema in Weimar Germany." *New German Critique* 51 (Fall 1990): 5–60.

Eggebrecht, Axel. Rev. of *Mädchen in Uniform*. *Die Weltbühne*: 26 December 1931.

Die Ehe der Maria Braun. Dir. Rainer Werner Fassbinder. 1979. 120 min.

Elsaesser, Thomas. *The New German Cinema: A History*. New Brunswick, N.J.: Rutgers University Press, 1989.

Fenner, Angelica. "Look Who's Talking: Pluravocity as Narrative Strategy in Helma Sanders-Brahms's *Shirins Hochzeit*." Paper presented at Coalition of Women in German Conference, Great Barrington, Mass., October 1993.

Fischetti, Renate. *Das neue Kino. Acht Porträts von deutschen Regisseurinnen: Margarethe von Trotta, Doris Dörrie, Helma Sanders-Brahms, Helke Sander, Ulrike Ottinger, Ula Stöckl, Jutta Brückner, Claudia von Alemann*. Dülmen-Hiddingsel: tende, 1992.

Frieden, Sandra. "'For Heaven's Sake, Anything But That!' Jutta Brückner's *Hungerjahre*." *Schatzkammer* 14.2 (1988): 80–86.

Frieden, Sandra, Richard W. McCormick, Vibeke R. Petersen, and Laurie Melissa Vogelsang, eds. *Gender and German Cinema: Feminist Interventions*. 2 vols. Providence, R.I.: Berg Publishers, 1993.

Grossmann, Atina. "Feminist Debates about Women and National Socialism." *Gender & History* 3.3 (Autumn 1991): 350–358.

———. "A Question of Silence: The Rape of German Women by Occupation Soldiers." *October* 72 (Spring 1995): 43–63. Earlier version in German appears in *Frauen und Film* 54/55 (April 1994): 15–28.

Hansen, Miriam. "America, Paris, the Alps: Kracauer and Benjamin on Cinema and Modernity." In *Amerikanisierung: Traum und Alptraum im Deutschland des 20. Jahrhunderts*. Ed. Alf Lüdke, Inge Marßolek, and Adelheid von Saldem. (*Transatlantische Historische Studien*, vol. 6.) Stuttgart: Franz Steiner Verlag, 1996, 161–198.

Happy Birthday Türke. (*Happy Birthday, Turk*.) Dir. Doris Dörrie. 1991. 109 min.

Hitlerjunge Salomon. U.S. Title *Europa, Europa*. Dir. Agnieszka Holland. 1991. 115 min.

Hungerjahre. (*Years of Hunger*.) Dir. Jutta Brückner. 1979–80. 114 min.

Huyssen, Andreas. "The Inevitability of Nation: German Intellectuals after Unification," *October* 61 (Summer 1992): 65–73.

Johanna d'Arc of Mongolia. Dir. Ulrike Ottinger. 1989. 165 min.

Johnson, Sheila. "The Crime: Rape. Helke Sander's 1992 Documentary, *BeFreier und Befreite: Krieg, Vergewaltigungen, Kinder* and Postmodernism." *Pacific Coast Philology* 28.1 (1993): 81–93.

Kaes, Anton. *From Hitler to Heimat: The Return of History as Film*. Cambridge, Mass.: Harvard University Press, 1989. Rev. and transl. version of *Deutschlandbilder: Die Wiederkehr der Geschichte als Film*. Munich: edition text & kritik, 1987.

Kaplan, E. Ann. "The Search for the Mother/Land in Sanders-Brahms's *Germany, Pale Mother* (1980)." In *German Film and Literature: Adaptations and Transformations*. Ed. Eric Rentschler. New York: Methuen, 1986.

Keiner liebt mich. (*Nobody Loves Me*.) Dir. Doris Dörrie. 1994. 104 min.

Knight, Julia. *Women in the New German Cinema*. London: Verso, 1992.

Koch, Gertrud. "Blood, Sperm, and Tears." Trans. Stuart Liebman. *October* 72 (Spring 1995): 27–41. Orig. German version in *Frauen und Film* 54/55 (April 1994): 3–14.

———. "Kurzschluss der Perspektiven." Rev. of *BeFreier und Befreite*. *Frankfurter Rundschau*, Nov. 17–18, 1992.

Koonz, Claudia. *Mothers in the Fatherland: Women, the Family, and Nazi Politics*. New York: St. Martin's Press, 1987.

Kosta, Barbara. "Rape, Nation, and Remembering History: Helke Sander's *Liberators Take Liberties*." In *Gender and Germanness*. Ed. Patricia Herminghouse and Magda Mueller. Providence, R.I.: Berghahn, 1997, 217–231.

———. *Recasting Autobiography: Women's Counterfictions in Contemporary German Literature and Film*. Ithaca: Cornell UP, 1994.

———. "Representing Female Sexuality: On Jutta Brückner's Film *Years of Hunger*." *Gender and German Cinema* 2 (1993): 241–252.

Kracauer, Siegfried. *From Caligari to Hitler: A Psychological History of the German Film*. Princeton: Princeton University Press, 1947.

Levin, David J. "Taking Liberties with Liberties Taken: On the Politics of Helke Sander's *BeFreier und Befreite*." *October* 72 (Spring 1995): 65–77.

Linville, Susan E. *Feminism, Film, Fascism: Women's Auto/Biographical Cinema and West German "Postwar" Culture*. Austin: University of Texas Press, forthcoming.

———. "The Mother-Daughter Plot in History: Helma Sanders-Brahms's *Germany, Pale Mother*." *New German Critique* 55 (Winter 1992): 51–70.

———. "Retrieving History: Margarethe von Trotta's *Marianne and Juliane*." *PMLA* 106.3 (1991): 446–458.

———. "Self-Consuming Images: The Identity Politics of Jutta Brückner's *Hunger Years*." In *Perspectives on German Cinema*. Terri Ginsberg and Kirsten Thompson. New York: G.K. Hall, 1996, 325–345.

Die Macht der Bilder. U.S. release title: *The Wonderful/Horrible Life of Leni Riefenstahl*. Dir. Ray Müller. 1993. 180 min.

Madame X—eine absolute Herrscherin. Dir. Ulrike Ottinger. 1977. 141 min.

Mädchen in Uniform. Dir. Leontine Sagan. 1931. 89 min.

McCormick, Richard W. "Confronting German History: Melodrama, Distantiation, and Women's Discourse in *Germany, Pale Mother*." *Gender and German Cinema* 2 (1993): 185–206.

———. *Politics of the Self: Feminism and the Postmodern in West German Literature and Film*. Princeton: Princeton University Press, 1991.

Münzberg, Olav. "'Schaudern vor der *bleichen Mutter*.' Eine sozial-psychologische Analyse der Kritiken zum Film von Helma Sanders-Brahms." *Medium* 7 (July 1980): 34–37.

Die Patriotin. (*The Patriot*.) Dir. Alexander Kluge. 1979. 121 min.

Peppermint Frieden. (*Peppermint Peace*.) Dir. Marianne Rosenbaum. 1983. 112 min.

Reimer, Robert C., and Carol J. Reimer. *Nazi-retro Film: How German Narrative Cinema Remembers the Past*. New York: Twayne, 1992.

Reisdorfer, Kathryn. "Seeing through the Screen: Women in Soviet and German Films from 1919–1939." Ph.D. Dissertation, University of Minnesota, 1993.

Rentschler, Eric. "Fatal Attractions: *The Blue Light*." *October* 48 (Spring 1989): 47–68.

———. *The Ministry of Illusion: Nazi Cinema and Its Afterlife*. Cambridge: Harvard University Press, 1996.

———. "Mountains and Modernity: Relocating the *Bergfilm*." *New German Critique* 51 (Fall 1990): 137–161.

Rich, B. Ruby. "From Repressive Tolerance to Erotic Liberation: *Girls in Uniform*." *Gender and German Cinema* 2 (1993): 61–96.

Rogoff, Irit. "From Ruins to Debris: The Feminization of Fascism in German History Museums." In *Museum Culture: Histories, Discourses, Spectacles*. Ed. Irit Rogoff and Daniel J. Sherman. Minneapolis: University of Minnesota Press, 1994.

Sander, Helke, and Barbara Johr. *BeFreier und Befreite: Krieg, Vergewaltigungen, Kinder*. Munich: Antje Kunstmann, 1992.

Das schreckliche Mädchen. U.S. title *The Nasty Girl*. Dir. Michael Verhoeven. 1990. 94 min.

Schulte-Sasse, Linda. "Leni Riefenstahl's Feature Films and the Question of a Fascist Aesthetic." In *Framing the Past: The Historiography of German Cinema and Television*. Ed. Bruce A. Murray and Christopher J. Wickham. Carbondale, Ill.: Southern Illinois University Press, 1992, 140–166.

Seiter, Ellen. "Women's History, Women's Melodrama: *Deutschland, bleiche Mutter*." *German Quarterly* 59 (1986): 569–581.

Shirins Hochzeit. (*Shirin's Wedding*.) Dir. Helma Sanders-Brahms. 1975. 130 min.

Smith, Sabine. "*BeFreier und Befreite: Krieg, Vergewaltigungen, Kinder*." Section in "Sexual Violence in German Culture: Rereading and Rewriting the Tradition." Diss., University of California, Davis, 1996. 258–284.

Thiele, Hertha. "Ein Gespräch mit Hertha Thiele." Interview in *Frauen und Film* 28 (1981): 32–41.

Weinberger, Gabriele. "Marianne Rosenbaum and the Aesthetics of Angst." *Gender and German Cinema* 2 (1993): 227–240.

———. *Nazi Germany and Its Aftermath in Women Directors' Autobiographical Films of the Late 1970s: In the Murderer's House*. San Francisco: Mellen Research University Press, 1992.

Zinn, Gesa. "The Controversy About a 'Grand Narrative': *BeFreier und Befreite: Krieg, Vergewaltigungen, Kinder*." In "Film, Fiction, and Feminism. Politics in Helke Sander's Cinematic and Literary Texts: Representation of Gender, Subjectivity, Humor and Music." Diss., U of Minnesota, 1995, 160–188.

Das zweite Erwachen der Christa Klages. (*The Second Awakening of Christa Klages*.) Dir. Margarethe von Trotta. 1977. 88 min.

Part VI

German Women after Unification (1989)

16

A Look at the Current Situation of Women in Germany

Renate Möhrmann

Germany has changed within the past five years—politically, economically, and socially. This has also had a tremendous impact on women, primarily on women from the former German Democratic Republic, who, for the first time in their lives, are confronted with unemployment and social decline. The public discourse hardly focuses on the special strains suffered by women and their specific political experience. And it is still true that our knowledge about the living conditions of women is far scantier than our knowledge about the living conditions of men.

Furthermore, it holds true that male experience enjoys a higher status than women's experience. Male experience apparently is more valid. Without reflection it is accepted as a synonym for "objective" experience and then becomes transformed as historic experience. At least this is how official historians still deal with the matter. Too often the female self gets lost in general catastrophies or disappears into private happiness. "No woman can say: I think, therefore I am" (Keine Frau kann sagen: Ich denke, daher bin ich; *Gestern war heute. Hundert Jahre Gegenwart,* 298),[1] explains Ingeborg Drewitz in her considerations regarding female self-realization. "Women lack time in their lives which really belongs to them. Because it wasn't customary in their parents' home and because it is not customary in their marriage. Because it was always self evident not to take oneself too seriously. (Frauen haben wenig Zeit im Leben, die ihnen gehört. Weil das zu Hause nicht üblich war und in der Ehe nicht üblich ist. Weil es immer nur selbstverständlich gewesen ist, sich nicht wichtig zunehmen; 297).

In this respect it is symptomatic that in the trendsetting postwar literature as well as in postwar theatre and postwar film the experience of women is scarcely depicted. *Des Teufels General* (*The Devil's General*) by Carl Zuckmayer, *Draußen vor der Tür* (*Left Outside the Door*) by Wolfgang Borchert, *Wo warst du, Adam?* (*Where Were You, Adam?*) by Heinrich Böll, and Wolfgang Staudte's film *Die Mörder sind unter uns* (*The Murderers Are Amongst Us*) are not exceptions but significant examples of this norm. More often than not in all of these cases women play the part of "silly geese" (alberne Gänse) or of the adulterous housewife who didn't expect the return of her husband from the war.

The same applies to the reappraisal of fascism. As late as 1987 the American historian Claudia Koonz emphasized in her book *Mothers in the Fatherland*: "I am always amazed that all theories about National-Socialism since 1945 without exception exclude the role of women" (11).[2] That, however, is gradually changing. It is mainly due to the impetus of feminist scholars who have continously and persistently challenged the traditional approaches of the social sciences and the humanities. They have introduced the category of "gender" into their research. Thereby, for the first time, a person's sex and gender are treated as a determining factor in perception. After all, one cannot accept that the social sciences and humanities make distinctions according to class or social status but not according to gender.

However, not only the academic but also the political scenery is changing in the Federal Republic of Germany. Particularly since 1989, Germany is no longer in a sheltered corner, safe from the storms of historic events. Right wingers are marching. Racist terrorism has flared up. Shelters for asylum seekers are burning. The crime rate is soaring alarmingly. The past seems to have returned. In the long term it cannot be held at bay. For decades history was allowed to be forgotten, due to the antagonism between East and West Germany, which—in hindsight—were transfigured into a kind of dual world order. Now, three years later, history is back with us. None of us was prepared for that.

In this chapter about the current situation of women in Germany, such indicators cannot be excluded. They must be considered and not only because women are particularly affected. Today women's research cannot be dealt with any more as a separate issue. That would only end up in a blind alley. With the end of the "grand narratives," the traditional stories of legitimation, the "grand recits" have to be told differently today—more paradoxically, more ambigously, and less normatively. Unambigous, one-dimensional images are transmitted via television. We should mistrust them. Unambigous, clear-cut images I neither can nor will offer you today. Hence, let me try to provide with each image its negative or its reverse so as to offer with each negative image a possible positive alternative. Because we all perceive things differently. In academic terms: Gender-determined perception often results in lopsided views, especially if women are concerned.

Scene One: Politics and Self-Interest or: The Disguise of Reality By Means of Statistics

The most recent analyses of demoscopic institutes reveal that even during 1992 the opinion prevailed within the German population that women are unpolitical by nature. The institutes for public opinion support this with appropriate figures. The considerable number of nonvoters—about one-third of eligible voters in the last Federal election in 1990—were mostly women (60 percent). This means there is not a deficit of male voters but of female voters. In the last election in the state of North- Rhine-Westfalia only 40 percent of young women between eighteen and twenty-four voted. Of the young women in the former German Democratic Republic, only 34 percent went to the polls in the federal election in 1990. The statistics indicate that in the old as well as in the new states (formerly GDR), nonvoting women belong to the economic lower strata of the population. Moreover, 75 percent of married women vote as their husbands do (see Kurt Möller, *Geschlechtsspezifische Aspekte der Anfälligkeit für Rechtsextremismus in der Bundesrepublik Deutschland*, 29-34).

But we should avoid hasty conclusions: All such statistical approaches taken in isolation don't say a lot: At least women's lack of political independence cannot be deduced from such statistics. Presumably also most married men vote as their wives do. Anyhow, statistical research reveals that the majority of married couples claim common interest as the basis of their relationship. Thus, we cannot consider every matrimonial agreement as a deficit of emancipation. Figures can be interpreted in many ways. However, when women are asked about the possibility of a political career, the picture looks quite different. Asked if they could envisage a political career, 75 percent replied negatively. Actually they can envisage becoming politically active in their local community, but not in the federal or state parliaments. And in fact only about 15 percent of federal and state parliamentary representatives are female. So much for statistics.

However, lack of political interest cannot be deduced from such figures. Because such a limited view of the statistics fails to take two facts into consideration: First, politics are not limited to institutions. Since the beginning of the 1970s at the latest, the political scenery of the Federal Republic of Germany has been decisively shaped by extraparliamentary movements, citizen's initiatives, ecological and peace movements, and by autonomous women's groups. Half of these extraparliamentary movements were sustained by women. This must be recognized. Today we have an antidiscrimination law, a new marital name law, improved old age pensions, representatives for women's rights and equality, community homes for abused women, and one year's fully paid leave of absence for one parent after the birth of a child. All this was primarily achieved by the angry young women of the 1970s. It is due neither to the attitudes nor to the understanding of politicians, regardless of party affiliation. Taking all this into account, it is rather shortsighted to maintain that women's autonomous groups have become ineffective in the meantime. It is shortsighted to say that they are not facing the future. That would lead one to accept the aforementioned statistics unquestioningly, and it would push women back into political no-man's-land—albeit for other motives.

Second, the fact that women prefer to involve themselves politically outside of parliaments has a lot to do with the parliamentary institution itself. To a large extent parliaments are hostile to women both psychologically and physically, as I experienced myself. After all—as a full professor at a conservative German university I was never spoiled by an excess of equality. Quite the contrary. The few women who teach in the capacity of full professor are regarded as some kind of exotic bird. At best they are tolerated as guests at the academic institutions that primarily nurture their male offspring. My appointment to parliament impaired my "guest status" even further, as I soon realized. As far as women's liberation was concerned I was going even farther downhill. Quite explicitly. At the university I at least enjoyed freedom of action where nobody could interfere. In parliament the guest was transformed into a "guest worker" within a male society that prefers to keep a closed male shop. My mistakes as a parliamentary newcomer were not the problem nor were my occasional and rather clumsy attempts to acquire the political skills by a do-it-yourself approach. This I would have understood and accepted. Here, however, something else was the actual issue: Woman constitutes a disruptive factor in parliament, which—despite all declarations of democracy—has a long history.

Louise Otto Peters, the German pioneer of the women's movement, declared as early as 150 years ago: "The political participation of women is a civic duty." (Die Teilnahme der weiblichen Welt am Staate ist eine Pflicht; 1847, 38). This legitimate request was not adopted by the male revolutionaries of 1848. They only gave their support to bondsmen, serfs, Jews, and to the Fourth Estate, which they claimed to liberate. On May 18, 1848, when the first German national parliament met, the participation of female partners such as Malwida von Meysenbug, Mathilde Franziska Anneke, or Luise Aston was prohibited—even their passive presence was not allowed. Politics was a matter only for men. It is ridiculous that they had to observe the conference through a hole they had secretly cut into a curtain, as Malwida von Meysenbug later reported (*Memoiren einer Idealistin*, 146). Although she was allowed to produce and distribute leaflets, she was excluded when the real action started and the parliament met for the first time. She had to remember her place, step aside, and remain a secret onlooker.

More than seventy years had to pass until the first woman was allowed to become a member of a German parliament. And when Marie Juchacz, Social Democratic member of the *Reichstag*, delivered her maiden speech as the first woman at all, her very voice was a cause of irritation. Until then power was only associated with the male voice. Even a microphone didn't help. Women were only considered to be a source of friction. Despite their thirty-six female colleagues, a large part of the male members in parliament continued to address their audience only with "gentlemen" (see Armin Burkhardt, *Sprache zwischen Militär und Frieden: Aufrüstung der Begriffe*, 123). Semantically, ladies didn't exist. The everyday sexism in parliament still produces strange effects. "Dear colleague, you look better than you speak," is a relatively harmless offense. Linguists such as Armin Burkhardt recently proved that women in their speeches get interrupted four times as often as their male colleagues.

One-half of such interruptions are aimed at creating a state of uncertainty or are simply insults. The parliamentary minutes do not reflect all the disparagements whispered to the female speaker while she is walking from her seat to the lecture stand. I often feel as if exposed at an Oriental cattle market, where it matters whether my dress fits, whether I am too big or too small, too chubby or too thin. Such comments I have had to face, before I could begin a speech. A highlight of these sexist observations was the publicly made remark of a Social Democratic party whig: "Female members of parliament are only half pints and they owe their mandate merely to the fact that they look different between the legs" (Weibliche Abgeordnete sind bloß Piepmäuse und verdanken ihr Mandat nur der Tatsache, daß sie zwischen den Beinen anders aussehen). When the women of all parliamentary parties got together and jointly requested the resignation of this male chauvinist, they were accused of lacking any sense of humor.

Scene Two: Against the Standard Male Biography or Legally Mandated Equal Rights

For a long time now politically active women have requested that the principle of equality be grounded in the constitution. We owe it to the "mothers" of the German constitution that in Germany—in contrast to other democratic countries—the equality of the sexes is secured explicitly in the constitution (Article 3, Paragraph 2). However, formal equality relating to family matters and private household affairs was introduced as late as 1977 by amendments to the family law. Further steps on the way to legal equality were:

- the change of the marital name law in 1979
- the law on maternity holidays, likewise in 1979
- the law on equal treatment of men and women at work in 1980
- the change of the law on old age pensions in 1983
- the alterations of the widow's pensions and the extension of educational grants in 1986
- and finally a second change of the marital name law in 1989. According to the current law women can keep their maiden names when they get married. Also, the children can take on their mothers' maiden name.

All this clearly indicates that the political determination has increased to effectively fight discrimination against women. And that applies to all political parties. In this connection the new law of equal rights that was presented to the *Bundestag* in Spring 1993 is certainly of interest. This new law deals for the first time quite concretely with the realization of equal rights, for its main aim is to reconcile family matters with the professional responsibilities of men and women. It is true that working women were legally supported during the 1970s and the beginning of the 1980s. But all such measures lagged behind the reality of women's life. Because they were based on the premise that women simply have to decide between family or profession. There were no legal attempts to make them compatible. The normal male biography was the yardstick, and there was only the career and nothing but the career. Family matters didn't require any solution.

Today such concepts are no longer acceptable. This is reflected in the new law of equality, which reminds men of their duty to attend to their family more than before. Any measure in support of women must be highly appreciated, such as vocational training for women, educational courses for mothers, rules to resume the profession once the children have left home, flexible working hours that are more suitable for families, part-time work also in key functions and so forth. The wish of the vast majority of German women to combine family and profession has, therefore, gained a solid foothold.

Scene Three: Rings of Candlelight against Xenophobia

Quite a variety of explanations are offered for what is happening in Germany today. One hits women particularly hard. Children and juveniles—so say the experts—don't find sufficient backing in their own families. Particularly due to their mothers' professions they are left to themselves and therefore turn to Nazi groups. These accusations are well known. With similar arguments the liberal-left historian Johannes Scherr railed against the first professional generation of female authors in Germany. "You can bet on it," we read in his reflections on 1848, "that the crowd of females pushing toward the public sphere without any justification consists either of hysterical old spinsters or irresponsible mothers. Their housekeeping books are in complete disarray, if they have got any at all. Their living rooms and bedrooms, their kitchens and wardrobes are in a state of chaos and their bills for dresses are enormous but unpaid and their children are physically and morally untidy" (Ihr könnt darauf schwören, daß das Kontingent der Weiber, welche sich unberufenerweise in die Öffentlichkeit drängen, entweder aus hysterischen alten Jungfern oder aus pflichtvergessenen Müttern bestehen, deren Haushaltsbücher—wenn sie überhaupt welche führen—in Unordnung, deren Stuben, Küchen, Speisekammern und Weißzeugschränke im Tohuwabo-Zustand, deren Modistinnenrechnung groß, aber unbezahlt und deren Kinder physisch und moralisch ungewaschen sind; 1875, 175).

The history of discrimination against women's gainful employment appears to repeat itself. On the one hand the working woman is criticized as promoting moral neglect and on the other hand as being responsible for right-wing violence today. It is not my intention to acquit women entirely of all guilt with regard to right-wing violence, even if the figures of the Office for the Protection of the Constitution prove that the culprits are almost exclusively male juveniles aged fifteen to twenty-two. One can also become guilty by applauding or passively looking on, as the example of Rostock shows. However, I am of the opinion that the asserted connection between female work and right-wing radicalism in itself is a dangerous example for right-wing thinking. Against that we must defend ourselves, and indeed we are doing it. Women as well as men. We are simply not willing to let our democratic constitutional structure be destroyed by 6,000 violent criminals. With only a few exceptions we have lived together as good neighbors and in peace with six million foreigners for years. We also will not forget that we ourselves invited these fellow citizens to move to our country. And certainly we remember how much we owe them. But suddenly these words are being kicked around: hostility toward foreigners. The new wording is in the papers, in the radio, on TV, it is being used in panel talks and in parliament. The *Institut für Angewandte Sozialforschung* (an opinion research institute) tries to make us believe that 25 percent of Germans do consent to the slogan "Foreigners out." This verbal assertion is followed by the visual proof: Skinheads with clubs admired by two elder gentlemen wearing Tyrolean hats.

And we who are watching TV and explicitly rejecting any hostility toward foreigners are suddenly reduced to a small minority. The media prevail over our own experience, because the TV presenter Pleitgen tells us "Friendliness of the Germans to working foreigners is simply a lie" (Die Ausländerfreundlichkeit der

Deutschen sei schlichtweg eine Lüge; WDR, 28.2.1992).[5] Almost with a feeling of satisfaction does he tell us that. But how does he know? What information does he have that I, as a politician, do not have? But the negative image seems to have magnetic attraction. This is also true for the press. The print media also adhere to the creed: good news is boring news. Only the spectacular makes good headlines. Thus, German TV stages right-wing extremism as a media event and thereby emphasizes violence as an experience that intensifies the quality of life. That is very dangerous, particularly for juveniles. Because he who offers violence as entertainment should not be surprised if that sets standards: the violence in their heads leads to knives in their school bags.

It is that which I am worried and concerned about. Real life differs from what is offered by the media. Besides this hostility toward foreigners, there are the rings of candlelight (candlelight demonstrations) on behalf of foreigners, increasing at a surprising rate. Citizens in almost all German towns are overcoming their passive attitudes. Joining hands and holding lighted candles, they are demonstrating against racism and hostility against foreigners. Recently in Frankfurt, Hamburg, Berlin, and Munich, 300,000 participated, the longest rings of candlelight against hostility toward foreigners. And there are more positive signs. Many businessmen are advertising with the slogan "No room for violence against foreigners." In numerous showrooms and thousands of shop windows you find insistent exhortations that read "We waive this advertising space in protest against violence toward foreigners."

Citizens are defending their democracy in a peaceful manner. This is new in German history. Only when you see these two, antagonistic pictures together—hostility against foreigners *and* rings of candlelight—do you get a little closer to the reality in Germany. And another remark: BONN is not Weimar. And Berlin will certainly not become Weimar. The inclination of many contemporaries to read the future of the Federal Republic of Germany in terms of the past doesn't clarify the issue. When history repeats itself it happens differently each time. Those who always expect the same thing to return run the risk of missing decisive differences. Germans, however, must face the present courageously, in order to ban the right-wing danger utterly and completely.

One of the first manifestoes against right-wing radicalism and hostility to foreigners was established by women long before the murders in the city of Mölln. It was jointly formulated by female politicians from all political parties, female clerical representatives, and other women. Let me finish my comments by quoting this manifesto, which is entitled "Women are transcending borderlines":

> We—the women—have united over and above political, ideological or confessional borderlines in order to participate from our point of view in resolving all matters of the future.

We want a multicultural society, a tolerant way of dealing with fellow citizens, who are of different origins and who have different attitudes.

We want the experience of other fellowmen—and -women—and other people to be accepted into and to enrich our life, and we want solidarity and social justice to form the basis for political and private activities.

We want to help children, senior citizens, and the handicapped, the socially weak and oppressed without forcing our ideas on them.

We women therefore direct our message to all citizens—male and female—to the churches, to the unions, to political parties, social movements, cultural institutions and to industry.

Please do assist us. Support the manifesto.

Do whatever is in your power to fight right-wing radicalism and hostility against foreigners.

(Wir Frauen haben uns daher über parteipolitische, ideologische und konfessionelle Grenzen hinweg zusammengefunden, um aus unserer Sicht zur Lösung der Zukunftsfragen beizutragen.

Wir wollen eine Gesellschaft mit kultureller Vielfalt einen selbstverständlichen toleranten Umgang mit Menschen, die andere Verhaltensweisen, andere kulturelle Herkunft haben.

Wir wollen, daß Erfahrungen anderer Menschen und Völker in unserem Leben Raum finden dürfen; daß Solidarität und Bereitschaft zur sozialen Gerechtigkeit zur Grundlage politischen und sozialen Handelns werden.

Wir wollen Kindern, älteren Menschen, Behinderten, sozial Schwachen und unterdrückten Völkern nicht erst dann helfen, wenn wir ihnen unsere Vorstellungen aufgenötigt haben.

Wir Frauen wenden uns daher an allen Bürgerinnen und Bürger, an die Kirchen, Gewerkschaften, Parteien, sozialen Bewegungen, Wohlfahrtsverbände, Kulturschaffenden, die Wirtschaft und an die Medien.

Helfen Sie mit, schließen Sie sich unseren Aufruf an.

Tun Sie in Ihrem Bereich und nach Ihren Kräften alles gegen das Anwachsen und die Duldung von Rechtsradikalismus und Fremdenfeindlichkeit in unserem Land.) ("Frauen überschreiten Grenzen,") 117.

Notes

1. All quotations are my own, unless otherwise indicated.

2. The German edition of Claudia Koonz's *Mothers in the Fatherland. Women, the Family, and Nazi Politics* (Mütter im Vaterland: Frauen im Dritten Reich) appeared in 1991. This edition is a revised version of the American edition and includes a new preface. My quotation is from the German edition since it does not appear in the American one. (Es erstaunt mich immer wieder, daß alle Theorien, die seit 1945 über den Nationalsozialismus entstanden sind, ausnahmslos die Rolle der Frauen ausklammern, 19.)

Bibliography

Drewitz, Ingeborg. *Gestern war heute: Hundert Jahre Gegenwart*. Düsseldorf: Classen, 1978.

Engelen-Kefer, Ursula, Liselotte Funcke, Hildegard Hamm-Brücher et al. "Frauen überschreiten Grenzen." *Feministische Studien* 9 (1991): 117–118.

Koonz, Claudia. *Mothers in the Fatherland: Women, the Family, and Nazi Politics*. New York: St. Martin's Press, 1987. (*Mütter im Vaterland: Frauen im Dritten Reich*, translated by Cornelia Holfelder von der Tann. Freiburg (Breisgau): Kore Verlag, 1991.)

Meysenbug, Malvida von. *Memoiren einer Idealistin*. Stuttgart: Deutsche Verlags-Anstalt, 1927.

Möller, Kurt. "Geschlechtsspezifische Aspekte der Anfälligkeit für Rechtsextremismus in der Bundesrepublik Deutschland." *Frauenforschung* 3.9 (1991): 27–49.

Peters, Louise Otto. *Amnestirte der Zeit*. Ed. Robert Blum. Leipzig: Verlag Robert Friese, 1847, 37–63.

Scherr, Johannes. *1849: Ein weltgeschichtliches Drama*. Leipzig: Otto Wigard Verlag, 1875, Second edition.

Sprache zwischen Militär und Frieden: Aufrüstung der Begriffe? Ed. Armin Burkhardt et al. Tübingen: Narr, 1989.

Part VII

Conclusion

17
New Scholarly Perspectives

Sara Lennox

To frame my commentary, I would like to turn to some of the issues raised by the last section of the 1992 *Women in German Yearbook*, "Positions and Provocations," and particularly by its final essay by Ruth-Ellen Joeres. In her essay, originally a controversial MLA talk, Joeres argues that there is no alliance at all between *Germanistik* and feminism. "*Germanistik* is a mostly male domain," Joeres maintains, "feminism is mostly the province of females. . . . But it isn't even a matter of apples and oranges. It is more like elephants and parsley" (248). Joeres goes on to assert that male American Germanists are at best ignorant of and bewildered by feminism, at worst actively hostile to it, in any case unconvinced, unlike their colleagues in other modern languages, that feminism has any utility for their own scholarly work on German literature. Meanwhile, Joeres asserts, "Feminists are increasingly losing interest in the *Germanistik* that ignores and/or minimizes our impact" (254). She predicts that, if *Germanistik* continues to disregard feminism, feminist Germanists will withdraw and align themselves with Women's Studies departments instead. Joeres's analysis raises questions that are of central importance to the project that underlies this volume of essays. If Joeres is right, why have the feminist authors of this volume nonetheless undertaken to investigate German women writers facing fascism and confronting the past? Is this feminist *Germanistik* after all? And if so, would we wish to argue that the feminist readings of women's texts advanced here are also of significance beyond the boundaries of feminist German Studies? Would we perhaps even maintain that the essays here raise issues that are central to our discipline? Might we even dare to argue that *Germanistik* will consign itself to the scholarly backwaters of literary, cultural, and historical studies if it fails to attend to the kind of feminist questions this volume poses?

It may be that the feminist scholars of this volume have been less concerned with transforming the field of *Germanistik*—Joeres's concern—than with discovering or devising analytical methods that offer new insights into German literature and culture. (It is then other Germanists' loss if they fail to understand why feminist methods are useful or important.) What recent investigations in many different fields of cultural studies have shown is that gender—femininity, masculinity, and their interrelationship—is always a potent factor, at work in every area of cultural activity including literary representation, that scholars ignore at the cost of misunderstanding the functioning of the aspects of culture they wish to study. In this spirit, Barbara Becker-Cantarino, also writing in the last section of the *Women in German Yearbook*, argues that a feminist *Germanistik* might work toward "eine integrative Erforschung der Geschlechterrollen und des Verhältnisses zwischen den Geschlechtern im historischen und sozialen Kontext, die auch Machtverhältnisse und Signifikationspraxis mit einbezieht" (228) (an integrative investigation of gender roles and of the relationship between the sexes in their historical and social context, which also includes power relations and significatory practices). In so doing, feminist scholars will need to take special care, as Gisela Brinkler-Gabler has also pointed out in that final section of the *Yearbook*, to address some of the thorny and unresolved questions that the new approaches to literary, cultural, and historical studies raise: "The problem, indeed, is the relationship between theory, social history, and the text itself. . . . What takes precedence, the general . . . or the specific? Or, if one proceeds from the assumption of a fragmented, disconnected set of phenomena, social relations, and discourses, what are the underlying principles governing selection and construction?" (240). To the degree that we feminists can offer answers to such vexing questions about the relevance of gender to representation and signification—to the degree that we have done that *here*—we will necessarily sooner or later command the attention of even the most reluctant scholars in our field.

Addressing these questions is nowhere more important than in investigations of what, for feminists and all other scholars of German Studies, must remain the central and unavoidable event of German history, National Socialism and the Holocaust. By focusing attention on German women writers from Weimar to the present facing fascism and confronting the past, the editors and authors of this volume have joined one of the major battles rending contemporary feminist scholarship in German Studies, the debate around women's relationship to, responsibility for, and complicity in German fascism. The spectrum of positions within this debate extends from the positions of Gisela Bock and Jill Stephenson at one extreme, who maintain that women, "themselves peculiarly resistant to National Socialism" (Stephenson, 18) were "only victims of a brutally misogynist regime," to Claudia Koonz at the other pole, who argues that most German women, like most German men, collaborated with the Nazis, helping "to stabilize a murderous regime precisely by their adherence to domestic and maternal values associated with a politically indifferent female separate sphere" (Grossmann, 351). As Atina Grossmann has maintained, these are questions not merely of interest to women's studies scholars alone:

> With the liquidation of conventional public sites of the political (parliament, political parties, trade unions, voluntary associations), much Nazi policy was directed at the appropriation and mobilization of the ostensibly private or reproductive arena where women had traditionally been situated and were perceived to have influence or even power. Arguments about women's role therefore cannot be separated from other questions that preoccupy historians of modern Germany, such as the reactionary or radically modern nature of the regime, and the degree of continuity or rupture with the era before 1933 and after 1945. Moreover, questions of gender are critical to an evaluation of the still unclear relationship between state social welfare and "racial" hygiene measures directed predominantly towards "Aryans" (such as marriage loans, sterilization, and "euthanasia") and the extermination of "inferior aliens," particularly European Jewry. (350–351)

Within scholarship on women, too, difficult and more differentiated conceptual questions will have to be asked as well before this debate can be resolved satisfactorily for feminism. Some of those questions have now emerged in recent highly contentious German feminist debates, some portions of which have been documented in the 1990 collection *TöchterFragen: NS-Frauen Geschichte*. Those questions might be clustered into several different areas. First, feminist scholars of National Socialism need still to clarify what actually happened to women under Hitler's rule. Is the Nazi conception of womanhood rooted in the nineteenth century, or did Nazi women's organizations deliberately offer women new and qualitatively different arenas of action? What continuities and breaks exist between the bourgeois women's movement and the Nazis' female leadership? Did Nazi policy relegate women to the family or seek to subordinate the family to the *Volk*? How did Nazi gender policies affect women of different classes, professions, regions, ages, religions, and ethnicities differentially? Were there gender-specific commonalities, as well as differences, among perpetrators and victims? What forms did female support for and resistance to fascism take, what kinds of activities count as support or resistance, how might both be related to and/or different from Nazi concepts of femininity? As well, feminist scholars must also raise questions about how to evaluate women's activities during the

Nazi period. Are all German women, whatever their support for fascism, victims of a patriarchal and misogynist regime, or, alternatively, are German women not explicitly targeted by the regime guilty of, or at least responsible for, complicity in Nazi crimes? Is Christina Thürmer-Rohr's conception of *Mittäterschaft* adequate to describe women's complicity in a male-dominant system, or is a more refined conception of "Täterinnenschaft eigener Art" necessary, as Karin Windaus-Walser has suggested (*TöchterFragen*, 69)? Can one speak of a "Handlungskollektiv Deutschland," as Lerke Gravenhorst argues in *TöchterFragen*, that bears a collective, undifferentiated responsibility for Nazi crimes? Or do conceptions of collective guilt blur concrete distinctions between individuals who are more or less guilty? Might such arguments for the necessity of one single relationship to the Nazi past even display an unintended similarity to Nazi conceptions of a single, unified German national identity? Is it proper to discuss the historical question of German women's role under fascism in moral terms at all; or, alternatively, is a moral or ethical approach the only one finally adequate to the horrors of the Holocaust? Finally, feminist scholars need to explore the relationship of present feminist debates about National Socialism to feminist needs of the present, questions that have recently been posed very sharply by the collective "Frauen gegen Antisemitismus" in the *beiträge zur femininistischen theorie und praxis*. Why has it taken so long for German feminists to ask questions about German women's role in fascism, and how is that long silence related to the course German feminism has taken? What ends are met by representing German women as victims of fascism, and what different purposes are served by demands that contemporary women assume their proper responsibility for a German past that includes National Socialism and the Holocaust? Does German feminists' fondness for portraits of German women as resistance fighters or as victims of German men, their elision of fascism and patriarchy, or even their lack of attention to National Socialism at all represent attempts to avoid dealing with women's—or, more specifically, their mothers'—complicity in Hitler's regime? If so, why has this topic emerged so powerfully right now? And more particularly how is the struggle over women and fascism today related to efforts since the *Historikerstreit* to normalize German history and reconstruct German identity, to German unification and the absorption of the GDR, to efforts to draw parallels between fascism and communism, to the upsurge of German racism and xenophobia?

Why and how are such questions relevant to us as literary scholars, how can we help to answer them, and why are they important for the work undertaken in this volume? As many recent theorists have pointed out, historical knowledge cannot be separated from its forms of representation. In *Writing and Rewriting the Holocaust*, for instance, James Young has observed:

> Scholars of the Holocaust have come increasingly to recognize that interpretations of both the texts and events of the Holocaust are intertwined. For both events and their

> representations are ultimately beholden to the forms, language, and critical methodology through which they are grasped. . . . What is remembered of the Holocaust depends on how it is remembered, and how events are remembered depends in turn on the texts now giving them form.
>
> Instead of isolating events from their representations, this approach recognizes that literary and historical truths of the Holocaust may not be entirely separable. That is, the truths of the Holocaust—both the factual and the interpretive—can no longer be said to lie beyond our understanding, but must now be seen to inhere in the ways we understand, interpret, and write its history. (1)

The study of representation and interpretation is our proper province as literary scholars. Our training in textual analysis can help other scholars of National Socialism to understand how discourses, representations, interpretations already influence how participants experience and evaluate events and that they affect again how participants or observers construct an account of what happened and what it meant. We can explore why the Nazi period is represented in certain ways rather than others, whence those representations derive, what sorts of writers employ what kinds of textual forms, and how and why representations of fascism change over time. Understanding that gender itself is a changing social construction, we can investigate its deployment in texts produced across the spectrum of possibilities during the Nazi period, from those in support of Hitler to those in resistance, in ideology, document, popular entertainment forms, belles lettres, exploring how representations of gender intersect with and influence other representations, showing how they may have produced the gendered subjects of the Nazi regime, or, alternatively, may have helped women to resist the Nazis. As Dagmar Reese has pointed out, this area of feminist scholarship—the "ideologiekritische Aufarbeitung von Weiblichkeitskonstruktionen im Nationalsozialimus in verschiedenen Bereichen von Politik, Literatur, Kunst, Medien, unter Zugrundelegung des bereits erarbeiteten sozialhistorischen Materials" (140) (the ideology-critical investigation of constructions of femininity within National Socialism in the various realms of politics, literature, art, media, drawing upon existing sociohistorical scholarship)—still remains almost entirely unexamined. If we succeed at these projects, we will add immeasurably to the historical understanding of National Socialism and women's role in it—and also demonstrate why feminist Germanistik is of absolute centrality to the field of German Studies.

How successfully have the discussions in this volume helped us to address this complex of issues? At their best, they foreground many of the difficult questions I have posed here, addressing them by looking specifically at how particular German women writers or filmmakers have represented the relationship of gender and fascism. In my view, the most useful contributions here have located their examination of specific texts within larger theoretical and historical contexts in several ways, and their treatment of representation, gender, and fascism could serve as models for investigations of the relationship of literary texts to the kinds of questions I posed earlier in my comments. Dagmar Lorenz's chapter on "The Interchange Between Experience and Literature: German Jewish Writers of the Holocaust," for instance, shows how even the attempt to determine what really happened in the Holocaust involves questions of narrative and representation. To document and comprehend the unprecedented events to which Nazi policy subjected them, the Jewish women Lorenz considers became writers, but they necessarily packaged their experiences in the traditions and structures available to them. Because most of those writers were of middle-class background with conventional middle-class educations, they drew in the main on the models they knew; thus, Lorenz concludes, "most Holocaust literature by women and men, both, is surprisingly conservative and conventional in terms of its form and ideology" (172). Moreover, Lorenz also shows that middle-class conventions not only determined writing about the Holocaust but also shaped and ordered her writers' actual responses to their experiences, explaining why, for example, cultural or aesthetic activities assumed such great importance as a form of resistance to the degradations of concentration camp life. Lorenz finally can demonstrate that her Jewish writers were so confined by the German discourses that produced them that they often even shared their oppressors' prejudices against race mixing, the lower classes, the mentally handicapped, or gypsies, gullibly accepted Nazi propaganda, or adopted Nazi terminology and jargon. Lorenz might have explored even further how gender is related to other categories and discourses of Nazi culture and also have pursued the relationship of representation in greater depth. Her essay seems still to propose that if writers had not clung so closely to bourgeois models they could have responded to their experiences in a way that was more spontaneous or less inhibited—instead of recognizing that other forms of representation would simply be different kinds of constructs, mediated responses to reality in a different way. Lorenz has, however, provided a methodology that could produce many more important investigations of texts written during the Nazi period, and feminist Germanists might now want also to apply similar methods to writing by German women who supported and opposed the Nazi regime.

Elke Frederiksen's chapter on "Luise Rinser: Dialogues with the Past? The Problem of *Vergangenheitsbewältigung*," offers a model for how feminist Germanists might approach moral questions about German women's complicity in the Nazi past. Drawing on Claudia Koonz's work, Frederiksen pleads for a more differentiated way of understanding women's moral agency under fascism beyond the simple perpetrator/victim dichotomy, instead attempting to reconstruct the social networks "in denen die Individuen die Vorteile der Kollaboration und den Preis des Widerspruchs gegeneinander abwogen, und Wege suchten, nicht Opfer des Systems zu werden" (Koonz, 21) (in which individuals could weigh the advantages of collaboration against the price of resistance and search for ways to avoid becoming victims of the system, Frederiksen, 190). She emphasizes that the questions we ask about texts will be influenced by the specific context in which particular readers read them and the questions they bring to them. And she raises doubts about the very project of *Vergangenheitsbewältigung* (coming to terms with the past) in the face of a past that can scarcely be comprehended, let alone mastered. Specifically, Frederiksen's essay reveals Rinser's quite deliberate silence about her early enthusiasm for the Nazis, despite the many literary texts in which she addresses the Nazi past and demands candor from herself and others. Frederiksen then explores how Rinser's apparent duplicity might change her own earlier feminist readings of those texts, and she now attempts instead to discern how Rinser's relationship to her own Nazi past might also have inscribed itself in her texts. Frederiksen's essay raises, though cannot solve, a whole range of troubling moral questions about the relationship of biography to text that, as she indicates, seem also to have emerged in more recent debates about GDR writers' relationship to their state. Frederiksen's essay takes the productive step of breaking with earlier feminist interpretive models that insisted on viewing women writers as inevitably on the right side. She leaves us with a moral quandary that only much more feminist discussion will be able to solve. Feminist literary scholarship needs many more studies like Frederiksen's that view women writers as potentially ambiguous figures living and writing within the political constraints of their time, and, as in the case of Rinser and Christa Wolf, we also need to develop more sophisticated criteria that enable us to assess the moral choices they made.

Finally, Robert Holub's chapter, "Fact, Fantasy, and Female Subjectivity: *Vergangenheitsbewältigung* in Christa Wolf's *Patterns of Childhood*," shows how literary works can contribute to the production or transformation of a discourse on women and fascism. As Holub details, Wolf's novel articulated new possibilities of *Vergangenheitsbewältigung* in both the GDR and the FRG, daring to acknowledge that fascism might also have left its imprint on the lives of Germans in the East, while adding a subjective and personal content to what had often been an abstract and quasi-religious discussion of moral responsibility in the West. As well, and even more importantly for our purposes here, Holub shows how *Kindheitsmuster* offers a new way of discussing women's involvement in fascism beyond the twin stereotypes of women as either docile, compliant tools of evil men or saintly innocents uncontaminated by political involvement. What is particularly useful in Holub's essay are his close textual analyses that reveal concretely how Wolf's novel appropriated, adapted, and transformed preexisting discourses on fascism. Wolf's text thus simultaneously succeeds in providing a more complex explanation for the production and functioning of subjectivity under fascism and in offering her readers a new discourse that allowed them to speak in new and different ways about their own involvement in National Socialism. Holub's essay shows us that and how literary works can intervene into political debates, and we need many more studies like his that investigate the relationship between larger political discussions about fascism—or other political issues—and the way in which those discussions are adapted and transformed by particular literary texts.

The film whose screening ended the conference from which this volume derived, Helke Sander's *BeFreier und Befreite*, poses very sharply the questions about facing fascism and confronting the past that this volume asks. The film demands that its viewers think about women as victims and men as brutal perpetrators, and forces them to ask to what degree it is fair or warranted to extract crimes against women from the historical context in which they occur: *is* what happened to women in Germany in 1945 the same as in Bosnia and Kuwait? Does what we think of those rapes depend in any way on how we judge German women's complicity in fascism? And are there ways in which the indignation about rape by Soviet soldiers, then and now, in reality and in Helke Sander's film, is related to Nazi racial propaganda: writing in *Die Zeit*, Volker Ullrich proposed, for example, that the feminist perspective of Sander's film unintentionally supported the Nazis' racist stereotypes about Russians, since, as her film presents it, in 1945 the soldiers of the Red Army behaved toward German women exactly as Nazi notions of subhuman Russians would have predicted. Finally, viewers of the film need to ask why this film was made now and what political function it performs. What role does Helke Sander's film play in the struggle to redefine German national identity after German unification? Are these rape victims "a kind of female equivalent to the valiant soldiers on the Eastern front invoked in the *Historikerstreit*, suffering and brave but loyal and without connection to or responsibility for the atrocities committed on their behalf?" (Grossmann, 354) Is Ullrich right to suggest: "All dies sind Symptome, Symptome für eine schleichende Veränderung des deutschen Selbstbildes. Und Deutschlands Nachbarn müssen auf der Hut sein, wenn Deutsche wieder anfangen, sich als Opfer zu stilisieren"? (All these are symptoms, symptoms of a creeping change in the German self-image. And Germany's neighbors had better watch out when Germans again begin to stylize themselves into victims.) The furor that Sander's film has aroused shows that it has become an intervention into a debate about the construction of Germanness and a German past that meets the needs of the present. That a debate about representation, gender, and fascism can play so important a role in Germany once more underlines the importance of the questions addressed in this volume—and is another indication that, even beyond the walls of the academy, feminist *Germanistik* matters.

Bibliography

Becker-Cantarino, Barbara. "Feministische Germanistik in Deutschland: Rückblick und sechs Thesen." In *Women in German Yearbook 8*. Ed. Jeanette Clausen and Sara Friedrichsmeyer. Lincoln: University of Nebraska Press, 1992, 219–233.

Brinkler-Gabler, Gisela. "Alterity—Marginality—Difference: On Inventing Places for Women." In *Women in German Yearbook 8*. Ed. Jeanette Clausen and Sara Friedrichsmeyer. Lincoln: University of Nebraska Press, 1992, 235–245.

Frauen gegen Antisemitismus. "Der Nationalsozialismus als Extremform des Patriarchats: Zur Leugnung der Täterschaft von Frauen und zur Tabuisierung des Antisemitismus in der Auseinandersetzung mit dem NS." *beiträge zur feministischen theorie und praxis 35* (1993): 77–89.

Gravenhorst, Lerke, and Carmen Tatschmurat, eds. *TöchterFragen: NS-Frauen Geschichte*. Freiburg i.Br.: Kore, 1990.

Grossmann, Atina. "Feminist Debates about Women and National Socialism." *Gender & History* 3.3 (Autumn 1991): 350–358.

Joeres, Ruth-Ellen B. "'Language is Also a Place of Struggle': The Language of Feminism and the Language of American Germanistik." In *Women in German Yearbook 8*. Ed. Jeanette Clausen and Sara Friedrichsmeyer. Lincoln: University of Nebraska Press, 1992, 247–257.

Koonz, Claudia. *Mothers in the Fatherland: Women, Family Life, and Nazi Politics*. New York: St. Martin's Press, 1987.

Reese, Dagmar. "Neuere Literatur zum Thema Frauen und Nationalsozialismus." *Feministische Studien* 10.1 (May 1992): 131–141.

Stephenson, Jill. The Nazi Organization of Women. New York: Barnes & Noble, 1981.

Thürmer-Rohr, Christina. Vagabundinnen: Feministische Essays. Berlin: Orlanda Frauenverlag, 1987.

Ullrich, Volker. "Die neue Dreistigkeit." *Die Zeit* 6 November 1992: 13.

Young, James E. *Writing and Rewriting the Holocaust: Narrative and the Consequences of Interpretation*. Bloomington: Indiana University Press, 1988.

Selected Bibliography

Bechdolf, Ute. *Wunschbilder? Frauen im nationalsozialistischen Unterhaltungsfilm*. Tübingen: Tübinger Verein für Volkskunde, 1992.

Berger, Karin. *Zwischen Eintopf und Fließband: Frauenarbeit und Frauenbild im Faschismus. Österreich 1938–1945*. Wien: Verlag für Gesellschaftskritik, 1984.

Bock, Gisela. *Zwangssterilisation im Nationalsozialismus: Studien zur Rassenpolitik und Frauenpolitik*. Opladen: Westdeutscher Verlag, 1986.

Böltken, Andrea. *Führerinnen im "Führerstaat": Gertrud Scholtz-Klink, Trude Mohr, Jutta Rüdiger, und Inge Viermetz*. Pfaffenweiler: Centaurus, 1995.

Burghart, Christina. *Die deutsche Frau: Küchenmagd, Zuchtsau, Leibeigene im III. Reich*. Münster: Verlag Frauenpolitik, 1978.

Capriolen und Vexierbilder: neue Studien zum NS-Unterhaltungsfilm. Marburg: Schüren, 1993.

Coosner, Sharon. *Women under the Third Reich. A Bibliographical Dictionary*. Westport, CT: Greenwood, 1998.

Czarnowski, Gabriele. *Das kontrollierte Paar: Ehe- und Sozialpolitik im Nationalsozialismus*. Weinheim: Deutscher Studienverlag, 1991.

Czech, Michaela. *Frauen und Sport im nationalsozialistischen Deutschland. Eine Untersuchung zur weiblichen Sportrealität in einem patriarchalen Herrschaftssystem*. Berlin: Tischler, 1994.

Decken, Godele von der. *Emanzipation auf Abwegen. Frauenkultur und Frauenliteratur im Umkreis des Nationalsozialismus*. Introduction Uwe Ketelsen. Frankfurt am Main: Athenäum, 1988.

Deininghaus, Theresa. "Medizinstudium von Frauen während der nationalsozialistischen Zeit. Eine retrospektive Betrachtung." Diss., University of Hamburg, 1992.

Dichotomie, Dominanz, Differenz: Frauen plazieren sich in Wissenschaft und Gesellschaft. Ed. Annette Bertrams. Weinheim: Studien-Verlag, 1995.

Dichtl, Gabriele. "Beiträge zur Frauenheilkunde und Geburtshilfe im Dritten Reich." Diss., University of Heidelberg, 1983.

Diester, Manfred. *Körpergeschichten: Eine Untersuchung zum Mythosbegriff am Beispiel der Darstellung von Mann und Frau in der Kriegsliteratur von 1939–43*. Frankfurt am Main/Bern/New York: Peter Lang, 1980.

Eldorado: Homosexuelle Frauen und Männer in Berlin 1850–1950; Geschichte, Alltag, und Kultur. Ed. Berlin-Museum. Berlin: Frölich und Kaufmann, 1984.

Elling, Hanna. *Frauen im deutschen Widerstand: 1933–45*. Frankfurt am Main: Röderberg, 1981.

Fascism, Aesthetics, and Culture. Ed. Richard J. Golsan. Hanover and London: University Press of New England, 1992.

Feral, Thierry. *La politique féminine du IIIième Reich*. Ed. Amicale Franco-Allemande. Paris: Amicale Fanco-Allemande, 1990.

Fine, Ellen. "Women Writers and the Holocaust: Strategies for Survival." In *Reflections of the Holocaust in Art and Literature*. Ed. Randolph L. Braham. New York: Columbia University Press, 1990, 79–95.

Frauenarbeit im Wandel: Vom ausgehenden Kaiserreich bis zum Ende des Nationalsozialismus. Ed. Museumspädagogischer Dienst der Kulturbehörde Hamburg. Hamburg: Museumspädagogischer Dienst, 1985.

Frauen gegen die Diktatur—Widerstand und Verfolgung im nationalsozialistischen Deutschland. Ed. Christl Wickert. Berlin: Hentrich, 1995.

Frauen im Nationalsozialismus: Dokumente und Zeugnisse. Ed. Ute Benz. München: Beck, 1993.

Frauen und Faschismus in Europa. Der faschistische Körper. Eds. Leonore Siegele-Wenschkewitz and Gerda Stuchlik. Pfaffenweiler: Centaurus, 1990.

Frauen und Nationalsozialismus: Historische und kulturgeschichtliche Positionen. Ed. Ortrun Niethammer. Osnabrück: Rasch, 1996.

Frauen unterm Hakenkreuz. Eine Dokumentation. Ed. Maruta Schmidt and Gabi Dietz. München: Deutscher Taschenbuch Verlag, 1985.

Frauen: Verfolgung und Widerstand. Ed. Wolfgang Benz and Barbara Distel. München: Deutscher Taschenbuch Verlag, 1993.

Frauen zwischen Grenzen: Rassismus und Nationalsozialismus in der feministischen Diskussion. Ed. Olga Uremovic and Gundula Oerter. Franfurt am Main/New York: Campus, 1994.

Frauenverfolgung und Widerstand. Dachauer Hefte 3.3 (1987).

Frauenleben im NS-Alltag. Ed. Annette Kuhn. Pfaffenweiler: Centaurus, 1994.

Friedel, Claudia. *Komponierende Frauen im Dritten Reich: Versuch einer Rekonstruktion von Lebensrealität und herrschendem Frauenbild*. Münster/Hamburg: Lit, 1995.

Fünfzig Jahre danach: Zur Nachgeschichte des Nationalsozialsozialismus. Ed. Sigrid Weigel and Birgit Erdle. Zürich: vdf Hochschulverlag, 1996.

Gättens, Marie-Luise. *Women Writers and Fascism: Reconstructing History*. Gainesville: Florida University Press, 1995.

Gehmacher, Johanna. *"Völkische Frauenbewegung": Deutschnationale und nationalsozialistische Geschlechterpolitik in Österreich*. Wien: Döcker, 1997.

Geyer, Michael, and Miriam Hansen. "German-Jewish Memory and National Consciousness." In *Holocaust Remembrance: The Shapes of Memory*. Ed. Geoffrey Hartman. Oxford: Blackwell, 1994, 175–90.

Grossmann, Atina. "Feminist Debates about Women and National Socialism." *Gender & History (Great Britain)* 3.3 (1991): 350–358.

Grunberger, Richard. *A Social History of the Third Reich*. Harmondsworth: Penguin, 1974.

Haidu, Peter. "The Dialectics of Unspeakability: Language, Silence, and the Narratives of Desubjectification." In *Probing the Limits of Representation: Nazism and the "Final Solution."* Ed. Saul Friedländer. Cambridge: Harvard University Press, 1992, 277–299.

Hancock, Eleanor. "Employment in Wartime: The Experience of German Women During the Second World War." *War & Society (Australia)* 12.2 (1994): 43–68.

Heinemann, Elisabeth. "The Hour of the Woman: Memories of Germany's 'Crisis Years' and West German National Identity." *American Historical Review* 101.2 (1996): 354–395.

Henics, Heidi. *Nationalsozialismus und Gegenwart: Eine empirische Studie über historische und aktuelle Kulturmuster von Frauen in der Region*. Hannover: Agis, 1996.

Hohmann, Joachim S. *Frauen und Mädchen in faschistischen Lesebüchern und Fibeln*. Frankfurt am Main/Bern/New York: Peter Lang, 1991.

Jacobeit, Sigrid. "Arbeits- und Lebensbedingungen der Bäuerin in Klein- und Mittelbetrieben. Ein Beitrag zur Lebensweise der Frau auf dem Lande in der Zeit der faschistischen Diktatur der deutschen Imperialismus 1933–1939." Diss., Humboldt-University Berlin, 1979.

fc

Jüdische Kultur und Weiblichkeit in der Moderne. Ed. Inge Stephan et al. Köln/Weimar/Wien: Böhlau, 1994.

Jugend, Frauen, Drittes Reich: Autorinnen im Exil 1933–1945. Ed. Eva-Maria Siegel. Pfaffenweiler: Centaurus, 1993.

Kessler, Hannelore. *"Die deutsche Frau": Nationalsozialistische Frauenpropaganda im "Völkischen Beobachter"*. Köln: Pahl-Rugenstein, 1981.

Kinz, Gabriele. *Der Bund Deutscher Mädel. Ein Beitrag über die außerschulische Mädchenerziehung im Nationalsozialismus*. Frankfurt am Main/Bern/New York: Peter Lang, 1991.

Klapdor-Kops, Heike. *Heldinnen: die Gestaltung der Frauen im Drama deutscher Exilautoren (1933–1945)*. Weinheim: Beltz, 1985.

Klaus, Martin. *Mädchen im Dritten Reich: Der Bund Deutscher Mädel (BDM)*. Köln: Pahl-Rugenstein, 1985.

Klaus, Martin. *Mädchen in der Hitlerjugend. Die Erziehung zur deutschen Frau*. Köln, Pahl-Rugenstein, 1980.

Kliner-Fruck, Martina. "Es ging ja ums Überleben: Deutsch-jüdische Frauen unter nationalsozialistischer Verfolgung, in der Emigration in Palästina, Israel und in der Remigration." Diss., University of Düsseldorf, 1994.

König, Cosima. *Die Frau im Recht des Nationalsozialismus: Eine Analyse ihrer familien-, erb- und arbeitsrechtlichen Stellung*. Frankfurt am Main/Bern/New York: Peter Lang, 1988.

Koonz, Claudia. *Mothers in the Fatherland. Women, the Family, and Nazi Politics*. New York: St. Martin's Press, 1987.

Koonz, Claudia. *Mütter im Vaterland: Frauen im Dritten Reich*. Reinbek bei Hamburg: Rowohlt, 1994.

Kopetzky, Helmut. *Die andere Front: Europäische Frauen in Krieg und Widerstand 1939 bis 1945*. Köln: Pahl-Rugenstein, 1983.

Korotin, Ilse Erika. *"Am Muttergeist soll die Welt genesen": Philosophische Dispositionen zum Frauenbild im Nationalsozialismus*. Wien/Köln/Weimar: Böhlau, 1992.

Kuhn, Annette. *Frauen im deutschen Faschismus. Eine Quellensammlung mit fachwissenschaftlichen und fachdidaktischen Kommentaren*. 2 vls. Düsseldorf: Schwann, 1982.

Kuhn, Annette. *Frauenarbeit und Frauenwiderstand im NS-Staat*. Düsseldorf: Schwann, 1987.

Kuhn, Annette. *Frauenpolitik im NS-Staat*. Düsseldorf: Schwann, 1982.

Leben, frei und in Frieden: Frauen gegen Faschismus und Krieg. Ed. Florence Hervé and Renate Wisbar. Frankfurt am Main: Röderberg, 1981.

Lehker, Marianne. *Frauen im Nationalsozialismus. Wie aus Opfern Handlanger der Täter wurden: Eine nötige Trauerarbeit*. Frankfurt am Main: Materialis, 1984.

Linville, Susan E. *Feminism, Film, Fascism: Women's Auto/biographical Film in Postwar Germany*. Austin: Univesity of Texas Press, 1998.

Lück, Margret. *Die Frau im Männerstaat. Die gesellschaftliche Stellung der Frau im Nationalsozialismus. Eine Analyse aus pädagogischer Sicht*. Frankfurt am Main/Bern/New York: Peter Lang, 1979.

Manns, Heide. *Frauen für den Nationalsozialismus: Nationalsozialistische Studentinnen und Akademikerinnen in der Weimarer Republik und im Dritten Reich*. Opladen: Leske und Budrich, 1997.

Meckel, Anne. *Animation—Agitation: Frauendarstellungen auf der "Grossen deutschen Kunstausstellung" in München 1937–1944*. Weinheim: Deutscher Studienverlag, 1993.

Mitscherlich Nielsen Margarethe. *Überlegung einer Psychoanalytikerin zum Hitlerreich: Weibliche und männliche Werte, damals und heute*. Münsterschwarzach: Vier-Türme, 1996.

Mutterkreuz und Arbeitsbuch: Zur Geschichte der Frauen in der Weimarer Republik und im Nationalsozialismus. Ed. Frauengruppe Faschismusforschung. Frankfurt am Main: Fischer, 1981.

Nach Osten: Verdeckte Spuren nationalsozialistischer Verbrechen. Ed. Theresa Wobbe. Frankfurt am Main: Neue Kritik, 1992.

Opfer und Täterinnen: Frauenbiographien des Nationalsozialismus. Ed. Angelika Ebbinghaus. Nördlingen: Reno, 1987.

Owings, Alison. *Frauen: German Women Recall the Third Reich*. New Brunswick, N.J.: Rutgers University Press, 1993.

Patriarchy, Gender, and Fascism in the Third Reich: The Response of Women Writers. Ed. Elaine Martin. Detroit: Wayne State University Press, 1993.

Paul-Horn, Ina. *Faszination Nationalsozialismus? Zu einer politischen Theorie des Geschlechterverhältnisses*. Pfaffenweiler: Centaurus, 1993.

Perchinig, Elisabeth. *Zur Einübung von Weiblichkeit im Terrorzusammenhang: Mädchenadoleszenz in der NS-Gesellschaft*. München: Profil, 1996.

Pilgrim, Volker Ellis. *"Du kannst mich ruhig 'Frau Hitler' nennen: Frauen als Schmuck und Tarnung der NS-Herrschaft*. Reinbek bei Hamburg: Rowohlt, 1994.

Plain, Gill. *Women's Fiction of the Second World War: Gender, Power and Resistance*. New York: St. Martin's Press, 1996.

Probing the Limits of Representation: Nazism and the "Final Solution." Ed. Saul Friedländer. Cambridge: Harvard University Press, 1992.

Ragwitz, Renate. *Die Frauenaußenkommandos des Konzentrationslagers Buchenwald*. Buchenwald: Nationale Mahn- und Gedenkstätte, 1982.

Rassenpolitik und Geschlechterpolitik im Nationalsozialismus. Ed. Gisela Bock. Göttingen: Vandenhoek und Ruprecht, 1993.

Reflections of the Holocaust in Art and Literature. Ed. Randolph L. Braham. New York: Columbia University Press, 1990.

Reuter, Angelika. *Seit 1848, Frauen im Widerstand, Frauen im Faschismus: 1933–1945*. Münster: Verlag Frauenpolitik, 1977.

Ringelheim, Joan. "Women and the Holocaust: A Reconsideration of Research." *Signs* 10.4 (1985): 741–761.

Rohr, Barbara. *Die allmähliche Schärfung des weiblichen Blicks: Eine Bildungsgeschichte zwischen Faschismus und Frauenbewegung*. Hamburg: Argument, 1992.

Ruland, Bernd. *Die Augen Moskaus: Fernschreibzentrale der Wehrmacht in Berlin. Mädchen gegen Hitler*. Zürich: Schweizer Verlagshaus, 1973.

Rupp, Leila J. "Women, Class, and Mobilization in Nazi Germany." *Science and Sociology* 43.1 (1979): 51–69.

Schmatzler, Uta Cornelia. *Verstrickung, Mitverantwortung und Täterschaft im Nationalsozialismus: Eine Untersuchung zum Verhältnis von weiblichem Alltag und faschistischem Staat*. Kiel: L & F Verlag, 1994.

Schmidt-Waldherr, Hiltraud. *Emanzipation durch Professionalisierung? Politische Strategien und Konflikte innerhalb der bürgerlichen Frauenbewegung während der Weimarer Republik und der Reaktion des bürgerlichen Antifeminismus und des Natonalsozialismus*. Frankfurt am Main: Materialis, 1987.

Scholtz-Klink, Gertrud. *Die Frau im Dritten Reich. Eine Dokumentation*. Tübingen: Grabert, 1978.

Schoppmann, Claudia. *Nationalsozialistische Sexualpolitik und weibliche Homosexualität*. Pfaffenweiler: Centaurus, 1991.

Schupetta, Ingrid. *Frauen- und Ausländererwerbstätigkeit in Deutschland von 1939–1945*. Köln: Pahl-Rugenstein, 1983.

Seidler, Franz W. *Frauen zu den Waffen? Marketenderinnen, Helferinnen, Soldatinnen*. Koblenz: Wehr und Wissen, 1978.

Siegel, Eva-Maria. "Weibliche Jugend im Nationalsozialismus: Massenpsychologische Aspekte in Exilromanen von Hermynia Zur Mühlen, Irmgard Keun, Maria Leitner." Diss., Humboldt-University Berlin, 1991.

Sternheim-Peters, Eva. *Die Zeit der großen Täuschungen. Mädchenleben im Faschismus*. 1987. Bielefeld: Verlag Wissenschaft und Politik, 1992.

Strobl, Ingrid. *"Sag nie, du gehst den letzten Weg": Frauen im bewaffneten Widerstand gegen Faschismus und deutsche Besetzung*. Frankfurt am Main: Fischer, 1995.

Thalmann, Rita. *Frausein im Dritten Reich*. Frankfurt am Main: Ullstein, 1987.

Theweleit, Klaus. *Männerphantasien*. 1977. 2 vols. Reinbek bei Hamburg: Rowohlt, 1980.

Thomas, Theodore N. *Women against Hitler: Christian Resistence in the Third Reich*. Westport, Conn./London: Praeger, 1995.

Thürmer-Rohr, Christina. *Vagabonding: Feminist Thinking Cut Loose*. Trans. Lise Weil. Boston: Beacon Press, 1991.

Tidl, Georg. *Die Frau im Nationalsozialismus*. Wien: Europaverlag, 1984.

TöchterFragen: NS-Frauengeschichte. Ed. Lerke Gravenhorst and Carmen Tatschmurat. Freiburg im Breisgau: Kore, 1990.

Traudisch, Dora. *Mutterschaft mit Zuckerguß? Frauenfeindliche Propaganda im NS-Spielfilm*. Pfaffenweiler: Centaurus, 1993.

Voigt-Firon, Diana. *Das Mädchenbuch im Dritten Reich: Weibliche Rollenangebote zwischen bürgerlichem Frauenbild, faschistischer Neuprägung und Staatsinteresse*. Köln: Pahl-Rugenstein, 1989.

Wagner, Leonie. *Nationalsozialistische Frauenansichten: Vorstellungen von Weiblichkeit und Politik führender Frauen im Nationalsozialismus*. Frankfurt am Main: dipa, 1996.

Weigel, Sigrid. *Bilder des kulturellen Gedächtnisses: Beiträge zur Gegenwartsliteratur*. Dülmen-Hiddingsel: tende, 1994.

Weigel, Sigrid. "Erinnerung vor Gericht: Zum Opfer-Täter-Diskurs über den Nationalsozialismus in Helga Schuberts 'Judasfrauen' und und ihre Geschichtsquellen". In *Bilder des kulturellen Gedächtnisses: Beiträge zur Gegenwartsliteratur*. Dülmen-Hiddingsel: tende, 1994, 198–321.

Weinberger, Gabriele. *Nazi Germany and its Aftermath in Women Directors' Autobiographical Films of the Late 1970s: In the Murderer's House*. San Francisco: Mellen Research University Press, 1992.

Wiggershaus, Renate. *Frauen unterm Nationalsozialismus*. Wuppertal: Hammer, 1984.

Winkler, Dörte. *Frauenarbeit im "Dritten Reich"*. Hamburg: Hoffmann und Campe, 1977.

Wittrock, Christine. *Weiblichkeitsmythen. Das Frauenbild im Faschismus und seine Vorläufer in der Frauenbewegung der 20er Jahre*. Frankfurt am Main: Sendler, 1983.

Zwischen Karriere und Verfolgung: Handlungsräume von Frauen im nationalsozialistischen Deutschland. Ed. Kirsten Heinsohn. Frankfurt am Main/New York: Campus, 1997.

Contributors

GISELA BRINKER-GABLER is a Professor and Graduate Program Director in the Department of Comparative Literature at the State University of New York at Binghamton. She has published *Poetisch-Wissenschaftliche Mittelalter-Rezeption; Deutsche Dichterinnen vom 16. Jahrhundert bis zur Gegenwart; Lexikon deutschsprachiger Schriftstellerinnen, 1800–1945*; and two volumes of critical writing on women authors of German-speaking Europe, *Deutsche Literatur von Frauen*. She started and edited the book series *Die Frau in der Gesellschaft* for Fischer Taschenbuch Verlag, Frankfurt. She also has published several women's autobiographies and anthologies of women's theoretical and political writings: *Zur Psychologie der Frau; Frauen und Beruf; Frauen gegen den Krieg; Fanny Lewald: Meine Lebensgeschichte; Toni Sender: Autobiographie einer deutschen Rebellin*; and *Kämpferin für den Frieden: Bertha von Suttner.* She recently edited *Encountering the Other(s): Studies in Literature, History and Culture*, and is co-editor with Sidonie Smith of *Writing new Identities: Gender, Nation and Immigration in Contemporary Europe* and the forthcoming *Polyglot Spaces, Polyglot Practices: The Politics and Poetics of Multilingual Textual Production*.

RUTH DINESEN is retired Lecturer of Modern German Literature at the University of Copenhagen, from where she also holds a doctorate. She has published several books and articles on Nelly Sachs and her poetry including the biography *Nelly Sachs. Eine Biographie* (Suhrkamp, 1991) which, in its Danish version (1994) was awarded the prestigeous literary prize of the State Foundation for Art by the Danish Ministry of Cultural Affairs.

ELKE P. FREDERIKSEN is Professor of German in the Department of Germanic Studies and an Affiliate Faculty member of Women's Studies at the University of Maryland. Her research and teaching focus on German and Austrian literature and culture of the nineteenth and twentieth centuries, with special emphasis on German women's social and literary history, as well as feminist literary and cultural theories, and post-colonialism. She has published five books and numerous journal articles and contributions to edited volumes. She is well known for her book *Die Frauenfrage in Deutschland 1865–1915* (1981, second edition 1994). Her book edition *Women Writers of Germany, Austria, and Switzerland* (1989) was selected by *Choice* as an "Outstanding Academic Book of 1989."

GERTRAUD GUTZMANN is Associate Professor of German Studies at Smith College. She has written on Anna Seghers and other exile writers, on issues of remigration and Post-World War II German society.

ROBERT C. HOLUB teaches German intellectual, cultural, and literary history in the German department at the University of California, Berkeley, where he has been employed since 1979. Among his numerous publications on these topics are *Reflections of Realism: Paradox, Norm, and Ideology in Nineteenth-Century German Prose* (1991); *Jürgen Habermas: Critic in the Public Sphere* (1991); *Crossing Borders: Reception Theory, Poststructuralism, Deconstruction* (1992); and *Friedrich Nietzsche* (1995). Recently edited volumes include *Impure Reason: Dialectic of Enlightenment in Germany* (1993); *Responsibility and Commitment: Ethische Postulate der Kulturvermittlung* (1996); and *Heine's Contested Identities: Politics, Religion, and Nationalism in Nineteenth-Century Germany* (1998).

RITTA JO HORSLEY is an Associate Professor of German at the University of Massachusetts-Boston, where she also teaches in the Women's Studies Program. She earned her Ph.D. in Germanic Languages and Literatures from Harvard University in 1970. Teaching areas include the Weimar Republic; women in European literature and thought; the European witch persecutions; twentieth-century German women's writing; Lesbian Studies. She has received university grants for curriculum development in German Studies and in Lesbian Studies, and her research has been supported by Fulbright and ACLS grants. Research and publications include work on Goethe, Ingeborg Bachmann, Irmgard Keun, Marieluise Fleisser, Lesbian Studies and the European witch hunts.

RUTH KLUGER, born 1931 in Vienna of a Jewish family, survived several concentration camps and emigrated in 1947 to the US. B.A. from Hunter College, M.A. and Ph.D. from University of California Berkeley. Taught at and chaired German departments at the University of Virginia, Princeton University and UC Irvine. Editor of German Quarterly from 1977–1983. Most recent publications: *weiter leben. Eine Jugend* (1992) which received several awards; *Katastrophen. Über deutsche Literatur* (1994), *Frauen lesen anders. Essays* (1996)

HELGA KRAFT is Professor and Head of the German Department at the University of Illinois at Chicago. She has published widely on gender issues and other topics in literature and culture of German speaking countries. Books are: *Ein Haus aus Sprache. Dramatikerinnen und das andere Theater.* (Metzler); *Mütter - Töchter - Frauen. Weiblichkeitsbilder in der Literatur* (co-editor Elke Liebs) (Metzler); *Erhörtes und Unerhörtes. Die Welt des Klangs bei Heinrich von Kleist* (Fink); *Auf Deutsch! Kompetenz durch kommunikatives Lernen* (co-author Barbara Kosta) (Prentice Hall).

SARA LENNOX is Professor of Germanic Languages and Literatures and Director of the Social Thought and Political Economy Program at the University of Massachusetts, Amherst. She is editor of *Auf der Suche nach den Gärtern unserer Mütter: Feministische Kulturkritik aus Amerika* (1982) and co-editor of *Nietzsche heute: Seine Rezeption seit 1968* (1988) and *The Imperialist Imagination: German Colonialism and Its Legacy* (1998). She has published articles on various twentieth-century German and Austrian authors, on women's writing in the Federal Republic of Germany and German Democratic Republic, on literary theory, feminist theory, feminist pedagogy, antifeminism, feminist German Studies, and the feminist movement in Germany and the United States.

ELKE LIEBS is Professor of German at the University Potsdam, in Germany. Her areas of specialization include literature of the 19th century, gender issues, children's (and young adults') literature, history of reception and cultural history. Books are: *Die pädagogische Insel* (on Robinson Crusoe) (Metzler); *Kindheit und Tod* (Fink) (Pied Piper Myth and history of childhood); *Das Köstlichste von allem* (cultural connection of love and food) (Kreuz); *Mütter Töchter- Frauen. Weiblichkeitsbilder in der Literatur.* (co-editor Helga Kraft) (Metzler); *Das Ich als Schrift, Festschrift für Winfried Pielow* (co-editors Jürgen Hein und Helmut Koch).(Schneider). Many articles on various issues in comparative literature.

DAGMAR C. G. LORENZ is Professor of German at University of Illinois at Chicago, and taught at the Department of Germanic Languages and Literatures of the Ohio State University from 1975–1998. She studied in Göttingen and received a Ph.D. in German (1974) and an M.A. in English (1975) from the University of Cincinnati. Her teaching and research interests include nineteenth and twentieth-century Austrian, German-Jewish, and women's literature. Her most recent book publications are *Verfolgung bis zum Massenmord* (1992), *Insiders and Outsiders, Jewish and Gentile Culture and Germany and Austria, ed.* With Gabriele Weinberger (1994), and Keepers of the Motherland. *German Texts by Jewish Women Writers* (1997).

ELAINE MARTIN is an Associate Professor at the University of Alabama where she teaches German, women studies, and world literature. She edited *Gender, Patriarchy and Fascism in the Third Reich: The Response of Women Writers,* and has written on contemporary German women authors and autobiographical literature about the Nazi era, as well as the theory and practice of comparative literature. She is currently writing a book about women who grew up in Germany during the Third Reich and wrote about the experience autobiographically.

RICHARD W. (RICK) MCCORMICK is an Associate Professor of German at the University of Minnesota, Twin Cities, where he teaches 20th-century German culture, film, and literature. He is the author of *Politics of the Self: Feminism and the Postmodern in West German Literature and Film* (Princeton University Press, 1991) and a co-editor of the 2-volume anthology *Gender and German Cinema: Feminist Interventions* (Berg Press, 1993). He has published a number of articles on the German cinema focusing both on postwar movements such as "New German Cinema" and its specifically feminist wing, as well as on the cinema of the Weimar Republic. He is currently finishing a book manuscript on the film and literature of the Weimar Republic titled *Identities in Crisis: Gender, Modernity, and 'New Objectivity' in Weimar Film and Literature*.

RENATE MÖHRMANN is Professor of Theater and Film Studies at the University of Cologne, and since 1989, visiting professor at the University of Vienna. She has held visiting professorships at the University of Mexico City, the University of Bari (Italy), the University of Toronto; she was Distinguished Max-Kade Professor at the Universities of California at Davis and at Irvine, at Washington University in St. Louis, and at the Summer School of Middlebury/Vermont. Recipient of the Canada Germany Research Award in 1994, she is on the Supervisory Board of German Public Television and of the Bavaria Film-Trust. Author and Editor of twelve books on topics ranging from women in pre-1848 Germany to a cultural history of female performers, MÖhrmann is particularly well known for *Die Frau mit der Kamera* (1980), *Frauen-Literatur-Geschichte: Schreibende Frauen vom Mittelalter bis zur Gegenwart* (edited with Hiltrud Gnüg, 1988) and *Verklärt, verkitscht, vergessen. Die Mutter als ästhetische Figur* (1996).

MONIKA SHAFI is Professor of German at the University of Delaware which she joined in 1986. She studied at the Universities of Aachen and Freiburg, Germany and received her Ph.D. from the University of Maryland in 1986. She is the author of *Utopische Entwürfe in der Literatur von Frauen* (1989), and of *Gertrud Kolmar: Eine Einführung in das Werk* (1995), as well as of articles on 19th and 20th century German literature, with special emphasis on women writers. Her current book-project is entitled *Germans as Foreigners - Foreigners as Germans.*

GUY STERN is Distinguished Professor in the Department of German and Slavic Studies at Wayne State University. He is the author of numerous articles on eighteenth- and twentieth century German Literature. Among this book publications are *War, Weimar and Literature, the Story of the "Neue Merkur"* (1971), *Literatur im Exil* (1989) and *Literarische Kultur im Exil* (1997). A festschrift, *Exile and Enlightenment* (1987) was published in his honor. He received the Goethe Medal, the Grand Order of Merit from the Federal Republic and an honorary doctorate from his alma mater, Hofstra University. He serves on the Executive Committee of the Leo Baeck Institute and of the Kurt Weill Foundation.

MARTHA KAARSBERG WALLACH is Connecticut State University Professor of German and Chair of the Modern Language Department at Central Connecticut State University, New Britain, Connecticut, and taught at the University of Wisconsin–Green Bay from 1970–1988. Born in Poland, she attended schools in Germany and Canada and received her Ph.D. in Modern German Literature from the University of Washington in 1972. Recent research and publications include articles on Heine, Therese Albertine Luise von Jakob (Talvj), mother-daughter relationships in German literature, translations of Barbara Frischmuth and the image of Poles in German literature.

MARGARET E. WARD is Professor of German at Wellesley College, Wellesley MA, where she has been teaching since 1971. Her areas of specialization include political drama, Berlin in the 20s, and 19th and 20th-century German women writers. She has published a monograph on Rolf Hochhuth, and articles on Bertolt Brecht, Armand Gatti, Volker Braun, and the theater of the GDR. More recently her publications have included several articles in books and *Festschriften* on Fanny Lewald and Ingeborg Drewitz. She is now completing a book, *Between Rebellion and Renunciation: Reading Fanny Lewald (1811–1889)*. Professor Ward's research has been supported by National Endowment for the Humanities, and Fulbright fellowships, and by grants from the Andrew W. Mellon and the William R. Kenan, Jr. foundations.

INDEX